. M. W. /Cint

School Reform, Corporate Style

5-7-06

Mike,

On deep appreciation in the
to kindling my interest in the
status of education and for
setting a high standard of
theory in practice —

Dorothy

STUDIES IN GOVERNMENT
AND PUBLIC POLICY

School Reform, Corporate Style

Chicago, 1880–2000

Dorothy Shipps

 University Press of Kansas

Published by the University Press of Kansas (Lawrence, Kansas 66045), which was organized
by the Kansas Board of Regents and is operated and funded by Emporia State University, Fort
Hays State University, Kansas State University, Pittsburg State University, the University of
Kansas, and Wichita State University

Library of Congress Cataloging-in-Publication Data

Shipps, Dorothy.
    School reform, corporate style : Chicago, 1880-2000 / Dorothy Shipps.
        p. cm. — (Studies in government and public policy)
    Includes bibliographical references and index.
    ISBN 0-7006-1449-4 (cloth : alk. paper) — ISBN 0-7006-1450-8 (pbk. : alk. paper)
    1. Education, Urban—Political aspects—United
States—Case studies.   2. Educational change—United States—Case
studies.   3. Business and education—United States—Case studies.   I.
Title.   II. Series.
    LC5131.S52 2006
    371.0109771'11—dc22   2006000285

British Library Cataloguing-in-Publication Data is available.

Printed in the United States of America

10 9 8 7 6 5 4 3 2 1

To Paul, who taught me about power,
and Fred, from whom I learned the art of collaboration.

Contents

Preface   *ix*

Introduction: Seeking Reform   1

1. Shaping the Modern System: Vocationalism, Managerialism, and
   Efficiency, 1880–1930   16
2. Confronting Race: Thwarted Reforms and Disillusionment,
   1930–1980   50
3. Improvising Decentralization: Uncommon Coalitions and
   Conflicting Agendas, 1980–1990   89
4. Perfecting Management: Standards and Control,
   1990–2000   130
5. Powering Reform: Corporate Influence, Civic Coalitions,
   and the Dynamics of Change   170

Appendix: Characteristics of the Commercial Club of Chicago and Its
   Network of Associated Organizations   211
Notes   *223*
Index   *277*

Preface

I began this study almost a decade and a half ago, drawn by Chicago's head-line-grabbing experiment in "parent power." As a graduate student, I studied the city's radical decentralization from the top-down perspective of its civic-minded elite. Chicago corporate leaders had sustained a coalition to create local school councils, lobbied alongside Latino community activists for passage of enabling legislation, and raised the lion's share of funding for the first elections to seat 6,000 parent and community volunteers as school board members. They seemed a breed apart from the indifferent executives I had encountered elsewhere.

Fascinated by a city that could foster so much civic engagement, I was initially hopeful, like much of the nation, that the problems of urban schooling would be solved in Chicago if nowhere else. But the Chicago public school system, like its urban counterparts nationally, remained trapped in cycles of reform with little substantive improvement. Puzzled, I returned to the city in 1996 for what amounted to a postdoc in the politics of urban school reform.

For the next three years, a broad range of civic activists were my teachers. They came not only from the corporate sector but also from every corner of the political geography in this famously balkanized city. African Americans brought a mix of patient boosterism and resistance to the racial barriers that were only slowly being dismantled. Deep connections to Mexico and the Caribbean gave Latinos a sense of community pride and the confidence to demand their rights through the schools. Teachers showed remarkable fortitude in the face of near-universal censure.

These dedicated Chicagoans convinced me that nothing is more important for educators than to master the politics of urban schooling. To many, urban politics invokes an irreversible social geography, spatial arrangements of poverty and wealth that separate residents and pit their interests against one another. This book examines the development of such cleavages in Chicago, tracing their roots to the early decades of the twentieth century. But I conclude that urban school politics is more fundamentally about power: historically contingent, institutionalized patterns of self-reinforcing ideas, influence, and organizational resources, hardened, to be sure, by income inequality and segregation, but not permanent because of them.

Urban regime theory provides the analytical tools to unpack Chicago's complex reform history without losing the centrality of power. It conceptualizes successful reform as a regime change, requiring concerted action by coalitions of resourceful civic groups that combine their influence to authorize and sustain an action agenda. New and institutionalized governing arrangements, and a fundamental altering of relations among educators and between them and the public, confirm the success.

Building on the concepts of Clarence N. Stone and his colleagues,* I construct a framework for the political analysis of urban reform, aiming to avoid the major problem that plagues most educational research on the topic: reform is divorced from the political processes needed to sustain it. At the same time, I aim to encourage political scientists to take account of educators' knowledge about what works, so that power and interest alone do not guide prescriptions.

To a remarkable degree, Chicago's corporate leaders have shaped the city's schools while constructing its economic and downtown development priorities, its response to racial segregation, and even its urban mythology. The same corporate club whose leaders' persistence impressed me in 1991 has led, abetted, or restrained nearly every attempt to improve the school system in the twentieth century. Such frequent, consistent behavior from powerful actors places them at the center of this narrative.

Power is a double-edged sword in U.S. public schooling. It can rearrange hierarchies, install new decision makers, create institutions that never existed before, and convince many that this is the way things ought to be. But in our democracy it also must be held accountable. This book asks a necessary but too frequently overlooked question: if corporate power was instrumental in creating the urban public schools and has had a strong hand in their reform for more than a century, then why have those schools failed urban children so badly?

The answer is no tale of conspiracy. I am deeply convinced that Chicago's business leaders want better schools for all the city's children. But their judgment has often been clouded by the limits of their experience and sometimes by an irrational antipathy to unions, the one organized group with enough resources and independence to challenge them as near equals. If corporate and union leaders worked together on behalf of school reform, they would be an un-

---

*Clarence N. Stone et al., *Building Civic Capacity: Politics of Reforming Urban Schools* (Lawrence: University Press of Kansas, 2001).

.

beatable combination. But in Chicago such comity has been rare, occurring only when neither was willing to risk the benefits it received under the complicated reciprocity of machine politics. Corporate executives are typically too wedded to a stunted view of educators to forge a productive partnership for change, and unionists may never accept the second-class status given to them by managers.

Yet an unlikely corporate-union coalition for school reform is not the only way forward. This book ends with an argument for teachers unions to forge a coalition with urban public school parents on behalf of their common interests, creating a new reform agenda, if possible—in opposition to the corporate agenda, if necessary. Teachers, like urban families, have too much to lose to remain on the sidelines of reform. If models and inspiration are needed, Chicago offers many examples. This book documents a remarkable diversity of reform coalitions and, in the early years of the twentieth century especially, a powerful and effective teacher-community partnership.

ORGANIZATION OF THE BOOK

The introduction explains why a study of twentieth-century Chicago school politics is germane to other cities. Following regime theory, I link school reform agendas to the civic capacity needed to enact and sustain change and clarify why business actors are at the center of my narrative.

Chapter 1, "Shaping the Modern System," reassesses the era between 1880 and 1930, when the city's public school system was being formed, and pays special attention to business's manifestations of interest. During this half century, Chicago's reforms were promoted as a national model of school system reorganization, but more often they served as a cautionary tale: draconian cost cutting and business's efforts to create a class-based system of schooling brought national approbation. Corporate leaders justified these and other reforms on their economic benefits, but different civic actors (albeit not the relatively weak politicians of the day) challenged their arguments and proposed options. Organized labor was business's main adversary. Teachers unions united with working-class industrial unions and middle-class professional associations to press for more democratic governance, an authentic pedagogy for working-class immigrant children in the regular schools, and a dedicated stream of funding. Although they won few outright victories, unions moderated the businessmen's ideas and kept the worst excesses of their economic functionalism at bay.

Chapter 2, "Confronting Race," covers the hitherto unexplored ground of business activism during the period from 1930 to 1980, when the racial concerns of a new group of civic advocates remapped city politics and civil rights came to dominate the school reform agenda. Many analysts have argued that business associations were passive regarding school reform politics during this half century. My research indicates otherwise. Corporate activism simply took a different form as did the interest group mediation of unions. Working behind the scenes to avoid offending the era's machine mayors, executives furthered their earlier management and efficiency agenda, while unions focused on collective bargaining. Mindful, too, that the city could explode into racial violence at the slightest provocation, business executives reached out to African Americans in a strategy of economic inclusion predating the political incorporation of blacks by more than a decade. Even so, by the end of the era, corporate leaders had helped precipitate a fiscal crisis in the schools that ruined desegregation prospects and redirected civic attention to the managerial and fiscal concerns they found more amenable.

Chapter 3, "Improvising Decentralization," examines the reform period encompassing the 1980s, ushered in by the death of Richard J. Daley and the disintegration of his Democratic machine, and closed down by the rise of his son, Richard M. Daley, with his corporatist brand of political centralization. In between, the populist African American mayor Harold Washington restructured civic participation, allowing black political incorporation to reach its apogee. For the third time in a century, a different range of civic actors entered the school reform arena to contend with business. Once again, corporate executives became strident, public critics of the schools, this time collaborating with emergent Latino grassroots organizations and white activists bent on radically decentralizing school governance. The resulting school law was a compromise, bearing the traces of every community interest involved, but deaf to the concerns of those outside the coalition, chiefly blacks and educators—in many cases, one and the same.

Chapter 4, "Perfecting Management," recounts the last decade of the twentieth century, which saw the fourth political sea change in the city's life: a hearkening back to the class cleavages of the Progressive era even as the political climate reverted to a centralization reminiscent of the machine era. It describes an uneasy cooperation among local business associations to install the mayor as the head of the school system. Basing their actions on mistrust of parents and arguments that mayoral control could be the apotheosis of managerial efficiency, they engineered revisions in the school law when the political opportunity arose. Mayoral control has now been in place for nearly a decade and has already endured the succession of the school system's chief executive officer, although not the city's mayor. Whether it will be institutionalized as the public schools' governing regime of the twenty-first century is Chicago's core debate. Its initial shape in the 1990s is being challenged by an alternative view of markets held by some corporate leaders who believe that privatization should displace managerial control as the preferred reform strategy.

Chapter 5, "Powering Reform," tackles the question: if business-led reform has so frequently been sustained, why do Chicago's schools remain problematic? It also points the way to alternatives, some by way of historical paths not taken and others derived from a view of school governing regimes that links reformers' intentions to the political coalitions needed to sustain them. I argue that the dominance of corporate solutions for Chicago's educational problems has several sources: extraordinary resources and cohesion, institutionalized patterns of access, a consistent corporate agenda, and the popular belief that schooling is a lever for economic development. The demonstrably poor results, despite such advantages, reveal corporate reform agendas to be more evolutionary than revolutionary: updates of the bureaucratic system their predecessors created.

Other civic actors—community groups and unions—have fewer organizational resources and are consequently required to join broader coalitions, expending significant time on coalition maintenance while negotiating a reform agenda. Bureaucratic rigidity, cross-class insensitivities, and mutual finger-pointing make it difficult for parents, community members, and teachers to trust one another. But reform coalitions led by teachers and activists may bring better results by providing an antidote to the generalized management and market solutions that tune up the bureaucracy but do nothing about teaching and learning. If reform is to reach deeply into classrooms and improve the curriculum and pedagogy on behalf of low-income, minority, and immigrant urban students, this lesson from the Progressive era may again be relevant.

Social scientists interested in the organizational attributes of Chicago's business elite or curious about how its civic activism was sustained for more than a century will find structural explanations in the appendix. Described are the membership rules, funding, decision-making practices, goals, staffing, and resources of the Commercial Club of Chicago and its affiliated associations. I discuss many attributes of the network, including how it achieved cohesion sufficient to speak with one voice on school reform. Such characteristics shaped individual members' attitudes toward the city and its schools, sustaining their local civic activism despite the nationalizing forces of corporate mergers and acquisitions.

* * *

I accrued many intellectual debts in the course of writing this book. I owe David Tyack, Larry Cuban, and Michael Kirst my deepest gratitude for encouraging my initial interest in school reform fifteen years ago and for showing me that every scholar, no matter how daunting the task she undertakes, stands on the shoulders of many others. Clarence Stone and Julia Wrigley were especially inspiring; both have broad shoulders and sure balance. David Tyack, Larry Cuban, Betty Malen, and John Portz gave the ideas in this manuscript their critical attention and offered many suggestions for improvement, a gift I can only hope to repay. None contributed as much to the shape of the prose between these covers as Fred Rosenbaum.

Many others provided unique assistance: Adrienne Booker, Rita Ghazal, Roseann Hugh, Linda Larach, Xu Li, Karin Sconzert, and Anthony Warn helped me shape my research in ways they may not even be aware of. Jeffrey Mirel encouraged me to keep writing when I was doubtful. Jeffrey Henig made useful editorial suggestions and aided me when other responsibilities competed for my attention. Sandra Jennings and Patricia Jones conscientiously transcribed interviews and transcripts, and Sonja Hubbert good-naturedly redesigned the illustrations more than once. I thank Fred Woodward at the University Press of Kansas for his cheerful patience. Susan Schott and Larisa Martin deserve special thanks for skillfully guiding this manuscript to publication. I am grateful, too, for early research support from the Spencer Foundation and to the Carnegie Corporation of New York, which made me a Carnegie Scholar, thereby permitting a year of relatively uninterrupted writing.

My biggest debt is to the Chicagoans who are described in these pages. The Honorable Mary Lou Cowlishaw, member of the Illinois House of Representatives, was extremely generous with her insight into the process by which the 1995 law was created. John Ayers pointed me toward individuals I might have missed, and Margaret Morrison and Carolyn Nordstrom corrected my early misimpressions of Chicago's business associations. My former colleagues at the Consortium on Chicago School Research have been an unfailing inspiration, as well as a source of some of the most reliable research on urban schooling in the nation. More than 150 activists, executives, teacher unionists, politicians, professors, journalists, and school leaders gave me their insights and perspectives. I hope they recognize my respect for their dedicated efforts to improve Chicago's schools.

School Reform, Corporate Style

Chicago Mayors and School Superintendents, 1880–2006

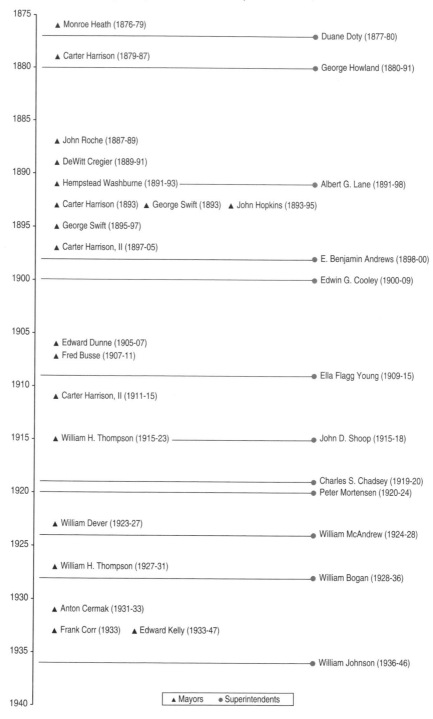

1875
▲ Monroe Heath (1876-79)
● Duane Doty (1877-80)

▲ Carter Harrison (1879-87)
1880
● George Howland (1880-91)

1885

▲ John Roche (1887-89)

▲ DeWitt Cregier (1889-91)
1890
▲ Hempstead Washburne (1891-93) ———— ● Albert G. Lane (1891-98)

▲ Carter Harrison (1893) ▲ George Swift (1893) ▲ John Hopkins (1893-95)
1895
▲ George Swift (1895-97)

▲ Carter Harrison, II (1897-05)
● E. Benjamin Andrews (1898-00)
1900
● Edwin G. Cooley (1900-09)

1905
▲ Edward Dunne (1905-07)
▲ Fred Busse (1907-11)
● Ella Flagg Young (1909-15)
1910
▲ Carter Harrison, II (1911-15)

1915
▲ William H. Thompson (1915-23) ———— ● John D. Shoop (1915-18)

● Charles S. Chadsey (1919-20)
1920
● Peter Mortensen (1920-24)

▲ William Dever (1923-27)
● William McAndrew (1924-28)
1925

▲ William H. Thompson (1927-31)
● William Bogan (1928-36)
1930
▲ Anton Cermak (1931-33)

▲ Frank Corr (1933) ▲ Edward Kelly (1933-47)
1935
● William Johnson (1936-46)

1940
▲ Mayors ● Superintendents

Chicago Mayors and School Superintendents, 1880–2006

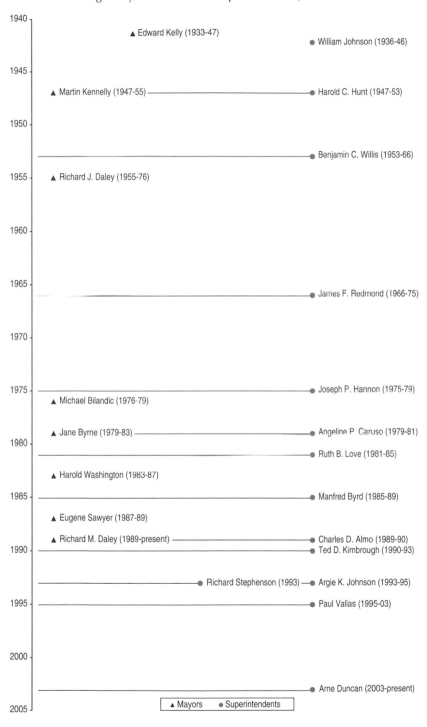

1940

▲ Edward Kelly (1933-47)

● William Johnson (1936-46)

1945

▲ Martin Kennelly (1947-55) —————————————— ● Harold C. Hunt (1947-53)

1950

————————————————————————————— ● Benjamin C. Willis (1953-66)

1955 ▲ Richard J. Daley (1955-76)

1960

1965 ———————————————————————————— ● James F. Redmond (1966-75)

1970

1975 ———————————————————————————— ● Joseph P. Hannon (1975-79)

▲ Michael Bilandic (1976-79)

▲ Jane Byrne (1979-83) ——————————————— ● Angeline P. Caruso (1979-81)

1980 ————————————————————————————— ● Ruth B. Love (1981-85)

▲ Harold Washington (1983-87)

1985 ————————————————————————————— ● Manfred Byrd (1985-89)

▲ Eugene Sawyer (1987-89)

▲ Richard M. Daley (1989-present) ——————— ● Charles D. Almo (1989-90)
1990 —————————————————————————————— ● Ted D. Kimbrough (1990-93)

—————————————— ● Richard Stephenson (1993) —● Argie K. Johnson (1993-95)

1995 ————————————————————————————— ● Paul Vallas (1995-03)

2000

————————————————————————————— ● Arne Duncan (2003-present)

▲ Mayors   ● Superintendents

2005

Introduction

Seeking Reform

This book is a story of power and agency, as well as one of schools and educators. At its heart is the paradox of school reform in one of our nation's largest cities. For more than a century Chicago's most powerful, persistent, and successful reformers have been its civic-minded corporate elite. Yet despite that activism, results have been disappointing.

Chicago has long held a place in the limelight, as a model to emulate or an example to avoid. In social science terms it is a boundary case: no muckraker uncovered more corruption in public schooling than in 1920s Chicago, mid-century school desegregation was nowhere so hotly contested with so little effect, and decentralization was never more radical than in the Prairie Metropolis during the 1980s.

Chicago is now known for being among the first cities to give its mayor, Richard M. Daley, control over the schools. This version of the "Chicago model" has spread to Detroit and Cleveland, as well as to New York City and to the troubled school districts of Los Angeles and Oakland, California, where the template barely fits the law. Even cities with unique governing arrangements, such as Washington, D.C., claim to be adopting the Chicago model of mayoral control.[1]

Although Chicago made school reform history in the twentieth century, the performance of the system's large majority of black, Latino, and low-income students has not met reformers' expectations. This failure lies at the heart of a question facing urban school systems across the nation: why, despite a century of reform, have city schools failed to become what their citizens want? Chicago's story challenges the conventional wisdom that state officials, school boards, and superintendents are initiators and sole implementers of urban reform and that greater bureaucratic accountability will increase the likelihood of success. Instead, it reveals school reform as part and parcel of urban coalition politics, initiated and sustained locally by business associations, unions, community-based organizations, good-government groups, and foundations.

In Chicago, civic activism explains which reforms will flourish or fade, but it does little to clarify why student outcomes have improved only slightly. Understanding this failure in performance requires close attention to the connections between the long-term goal of school improvement and the immediate action agenda, including the politics that sustain it. Combining Chicago's twentieth-century experience of coalitional politics with educational research—most of which emphasizes the centrality of teacher-student relationships to performance improvements—reveals that some action agendas have better prospects than others of improving urban schools for low-income and minority students.

Agendas less likely to affect pedagogy and student performance are easier to bring to fruition because they require only narrow coalitions to sustain and draw on resources concentrated in the hands of an elite. Reform agendas with better prospects require unusual cross-sector coalitions that are difficult to initiate and even harder to sustain in our current context of mistrust between professional educators and the public.

All reform produces unpredictable political consequences, making it difficult to maintain any coalition long enough to institutionalize change. Moreover, even subtle changes in a coalition can alter its agenda. Chicago's reform history illuminates this process, and its status as a national exemplar suggests that lessons learned there can have far-reaching effects.

THE CHICAGO MODEL

What makes Chicago a national model of urban public schooling? Part of the answer is found in its social ecology, an intensified version of the perpetually renewing diversity of city life in the United States. In the decades between 1880 and 1900, Chicago grew more rapidly than any U.S. city up to that time, largely because of massive immigration from southern and eastern Europe. City resources strained to respond to the needs of children whose Italian, Polish, and Czech parents did not speak English or read and write any language. The newcomers were drawn by the promise of work in its Fordist factories, far larger than those in New York City. By 1919 nearly one-third of Chicago's industrial wage earners toiled in an establishment with more than 1,000 workers. Ninety percent of them worked for corporations, and two-thirds of the firms had over $1million in product worth.[2]

Chicago next became an internal mecca, exceeded only by New York. From 1915 through the end of World War II it drew many thousands of black migrants each year, fleeing the impoverished rural South and searching for freedom and work up north.[3] The famously segregated city jammed black children into old schools and trailers, unwilling to let them attend more spacious and up-to-date facilities outside the dense "black belt." A generation later, the cruelty of this inequity led Martin Luther King Jr. to select Chicago for his northern campaign for civil rights, but it also encouraged racial confrontations over school deseg-regation, which resulted in white flight that rivaled Boston's. By 1980, blacks composed nearly 40 percent of the city, their children occupying 61 percent of the still highly segregated public school seats.

Despite its "rust belt" moniker, Chicago has continued to attract immi-grants. Latinos became the fastest growing population in the city by the 1980s. Today, the Cook County Latino population is exceeded only by that of Los Angeles County, New York City, Miami–Dade County, and Houston's Harris County.[4] Overwhelmingly from Mexico, but also from Puerto Rico and more recently from Central and South America, the Latino population in Chicago has grown rapidly—to 26 percent by 2000—magnifying the challenges faced by Chicago educators. One-quarter of sixteen- to nineteen-year-old Latinos were not in school in 2000, more than half reportedly did not speak English well, and 35 percent were linguistically isolated in Spanish-speaking households.[5] In part, Chicago is paradigmatic because its schools have been required to respond to the changing racial and ethnic demographics faced in most U.S. cities.[6]

The Chicago public schools mirror the thirty other largest urban school systems in other respects. With 435,000 students and about 600 schools, Chicago's system shares some characteristics with the nation's two giants, New York City and Los Angeles, but it also shares attributes with many cities that are less than half its size.[7] Black and Latino students currently make up more than 80 percent of the students, "minorities" represent 90 percent overall, and the proportion from low-income families has risen sharply from 47 percent in 1983 to 85 percent in 2001.[8]

Like its counterparts, the Chicago public schools have also endured a half century of relatively poor performance, punctuated by small improvements. The current four-year dropout rate of about 43 percent remains unchanged from the 1980s, although the twelfth-grade dropout rate of 9.8 percent is below the average for many of the nation's other large cities.[9] Average student perform-ance is well under national norms on the Iowa Test of Basic Skills, in spite of two waves of test score improvements in the last twenty years. As before, the recent rise shows no evidence that the black versus white achievement gap is closing, and the Latino gap is a growing source of concern.[10]

In all these ways and more, Chicago is a city of stark contrasts. Janet Abu-Lughod perceptively noted that the city's negative image comes from its actual past, rather than from an exaggeration of the metropolis gone astray, as is often the case for New York and Los Angeles.[11] The city is a clean, architecturally stimulating monument to human ingenuity and determination, and its citizens display an uncommon sense of civic pride. Yet, it is simultaneously the site of radically segregated ghettos lined with sterile rows of poorly constructed blockhouses and high-rises, and neighborhoods with grossly inadequate schooling and other social services.

The contrasts in school reform have been no less dramatic. Even though Chicago was not the first city to attempt vocationalization early in the twentieth century, it did so in an extreme way, seeking to create two separate school systems—one for manual workers that business tycoons would control, and another for the city's future civic leaders. Most cities cut back on school services during the Depression, but Chicago put its schools under the command of the city's financially strapped bankers, who slashed budgets and programs even as they themselves reneged on back taxes.[12] Nearly half a century later the city's corporate leaders again declared the school system bankrupt and, once again, drastically reduced the budget in the name of efficiency.

Since adopting mayoral control, Chicago has instituted an exaggerated form of another currently popular reform trend: student accountability. Chicago's "no social promotion" policy reinvigorated the once taboo practice of retaining underperforming students because of a single low test score. The city's example helped popularize high-stakes testing as an urban school reform, despite decades of research concluding that the practice has large negative consequences. In instance after instance, Chicago has been a national example, pointing the way or signaling a warning.

Chicago did not become famous as a reform leader simply because new needs arose. Nor have the city's educational leaders, a force of conservatism since midcentury, led its reform efforts. Chicago served as both a model and a cautionary tale throughout the twentieth century because it developed an uncommon citywide capacity to engage in local political debate about its schools, form coalitions, and sustain a program of change. "Big-shouldered" civic leaders vigorously adopted popular national reform initiatives, but they were not alone.

A dense network of community-based organizations with roots in the city's settlement houses, good-government clubs, and unions of the 1910s has invented new reforms to fit the city's neighborhoods and extend educational opportunities to vast slums of immigrants, black ghettos, and low-income-housing blocks. A legacy of black activism exists from the 1960s; Saul Alinsky's form of grassroots organizing was tested in the same decade.

Moreover, Chicago's public schools have always had close links to city hall. Unlike many cities in the East, Chicago never abandoned mayoral selection of the school board in favor of an elected one. Nor did it fully separate funding from city hall, even when the state legislature intended to cut the tie. Accordingly, school governance has always been colored by city politics. For five decades, that meant the Chicago Democratic machine.

Neither mayoral influence nor volunteer activities and community organizing, however, could have put Chicago so often in the national spotlight without the assistance of the city's industrial and commercial titans. For more than a century these powerful business executives have used their influence over local and state politicians, and have occasionally dipped into their own pockets and their corporations' wealth, to support their version of Chicago school reform. As important, they institutionalized a concern for the public schools in the business associations that represent them, beginning in 1877 with the Commercial Club of Chicago.

In this study, I draw attention to the links forged among the city's three governing systems—its civic groups, city hall, and economic leaders—and to the interpenetration of their separate interests and values. These political struggles, coalitions, and accommodations, more than anything done by educators, have produced the current school system's governing structure, including its reform agenda at the turn of the millennium. Such political interactions help explain why Chicago's repeated attempts to restructure its public schools have so often caught the nation's attention, and why some of the city's reform efforts became institutionalized, while others quickly faded.

URBAN SCHOOL REFORM

Mobilization for urban school reform—David Tyack and Larry Cuban define the term as "planned efforts to change schools in order to correct perceived social and educational problems"—has been common enough in the last century to be considered a regular occurrence.[13] This book focuses on planned efforts to institute systemwide change, rather than the change that occurs when one or a few schools seek improvements. Describing such citywide reform coalitions and their animating ideas is a staple of historical writing, as is the observation that one era's reform begets problems that must be solved by the next generation of reformers. Few reform efforts, we are told, last long enough to alter the behavior of most teachers, change the way everyday decisions are made, or reconfigure the relationships between urban educators and the city's residents.[14]

For many, such observations engender skepticism, even cynicism, about urban schools' capacity to change. Almost inevitably, some argue, attempts to reform urban schools are no match for the habits, "trained incompetence," or material interests and limited vision of those—often educators—who would prefer to keep the system as it is.

Educational bureaucracies were themselves once a reform, established to manage and coordinate hundreds of relationships within urban school districts. They have come to foster conservatism based on the defined roles, rote functions, and perquisites of professionalism that can hide incompetence and sustain dysfunctional practices. Bureaucratic accountability means that no employee can initiate substantial change without requesting approval from higher-ups and simultaneously engaging the support of peers and underlings. The result is incremental, localized, and ephemeral improvements; systemwide change is resisted. As a result, some have described bureaucracies as being "at war" with democracy.[15]

Many political scientists and reformers respond by seeking new governance arrangements intended to break the bureaucratic stranglehold. Some advocate political decentralization to increase citizen influence; others espouse centralization to bolster bureaucratic accountability.[16] Desegregationists have focused on structural changes such as districtwide open enrollment.[17] Underlying all these efforts is the implicit assumption that urban residents can improve their schools only when the formal institutions of citizen deliberation change, and this requires the active engagement of officials, elites, and residents.[18]

This consensus that educators cannot or will not initiate and sustain change is paired with the ubiquitous observation that educators and educational bureaucracies are crucial to any successful reform implementation, making the prospects for systemwide reform appear bleak. Chicago's story supports the concept that any enduring change in an urban school system must have lasting external support. However, I would argue that educators are as important in initiating some types of reform as they are in implementing and institutionalizing most school change.

In the first instance, this means that powerful ideas and dedicated resources from outside the system must be mobilized for improvement; urban school systems become arenas for political action when performance lags behind expectations. This type of politics has remained primarily local, despite homogenizing national interests such as testing agencies and textbook publishers or the waves of reform that seem to sweep across the nation's cities. Localism explains why Progressive era reforms were hard fought and produced city-to-city variation, but it also explains why currently popular reform agendas such as privatization appear in many guises and are embraced in one community but rejected in another.

Second, the importance of educators and their formal organizations cannot be overlooked in any type of reform that aims either to devolve authority to school communities or to improve teaching and learning in urban class-rooms. Chicago's experience demonstrates that the details of reformers' plans, far from being technical matters, are intimately bound to the politics of build-ing civic capacity for change.

CIVIC CAPACITY

Clarence N. Stone and a group of collaborators characterized the external sup-port needed to reform urban schools using theories of neighborhood devel-opment, resource redistribution, and economic growth, focusing on a triangle of relationships among the city's political authority structure, local civic and economic actors, and the bureaucracy. Large cities change, they argue, when a cross-sector coalition of external actors and bureaucrats commits resources to the effort, and there is political leadership to sustain the momentum. These preconditions for change, a city's *civic capacity,* make the difference between efforts that endure and those that fade.[19] In adapting this concept, I build on Stone and colleagues' comparative analyses by examining one city's history of successive school reform attempts over time.

Civic capacity is created and maintained by a combination of governmen-tal and nongovernmental partners and resources, hence its *civic character.* To be successful, civic capacity requires not only agreement on an agenda but also "a significant degree of loyalty to the effort," going well beyond the enactment of laws or regulations and the insistence that educators comply with their inten-tions.[20] Reformers must contribute their own energy and resources throughout implementation.

The link between civic capacity and a viable reform requires knowing which "core elements . . . have the most to contribute to educational improve-ment," based on the program at hand.[21] School reform requires the participation of nongovernmental actors because many essential educational activities are carried on outside of government (e.g., child care, medical screening, job design), but also because parents must agree to enroll their children. Of all the potential external actors, a broad consensus of political analysts agrees that business groups are structurally advantaged to sway coalition outcomes because they dominate local economic policy and have privileged access to politicians, the wealth of corporations, and ready-made organizations.[22] Participation by lower socioeconomic groups must be weighted to compensate for business's resource advantages.[23] Reform coalitions also require the active participation of politicians; without them, state resources (e.g., taxes, employee time and knowledge) can be used to resist change. And without a key bureau-crat or two, school reform can become rhetoric without action.

Although the stimulus for action may be an unpredictable event—a financial inducement, economic restructuring, the transfer of power to a different political party, or a crisis such as a race riot—leadership is essential. Leaders reframe problems that the stimulus reveals, maintain the coalition, modify institutional constraints, provide a policy forum, and mobilize additional resources.[24] Coalitions must be sustained by dampening the rivalry and competition between groups, steering them instead to cooperation and compromise. The task involves forging new relationships among the coalition members, and in this regard, material resources can be especially important assets because they attract constituents who do not know or trust one another.[25]

Each coalition determines its own reform agenda, reflecting the core constituents' interests, experience, values, and material interests, which may initially take the form of a shared critique or an abstract policy preference.[26] But they must eventually establish a feasible and consensual action agenda that matches the available expertise, organizational resources, and financing.[27] The agenda itself requires a particular configuration, sometimes unforeseen by the coalition participants, of technical expertise, logistical support, organizational capacity, inspiration, and sanctioning authority. The broader the coalition, the more this action agenda will involve collective deliberation and compromise, backed up by an investment of personal resources and loyalties. If not, it risks exploiting divisions among the constituents.[28] For all these reasons, the composition of a reform coalition has policy consequences.

Because civic capacity is agenda specific and not transferable, a coalition successful at redeveloping downtown business cannot automatically replicate its success in the public schools. Yet joining one school reform coalition creates the organizational proclivity to participate in the next, and each reform attempt shapes future possibilities by restricting the goals and prescriptions to those the constituents consider legitimate improvements. Applying these constructs to the broad history of school reform partly explains the historians' observation that what is promoted as radical change is often an incremental adjustment of the last reform agenda. This also helps explain why broad coalitions of constituents with widely differing definitions of the problem have so often agreed to support governance reform: their action agenda gives each one control over some part of the new structure without requiring immediate substantive compromise.[29]

Thus, a sustained civic coalition is the missing ingredient in potentially effective but stillborn reform, rather than a structural deficiency in the system. But there is no template; the composition of a reform coalition and the viability of its agenda are contingent on the institutions—the local economy, community demographics, political history—and traditions of school governance (e.g., elected or appointed school board, independent or dependent financial authority, the strength of collective bargaining). There are also variations from city to city and over time, making comparisons difficult to summarize without more analytical tools.[30] This requires an examination of how school politics is embedded in city politics.

REGIME CHANGE

School politics and city politics are inseparable and interdependent, and studying school reform as one case of interest-group politics—often with the mayor at the center—has a tradition in urban studies that fell dormant in the last two decades of the twentieth century. The decline in such studies may have been precipitated by the economic competition among cities that accompanied suburbanization. This, Paul Peterson argued, forced political leaders into a narrow set of policy options: an urban development strategy favored by business interests that creates jobs and tax revenue, a redistributional strategy that pleases community groups but leads to economic decline, and a patronage strategy that forces constituents to compete for jobs, city contracts, and appointments but does not improve the economy. With only one good choice, the end of politics in urban studies seemed near.[31]

Yet the politics of urban education is not so clear-cut. Whereas suburban school systems take the optimal developmental path by providing educational services in proportion to the residents' ability to pay for them, according to Peterson, city school systems seem to make the redistributional choice. They receive state and federal resources that the city's own tax base cannot provide, redistributing these resources to schools in poor neighborhoods and damaging the entire metropolis's development prospects in the process. This conception of the relation between urban schools and the city has been warmly embraced by Chicago's corporate leaders because it suggests that the resources needed to improve schools cannot come from government; they require privatization.

Some argue that the developmental model of urban school reform has its own problems for democracy. When "the politics of schooling [is subordinated] to the imperatives of the market," Ira Katznelson and Margaret Weir remind us, we lose sight of the public schools' republican purpose—to provide all children with the ability to participate as democratic citizens. The new social geography of segregation, from their perspective, makes it nearly impossible to organize the broad coalitions of community groups that would support the republican purpose. Labor's waning influence and its apparent disinterest in reform also contribute to the decline in political possibilities for reform.[32]

In this now-dominant paradigm of limitations and missed opportunities, Stone's work gives us hope by exploring the possibilities of change, rather than what impedes it. He and his colleagues reintroduce human agency and coalitional politics in the choices cities face about their schools.

Regime change is the term Stone uses to describe the thoroughgoing reconstruction of a school system. It includes altering underlying values (e.g., equity, efficiency, choice) and shifting the criteria for evaluation, but it also changes the relationships among politicians, agencies of city government, and school leaders, as well as among business leaders, unions, parents, and teachers. No regime change has occurred until all the required substitutions are institutionalized: educators' perceptions of their material interest and the way they talk about the responsibilities of their jobs, as well as how citizens assess their schools. The entire system is overhauled, and the existing governing regime is replaced with another. Regime change is therefore difficult to achieve, and most attempts at reform never reach the goal.

Regime change goes well beyond ousting leaders and ensconcing new ones. The electoral coalition that can amass enough votes to win may not have the resources needed to help an officeholder deliver on promises. Successful governance often requires a separate coalition of support—a governing coalition.[33] If the governing goal includes reform, the constituents of the coalition must be willing to help develop and sustain that agenda. Voters may hope that elected school officials will do their bidding, but the politicians must rely on others to make it happen. This distinction between electoral and governing coalitions is used in the chapters that follow as a way to clarify why some constituents are left out of reform, even when they vote for the politician who pledges to lead them.

Stone and colleagues describe the status quo as an employment regime, so named because its core rationale is the protection of teachers' and administrators' jobs and careers and school board constituency services. "Teacher defensiveness," justified by public opinion polls that identify their unions as "a major obstacle in school reform," accounts for some of this preoccupation.[34] But schools are also important sources of employment, often the largest in a city; they provide middle-class jobs to many who grew up in low-income households and are thus an important avenue of social mobility for adults as well as for children. When a coalition seeks regime change, it jeopardizes this employment structure and challenges educators' social standing. Resistance from an employment regime is an obstacle that all reformers face; it can undermine an agenda's feasibility and fracture a coalition.[35]

A performance regime, in contrast, actively seeks to improve the performance of children. In Stone and his colleagues' view, it always includes parents, business elites, and some educators. Performance regimes begin as reforms initiated by reform coalitions. Only when the coalition partners' agenda is realized and their common core beliefs and commitments are institutionalized has the process of regime change created a performance regime. Throughout, constituents must remain loyal to the reform's animating ideas, even in the face of compelling and crosscutting material interests.

The tasks of initiating a performance regime are so difficult that few city school systems could be so designated in the mid-1990s, despite an abundance of critical commentary on the schools and no dearth of reform ideas.[36] In addition to the daunting tasks of forming an agenda and amassing the appropriate coalition are problems of class. Middle-class parents are more likely to participate in reform coalitions than are low-income parents, who lack political clout and resources and need a greater degree of change from their schools.[37] Business groups do not always recognize the relationship between the relatively unfamiliar territory of reforming schools and the interests that routinely draw their attention—development, taxes, short-term city booster projects.[38] Because Stone and colleagues consider these two constituents key to any performance regime, the hopefulness of regime change seems to founder on social geography.

Chicago's history suggests a different approach to regime change. Close examination of the reforms attempted, supported, and defeated reveals more than one type of reform agenda and three potential types of activist school governing regimes. Business leaders are required for only one type, and middle-class parents may not be needed at all.

This means that the reform agenda is as important to the formation of the coalition as the coalition is to the maintenance of reform. Some reforms seek deep but targeted pedagogical change, intending that a few key alterations will produce ripples throughout the school system as relationships become altered and rules for decision making change. Others focus on changing the decision makers and the institutions of governance, expecting that better decisions will result. Still others begin with models of market accountability, hoping to steer change by tinkering with systems of punishment and reward. Conflating such disparate reform agendas means that Stone and colleagues miss the distinctions between the constituents and resources needed to sustain each. The overall effect of their two choices—either resisting reform or embracing it—creates the impression that nearly all school reform is the same, and the more the better. If any reform agenda will do, then the central question remains: why have institutionalized governance changes occurred in urban schools throughout the twentieth century without tangible improvements in student performance?

The alternative approach taken in this book is to assume that some reforms are more effective at improving student performance than others. The questions then become: Which reform coalitions and agendas are more likely to improve the educational performance of low-income, urban children of color? When, if ever, have these coalitions been mobilized to create a regime change in urban education, and what can we learn from that experience? What other types of regime change have occurred, and what have been the consequences for the children?

These questions focus my attention on Chicago and justify this volume. The well-documented history of Chicago's schools reveals that reforms can be organized by type, each requiring a different combination of coalition partners and resources to initiate and sustain it, and each aiming for regime change of a particular kind. Each has its own characteristic problems with institutionalization. The last chapter of this volume outlines my version of this typology in the hope that it will be a useful analytical tool for further research.

Although most efforts fail to become institutionalized, Chicago's 120-year reform history reveals some that did, demonstrating that urban school systems have been changed, albeit with great difficulty, and local interest in doing so again has not died. Because regime change is a decades-long process, it is easier to observe using the historical approach taken here than it would be using cross-sectional research with a limited time frame.

If a regime analysis of Chicago helps clarify that cities do have choices, and that building cross-class civic capacity is still a viable method of changing schools, it is partly because of the remarkable role that business has taken throughout the century.

THE CORPORATE ROLE

Corporate executives enjoy resources and influence that are not available to other civic actors. They can tap the wealth of their enterprises, and their business associations provide professional expertise, private debating forums, and networks of colleagues who can be called on for support. Their authority to make economic decisions in capitalist societies gives them uncommon influence over politicians, who must worry about the political consequences of job creation, plant sitings and closings, and the business cycle. Access to resources and politicians means that their influence can achieve many kinds of results unaided, whereas other community actors with fewer resources must find collaborators.[39]

The structural aspect of business power is especially salient in cities where a major firm's ability to leave town is taken quite seriously by politicians, because cities serve as economic "substitutes for each other" in average worker productivity or transportation costs.[40] Business influence is strongest when it is directed toward political executives rather than legislative bodies, where logrolling and compromise make it more difficult for corporate executives to hold individual politicians accountable. Each of these elements of corporate power is apparent in Chicago.

Nor are such advantages new. Historians have taken note of the influence of corporate leaders when our urban school systems were formed, although their precise role has been hotly debated. A revisionist literature argues that business tycoons, with the willing support of the state, imposed a school system on the lower classes,[41] while others counter that rival good-government groups were more influential in shaping urban school systems.[42] Some highlight the divisions among business leaders themselves.[43] Julia Wrigley has emphasized the intense class conflict that existed between business organizations and labor unions. In her view, business leaders' insistence on cheap and limited versions of schooling for the working class were effectively countered by labor groups that believed that working-class children should receive a broad liberal education.[44] Such disagreements are important because each side recognizes that the groups responsible for forming the system in the early years of the twentieth century bear part of the blame for its failures today.

Quite different disagreements about the corporate impact on schools characterize the civil rights era. Although it was common for political scientists to notice business's intervention in urban policy making between World War II and 1980,[45] educators tended to take more notice of business's absence, and a few young Chicago scholars wrote in business's defense.[46] For this period, the argument turns on whether business leaders hurt or helped desegregation efforts.[47]

The extensive literature on business involvement since the 1980s is heavily weighted toward its national influence. Some parse the differences between local corporate involvement that provides philanthropic assistance and that of nationally oriented firms, which is often at odds with the interests of local school systems and students.[48] Others suggest that the debate hinges on whether reforms attempt to promote greater inclusion or improved instruction.[49] Yet another segment examines business efforts to provide services to schools, abetting their commercialization.[50]

The eleven case studies discussed in Stone and colleagues' work provide strong evidence of corporate involvement that was advantaged by robust associations and experience with informal policy networks; their informants mentioned no group more often, with the exception of mayors and school boards, when asked about key reform actors. But they focus on the obstacles to business groups' becoming effective coalition partners, including their tendency to see educational problems in economic terms and the proclivity to lose interest if courts or the federal government get involved. Stone identified the cohesion and organization of the corporate sector as a key measure of civic capacity for reform.[51]

This book confirms many of these themes. Chicago's business associations have been consistent and powerful actors, engaged in nearly every effort to improve the city's public schools during the twentieth century. The corporate leaders described in these chapters were vitally interested in the nature of reform, and their ideas about management and efficiency, governance, and social stability determined their goals. Their motives varied from material self-interest—attempts to sell their goods to schools, efforts to keep the costs of city services low—to the altruistic desire to improve the civic life of a city by fostering better citizens.

Although corporate leaders were not limited to a single blueprint, a dominant business reform agenda—managerialism—emerged in the late nineteenth and early twentieth centuries and has been remarkably influential in shaping the structure of Chicago's schools ever since. Business leaders brought their expertise as senior managers to the coalitions they joined or led, steering agendas toward a prominent role for executives who directed a hierarchy below them and adjusted accountability sanctions and rewards. Their efforts at institutional redesign have emphasized separating and routinizing the system's business and educational practices to make them more susceptible to planning, prediction, and managerial manipulation. Since the Depression, this agenda has been altered to fit shifting definitions of modern managerialism (e.g., depending on the era, managerialism may encourage devolution or centralized decision making), but the idea that a large urban school system can be substantially improved through better management has remained essentially unchanged.

The early decades of the twentieth century fostered managerialism, but also saw the development of a more extreme and (at the time) less successful business program. It insisted that urban schools not only be run like businesses but also serve corporate ends: the training of workers and the discouragement of labor unions. This competing business agenda has an analogue today in some executives' preoccupation with remaking urban public schools in the image of market firms, to be guided primarily by competition and customer choice. At times the two business agendas have clashed, creating a schism, but never one that attracted much public notice.

Whether Chicago's business associations act unilaterally or in concert with other civic actors, their goals have always been contested, leaving outcomes far from certain. Business associations have repeatedly formed narrow coalitions, lobbying sympathetic officials on behalf of their agendas at the exclusion of everything else. But their unilateralism has drawn criticism and competition, even as it made corporate leaders the primary agents of change. They have also cooperated with other civic groups in a grand alliance. Collaboration both moderated the corporate leaders' plans and facilitated implementation by broadening the base of civic support for innovation. And when corporate leaders anticipated that planned improvements might be costly, socially destabilizing, or reduce their influence, they proved adept at stalling change.

If Chicago's history of attempts at urban school regime change is worth understanding, it is also because there are practical lessons to be learned. These include the importance of teachers and low-income parents as reform actors. Neither group, nor the organizations each has chosen to represent it—teachers unions and community-based organizations—can be dismissed as an impractical coalition partner if the goal is to improve the school experience and the performance of minority and low-income students. It is also clear that middle-class professional associations and researchers have a role to play, for they lend crucial legitimacy to reform plans and can shift agendas. Too little of the research that examines the performance of urban students directs itself to any of these audiences. And there are too few attempts by professional education researchers to focus on the reform of one city's schools over time.

Moreover, Chicago clarifies that civic debate is an essential ingredient in successful reform, rather than something to avoid in the interest of harmony. The public forums through which that debate occurs—neighborhood associations, community organizations, and summits; the new and old media; formal courses and informal gatherings; polls and focus groups—are no less significant to the politics of urban school reform than they are to the politics of democratic governance.

There are less felicitous lessons as well. At a time when it is common to assume that the economic imperatives of a city's competitive advantage require intent focus on the preferences expressed by its corporate leaders, Chicago's experience suggests that this might be an inappropriate emphasis for school reformers. Just as they dominated so much of the civic agenda in the years when the city's physical and social contours were shaped—by commissioning the Plan of Chicago, sustaining the city's radial center–periphery grid, and reifying the city's racial and ethnic distinctions—corporate executives have often set the agenda for the public schools. Even when they looked the other way, their absence was felt. Yet they are seldom required to justify or account for their actions. Indeed, their role is poorly understood, even in Chicago. Thus, I place the city's most influential civic actor at the center of its school reform narrative.

1

Shaping the Modern System

Vocationalism, Managerialism, and Efficiency 1880–1930

For most of its first fifty years, the Commercial Club of Chicago competed as one of many private interests attempting to influence public policy in the growing city. Other business associations, among them the Merchant's Club of Chicago, the Illinois Manufacturers Association, and the Chicago Association of Commerce, were also framers of the young city's social and economic infrastructure. Professional, reform, and labor groups vied for influence as well. But the Commercial Club had an advantage: its founding members were among the metropolis's wealthiest men and its commercial and industrial leaders. They personally symbolized the best of "scientific" management and business efficiency at a time when these phrases evoked modernity, progress, and the highest achievements of Western civilization.

This half century, which includes the Progressive era, began after the Industrial Revolution and workplace efficiency made millionaires of nearly 300 adventurous men who journeyed west to Chicago.[1] It closed with the Great Depression, in which many were ruined. During this era Chicago became the nation's "second city" and the industrial and transportation hub of the heartland. In 1870 it had about 300,000 people living on 35 square miles. Over the next twenty-five years it swelled to 1.3 million people living on 185 square miles, growing faster than any other city in the United States. This period established the city's industrial foundation, its spatial patterns, and its civic habits along "sharp cleavages based on class, ethnicity and race" that resonate today.[2]

In 1877 Chicago's business titans established the Commercial Club as their private debating forum. From the first, their elite status and the far-flung markets they commanded gave them the social and economic security to concentrate their discussions—and soon their activism—on local civic affairs, including public schooling, a passion they inherited from an earlier wave of pioneer businessmen.[3]

By its fifth year, the club had built the city's first vocational school. Within a decade the group was cosponsoring legislation to centralize, bureaucratize, and bring business efficiency to all the public schools. By the end of this half century the club controlled the school system's budget and financing. Yet each time legislation was sponsored with the Commercial Club's imprimatur, it attracted a different group of opposing forces—civic reform groups, the Democratic Party, and other business associations among them. Mayors were frequently supportive of business plans for the schools, but not always so. In Chicago's fractious, pluralist political culture, the Commercial Club was merely one exceptionally well endowed private-interest group vying for influence over a shifting array of politicians.

No socioeconomic cleavage was more persistent than the one between club members and organized labor. If the late nineteenth century was a period of commercial and industrial consolidation and huge profits, it was also a time of company towns; exploited, often immigrant labor; and militant trade unions. The club's first and strongest adversaries in all its public school initiatives were the unions and workers movements that transformed labor in Chicago. They characterized the elite executives of the club as essentially conspiratorial profiteers.

Club members self-righteously believed that the rapidly growing public schools could simultaneously upgrade the masses, preserve order, and provide young workers. They sought to vocationalize, economize, and rationalize schooling, steering it by judicious application of the same governing principles they thought best for their own businesses: keep taxes low, organize the work "scientifically," and, above all, trust in management. Labor groups provided an alternative vision of schooling that emphasized worker democracy in governance, social change through education, and equal access for all students to the highest levels of public schooling.[4] Teachers federations and industrial unions fought to maintain teacher autonomy, union control over workplace skills, and a secure flow of public funding.[5]

Union and Commercial Club members agreed that most students were destined for agricultural, industrial, or commercial employment, but they differed on how education ought to prepare them. While unions fought for regular increases in school funding, the club wanted to link the funding of public education to its own members' financial circumstances: encouraging generosity when profits were high, insisting on cutbacks when they dipped. The public debate fostered by these opposing forces was the raw material from which the city's twentieth-century public school system was formed.[6]

This labor-capital antagonism produced more conflicts than the relationship between the club and the city's politicians, who routinely sold their favors and votes. County tax assessors imposed scandalously low valuations on club members' personal property and real estate, shifting the tax burden onto shopkeepers and the middle class.[7] Corrupt aldermen sold city franchises for a few hundred dollars per vote.[8] City and school board property was bought or leased by private investors at prices far below market value.[9]

Although club members benefited from municipal corruption in these and other ways, many were offended when the same practices succored the outlawed businesses of prostitution, gambling, opium, and alcohol. Their moralizing put them at odds with some mayors and aldermen, and their business ethic put them in conflict with others. For the first fifty years of the Commercial Club's existence, local politics was fragmented, and until 1907, their two-year terms produced mayors who frequently had to choose whether to antagonize club members with "clout," union members with votes, or reformers with access to the media.

To George Counts, the city was "a population that finds itself organized, either by design or by the accidents of association, into hundreds, even thousands of organizations, each demanding a more generous portion of the social income."[10] In this fractious environment, club members expected to do good while doing well. Goaded by muckrakers, other reformers, and their own wives, and aiming to distinguish themselves from the notoriously rapacious among them, many joined civic groups such as the Citizen's Association of Chicago (1874), the Civic Federation (1893), the City Club (1903), or the board of Hull House (1889).[11] Social critics such as William T. Stead, Jane Addams, Upton Sinclair, Graham Taylor, and economist Thorstein Veblen exposed the awful plight of workers, convincing a few businessmen and their wives to become "genteel" reformers. They sought relief for the poor, better sanitation and housing, and more efficiency and less corruption in municipal government, aiming for a community in which the laboring classes would accommodate to their dependence on the wealthy.[12]

CIVIC BETTERMENT AND "THE SUBJECT OF EDUCATION"

Chicago's titans were among the wealthiest capitalists in the nation. As Frederic Jaher described them: "Money making was the chief aim of these volatile manipulators and those with the largest fortunes received the most respect."[13] Some acquired their fortunes with innovations in wholesale marketing, meat and grain processing, department store retailing, textile and shoe manufacturing, farm machinery assembling, or furniture making. Others constructed the city's canals, streetcars, railroad cars, and elevators. About 60 percent had migrated west from Massachusetts, New York, or Pennsylvania to watch over the speculative ventures of patrons or to seek their own fortunes in the city "atop the urban hierarchy" of its region. Later, the same group controlled the city's utilities, steel and iron production, and banking and insurance firms.[14]

Whatever source generated their wealth, most also speculated in Chicago real estate, especially in the Loop, the city's central commercial and financial district, where astonishing profits were made. Thus began a century-long pattern of concentrating development in the Loop, at the expense of Chicago's other neighborhoods.[15] Between 1873 and 1892 aggregate land values (within the 1933 city limits) multiplied twelvefold and exploded in the Loop.[16] Land speculation, in turn, fueled local credit markets. By 1877 Chicago's financiers were able to provide more than half the credit needed by local merchants and industrialists, and by 1900 Chicago ranked second only to New York as a money market.

Market growth reinforced business leaders' vision of a heroic future for the city and their belief that it would result quite naturally from Chicago's unique assets: its "natural" port, the trade advantages afforded by its railroads, and a concentration of commercial and industrial firms led by the rugged pioneers they saw themselves to be.[17] Even so, ties to eastern capital, nurtured by personal relationships, remained crucial.[18]

Twenty-eight of Chicago's tycoons formed the Commercial Club after hosting a three-day visit by a delegation from the nine-year-old Commercial Club of Boston.[19] Among the first members were William T. Stead's "Chicago Trinity" of capitalists, whom he claimed were "worshiped" for their moneymaking powers: Marshall Field, Phillip D. Armour, and George M. Pullman.[20] Levi Z. Leiter, a partner with Marshall Field in the department store business and the father of an infamous and self-destructive commodity speculator, was chosen the club's first president.[21] These "Anglo-Saxon Yankees," as the press referred to them, had arrived in the 1850s and created their wealth in Chicago during the intervening two decades.[22] The members were well acquainted, investing in one another's businesses and sending their children to the same elite New England and New York schools. Two-thirds of them had rebuilt their homes after the Great Fire of 1871 within a five-block radius around Prairie Avenue.[23]

The official history of the club describes how they saw themselves: "To be eligible for membership a man must have shown conspicuous success in his private business with a broad and comprehending sympathy with important affairs of city and state and a generous subordinating of self in the interests of the community."[24] In addition to their discussions of the public schools, members debated municipal reform, Chicago's infrastructure development, labor issues, and taxation.[25]

Building local commercial and financial networks while enhancing Chicago's reputation as a great metropolis did not limit the club's contacts or its members' interests. About half of the club's meetings in this era were devoted to national politics, federal trade regulation, foreign policy, or war.[26] Information about "the affairs of the entire country," as one New York journalist described Chicago's business discourse, permeated their meetings.[27] Club members frequently traveled to Cincinnati and St. Louis to further ties to those rival commercial centers and to help establish Commercial Clubs in those cities. By the beginning of the twentieth century, the nation's four Commercial Clubs organized joint expeditions to new markets, first to San Francisco, and then to Cuba and Panama.[28] Such contacts permitted the easy exchange of new ideas about the organization of social life and the design of civic institutions, providing a means by which a member's national or international interests could be furthered at home.

Consequently, the club's local initiatives both reflected and influenced national concerns. When club members championed a separate system of vocational schools for Illinois, they also helped spur a national debate by unions, business associations, and intellectuals in other states.[29] The club's efforts to centralize and rationalize the schools coincided with a national movement also spurred by events in Chicago.[30] Its attempts to cut public school costs during the 1930s drew criticism from across the nation, although urban reformers and business groups in other cities were also worried about misspent taxes.[31] Its national reach and its members' blend of boosterism and cosmopolitan attitudes made it a conduit for big ideas with widespread applications.

More meetings were held and more committees were formed on education than on any other local issue during the club's first fifty years.[32] The chairman of its Education Committee in 1915, Theodore W. Robinson, confirmed this with pride: "It is a fact that in the thirty or more years of [its] existence there has been no activity with which this Club has concerned itself in some phase or other for so long a time and in so expensive a manner as the subject of education."[33]

VOCATIONAL EDUCATION

The club's initial effort to change the course of public schooling was to build the Chicago Manual Training School on Michigan Avenue and Twelfth Street as a model for the efficient preparation of boys for engineering and industrial work. At a club meeting in 1882, Marshall Field pledged $20,000 for its construction and challenged his fellow members to match his gift, raising $110,000. George M. Pullman, N. K. Fairbank, Richard T. Crane, Field, and five other club members became the school's board of trustees.[34]

They anticipated that the public school system would copy their prototype and succeeded in encouraging the opening of a public manual training high school in 1890, while club financing paid for shop classes in elementary schools.[35] After operating the Chicago Manual Training School for fourteen years, the club transferred ownership to the University of Chicago. University president and club member William Rainey Harper sustained the school for a few more years.

But technical training in industrial skills developed strong opposition. The school was entirely reorganized in 1902 when the university received a $1 million gift from the heir to the McCormick fortune, Anita McCormick Blaine. She stipulated that the school be combined with the South Side Academy and put under the overall direction of University of Chicago professor John Dewey, who saw manual training as "methods of living and learning, not as distinct studies."[36] Despite strong letters and threatened lawsuits from businessmen and parents who protested the "extremely wide departure" from the club's initial impulse, their industrial education prototype succumbed to Dewey's vision of active learning. They referred to Dewey's concept as "cultural training," by which they meant socially useful but not vocationally useful education.[37]

Club members concluded that their ideas about vocational schooling would be better institutionalized if they were enacted into law by the Illinois legislature and governed by business leaders, independent of the public schools. Believing that their original attempt had been fatally compromised, their new plan was to create a parallel ("dual") system of secondary vocational schools for Chicago under the direction of a board made up of two businessmen, two workers, and the regular school superintendent as an ex officio member. It would have separate funding and would be part-time (six hours per week) and compulsory for children aged fourteen to eighteen who had completed primary school and did not attend an academic high school (estimated at about 80 to 90 percent of the age group at the time).[38] A state commission was to approve courses and schools "to secure uniformity."[39] According to the enabling legislation, club members expected to have representation on both the state commission and the local board, ensuring an ongoing influence on the curriculum. Their primary justification was "new and rapidly expanding economic forces" brought about by international competition that were "demanding an elementary training for industrial workers."[40]

In 1909 the club commissioned outgoing superintendent of schools Edwin G. Cooley (1900–1909) to develop its vision and draft a law. Cooley was an apt choice. He had grown frustrated by the slow spread of manual training programs in his second term as superintendent and did not question the businessmen's rationale. Like them, Cooley believed that centralized control using modern management techniques was the best way to ensure efficient implementation of vocational schooling and other reforms. He envisioned the superintendent as the primary educational decision maker, and he saw his relationship to an ideally business-led board as analogous to that of a corporate president to his board of directors. He did not view himself as a municipal agency head because that involved working in the arena of party politics, with its attendant corruption and patronage. While superintendent he had been able to cut (temporarily) the number of Chicago school board committees from seventeen to four, demonstrating his version of a nonpolitical school system. It did not hurt that, in the process, he curtailed the board's ability to gather independent information with which to countermand his decisions.[41]

In his view, solving the dropout, overcrowding, and motivational problems that many observers agreed were widespread in the schools also required a systematic approach. And, like other reformers of the time, he addressed the "moral reformation of the child," by which he meant industry, punctuality, and obedience, expecting these virtues to be taught in the schools as well.[42]

Cooley freed himself to work for the club by resigning the superintendency in March 1909. Though the Club's offer was attractive, he was also pushed out by one of several mayoral attempts to refashion the school board in the image of city hall politics. In this case, the mayor was Edward Dunne (1905–1907), one of very few municipal reformers who held the office. Dunne thought that government ought to guard against the "machinations of predatory private interests."[43] His reformist credentials were strong: a former judge with no hint of personal scandal, he regularly wrote for progressive journals and ran for office championing the immediate municipal appropriation of Chicago's transit system. The issue had tremendous appeal by 1905, since its private owner, Samuel Insull, was notorious for bribing elected officials to gain scandalously low franchises and providing poor service in the bargain. Many of the club's leaders condemned the corruption he represented. Even though they were deeply committed to privatism, Insull was so despised that they set themselves apart from him by arguing that "the answer lay in better-managed, or at most, more regulated private enterprise." Yet Mayor Dunne's position was beyond the pale, representing in their view the "socialist" enemy.[44]

Dunne used his appointment power to remove the school board's pro-business members. Contending that "labor and middle class people are better able to determine what is good for them than the Merchant's Club," and turning for advice to union leaders, he appointed a slim majority of good-government reformers and union supporters, including settlement workers Jane Addams and physician and kindergarten advocate Cornelia B. De Bay; "single-tax" supporters Wiley Wright Mills and Louis F. Post, editor of the progressive weekly *The Public;* union leaders John J. Sonsteby of the Garment Workers Union and John C. Harding of the Typographical Union; and patron Anita McCormick Blaine, a supporter of Addams, Francis Parker, and John Dewey.[45] Together this board crafted a majority in favor of suing for the collection of underpaid corporate property taxes, renegotiating the undervalued 100-year fixed-rate leases that several corporations held on downtown school property, and championing the teacher's voice in school governance. All these changes put them at odds with Superintendent Cooley and his business supporters. For their trouble, the reformers were dubbed "freaks, cranks, megalomaniacs and boodlers" by the *Chicago Tribune,* and twelve of them were illegally removed from office by the next mayor, coal merchant Fred A. Busse (1907–1911), who promptly replaced most of them with businessmen.[46]

Cooley served as the club's resident education adviser for about ten years. Steel magnate Theodore Robinson made it clear that Cooley spoke for them. When Cooley opened his mouth or lifted his pen, Robinson asserted, "it is The Commercial Club that is speaking or writing."[47] Unconstrained by having been appointed president of the school board by Mayor Busse, Robinson also spoke up on behalf of the club. He believed that well-designed vocational schools could enhance the productivity of each worker by as much as 10 cents a day. He saw a causal relationship and a model for Chicago schooling when he looked to Germany's early-twentieth-century economic rise and its two-tiered system of schools.[48] In arguments aimed at convincing his fellow club members to lobby for a "Cooley bill" in the Illinois legislature, he identified vocational education as "a question of property and property rights . . . not only a question of the economic efficiency of this nation . . . that directly concerns not only the production of wealth, but [also] the distribution of wealth."[49]

At least one of the trustees of the Chicago Manual Training School disagreed. Richard T. Crane Sr., who had personally donated hundreds of thousands of dollars to Chicago schools for vocational training classes, argued that such training had never been more than "ancillary" to public schooling and was ultimately transformed by its association with the public schools into cultural work. He also disputed Robinson's premise that Americans had cause for alarm because of Germany's labor force, citing Frederick Winslow Taylor's metallurgy advances at Bethlehem Steel as evidence of U.S. industrial superiority *without* vocational schools.[50]

Crane's dissent was read to the club at a 1911 meeting, but the reader felt compelled to disavow its sentiments, adding his own rationale for vocational schooling: "Statistics show that there are about 30,000 boys between the ages of fourteen and sixteen who are neither in school nor at work . . . this vocational education that we are favoring is to do something for that boy after he leaves the elementary school."[51]

The main argument of Cooley's two-volume report supported Robinson's belief that the vocational schools of Germany had accelerated its industrial development and solidified its nation building. For club members, the examples of Germany and, to a lesser extent, Scotland, Switzerland, and Austria pointed to one answer for the educational and economic future of the United States: a wholly independent system of public vocational schools to ensure that the nation used its labor resources efficiently.[52]

If there was a time when political influence and economic power should have won the day, this was it. Chicago's corporate leaders were well organized and willing to invest their own resources, had great influence in city hall and a clear plan for what they wanted, and could tie their vision to the economic productivity of the city and the nation during a period of rapid economic change. Moreover, the Chicago Association of Commerce, the Civic Federation, the Hamilton Club, the Illinois Manufacturers Association, and several other manufacturers groups all endorsed the Cooley bill. To garner popular support they distributed more than 2,000 copies of Cooley's report and 3,000 copies each of four related pamphlets. They enlisted Cooley to give thirty-seven lectures outside of Chicago and twenty lectures in town. Their efforts brought praise in the national press, as well as the support of leading intellectual adherents to the corporate efficiency cause, such as Massachusetts commissioner of education David Snedden and Columbia University president Nicholas Murray Butler.[53]

Yet the Cooley bill drew strong local opposition. The reformist City Club opposed the Commercial Club's plans, suspecting that a separate vocational system would "encourage professional jealousy" among teachers. It might stigmatize vocational students or simply fail to attract them, because working-class parents "have an unshaken confidence in the democratic character of the 'regular' public school."[54] Notwithstanding such qualms, the City Club, the City Women's Club, and the Chicago Women's Club, as well as Jane Addams and Cooley's successor as superintendent, Ella Flagg Young, all acknowledged the powerful argument that the public schools ought to prepare students for their destined work in the region's large-scale industrial and commercial economy.[55] City Club members justified their position by referring to the high dropout rate and claiming that a vocational program was required to sustain student interest. Addams thought that properly organized vocational schools could overcome class alienation by teaching "the implications, the connections and the relation to the industrial world."[56] On such grounds they commissioned an alternative bill, specifically designed to counter the club's emphasis on creating a separate system. The City Club's plan engaged the regular public schools in the provision of vocational education (the "unit" system).

John Dewey, by then at Columbia University, also criticized the Cooley bill. He was concerned not only that it increased the "tendency for stratification of the classes" but also that "it prepares the way, if it passes, for future separations" between state-supported religious schools, labor-run schools, and ethnically distinct schools, all under their own separate sectarian administration.[57] In any case, vocational education of the sort that he embraced and Ella Flagg Young advocated would "alter the existing industrial system," not "adapt" students to it.[58]

Support for some sort of legislation was bolstered in 1912 when a City Club survey revealed that 86 percent of 300 "leading" Chicago employers were dissatisfied with the skills of job applicants.[59] Since both sides accepted the argument that the new industrial economy created the need for vocational schooling, the differences between the "dual" and the "unit" systems were fought out over elite dinner tables and in the press.[60] Neither faction could persuade the other, however, and neither the Cooley bill nor the City Club alternative became law.

THE LABOR-CAPITAL CONFLICT

Competition between the Commercial Club and the City Club might have led to a compromise. Not so opposition from the city's labor unions. In *Class Politics and Public Schools,* Julia Wrigley writes persuasively: "The most fundamental dispute in Chicago's educational history occurred over the scope of education for working class children."[61] The terms of this larger debate were set by the Commercial Club and its various business and professional supporters at one pole and the Chicago Teachers Federation and its union and professional supporters at the other.[62]

Conflicts between labor and business had begun even before the Commercial Club's first forays into vocational education. The year of the club's founding, 1877, also brought a railroad strike that nearly came to open warfare between workers and the industrial elite. The Haymarket bombing in 1886 dramatized industrialists' efforts to keep Chicago's labor force docile and its organizations quiescent. National attention was riveted on Chicago again in 1893–1894 during the Pullman strikes. Throughout, only passing notice is given to the suffering of the laboring classes, immigrants, and the poor in club records.[63] The plight of workers was also a minor factor in its first Plan of Chicago (1909), begun a week after the Columbian Exhibition of 1893–1894 and the same year that William T. Stead gave his fiery speech indicting Chicago government for failing to protect the working class from the excesses of capitalism.[64]

The struggle centered on the dual system. Like City Club reformers, the Chicago Federation of Labor (CFL) and its affiliate, the all-female elementary school Chicago Teachers Federation (CTF), agreed with the Commercial Club that a vocational program was needed for working-class children. A CFL report conducted in 1902 deplored the 50 percent dropout rate among ten- to twelve-year-olds and called for some form of vocational education that might better prepare them for work while encouraging longer school attendance. Agreeing with the City Club, unionists endorsed vocational training as an addition to the regular curriculum, not a replacement of it. Unionists were also worried that a dual system of schools would deny working-class students the opportunity to learn academic subjects and thus block their social mobility. They were opposed to any vocational education that prepared children for the "nerve-destroying" aspects of factory work and worried, along with Dewey, that permitting a separate system would make it more difficult to change "mechanical" and "monotonous" industrial processes. Further, they suggested that the dual system was a "ploy" to divide teachers into classes and reduce their salaries to pay for redundant administrations.[65]

The result was an intense battle in the state capital that extended over the legislative sessions of 1913, 1915, and 1917. The CTF, CFL, and Illinois Federation of Labor, with help from a shifting array of civic groups, succeeded in defeating the legislation each time, but only after it had become a political issue throughout the state and nation. In 1913 these labor groups opposed the Cooley bill chiefly because it would set up a system run by and for businessmen. In 1915 the contest was less a struggle between rival vocational education bills and more a fight for or against the Cooley bill. Again the bill was strongly opposed by "selfish self interested and labor politics," according to Robinson, and "a number of professors of the large colleges," as another club member acknowledged. Yet it was defeated.[66] By 1917 there was only a slight chance of passage.

After the federal Smith-Hughes bill was signed into law on February 28, 1917, Illinois passed the required enabling legislation that brought federal matching funds for the training and salaries of vocational education teachers. Club members had lobbied for this bill in Congress and took credit for its passage.[67] The club's Education Committee chairman, Sewell Avery, soothed the sting of the Cooley bill's third defeat; "the big problem with which the Club has been laboring in the past several years may have been answered in the passage of the Smith-Hughes Bill."[68] With this weak declaration of victory, Avery also acknowledged that the club had heightened the class-based animosity in the city by pursuing its own school system. Perhaps unintentionally, according to historian David Hogan, the club had also initiated a process that led to the institutionalization of vocational, industrial, and commercial tracking in regular schools for a significant minority of Chicago students.[69]

CENTRALIZATION AND EFFICIENCY

Although the Commercial Club did not succeed in its legislative attempt to put vocational schools under business control, members could claim more success in centralizing and bureaucratizing the governance of the regular schools. Here too they championed management changes that could be enacted by legislation. This time, the legislation they sought was presented as the rational alternative to political favoritism and graft, as well as being linked to the global economy. George E. Vincent, president of the University of Minnesota, helped provide their justification. In a 1912 speech to the club, he claimed that the frontier ethic of American individualism was being challenged by international competition: "The stress used to be put on opportunity for the individual. Now it is laid on efficiency for the factory, the railway, the city government, the nation as a competing unit."[70]

The twin ethics of efficiency and "scientific" management so permeated U.S. culture at the turn of the nineteenth century that it is impossible to pinpoint the precise source or significance of business in advancing those ideas.[71] Even so, the Commercial Club was more of an advocate in this regard than many business organizations of the time. Its official historian clarified the members' goal: "What they meant by 'business matters of the public interest' was found to be the application of business principles to the minutest detail of providing for the comfort and betterment of the poorest, the most illiterate, as well as the rich and cultivated."[72]

The club's first legislative efforts to reorganize public schooling along "business principles" drew on work commissioned in 1898 by Chicago's mayor, Carter H. Harrison II (1897–1905, 1911–1915). Harrison was a compromiser, championing a businesslike administration in city hall but also the rights of the working class to enjoy their vices. This made him unpopular among the city's moral reformers, who would have closed down the saloons, gambling dens, and brothels. Nor did patronage and partisanship trouble him. Harrison's only consistent interest in reform was to make government more efficient. He created a bureau of statistics, a city manual, and a municipal library. He championed the municipal ownership of transit only to curtail aldermanic boodling (use fees, he reasoned, should go to the city rather than into their pockets).[73] Like Cooley, he accepted the arguments of business leaders and educators when they said that the school system was inefficient, and he assumed that businessmen could recommend useful changes.

One way was to charge business leaders with fixing a "system in operation for the government and supervision of the public schools of Chicago [that] is not giving a measure of results commensurate with the generous financial resources furnished by the people." He accomplished this by appointing an eleven-person blue-ribbon Commission on Educational Reorganization in 1898. Its problem was framed as a lack of efficiency and economy in school governance, including "grave defects" in the administration of the schools, "unsatisfactory" delegation of school board powers to subcommittees, and a lack of teacher "incentive" due to varying pay and performance standards.[74]

The head of this commission was William Rainey Harper, president of the University of Chicago, school board president, president of the Civic Federation's Education Committee, and Commercial Club member. The other commissioners consisted of one rabbi, three aldermen, and six businessmen, including at least one other club member.[75] The Harper Commission was heavily influenced by fifty or so members of what David Tyack and Elisabeth Hansot called the "education trust," which was preaching the virtues of centralization and expert efficiency in public schooling; among them were thirteen presidents of elite colleges and twelve superintendents of large urban school systems.[76]

The commission's report had twenty specific recommendations, most of which supported the management proposition that there should be a professional head of the school system who made the educational decisions, with a business manager to run financial affairs. The existing structure gave a twenty-one-member mayor-appointed school board nearly complete authority to make all decisions, with advice from many (seventeen, at the time) citizens committees with broad jurisdiction over teacher appointments, textbook selection, supplies, and buildings. The superintendent and other officers served as staff. The image the commission used to convey its "essential" changes in governance was political—the superintendent and his staff would be the executive branch of school governance, and the board would be the legislative.[77]

The political imagery was ironic, for the commission sought to take party loyalty and patronage out of the school system by replacing school board authority with a professional loyalty to hierarchy and efficiency, while retaining mayoral appointment of the board. Most decisions would be made by the two key executives who ran the system: an independent business manager would mimic "the executive in any well-conducted business enterprise," having the authority to appoint and remove subordinates and determine the financial feasibility of projects. The superintendent would hire and fire teachers and principals, arrange the course of study, choose textbooks, and determine the methods of student examination. The board itself would be cut in half to eleven members, and its authority would be delegated to the two executives.[78]

Other features of Harper's report fit the corporate model as well, including a hierarchy of managers from general superintendent through school principals to teachers, performance-based promotion, and differential pay based on gender. Less attractive to club members were the commission's embrace of teachers federations and its encouragement of teachers councils, designed to "offer the teachers an opportunity to make their experience profitable to the whole system." The inclusion of "resident commissioners to represent the people in oversight of the schools in various sections of the city," or mayor-appointed lay school inspectors, were also elements of the Harper Commission report they disavowed.[79]

The Teachers' Democratic Challenge

Critics of the report, including the fiery Margaret Haley, cofounder with Catherine Goggin of the CTF, agreed that the Harper Commission's model for school governance was borrowed from private enterprise: the company president, his fiscal officer, and the corporate board.[80] Sharing a mistrust of business motives with single-taxers, socialists, and religiously motivated reformers, Haley complained that, having founded the University of Chicago and ensconced Harper as its president, Rockefeller money and influence were now forcing the "power in American business" on the schools.[81]

Not surprisingly, the CTF had a different vision of school governance. Harper, other administrative progressives, and business elites agreed that education should be organized from the end point backward—assuming that college-educated or factory-trained gainful employment and corresponding civic responsibilities were the outcomes of interest. The CTF convinced middle-class reform groups and working-class unions that education in a democracy had to be organized from the beginning forward. Universal kindergarten undergirded the CTF's model for public schooling, rather than university education for the few and factory drudgery for the masses, which seemed to guide businessmen's thinking. Opportunities for children of all social strata to make informed choices about their lives based on experiences and ideas they had been exposed to in the public schools constituted the essence of civic reform. To the CTF, the machinery of government should be reorganized to serve this purpose.[82] In the words of one incredulous superintendent, it was the concept "that the public school system should be a democratic institution, and that the body of teachers constitute the democratic government."[83]

By 1897, when Haley was elected vice president of the CTF, she had already developed a presence in Chicago's dailies as a corporate critic and was frequently derided for what was perceived as her Irish-Catholic pro-labor bias. Both she and Goggin had been elementary school teachers in Chicago's overcrowded immigrant and African American South and Westside schools for about twenty-five years. Their political skills complemented each other: Haley was convinced that through political education teachers could improve their circumstances and rebalance civic power, which was tilted in favor of "machine civilization which tries to extinguish all leadership other than its own."[84] Disagreeing with many suffragists, she did not think that female teachers' civic responsibility began at the ballot box, but rather with political organizing, grassroots petitioning, lobbying, and deep analysis of the sources of power in democracy. A consummate negotiator, Goggin's charm and humor could bring a room to consensus and action after it had been roused to heated debate by Haley's partisan oratory. Their paired skills were recognized in 1903 when the CTF voted to pay them both as full-time staff members. By then, historian Kate Rousmaniere tells us, the teachers' cause was already woven into "the broader fabric of progressive municipal reform."[85]

The Harper Commission produced draft legislation aimed at enabling the management changes but leaving out those that were offensive to Commercial Club members. Particular attention was paid to maintaining the close relationship between city hall and the board of education: the board was to keep its funds in the city treasury, and the mayor was required to cosign all real estate and budget transactions.[86]

The Harper bill was vigorously opposed by the CTF because it overly centralized decision making and established "efficiency" as the primary performance criterion for teachers. It also required a college degree for teachers, in effect limiting the social mobility of working-class women at a time when 80 percent of the female teachers were Catholic and up to 33 percent were Irish.[87] As would soon be the case for union opposition to vocational education, opposition to the Harper bill centered on the question of control, and the position of business leaders and administrative reformers would harden on this issue too. Cooley's predecessor, Superintendent Benjamin Andrews (1898–1900), characterized the CTF stance as "protecting mediocrity and incompetence."[88]

Each time legislation of this sort was proposed over the next decade, the CTF assembled a larger group of allies to oppose it. In 1899 it gathered 50,000 signatures on an opposing petition. In 1901 Superintendent Cooley collaborated with club and school board member Clayton Mark and the Civic Federation to draft a second Harper bill, destined, Cooley hoped, to give him the legal authority that he was slowly wheedling from the board. But defeat came again, this time from the combined opposition of the CFL and the CTF.[89]

Their cooperation led the two labor organizations to affiliate one year later in a historic and widely decried alliance. Whereas the typical administrative progressive assumed that female teachers should associate with school administrators and university professors as their junior partners in a common profession, the CTF's strategy was to link working-class parents with working-class teachers. Haley admitted that in doing so the teachers joined forces with often disorganized, discordant, and sometimes corrupt labor organizations, but she believed more strongly that "the school alone was powerless against organized wealth."[90]

John Fitzpatrick, the CFL president in 1902, extended the invitation to the CTF as part of his effort to encourage a progressive orientation with democratic processes, including "a demand for justice for the teachers and the children so that both may not be crushed by the power of corporate greed." He sweetened the offer by clarifying that the women teachers, still portrayed as caring, community oriented, and self-sacrificing, need not honor the men's strikes.[91] The benefits of unionization were unusually clear to the CTF's heavily Irish-Catholic membership, whose fathers and brothers, like Haley's, were union men; the women deliberated for only five weeks before joining. After affiliating with the CFL, the CTF also joined the new National Women's Trade Union and the Illinois Federation of Women's Clubs.

Infuriated but undaunted by the labor union coalition, club members pressed on. Clayton Mark coauthored with Cooley another version of the Harper bill in 1903 and submitted it to the state legislature as an alternative to that year's Civic Federation bill, although the two differed only in the size of the board.[92] Both were defeated again by the combination of the CTF, the CFL, and their growing coalition of civic reform groups and unions.[93] By 1904 the CTF took the offensive in the battle for control, organizing a drive to put the democratic concept of an elected board to the vote on a citywide referendum. Although only advisory, it passed by a two-to-one margin.[94]

After suffering successive legislative defeats, punctuated by the election of the "radical" reformer Mayor Edward Dunne, the Commercial Club used the opportunity of a new city charter to restructure the schools. Between 1904 and 1906 club members prepared the education recommendations for the Charter Convention.[95] In 1907 the new city charter went before Chicago's voters in yet another referendum, and again the CTF and the CFL defeated the measure.

By this time, Mayor Fred A. Busse (1907–1911), a mainstream Republican businessman, had ousted Dunne's "radical" school board members, appointed business executives to half the vacant seats, and installed Theodore Robinson as board president.[96] For a time it looked as though this reconstituted business board, working with Superintendent Cooley, might achieve managerial centralization informally. In the hope of sanctioning their arrangements by law after the fact, Robinson wrote yet another version of the Harper Committee legislation on behalf of the club in 1909. The same labor opponents that had defeated each of its predecessors defeated Robinson's bill as well. Cooley gave up the superintendency soon after, frustrated that efficiency and centralization had not been enshrined in law and convinced that "no reorganization program would be successful so long as the CTF existed."[97]

When Busse's business board hired Ella Flagg Young (1909–1915) to replace Cooley, Chicago's first female school superintendent won some measure of labor peace. A brilliant student of John Dewey, Young had been a Chicago teacher, a district superintendent, a college professor, and principal of the Chicago normal (teacher training) school. A feminist, she was a champion of teachers councils, having argued for them in her dissertation, which was published in 1900 as *Isolation in the Schools*.[98] Teachers councils had been accepted by the 1898 board but sporadically implemented; the Dunne board had tried to organize them, but Cooley objected. Nor were teachers councils supported in any version of the Harper bill, because club leaders objected.

Preferring to create good working conditions and build on teachers' inner motivations in lieu of offering pay incentives, as the Harper Commission had sought, Young authorized the teachers in every elementary school to meet regularly and during school hours to debate curriculum, salary issues, working conditions, or classroom duties, as they saw fit. Each school council sent a representative to one of thirty-five district councils, which in turn sent delegates to a systemwide general council that met with the superintendent every five weeks. Though some teachers councils were unproductive, they gave classroom educators an unmediated voice in school decision making. For Superintendent Young, councils were the teachers' representative assembly. Even her business board preferred council advice to the CTF's accusations.[99]

Young also dismantled or ameliorated Cooley-era management initiatives by increasing salaries and altering promotion criteria. The business board showed little enthusiasm but supported her decisions until she joined the City Club in opposition to the Cooley bill, calling it "undemocratic." Young had long enjoyed strong teacher support; now she and the board became open adversaries.[100]

Cooley had provided managerial leadership that the Commercial Club members trusted. His style of decision making reduced the board's discretion, and the Harper bill would have institutionalized the changes. Yet under Superintendent Young's leadership, club members on the school board clung to their pre-Harper prerogatives, curtailing her authority whenever possible, even to the point of removing her ability to establish the curriculum.[101] Twice in 1913 she resigned over the board's efforts to shut down teachers federations, narrowly being reinstated each time only after pressure from an "ambivalent" Mayor Harrison, who was serving his final term (1911–1915).[102]

It was not until after Young was replaced that a centralization and efficiency law patterned after the Harper Commission report was enacted. The 1917 Otis law sanctioned the superintendent's authority over texts and instructional materials, school sites, educational approaches, and teacher appointments and transfers. It also created the positions of business manager and board attorney and reduced the number of seats on the school board. Legally the superintendent became the equivalent of a corporate leader, and school governance was centralized and professionalized.

An Impersonal Bureaucracy

Commercial Club members were a leading force behind passage of the Otis law, although by 1916 they had chosen to work through another organization. The Otis bill—named after its author Ralph Otis, a school board member and a relative and neighbor of Commercial Club member Joseph E. Otis—was championed primarily by the Public Education Association (PEA), formed in 1916 for that purpose. The founding president of the PEA was Commercial Club and Education Committee member Allan B. Pond. Two other club members served on the PEA directorate as well, one of whom sat with Pond on its Executive Committee and helped him supervise the publication of four "bulletins" to promote the bill.[103]

Although claiming to be "impartial statements of facts," the PEA bulletins attacked the democratic version of school governance promoted by the CTF, Dewey, and Young. In patronizing terms they asserted that Americans were "wrong" to believe that a board of education is "the means employed by the people to conduct the schools." Centralization was declared necessary to obtain "expert people," including a superintendent who "does exactly what the head of any great corporation does, he organizes the undertaking." "The board," they intoned, "should be small enough to meet around a single table to discuss matters in a simple, direct and business-like manner," and teachers were to be evaluated on "a scientific impersonal determination of the progress of the pupils."[104]

Several of these elements were present in another school reorganization bill before the legislature in 1917, but the Otis bill had two unique features designed to please businessmen. It required the board to hire a certified public accountant, who would report to the city on financial affairs every year, and it prohibited the board from usurping the functions of the independent business manager.[105] The Otis bill also reinstated tenure, an inducement to which the CTF was uniquely susceptible by then.[106] So, despite their long-standing resistance to centralization and expert efficiency, the CTF and the CFL did not oppose the Otis bill, effectively ensuring its passage.

The CTF's vulnerability had become clear two years earlier, in 1915. The Loeb rule, a thinly veiled attack on the CTF, was a board directive prohibiting teachers from affiliating with trade unions. It had been passed over Superintendent Young's strong objections. Board president Jacob Loeb could have been speaking for the ideologically laissez-faire industrialists of the Illinois Manufacturers Association when he justified his resolution: "Trade unionism is inconsistent and unnecessary to a professional career . . . it makes for divided allegiances . . . breeds suspicion and discontent . . . destroys harmony and creates strife . . . interferes with discipline and halts efficiency." He added, "We'll cut their professional throats if we have to."[107] The newly elected mayor, William Hale Thompson (1915–1923), supported the rule by delaying the naming of his new board appointees, who would have voted against it, but he was otherwise silent.[108]

After sixty-five teachers were denied reappointment for union organizing under the rule—thirty-eight of whom were current or former CTF officers—the unionists collaborated with the City Club, the Women's Club, and Hull House on an ill-fated governance bill of their own in a final attempt to undermine board authority. The Buck bill would have given teachers councils statutory authority, created an elected school board, and enshrined teacher tenure into law. Ultimately, however, the Loeb rule was upheld by the Illinois Supreme Court under the judicial argument that "the board has the absolute right to decline to employ or re-employ any applicant for any reason whatever, or no reason at all." The ruling forced the CTF to disaffiliate with the CFL and all other unions, including the Illinois Federation of Labor, the national Women's Trade Union League, and the American Federation of Teachers.[109] Using the same reasoning, the court also upheld a separate board rule that voided twenty-two years of teacher tenure, initially granted by Governor Altgeld as part of a pension arrangement in 1895.[110] The ruling came on the same day, April 5, 1917, that the Otis bill passed in the legislature. Only under this intense pressure were unionists willing to trade the central authority of the superintendent for the security of tenure.[111]

With the Loeb rule drawing nationwide approbation, including outraged articles in *American School* and *New Republic,* cleavages over school governance surfaced in the business community.[112] The Illinois Manufacturers Association had developed an ill-fated fourth option: the Baldwin bill, or the "business alternative" to the Otis bill.[113] The Illinois Manufacturers Association had formed the Public School League in 1916, "dedicated to the elimination of teachers federations" and opposed to the Commercial Club–backed PEA.[114] Had the Baldwin bill passed, it would have reaffirmed the Loeb rule and increased the board's power to sell school lands without city council approval, but it would have changed little else.[115]

Quite intentionally, the Commercial Club did not take a public stand on the Otis bill; it was unnecessary, since its influence in the PEA was strong. At the same time, club members sought to avoid antagonizing the teachers further or alienating the good-government groups. After decades of legislative defeat at the hands of the CTF and its labor allies, the club was no longer sanguine about its independent legislative effect. In the PEA, club leaders saw an opportunity to work through an intermediary organization. Furthermore, a few club members sided with the Illinois Manufacturers Association on the Baldwin bill. Thus, without a clear consensus, any public statement might have divided the club. And with war imminent, the attention of some members was shifting to military preparedness and homeland security.[116]

After World War I, club members let several years pass without mounting a major reform effort for business-style management of the schools. Instead, they formed short-lived committees to examine citizenship, Americanization, and the expansion of institutions of higher education as postsecondary enrollments burgeoned. They also quietly endorsed, over strong labor objections, the development of junior high schools, partly designed to "hold" workforce-bound students, and the platoon system; the latter was an efficiency measure requiring students to shift from room to room and each teacher to see as many as 400 students a day, but it also exposed children to longer periods of active learning. Superintendents Peter Mortensen (1920–1924) and William McAndrew (1924–1928) championed these pedagogical changes, and the businessmen's interest in them was fleeting.[117] But as the Depression arrived, club members were drawn into another long-standing goal: containing school costs.

SLASHING COSTS AND CONTAINING CORRUPTION

The class conflict reflected by unions and big business struggling over control of public schooling was also played out in arguments over school funding. The Chicago business community's concern about school finances and cost containment was partly a reaction to the lawsuits brought against tax-delinquent corporations by the CTF. Club members were also interested in securing economic stability and achieving the goals of public schooling at the least possible cost to themselves.

The open hostility between the unionized teachers and club members starkly exposed the school system's financial problems. In 1897 Margaret Haley and Catherine Goggin held their first meeting of the CTF to insist that the school board honor its promise to deliver salary increases that had already been approved but were delayed because the board claimed insufficient income. The injustice struck such a responsive chord among the female elementary school teachers that more than half of them (2,567) enrolled in the new federation within six months.[118] Convinced that corporate tax dodging was the root of the shortfall, Haley and Goggin wanted business tycoons to pay what they owed. In 1900 the CTF filed a lawsuit charging that the city's private utilities—all club member corporations—had failed to pay the required taxes on their monopoly franchises.[119] The corporations defended themselves in court until 1901, when they were finally defeated, but despite the Illinois Supreme Court ruling, they stalled their delinquent payments until 1904.[120]

Teacher anger over unpaid corporate taxes continued for decades. As late as 1926 the fourteen-year-old Federation of Men Teachers of High School embarrassed fifteen corporations by publicizing that they had not paid their share of school and city taxes due to unreasonably low assessments.[121] These corporations included the Pullman Car Company, Swift and Company, and Crane and Company, their owners among the now 100 members of the Commercial Club. The overall effect of these repeated public disclosures and lawsuits was to keep businessmen on the defensive.[122]

Thus, one reason the club became embroiled in the conflict over school funding was that its members were under attack. Between 1894 and 1902, the club held seven meetings during which members debated such topics as "How Can the Evils of Our Present System of Taxing Personal Property and Levying Special Assessments Be Reformed?" (1894) and "The Financial Aspect of the Chicago Public School Question"(1902).[123]

Union lawsuits against individual club members were common for the next two decades. But the club as a whole was not drawn further into the school funding debate until the eve of the Depression, when its members began to serve on the state and city commissions that reformulated tax and spending policy. By then, teachers' paychecks were routinely late, paid in scrip or tax-anticipation warrants. Teachers unions protested mightily, but to no avail.[124]

Other problems added to the school system's rising costs. Increased expenses came from ballooning enrollments: the citywide system of about 300,000 students in 1910 grew by nearly 100,000 in ten years and another

50,000 by 1930, and high school enrollments grew from 25,322 to 31,500 between 1915 and 1920 alone. New school services, such as vocational and manual training programs, guidance counselors, and junior high schools and kindergartens, as well as debt service, added expenses too.[125]

The close political link between city hall and the school board exacerbated the system's budgetary problems. Chicago had less economic stability than most big cities in the early twentieth century because of the erratic and inflammatory behavior that characterized William Hale Thompson's three terms as mayor, (1915–1923, 1927–1931). Simply put, Thompson's city hall was supported by organized crime. Phony patronage positions, including school janitors, clerks, and engineers, were rampant. Bookkeeping practices were lax, and boodling was at its height. The mayor himself substituted personal political ambition, theatrics, and evangelical hubris for any sort of commitment to the public welfare.[126]

Republican "Big Bill" Thompson presaged Chicago's twentieth-century "builder" mayors, adopting parts of the Commercial Club's Plan of Chicago (essentially the Burnham Plan) as his own and arguing for grand public works, even in wartime. Although nothing came of the lakefront development, monorail, and subway system he patterned after the Plan of Chicago, he earned club members' loyalty in his first two terms simply by focusing on downtown bridge construction and street renovation.

But Thompson owed his narrow primary victory in 1915 to black Chicagoans, who had become a large enough group to turn a close election. He repaid them by hiring some blacks among the 9,200 "temporary" city workers employed in his first five months to circumvent civil service laws.[127] At the same time, he ignored the competition for housing and gang tensions brewing between white ethnics and the rapidly concentrating population of blacks at the edges of the extremely congested black ghetto.[128] "Between March 1918 and August 1919, 25 bombs were exploded at the homes of blacks and at the homes or offices of blockbusting realtors." This violence escalated to thirty-four bombings in the eighteen months after the 1919 race riot, touched off when an African American boy strayed over the invisible color line while swimming in Lake Michigan.[129] Thompson ignored the racial crisis, just as he ignored the schools.

During his first two terms, Thompson's official stance on the public schools was noninvolvement, but he showed his disdain in myriad ways. He selected the first, second, and third school boards under the Otis law, but their reduced size did not bring efficiency and economy to the system. Several members of these boards were fined and jailed for looting the system "wholesale" and for illegally unseating a superintendent. Thompson fought near-continuous court battles with other board members over the superintendent's authority. His belligerence pushed administrative reformers into the arms of his board enemy, Jacob Loeb, who had proposed racially segregating the schools in the face of burgeoning enrollments and a 37,000-seat shortage.[130] Three successive superintendents were unable to contain these crises despite their newly centralized powers. They vacillated in their approach to teachers, prompting Haley to encourage the mayor's flagrant opportunism in his last term and lose some of her own stature in the process.[131] Facing heightened approbation for patronage, social turmoil brought on by racial conflict, and mounting city debt, Thompson lurched from one outlandish political scheme to another.

Commercial Club businessmen were not as indecisive. Thompson had wooed business by declaring, "City employees should be prohibited from organizing against the municipal government," and businessmen had returned the favor by largely ignoring the rank venality in Thompson's first two terms.[132] Yet when economic ruin loomed, as it did in the two years preceding the Depression, they became obsessed with cutting costs and rationalizing the tax system. From another perspective, the club's decision to develop, and then use, a financial "veto" over city and school expenditures was a highly controversial but innovative way for corporate executives to stabilize a potentially dangerous social situation, using their lending power as leverage.[133]

But first, club members would be lulled into believing that they might accomplish their efficiency goals simply by putting the right man in the mayor's office. When Thompson wisely declined to run for a third consecutive term, William E. Dever (1923–1927) crushed his Republican opposition, even though the two candidates "agreed on nearly everything."[134] A Democratic boss attempting to unite the several factions of the party behind a compromise candidate had recruited Dever for mayor. He was for "clean" government—initiating a survey of city agencies, firing many of Thompson's temporary workers, and finally achieving municipal ownership of the traction lines (streetcars and elevated trains). A builder as well, he opened more parks, beaches, bathhouses, and schools than any previous mayor.[135]

Mayor Dever also promised to take the schools out of politics, the classic administrative reformer's position. He followed through by putting four businessmen back on the school board and by refusing Haley's entreaties to intervene when Superintendent McAndrew—more like Cooley in style than any superintendent between them—recentralized decision making and permanently dismantled the teachers councils that his immediate predecessor, Peter Mortensen, had reinstated.[136] Dever promptly lost the support of the teachers unions and the backing of many other working-class Chicagoans, who also disliked McAndrew's plans to introduce platoon schools, junior high schools, and intelligence testing for tracking, all pedagogical innovations then sweeping the nation.[137]

McAndrew claimed that the aim of schooling was "to produce a human, social unit, trained in accordance with his capabilities to the nearest approach to complete social efficiency possible in the time allotted."[138] He ran a tight central office; according to one reporter, "everyone from assistant superintendents down to office boys [were] as uncommunicative as a wartime censor's bureau."[139] Club members, professionals, and most good-government reformers gave his team their approval, applauding McAndrew's efficiency as often as his rectitude.

Even with a "manager" mayor and a businesslike superintendent firmly in control of the schools, the business model could not forestall budgetary shortfalls. There were technical reasons for the deficits that lay in the businessmen's own recommendations. In 1917 and again in 1925, bookkeeping procedures had been adopted to give the board "windfall" access to funds, each an attempt to stem the school system's financial hemorrhaging. Both sanctioned the use of tax-anticipation warrants (essentially loans against future taxes) to balance the system's books. Such contrivances helped push the schools further into debt and eventually prostrated the system to the city's bankers, the only creditors willing to buy the warrants.[140]

IN THE GRIP OF THE DEPRESSION

The Commercial Club's direct intervention in school finances began as a routine fight over property tax assessments, a staple of Chicago politics for decades. A committee of businessmen had been asked by the Cook County Board of Commissioners to participate in the quadrennial reassessment of all property, just before Thompson took back the mayor's office to serve his last term. They were joined by the financially sophisticated Margaret Haley.[141] Although Illinois law required that property be assessed at 100 percent of its value, it was routine practice throughout the state to use a much lower basis, averaging about 40 percent. In Chicago even this low valuation was routinely violated, with some parcels being assessed at closer to 10 percent. The committee exposed these gross, long-standing irregularities, drawing support from women's groups, the CTF, and others who had championed clean government in the past, but it was ignored by the elected tax assessors and Mayor Thompson.

This led the CTF to call on legislators and the state of Illinois to recalculate the 1927 reassessment. Although the state agreed, this too was delayed in the courts, giving many property owners a two-year tax holiday. By the time the reassessment was complete, the Depression had lowered the total assessed value of land in the county by $2 billion.[142] In the meantime, the schools (and the city) had spent money based on tax-anticipation estimates that assumed that property values would rise. Nearly 500,000 property owners, large and small, challenged their 1927 assessments, including some "apoplectic" club members. The Depression had made the reassessments irrelevant for others; layoffs, bankruptcies, and declining paychecks were already being felt before the calculations were complete.[143] As one political observer remarked, "Chicago entered the Depression already on the verge of bankruptcy."[144]

At this point, the club offered to finance (with a $50,000 subscription) and assemble a so-called citizens committee on taxes, which was given statutory authority to audit city finances by the Illinois legislature and governor. Club member Silas Strawn led the fifty-eight-person group. At meetings devoted to the topic, members convinced one another that the malfeasance was less the result of their "pull" than corruption by elected officials and a lack of centralized management accountability. They recommended that the eight elected property tax assessors, long known to take bribes to fix assessments, be replaced by an assessor appointed by the mayor, "so that we can keep our hands directly on the man who is responsible for putting him there."[145]

The Strawn Committee also determined that Chicago was "broke." The city had spent $23 million above its income. Club bankers raised $20 million in emergency funds for city agencies, including the schools, but refused to let Mayor Thompson have access to the funds unless he gave the committee control over future expenditures.[146] Thompson initially resisted, then ultimately agreed to the Strawn deal, which required that the city sell $74 million in tax-anticipation warrants to delinquent corporate taxpayers. But in the rapidly deflating economy, even the warrants lost value and could not be redeemed one year later.[147]

The short-term effects of the Strawn Committee were to keep the schools open and teachers paid (though frequently late and sometimes at a discount) until 1931. Firemen, policemen, and nurses began going without pay in 1929, the last for as long as one year.[148] By 1930, 45 percent of Chicago's total workforce was unemployed.[149] Schools were 50,000 seats over capacity and deeply in debt. Ten thousand property tax payers were on strike, and across the country the city was the butt of jokes.[150]

Only two months after Thompson lost his bid for a fourth term to Anton Cermak (1931–1933), the governor called a tax conference to resolve the growing crisis. McCormick, Strawn, Fred Sargent of the Chicago and Northwest Railroad, and Samuel Insull of Commonwealth Edison and People's Gas, Light and Coke, the infamous purchaser of council votes, joined other Commercial Club leaders who were also the heads of the city's three largest banks in a series of meetings with labor, civic leaders, and Mayor Cermak to "undertake a comprehensive study of the entire question [of taxes]."[151]

The group adopted the Strawn Committee's recommendations, adding property tax relief by instituting a graduated income tax and a tax on tobacco.[152] But no legislative agreement was forthcoming. In the meantime, teachers began to be paid in scrip stamped "insufficient funds" or tax warrants, neither of which was worth its face value for purchases. Unpaid school board liabilities approached $135 million.[153]

Members of the Joint Commission on Real Estate Valuation, the Strawn Committee, and the Governor's Tax Conference then united to form a fourth group, the Committee on Public Expenditures, otherwise known as the (Fred) Sargent Committee. It was large but dominated by club members, including five who were on the boards of the four major banks in Chicago: First National, Harris Trust and Savings, Continental Illinois, and Northern Trust. Sargent defined the committee as an "extralegal body" made up of "the people who pay the biggest tax bills" whose power was based on the fact that "the banks had decided our committee's judgment could be trusted."[154] John O. Rees, the paid executive director of all the previous committees as well as this one, concurred: "It was all sort of informal."[155]

The formation of the Sargent Committee was announced in the *Tribune* the same day, March 14, 1932, that Chicago's investment bankers advised against further purchase of school tax-anticipation warrants. Six months later, representatives of Chicago's major banks and others in the inner circle of the Sargent Committee announced that no more warrant credit would be offered unless the school board *reduced* its property tax levy. The group then began a series of ten meetings with the school board to discuss "retrenchments."[156]

At one of these meetings the committee proposed a deal: make $15 million in cuts, or the banks will buy no more warrants. If the board agreed, the committee held out the promise that it would "use its best efforts to secure sufficient cash" to keep the schools open. Mayor Cermak also offered $3 million toward teacher salaries, but only if the Sargent Committee's recommendations were accepted. The committee was successful, and a second, similar "deal" was extended before the end of the year. The committee's influence was underscored when Columbia University professor George Strayer's recommendations to lay off patronage employees and cut administrative expenses (double those of New York City at the time), detailed in his 1932 school survey, were ignored.[157]

Mary Herrick, a former president of the Federation of Women High School Teachers (1914), detailed the cuts.[158] In one agreement alone, in July 1933, the board eliminated the following items: the junior college, all junior high schools, the Bureau of Curriculum, the Bureau of Vocational Guidance, the Bureau of Special Education, manual training from elementary schools, home economics from elementary schools, 50 percent of kindergartens, 50 percent of high school physical education teachers, all but one continuation school, visiting teachers, parental schools, textbook purchases, two of five assistant superintendents, five of ten district superintendents, all deans, half of all bathing rooms, and much of the lavatory maintenance. In the process, 1,400 teaching jobs were lost. Significant cuts in the building program had already been made.[159] In a pamphlet sent home with schoolchildren, the board explained that these "fads and frills" were superfluous and, in any case, their elimination was required to keep the schools open.[160]

An independent, quasi-legal committee of businessmen to oversee public school expenses was, in Sargent's view, a necessary antidote to irresponsible politicians who increased expenses without limit in order to sustain a political advantage. After the 1933 cuts were in place, the board no longer made any pretense of resisting the Sargent Committee's demands; it voluntarily consulted the Sargent Committee before acting. The governor also agreed not to consider any tax legislation unless he had the approval of the committee.[161] Mayor Cermak and his successor, Edward J. Kelly (1933–1949), were both strong supporters of control by the businessmen, who returned the favor at election time.

Anton Cermak did not live long enough to affect school policy beyond pressing hard for the businessmen's cuts. In 1933 he was killed in Florida by a bullet intended for President Franklin D. Roosevelt. Cermak's successor, promoted by Democratic boss Patrick Nash and appointed by the city council, had been the chief engineer of the sanitary district for the past thirty-nine years. Not yet subject to civil service laws, the sanitary department had tripled in size under his leadership.[162] Besides being notorious for making a fortune in kickbacks, Kelly was appreciated by Chicago businessmen for his leadership of the South Park Board, building a host of urban parks, museums, and streets originally laid out in the club's Plan of Chicago—all downtown services he continued to develop while mayor.

Kelly also intended to maintain the support Cermak had garnered from unionized labor. On the day he took office, 14,000 teachers stormed the city banks and picketed in the financial district. His first official act was to ensure that they received paychecks by signing $1.7 million in tax-anticipation warrants. Then he proceeded to defend the Sargent Committee's cuts, claiming that the alternative, closing the schools, was worse.[163]

Justifying its behavior to a skeptical nation, Sargent acknowledged that his committee had first sought to reduce expenditures and only secondarily to collect delinquent taxes because, as committee members saw it, the problem was a tax based on property.[164] The committee preferred more regressive ways to raise revenue: "a tax universally spread rather than a scheme based on the fallacious theory that taxes are something to be collected from a few rich men."[165] It was most important to keep business leaders satisfied, the committee argued, because they were the only group wealthy enough to purchase the city's tax warrants. To this end, not only tax policy but also the "reorganization of government with a view to centralization" was crucial.[166] This made troublemaking female teachers more expendable than male patronage janitors, who were at least loyal to the mayor.

Not everyone knew about the connection between the Sargent Committee and the Commercial Club, but club minutes from 1939 acknowledged that the group had initiated the Sargent Committee and intended to sustain it indefinitely.[167] "The businessmen of Chicago have learned their lesson. We shall not again let the mechanism run wild. . . . Eventually we may have a permanent organization to embrace the general purposes of the [Sargent] committee."[168] By the end of the Depression, club leaders concluded that there were two crucial prerequisites to this plan: a fiscal crisis severe enough to put their "private" money in charge of the school's finances, and a mayor who had "complete political power to see that his orders were carried out."[169]

THE COALITION POLITICS OF EARLY SCHOOL REFORM

Civic actors were the key constituents of school reform coalitions in this era. State and local politicians and the courts sometimes aided their efforts but just as often complicated them. Corporate leaders, union members, and local activists developed the reform agendas, established the lines of debate, and used their political and material resources to sustain governmental interest. Usually two or more civic coalitions competed, their different goals fostering arguments about which services should be offered, what subjects ought to be taught, and, most importantly, who should have the authority to control decision making in the future. The stakes in these debates seemed high to all involved. Every social class agreed that how youth were educated, especially the large number of immigrants, would determine the city's future.

Notwithstanding their authority to select the school board, the era's mayors, constrained by competing sources of political power and frequent elections, had limited impact. Characterized as the "age of personality politics," the long stretch of individualist mayors from 1880 to 1930 echoed the fragmentation in party politics: Democrats and Republicans typically had several factions, rival ward bosses and third and fourth parties were common, and many aldermen had an independent base of support and separate patronage. This led to high mayoral turnover; there were fourteen mayors in this fifty-year period, compared with only four in the next.[170] Unstable electoral coalitions—the groups that backed a candidate for election—seldom provided support sufficient for a mayor to initiate major social or political change.

Those mayors participating in school reform coalitions typically used their board appointment powers to back the favored approach of the city's wealthy corporate leaders. Nineteenth-century mayor Carter Harrison II was the first to do so by establishing the Harper Commission, which developed a template for efficient school governance that was frequently referred to by others. Two years later, Fred Busse reinstated corporate control of the school board after it had briefly lapsed, risking legal censure in the process. A dozen years later, William Dever, responding to the flagrant corruption of William Thompson's last term, appointed another business board. This cyclical pattern reinforced many reformers' conception that the antidote to school corruption was a businesslike governance structure. Even Anton Cermak, determined to appear managerial but relatively uninterested in the schools, supported the Commercial Club's cost cutting and control while he focused on building the multiethnic Democratic machine that was to be his political legacy.

The mayors who did not routinely back business either were disinterested and corrupt or, more rarely, supported another faction in reform debates. William Thompson was the iconic mayor whose goal was to use the schools as a source of patronage, but even he occasionally backed corporate leaders, as evidenced by his failure to object to the Loeb rule outlawing unions, although organized labor had voted for him. Mercurial when it seemed useful to his reelection campaign, he also shamelessly castigated the business-backed superintendent William McAndrew, turning board meetings into his own political stage and circus. Only Harrison's immediate successor, Edward Dunne, actively supported a labor democracy position on schooling.

Superintendents choosing to lead reform were limited by their uneasy relationships with school boards and their lack of an independent relationship with the city's civic groups. The mayor frequently removed board members before their three-year terms expired, leaving superintendents with the difficult task of amassing a stable coalition of support from among a shifting array of community figures. In their competition to gain an advantage over district finances and jobs, powerful business and labor groups also swayed board members. Facing such impediments, Edwin Cooley actually found it easier to lead reform in the employ of the Commercial Club than as a superintendent. Board resistance also stifled Ella Flagg Young's ideas about teacher professionalism. William

McAndrew's many pedagogical and structural innovations (e.g., junior high schools, platoon schools), hampered by Mayor Thompson's corruption and union resistance, could not be sustained in the face of cost cutting during the Depression because he was unable to engage a sufficiently committed civic coalition, even though business executives nominally approved of his efforts.

With mayors uninterested or merely reactive and superintendents ill positioned to amass long-term support, the city's business elites and labor leaders led most school reform efforts. Every coalition needed as many partners as it could muster. Committee chairmen and paid professionals affiliated with the Commercial Club were the consistent leaders of one coalition, although they drew opposition from among competing business associations. Vocal feminists in the CTF were equally visible as leaders of the other large coalition, although unanimity eluded the dozens of associations that represented educators as well. These two competing coalitions represented the Progressive era's great fissure between a tiny, wealthy capitalist elite and the working and laboring masses. A third civic sector consisting of the city's good-government and social reform groups—almost always comfortably middle-class socialists or religious moralists—typically aligned with one or the other of the two class-based coalitions and could shift the balance of influence, but it had too few resources to sustain a coalition for long and was also divided internally.

Each group brought different resources to its activism. When cohesive, the CTF, CFL, Illinois Federation of Labor, and other labor unions could sway both municipal and statewide elections on school issues because they represented large numbers of voters; estimates at the time put 80 percent of the families of public school students in the ranks of union-eligible workers. Strength came as well from the large number of members they could call on for pamphleteering and debating, rallies, subscriptions, and, when necessary, civil disobedience. Skeptical of the reform agendas created by business elites who refused to pay their taxes for the upkeep of the schools, unionists used their large numbers, cohesiveness, and organizing strength to hold back the Commercial Club's threatened dual system of schooling while a more moderate pedagogical approach to vocational education developed its own coalition of support. In a similar way, organized labor defeated attempts to bureaucratize and centralize the governance of schools for nearly two decades. Only when unions failed to use their legislative veto could the Otis law pass.

Business was sometimes less cohesive than labor during these years, but the Commercial Club gradually developed the discipline to speak with one voice by the era's close. In the early school reform debates over vocational education, the club had been internally divided between Robinson's advocacy and Crane's dissent. It could be argued that the club was tactically reactive as well:

Cooley's multicity tour advocating a dual system was an effort to compete with Margaret Haley's national reputation as a sought-after speaker on corporate scofflaws. In 1903 alone she covered 7,500 miles in thirty-five days.[171] Likewise, during the debates over the Otis bill, some members endorsed the more anti-union Baldwin bill. But by the Depression, such internal differences were entirely hidden from the public. The Sargent Committee did not reveal the names of club members who were worsening the city's financial problems by their own tax delinquency, and, breaking a fifty-year precedent, it stopped recording its debates in meetings. Club leaders had learned to treat internal division as a private matter.

But cohesive or not, the Commercial Club, the Industrial Club, the Merchant's Club, and other business groups dominated school reform debates only when school financing was the primary issue, as it was during the Depression. When faced with a fiscal crisis that enhanced the influence of their access to private capital, club members found it more efficient and effective to act unilaterally, safeguarding their own interests without the compromise required in coalitional politics.

Club members had other political resources that they used in this era. Their cultivated identification with efficiency, good management, and (moderately) profitable enterprise was one. Partly intended to counter the Progressive era's image of corporate leaders as robber barons, it also reflected a growing middle-class belief in managerial techniques as a means of harmonizing class conflict. Pressing this argument, club leaders worked through good-government groups to convince politicians and other reformers that a more centralized and businesslike city was in their interests; for example, they used their leadership of the City Charter Commission and the PEA to build support for club reforms ultimately embodied in the Otis law. Yet this collaborative strategy required club members to moderate their positions to take into account their coalition partners' objections and frequently led to less satisfying compromise legislation.

Their control of industrial and commercial job opportunities in the city and the ability to withhold taxes gave club leaders a third political resource: routine access to state and local politicians. In this era they made frequent use of their ability to pit one politician against another. But the importance of access could be overstated when electioneering distracted politicians, as it so frequently did in Chicago. In this respect, the club's influence would not reach its peak until the political culture of the city was more unitary and more stable.

For their part, good-government and social reformers brought research, ideas, moral righteousness, national visibility, and volunteers to any coalition they joined. These resources were crucial in drafting laws, creating watchdog groups, and documenting abuses, but they were less politically compelling than the unions' ability to arrange demonstrations, mobilize supporters, and, ultimately, deliver votes. And they were less easily transferable to coalition partners, including politicians, than were the funds controlled by business leaders. These assets, though useful, kept good-government groups in a secondary position relative to big business and labor.

The reform ideas and coalition agendas of these civic reformers encompassed the very purposes of public education. They debated elaborate and detailed positions on school organization and vocational pedagogy, school governance and economizing, often drafting the language that was found in enabling legislation. Multiyear battles within and between these competing civic coalitions determined which type of school reform would prevail.

Governance reforms dominated the era because each of the two main reform coalitions hoped to institutionalize its view of schooling and its own role in defending that purpose. Unionists wanted schools to change the social structure, or at least the life opportunities of working-class children. Had they been able to, they would have changed industrial capitalism as well.[172] In winning the right to secure employment through tenure, unions expected that teachers would be able to influence, without fear of reprisal, what was taught to working-class children. Unions also set a precedent, albeit one that would soon be forgotten, for teacher influence over the fiscal and programmatic priorities of the district through teachers councils.

Business elites wanted to harmonize the industrial order and ensure Chicago's place in the nation's economy. They sought to keep government expenses low but also to dampen the allure of socialism. Club members believed that their own financial success came from superior organization and discipline. If these principles were applied to schooling, they reasoned, all students would learn to live untroubled by the economic limits of their station in life. Thus, they saw victory in institutionalizing business influence over the new vocational curriculum—future corporate executives would have to be consulted when changes were anticipated in the preparation of students entering the workforce—even though their idea of a separate system under their control was rejected.

The Commercial Club was on the winning side of most governance battles. A management hierarchy very much like the one club members envisioned in this era would direct schools for most of the twentieth century. They were successful in modeling the structure of the school system on the industrial corporation, and the bureaucratic governance structure adopted in the Otis law facilitated the transfer of modern management techniques in successive eras. Club members in this era believed that good management principles required that educational and business functions be administered separately. But they would later prefer a unitary management approach when corporate models shifted, and they tinkered with the precise scope of executive authority for much of the twentieth century. Such innovations would be more easily rationalized to the extent that they fit the Progressive era standards of being "nonpolitical," quantifiable and measurable, and justified by a business efficiency rationale.

If big business had won every battle, however, the schools would have been governed quite differently. Because unions won tenure and a small measure of governing authority during this era, they secured for teachers a decision-making role sufficient to influence changes in the future system.

Not every battle hinged solely on its governance implications. In defeating the Cooley bill and vigorously campaigning for a version of vocationalism that altered the pedagogy and curriculum of regular schools—but not their governance structure—unions and their civic partners attempted to prepare working-class students for their economic roles without forgoing their access to a liberal curriculum. And they ensured that teachers and parents would have an ongoing influence: in order for changes to be implemented for more than a tiny number of students, parents would have to alter their expectations of schooling, and teachers their practice. By acting in concert across workplace boundaries, this vocational education coalition ensured that the public schools would remain one system, obliged to provide some form of academic opportunity to working-class, immigrant, and other less advantaged children, as well as to the affluent and the middle classes.

The much more controversial progressive pedagogical techniques championed by some reformers developed only a relatively small following. As a result, few of these child-centered curricular ideas were initiated in more than a handful of schools; most were readily abandoned when resources dried up. The curricular and instructional changes that were sustained during this period were the by-products of governance reform, supported less for their pedagogical significance than for the ease with which they could be absorbed in the new hierarchical structure or the implications they had for control of the workforce.

By the end of the Progressive era, neither business nor labor had won the war for control of the schools, although each had bested the other in separate battles, and both had formalized their influence over future school decision making. The school governance system forged in their conflict was an amalgam of centralized bureaucracy and managerial direction by principals, superintendents, and business-led school boards and the classroom influence of teachers on instruction and curriculum, solidified by tenure. In this era, unions and those who provided them with intellectual support effectively countered the structural advantages of corporate wealth, helping to institutionalize broader purposes of education than would have emerged had business plans been adopted and implemented without opposition. Over time, tenure would make teachers a voice of moderation, even conservative reaction, and teachers themselves would serve as the system's institutional memory. Business leaders would become no less conservative. But the initial purposes over which the two groups fought in this era were embedded in the structure of the system through those early governance victories.

After the Depression, fragmentation and competition among the city's reform coalitions would be transformed into a political problem for the mayors who headed Chicago's Democratic machine. The ensuing fifty years would link business and labor interests as beneficiaries of machine politics, and greater political stability would both limit and consolidate the two sectors. The next era's political cleavage divided those with personal access to the mayor from those denied it, a racial fault line that would shape the city's school reform debates for much of the next half century.

2

Confronting Race

Thwarted Reforms and Disillusionment 1930–1980

Both Chicago and its public schools were irreparably altered by the Depression. Deep budget cuts decimated teacher salaries and programs, nearly eliminating some long-standing reforms in a matter of months.[1] The same dark days of market failure and unmet needs also spawned the city's famous Democratic "machine" politics.

The consolidating effects of this new regime were gradually institutionalized by Anton Cermak, Edward J. Kelly, Martin Kennelly, and Richard J. Daley. Well known for its complete control of patronage employment, tolerance for graft, pragmatic orientation to conflict management, and symbiotic relationship between city hall and Washington, D.C., Chicago's machine depended equally on a unified electoral coalition and a strong governing coalition. In addition to assembling a multiethnic mixture of loyal voters, these four mayors cultivated business and union leaders to help them govern. They wooed corporate leaders by adopting the rhetoric, and occasionally the trappings, of business efficiency and by doling out a host of material incentives. They courted workers with high wages and benefits and, ultimately, collective bargaining. The resulting governing coalition of labor, business, and the electoral machine insulated the school system from substantial change for nearly five decades.[2]

To private-sector actors, machine-era consolidation meant that personal access to the mayor was a precondition for political influence. Commercial Club leaders, already powerful spokespersons for a centralized corporate sector, intensified their personal relationship with the Democratic mayors. In addition to the economic resources they could bring to governing, they represented a cohesive business association and reliably spoke with unanimity for corporate Chicago. Unions combined to increase their influence on city hall and use electoral politics as a way to achieve their economic agenda. Teachers union leaders sought higher wages, of course, but that was only one of many workplace demands. Trading member votes for political favors from a cooperative regime won them collective-bargaining rights. The reward of stable employment brought them into the regime's governing coalition.

Machine governance brought centralization and bureaucracy to both city hall and the schools. Community groups without access to the mayor were shut out, and all efforts to influence the inaccessible administrators of the 600-school system were fiercely resisted. Professional prerogatives increasingly animated district leaders between 1930 and 1980, but they drew their authority from city hall more than from their expert standing. An appointed school board continued to ensure mayoral influence over the schools, and city hall governing practices—including patronage employment—became routine. Another series of centralizing regulations, a succession of superintendents resolutely protecting their management prerogatives, and, ultimately, Mayor Richard J. Daley's direct intervention on behalf of the teachers union added to the consolidation of power and the sense of community isolation. Together, this pattern of choices shifted decision making from civic actors to the superintendent and his chief patron in city hall.

Centralization and bureaucratization served to mask festering problems. The Sargent Committee's legacy of cutbacks led to double shifts and overcrowding that spawned enormous elementary schools, made even larger by the absence of junior high schools. Teacher salaries remained pitifully low for decades. A bare-bones curriculum sustained fewer of the special services once offered to immigrant children. Meanwhile, high-wage school custodians and other patronage employees, tolerated by the Sargent Committee, guaranteed that administrative costs would remain high despite their draconian belt-tightening. These and other problems left parents and citizens with much to protest. However, the new governing arrangements gave them few opportunities to be heard, forcing them to seek allies outside of Chicago.

Civic reform groups blamed the mayor and a culture of municipal corruption for the school problems. In doing so, they gave each Democratic mayor greater incentive to trade wages and class sizes, schools and services, for votes and machine loyalty. Business leaders, in contrast, praised the Sargent Committee's legacy and mayoral influence over the schools as evidence of sound fiscal management. For them, all that was needed was a continuation of centralized control and as much influence over the district superintendent as they were accustomed to having in city hall.

The half-century-long class-based political cleavage between labor and business gradually diminished when both became governing partners in the Democratic machine. Each suppressed its earlier differences with the other to obtain the favors and rewards now available. In place of class conflict, a racial divide emerged, separating those with access and influence from the marginalized.

Chicago's growing black population had been in the minority when the Sargent Committee's retrenchment occurred. But increased migration, white flight, and discriminatory housing and school assignment policies meant that they soon became the majority and would bear the greatest burden of the cuts over the long term. Because blacks lacked personal access to city hall and school district leaders, their protests over such inequities were dismissed by the mayor and the superintendent, ignored by the teachers unions, and played down by corporate leaders, even after the civil rights movement had divided the city. This racial cleavage grew to overshadow all others until reform meant finding some way to address the resulting inequities. But Chicago, so proud of its big shoulders and big plans, was not yet ready for *that* reform.

A NEW EQUILIBRIUM

Political machines were not new to Chicago. Yet the election of Anton Cermak (1931–1933) marked the beginning of nearly fifty years of unbroken Democratic rule that grew increasingly mayor-centric, consolidated, and patronage ridden. Cermak won an unprecedented majority of votes among every segment of the population except blacks. He unified the white ethnic factions by becoming the "wettest man in Chicago," according to the *Chicago Tribune*.[3] All this was made easier by a weak opposition. "Big Bill" Thompson's Republicans, who over the previous fifteen years had won city hall, lost it, and won it again, were always hampered by hotly contested primaries within the party.[4] Thompson also lost votes due to corruption, the Depression, and the onset of a white Protestant flight to the suburbs in the 1920s.[5]

Cermak's brief tenure (shortened by his untimely death) began a fifty-year period in which Democratic machine mayors cloaked themselves in the rhetoric of efficient management. He wooed business leaders, women's groups, and good-government organizations to his governing coalition with promises to cut back on corruption, and he was effective enough to be referred to as a "master public executive." Cermak strongly supported the Sargent Committee's belt-tightening and delivered blue-ribbon committees and the latest management technology in city hall, while fashioning himself a "workaholic."[6]

He also began a trend toward centralization. Before Cermak, patronage and other economic favors of machine politics were decentralized—doled out from both parties, including out-of-office factions, and from many city agencies such as the school board, the sanitation district, and the parks department. Patronage employees also collected kickbacks from organized crime. After consolidating all this in the mayor's office under his direct control, Cermak offered even more city jobs through contracts supported by New Deal aid. The city's relief expenditures soared to $35 million in 1932, triple the amount spent in his first year in office.[7] Yet not everyone benefited. Annoyed that he had received only about 18 percent of the black vote, Cermak fulfilled an anti-crime campaign promise by selectively raiding black "policy" syndicates. He further punished black voters with the loss of over 2,000 patronage jobs.[8]

Cermak's immediate successor adopted a different tactic. Edward J. Kelly (1933–1947) incorporated black voters in his electoral coalition by appealing to their racial pride and desire for integration.[9] He made symbolic gestures such as banning the inflammatory film *Birth of a Nation,* attending the Wilberforce-Tuskegee football game, and publicly defending integrated schools and housing. For speaking out, he earned the "respect and confidence of every citizen of every color and creed whose mind is not blinded by hate, prejudice and bigotry," according to the city's black newspaper of record, the *Chicago Defender.*[10]

Although Kelly's overtures were a first step, it would take decades before blacks joined ethnic whites in the Democratic electoral coalition.[11] Already a demographic force in Chicago after their post–World War I migration, blacks had been forced to settle on a narrow strip in the near South Side, the "black belt," only a few blocks from the Prairie Street mansions of the Commercial Club's founders.[12] By 1930 restrictive housing covenants covered 75 percent of the city's residential property, reinforcing this dense confinement. As congestion deepened, tensions rose.[13]

White resistance to African American migration was spurred by Cermak's racist political tactics but had been evident long before the Democrats captured city hall. In 1919 twenty-three blacks and fifteen whites had been killed, hundreds injured, and nearly fifty homes destroyed in full-scale race riots. Mayor Thompson did not react until most of the damage had been done.[14] Despite the racial segregation and white enmity, blacks turned their increased numbers and heightened concentration into political gains, at least before the Depression and Cermak's favoritism wore them away. Black voters sent four representatives to the state legislature; elected an alderman, state senator, judge, and congressman; and gained footholds in patronage jobs, all because they consistently voted between 70 and 90 percent Republican.[15]

To blacks and whites alike, Mayor Kelly's support for integration seemed to be a return to Thompson-era politics. Kelly slated Republican William L. Dawson to be alderman of the black belt's Second Ward and enticed him to switch parties in exchange for Democratic patronage and a commitment not to challenge the party on race issues.[16] Dawson's response was to deliver 80 percent of the black vote to Democrats in 1935.

African Americans were heartened by the changes in city hall, but bigoted whites were enraged, and they countered with civil disobedience and violence. In 1934 white parents threatened boycotts to keep black students out of "white" high schools. Kelly responded by rescinding the school board's order to remove the black students, as much a clarification of who was in charge of the schools as a testament to his desire for black votes. Kelly's assertion of authority changed few minds, of course, and both violent protests and school boycotts became routine. Even so, he lasted for three terms, partly because the city's newspaper editors agreed to limit their coverage of the social disruption.[17]

CONSOLIDATION AND SCHOOL CORRUPTION

If blacks received mixed signals from city hall, the Commercial Club attracted clear support, and by the end of Kelly's last term, the club had linked its fate to the machine. Treasurer John Nuveen described its strategy in 1943: "An organization such as this club is never going to accomplish very much in civic activities, the kind of operations we have had in the past, unless they are willing to get into the political life of the city."[18] In the referenced "past," club members had functioned openly through volunteer committees. The Democratic machine's dominance of previously private arenas now required new political alignments. The machine interfered with wage rates through its control of patronage and siphoned off consumer dollars in its support of gambling and other vices. Moreover, unlike Progressive era politicians who responded to private-sector advocacy and (sometimes) to good-government research, the new Democratic mayors were rapidly monopolizing information about public services even though what they revealed was not always accurate.[19] Club members wanted access to inside information as well as guaranteed influence. To obtain both, they agreed to collaborate with the machine as a governing partner.

The club consolidated and centralized its organizational structure, absorbing its only rival, the Industrial Club, in 1932 and subsequently identified a few leaders, already friendly with the mayor, who became its spokesmen in city hall. Members also agreed to do away with the committee structure that had fragmented formal leadership before 1930 and to eliminate the public airing of disagreements.[20]

Even though Kelly had been the infamous chief engineer of the sanitary district for thirty-nine years, tripling that agency's patronage appointments and raking off a fortune in kickbacks, and even though he had been selected to run for mayor by notorious party boss Patrick A. Nash, club leaders supported Chicago's second Democratic machine mayor, as they had the first.[21] They also approved of his consistent opposition to taxes on personal property and income, a position made possible by New Deal administrators in Washington, D.C., who continued to funnel "extra" money to Chicago in exchange for votes. Like Cermak, Kelly cultivated the reputation among business executives of being a good manager, turning "one of the worst-governed cities into one of the best-governed," according to the distant and undiscerning *New York Times*.[22] Before and after becoming mayor, Kelly returned the corporate leaders' favors with multimillion-dollar contracts for urban parks, museums, and streets that had originally been conceived in the club's Plan of Chicago.[23] Rather than reforming Kelly's machine, club leaders sought accommodation, looking the other way at corruption and patronage, while ensuring that downtown development, city contracts, low taxes, and a steady flow of government dollars for Depression-era loan repayments were all sustained.

Grateful to business, Mayor Kelly was ambivalent toward unions. Making amends for the infamous Memorial Day massacre of 1937, in which Chicago police fired on fleeing picketers, he bargained for the votes of the Chicago Council of Industrial Organizations (CIO) by offering its members future exemption from interference. He kept his promise by ignoring the excessive number of union workers on Works Progress Administration construction projects. Kelly briefly courted teachers' support too. Early in his first term, he signed $1.7 million in tax-anticipation warrants after 14,000 teachers stormed the city banks and picketed in the financial district over the near-worthless scrip they were being paid.[24] But on school issues in general, he judged business backing more valuable. Like Cermak, Kelly aggressively supported the Sargent Committee's cuts and expanded school district patronage, often at the expense of teachers.

Meanwhile, good-government groups opposed the machine by using the same tactics that had worked in earlier decades and succeeded in destabilizing Kelly's administration, if not the machine regime itself. Like business associations and the unions, the many competing and overlapping civic groups found it necessary to join forces in their bid for political influence. But unlike the former two sectors, civic reformers and good-government groups received no favors, were not privy to inside information, and did not participate in governing the city or the schools. Their consolidation strategy—organizing by wards to elect a few representatives to the city council—put them in direct conflict with the Democratic machine.[25] The City Women's Club, the League of Women Voters, the local parent-teacher associations, and eventually about seventy-two other groups unified around this strategy under the banner of the Citizen's Save Our Schools Committee of Chicago, later shortened to Citizen's Schools Committee (CSC).[26]

The 1933 Sargent Committee's "wreckage" of the system was the impetus for the CSC, and for a time it became the school system's main gadfly. Although the CSC's influence in city hall and the school board rapidly waned, private professional groups, state officials, and the national media took notice.[27] A protest rally of 25,000 sparked a petition drive to reinstate school services and secured 300,000 names in nine days. These demonstrations forestalled some cuts to high school electives and reopened junior colleges, but redeeming worthless paychecks for teachers took a broader coalition and a national campaign.[28]

The North Central Association of Colleges and Secondary Schools (NCACSS) was persuaded to drop its accreditation of Chicago high schools, sparking nationwide condemnation that embarrassed the city's boosters. Club leaders responded by agreeing to underwrite a federal loan to the schools for teachers' back wages, which gave Kelly his brief honeymoon with the unions.[29] Yet settling the salary arrears addressed only one of the Sargent Committee's cuts. Others, such as the loss of junior high schools and overcrowding, became defining characteristics of the system for decades to come.

Although the machine was not brought down, repeated school scandals indelibly stained the mayor's image as a good manager. In addition to holding him personally responsible for patronage employment in the schools and outrageously high contracts, the CSC targeted Kelly's close friend, school board president James B. McCahey, and his poorly qualified superintendent, William H. Johnson (1936–1946). They disparaged McCahey as "the spectacle of a *businessman,* with no knowledge or equipment for the purpose, actually dominating every feature of the schools system . . . [with the result that] expenditures for education purposes are curtailed at every chance and expenses of the business organization are constantly enlarged."[30] They saw in Johnson an "utter lack of ethical and professional standards," a man who routinely engaged in favoritism and plagiarism in the books he "authored" and cavalierly adopted for the school system.[31]

It took nearly a decade, but the CSC eventually managed to convince another outside agency, the National Education Association (NEA), that the Chicago schools were severely compromised by cutbacks and corruption. In 1944 the NEA conducted its own investigation and found "undemocratic and even fascist" policies in place, by which it meant rampant corruption, patronage, and a lack of professional accountability in hiring principals, teachers, and faculty of the Chicago Teachers College. Without tenure, the NEA investigators surmised, "it is possible that the schools of Chicago would be hopelessly disarrayed and completely decimated by politics and corruption."[32] The published findings denounced the mayor, board president, and superintendent equally. The "city is in excellent financial condition," the NEA insisted, so there was no fiscal excuse for the overcrowding that had pushed class sizes above forty everywhere, or for the double shifts in black areas, where congestion was "at its worst."[33]

Two years before NEA investigators were called in, another survey team, led by local business executives, had reached opposite conclusions about the strength of the school system.[34] Despite recommending dozens of detailed business office changes, the executives found the district "highly competent," only mildly faulting civil service (patronage) hiring policies for high wages, padding of the payroll, and excessive decentralization that created a number of coordination problems. They recommended an *increase* in the average class size to forty-three students to avoid financing more school construction and saw no need to end double shifts among black students. Eschewing the Otis law's fragmented, tripartite executive that their predecessors had won, they argued most stridently for aligning the schools with the modern practices of their own corporations; in their view, a single executive should be responsible for the entire system.[35]

Corporate executives and NEA educators both sought increased professional centralization and accountability from the schools, but with one striking difference. The executives wanted a chief executive officer with "broad qualifications and experience in the business and operational management of a school system," to whom a superintendent of education would report as only one of seven "bureau and department" heads. The NEA educators felt that the business manager and the attorney ought to report to a "fully responsible" educator.[36]

Mayor Kelly took neither recommendation seriously.[37] But with the school scandals greatly exacerbated by the NCACSS's continuing threat to withdraw accreditation, and with his political standing already damaged by the white ethnic backlash over his integration rhetoric, Kelly acted to squelch the controversies. He asked for recommendations from a blue-ribbon commission of university presidents, which demanded a citizens advisory committee to screen candidates for the school board. Since following the advice of this Advisory Commission on School Board Nominations would be voluntary, Kelly considered it a small price to pay for maintaining control of the schools, as well as their patronage.[38] Even so, the seventy-year-old mayor had outlived his usefulness to the machine, and a new Democratic Party boss, Jacob Arvey, slated someone with nominally "reformist" credentials to run for mayor in 1947.[39]

REFORM, MACHINE STYLE

Kelly's successor was Martin H. Kennelly (1947–1955), a founding partner of Allied Van Lines in 1929 and a civic-minded businessman with a "squeaky clean" image. In his nomination speech, Kennelly, a self-styled reformer, pledged to eliminate patronage. "He spoke of efficiency, of economy, of curbing waste, of running the city on a non-partisan basis, and of treating public offices as public trusts," going so far as to describe Chicago as a "cooperatively-owned municipal corporation." During his eight-year tenure, he cut jobs in city hall by 40 percent, to 18,000, and modernized the civil service system.[40]

All this endeared him to his fellow Commercial Club members, who were given a free hand to redevelop the city and reorganize its housing patterns. Marshall Field and Company (Kennelly's first employer) and the (segregationist) Chicago Title and Trust Company were key benefactors of the Illinois Blighted Areas Redevelopment Act (1947) and the Community Conservation Act (1953), which business leaders wrote and for which they lobbied.[41]

In keeping with his corporatist view of the city's economy, Kennelly showed little interest in city hall politics or in the schools. He allowed a small group of Democratic machine aldermen, the "Grey Wolves," to run the city while he functioned, in effect, as chairman of the board. Boss Arvey tolerated Kennelly because the machine needed his image to win elections. Kennelly and his fellow club members, in turn, accepted the machine and ignored city hall corruption. He also left a few machine stalwarts on the school board, even though it meant rejecting the nominating commission's recommendations.[42] He had inherited five new board members from Kelly, as well as the resignations of Johnson and McCahey as superintendent and school board president, respectively, but his own activity was limited to backing a new law uniting the business and educational functions of the school district under one man. The superintendent became "the Chief Executive Officer of the Board" in a compromise between NEA and business recommendations.[43]

The new school law encouraged Harold Hunt (1947–1953), a nationally known administrator, to accept the more centralized school leadership position. Hunt was immediately lauded by the CSC for bringing "a refreshing atmosphere" to the district office and foreshadowing "a new spirit of democracy" in the operation of the schools.[44] His management credentials were also strong enough for the Commercial Club to offer him membership, the first Chicago school superintendent so honored.

He reined in some school patronage, as anticipated, but also functioned as a modern corporate manager, excelling in the use of data to clarify problems.[45] In 1947 he seemed to be tackling racial issues when he called for a Technical Advisory Committee on Intergroup Relations, but it made only minor adjustments to elementary school attendance zones.[46] Three years later, his data gathering produced a public report that reframed two more long-standing concerns:

civil service salaries (those of patronage engineers and custodians) were documented to be much higher than those of either teachers or principals, and, despite constant overcrowding, there had been a decades-long decline in elementary enrollment that was reversed only after the second major wave of black migration during World War II.[47] In all his reports, whether on selective overcrowding or patronage employment, it was assumed that technical adjustments could rectify the problem.

In addition to expanding the black belt on the South Side, the second African American migration created another black ghetto in the formerly white ethnic and Jewish West Side districts of East Garfield and North Lawndale.[48] Chicago's black population grew 77 percent in the 1940s, almost doubling the proportion of blacks in the city. Adding to the housing pressure were the city's returning war veterans, 20 percent of whom were black.[49]

After racial covenants were ruled unconstitutional in 1948, an enormous exodus occurred: middle-class blacks abandoned the black belt. In 1950 three-quarters of Chicago's black population was cramped into the ghettos; ten years later only one-quarter lived within the same boundaries.[50] But under Mayor Kennelly, the Chicago Housing Authority (CHA) became a new mechanism to enforce segregation. Although its director, Elisabeth Wood, was committed to building CHA housing in white neighborhoods, she noted that Kennelly "could see no sense in calling out a thousand policemen at a fantastic cost per day, just to protect . . . Negro families."[51] Integrated public housing would not be built. Blacks occupied 99 percent of CHA housing, nearly all of it located in black or industrial areas. Nor did open housing fit into the business executives' redevelopment plans for the central city.[52]

Like Cermak a decade and a half before him, Kennelly was "uncomfortable with blacks," except for a handful who were "respectable" and with whom his white business friends had frequent contact. He antagonized those he did acknowledge simply by ignoring their social justice concerns.[53] CHA homes were the site of riots in 1947, 1949, and again in 1954 in reaction to Kennelly's insensitivity and outright appeasement of white bigots. When the mayor blamed the violence on "insurgents," the head of the Chicago Urban League called for his impeachment, but that intemperance only lost the league its local corporate financial support, forcing it to close down for six months.[54]

Kennelly's arguments against open housing and his crackdown (as Cermak had once done) on gambling in the black neighborhoods, which financed Congressman Dawson's submachine, squandered the declining support blacks had given his immediate predecessor. Blacks responded again to a new Democratic challenger who promised deliverance from a callous city hall. The *Chicago*

Defender editorialized that Richard J. Daley's candidacy was a continuation of an earlier, more paternalistic machine, "like . . . when Ed Kelly and Pat Nash ran it."[55]

A MYTHIC LEADER

When he took office from Kennelly, Richard J. Daley (1955–1976) reinstated patronage with a vengeance. He had already been the Cook County Democratic Party leader for three years and had engineered changes that would make his machine more centralized and unitary than any before. As his own "boss," Daley shifted Chicago's budgetary authority from the city council to the mayor's office just before he was elected, thereby controlling more patronage than any of his mayoral predecessors.[56] He kept patronage alive by refusing to schedule civil service examinations for long periods, reinstating the earlier era's practice of hiring "temporary" employees on a permanent basis, and keeping loyalists employed whether they demonstrated competence or not. He also used his school board and city commission appointment authority to centralize the remaining patronage.[57]

Daley became a crucial political ally for every statewide Democratic officeholder by virtue of his ability to direct the votes of most Chicago Democrats.[58] City hall functioned as his "rubber stamp." Between 1958 and 1965, 78 percent of Democratic primary elections in Illinois were uncontested, largely due to the control he exerted. His influence over party loyalists and machine voters also gave him great leverage over the Democratic administrations in Washington, D.C.[59] By the early 1960s Daley was running a fully consolidated political machine.

Although Daley campaigned in 1955 as an anti-business mayor, insisting that he "would never permit politics or big business to interfere in any way with the Board of Education," he nevertheless "wooed business from the start."[60] In his first speech at a Commercial Club meeting only a few months after his election, Daley's topic was a redevelopment plan modeled after the club's Plan of Chicago.[61] Charles Davis, a moderate leader of the National Association for the Advancement of Colored People (NAACP) with club connections, recalled, "If you'll remember, that was during the years that the term 'establishment' was quite popular . . . it came into the lexicon as a result of the story in *Fortune* magazine describing Daley's relationship with the business community. He understood they were players."[62]

"Never an effective speaker," and with a seeming disdain for issues, Daley ran for office on the strength of the Democratic machine's electoral coalition.[63]

At the same time, Daley was able to benefit from its stronger governing coalition. Mayor Kennelly's business instincts and his anti-patronage stance had secured the city's corporate elite. Daley kept their allegiance partly by increasing centralization. He made, or at least approved, all major deals, doled out favors, and, above all, rewarded loyalty. He also continued the machine's Depression-induced reliance on job creation, expanding Kelly's use of public construction contracts to provide quasi-patronage to business and private union workers.[64]

Daley cultivated the reputation of a "builder" by revitalizing the city center with new transportation, universities, and urban renewal, and he advanced his reputation as a good manager by facilitating these projects with property tax incentives and the use of eminent domain and selective zoning. The Commercial Club's century-long focus on downtown development (at the expense of neighborhood development) was doubly rewarded because most of the construction was paid for by federal dollars, keeping taxes low.[65]

Following the precedent of the three machine mayors before him, Daley cultivated personal relationships with the city's elite Commercial Club leaders. Mayor Cermak had been close to First National Bank president Melvin Traylor, whom he nominated for U.S. president as a favorite-son candidate in 1932, as well as Julius Rosenwald, Silas Strawn, Sewell Avery, and Robert McCormick.[66] Many of these same men were Mayor Kelly's confidants, but Colonel McCormick acted as his "guiding light" in the use of federal dollars for downtown urban renewal.[67] Kennelly's fellow club members knew him well even before he was elected mayor.

Thomas Ayers, chairman and chief executive officer of Commonwealth Edison, was one of the Commercial Club leaders that "Dick" Daley trusted. A native of Detroit but a longtime Chicago resident and businessman, Ayers is frequently cited as one of the most influential Chicagoans during Daley's five and a half terms. Listed as one of the "top fifteen business leaders in Chicago," he was called the closest thing to "glue" in the business community.[68] Ayers described his relationship to Daley as typical for club leaders at the time: "Corporate Chicago had a pretty good relationship with the mayor. He would back Corporate Chicago. . . . The mayor wasn't crooked. He wanted people on the board of education, or what have you, that he could control. Those were things that were important to him as a politician. I don't find that repulsive. . . . He was not an anti-business mayor, he would come to the business community to talk about problems . . . but he was also careful of his own turf."[69]

Club leaders like Ayers worked quietly and behind the scenes with Daley, a task facilitated when they made him an ex officio club member. Their more public ties to Martin Kennelly had proved to be a political liability. That, along with their memories of the rough-and-tumble interest-group politics in the past generation, was more than enough reason to prefer the back door of the mayor's office and private discussions. Club leaders and political operatives alike knew that effective machine politics depended on "the politics of secrecy." Patronage-ridden bureaucracies were "steadfastly committed to the protection of information and were adept at a variety of strategies aimed at excluding the public."[70]

The alliance between club leaders and the mayor did not consist simply of their acquiescence to his political wishes in exchange for city franchises, downtown redevelopment, and other side benefits. Those who had the mayor's ear were also expected to assist him in running the city.[71] Ayers reported, "[Daley] wanted to build some new schools and some new firehouses throughout the city, [so] he got a group of businessmen . . . and he said, 'We got to finance this and pay for it, and I want you to help. How are we going to do it?' "[72] For their part, club leaders were proud of their easy access and their role as special advisers. If the bargain required them to assist the mayor in carrying out his plans, those responsibilities also facilitated their involvement in the municipal budgets and management tasks they had always sought to influence.

By the time of Dick Daley's tenure, the industrial Chicago Federation of Labor (CFL) was not only an influential part of the machine but also a reliable and well-rewarded ally.[73] The CFL had long since traded member votes for prevailing wages on the city payroll, an elaborate building code that kept construction costs high, and a guaranteed seat on nearly every city board and commission, including the school board. The American Federation of Labor (AFL) followed suit, earning the same privileged status.[74] Like other machine politicians, Daley incorporated private-sector unions in his electoral and governing coalitions while officially opposing public-sector bargaining as a threat to patronage. In return, private unions strongly supported the Democratic machine candidates. However, the uncommon status of the Chicago Teachers Union (CTU) as a professional, nonpatronage, public-sector organization meant that it posed a threat at election time. When the teachers' pent-up demands for reasonable wages led to a series of strikes, the CTU threatened Daley's governing coalition no less than any other private-sector union.[75]

Patronage angered teachers, who were aware that they were paid far less than the custodians assigned to the schools by city hall. To put pressure on Kelly's city hall, all the teachers unions, except for Margaret Haley's Chicago Teachers Federation (CTF), banded together in 1937 under a single charter as the CTU, having reaffiliated with the American Federation of Teachers when the Loeb rule was rescinded in 1924.[76] But teachers remained ideologically fractious throughout the 1940s and 1950s, unable to take full political advantage of their large numbers. During Daley's tenure, a trade union–oriented faction of the CTU initiated a campaign to achieve collective-bargaining rights, directly confronting the patronage machine and Daley's avowed resistance to public-sector unions.[77]

Yet, as William Grimshaw points out, the members of the CTU did not win collective bargaining so much as "they had the right thrust upon them" by Daley.[78] The trade union faction narrowly secured a strike vote on the issue of bargaining in 1964 and threatened to strike again a year later because Superintendent Benjamin Willis had offered them a raise without any attempt to negotiate. Three days before the strike was called, Daley personally guaranteed their bargaining rights and the promised raise. He then sent AFL representatives and other party loyalists to the school board to obtain its agreement. "Board members who were adamant against granting the union this right changed [their minds], just like that."[79]

Daley's preemptive decision brought the CTU into the machine's governing coalition and ensured that he would remain at the head of the school bargaining table, a role he never attempted to hide. CTU strikes, followed by settlements that Daley negotiated, became a habit after 1968. Paul E. Peterson calculated that by 1973 Chicago teachers were making, on average, 15 percent more than their big-city counterparts as a result.[80] But the offer of collective bargaining also had racial implications at a time when civil rights struggles were beginning to polarize the city. The forthcoming raises did not apply to the vast majority of the system's black teachers, who were mostly untenurable full-time-basis substitutes, ineligible for raises. Only when black teachers crossed the CTU's picket lines during the strikes of 1969 and 1971 did the union make them eligible for tenure and, along with it, the raises already paid to whites. Daley's none too subtle message to protesting blacks was to join the system if they wanted a better deal. Two strikes later, by 1975, internal opposition to the union's bargain with the machine was virtually nonexistent because the strike strategy was always successful in providing teachers with a generous settlement engineered by the mayor.[81]

Continued efforts to meet the teachers' demands demonstrate that union peace was at least as important to Daley's governing coalition as the mayor was to the union. Daley sought property tax hikes in 1966, 1967, and 1968, used Great Society dollars, and took advantage of an Illinois income tax passed in 1969 to fund the first pay raises. Nevertheless, the school district had amassed a huge deficit by the 1970s.[82] Each strike settlement after 1969 added to the debt, totaling $95 million in 1975 when Joseph P. Hannon, a "dedicated budget balancer," was appointed superintendent.[83] Since settlements after 1971 were financed with loans against future tax receipts, the situation was even worse by the time Hannon was forced to resign four years later. The mounting debt bears witness to a CTU leadership that took advantage of the vulnerability of the mayor's boast about his "city that works." The union thus became the second most powerful force in school policy making for more than a decade, second only to the mayor himself.[84]

Business and union ties to the machine grew more important after a series of lawsuits threatened its patronage base. One suit brought against the city in the mid-1970s (*Shakman v. The Democratic Organization of Cook County et al.*) revealed that more than half of municipal jobs were patronage, spurring a federal court order to outlaw political criteria in city hall employment. Under this pressure, public building programs that were underwritten by private loans and employed union labor, city services contracted to local businesses, and public-sector union "bargaining" became substitutes for the proscribed patronage. The new system had its own political advantages: Daley took the credit, business was permitted to negotiate the deals, unionists kept working, and, whenever possible, the federal government was billed.[85] By 1971, John Allswanger argues, the Daley machine had absorbed unionized labor to such an extent that "no one important was against the unions, not even his upper-class supporters."[86]

The school system's governing regime was a by-product of these arrangements with city hall. It allowed business and labor to debate the broad outlines of educational policy with Daley while sustaining the employment of adults who worked in the schools. To openly oppose teachers unions, as the Commercial Club and other business groups had done before the Depression, would have been political suicide in Daley's time.

This long-developing and, by the 1960s, quite stable near-corporatist governing arrangement largely ignored another cleavage that had reopened like an old wound while teachers were winning their rights. Blacks were already one-third of the teaching force, yet most were relegated to second-class status throughout Daley's tenure; it was not until 45 percent of the African American teachers refused to cross picket lines during the 1969 strike that the union even considered bargaining over their full-time-basis status.[87] Chicago's black and white rift festered in the schools among teachers and students alike. For the first time it seriously threatened the machine.

CHICAGO'S CIVIL RIGHTS STRUGGLE

Daley knew that it was time to court black votes when he ran for mayor in 1955. Although he did not personally campaign in a black ward until 1963, he turned to Congressman Dawson and his growing number of ward loyalists. Restricted housing had combined with black migration to create African American majorities in half a dozen wards. Daley offered black politicians more patronage in exchange for their loyalty, and they accepted the deal, although the booty amounted to less than half that dictated by their proportion of the population.[88] Under this bargain, black votes fueled the Democratic voting machine for the remainder of Daley's tenure.[89]

But blacks had no more access to Daley than they had enjoyed under earlier Democratic machine mayors. Although now crucial to the machine's electoral coalition, they were never admitted into its governing coalition. When forced to choose between ethnic whites and blacks, Daley "would choose his own people every time."[90] Moreover, he steadfastly insisted that the only representatives of the African American community worthy of his attention were those black elected officials and the "inner circle" of civic leaders beholden to him. Unlike the business associations or the unions, independent black organizations were not permitted a hearing.[91]

Growing inequalities and political neglect spurred Chicago's black rebellion in the 1960s. The city's famous civil rights struggles and Daley's lukewarm response shook some black voters from their machine allegiance and revealed that many of the black aldermen who served the machine were out of touch with the racial anger in the streets. Neither Daley nor these black leaders could control the newly enraged black population, especially its growing Black Power faction. By 1968 race had superseded all other social cleavages.

The trouble began over Chicago's segregated, unequal schooling.[92] Aided by a white flight so swift that it outstripped black demand for the abandoned housing and left formerly white neighborhoods nearly deserted, the black population increased rapidly as a proportion of the city, doubling to 30 percent in the decade since 1955. A 1963 census revealed that 48 percent of all schoolchildren were black. As early as 1940, all double-shift schools had been located in black neighborhoods, and little changed thereafter, even though empty classrooms in white schools multiplied.[93] By 1962 thirty-seven black elementary schools were larger than the district's "maximum size" of 1,200 students.[94]

Chicago's black parents, clergy, and civil rights groups protested such conditions between 1956 and 1966.[95] Their main achievement was to bring public attention to the overcrowding and poor conditions in the "black" schools.[96] Data were closely guarded by the school system, and it took lawsuits and sit-ins before the district would agree to conduct an accurate demographic study to validate or refute the accusations. The board and superintendent stalled, repeating the same justification for any perceived inequities: the policy of "maintaining no records concerning race" meant that they were impartial.[97] In the meantime, the NAACP and the Chicago Urban League were forced to extrapolate from housing and census data or from incomplete survey data prepared by the CTU. Their guesses were not far off the mark, however. When independent academic studies were finally completed in 1964, the broad outlines of the long-standing inequities were confirmed and acknowledged, but they were not altered.

At the center of the controversy was Superintendent Benjamin C. Willis (1953–1966). He refused to give researchers access to the schools or allow district staff to provide data. His fierce determination to maintain "neighborhood schooling"—which meant that students were assigned to one school based on attendance boundaries that he drew—gave him the appellation "the Governor Wallace of Chicago . . . a one man John Birch Society, incarnate and inviolate."[98]

Many whites nonetheless considered Willis a courageous leader, willing to stand up to intimidation. He met all the NEA's criteria for a general superintendent. After a brief stint as a teacher, he had been a school administrator for twenty years when he accepted Chicago's offer; eight years later he had received four honorary degrees, been elected president of the American Association of School Administrators, and been named to President Kennedy's Vocational Education Commission.[99] The CSC welcomed Willis and supported his responses to overcrowding and other issues. Although the CSC acknowledged that black schools were the most overcrowded, it stated, "many of us do not share the insistent objections voiced particularly by our Negro friends," explaining that "the critical education issues of today are not the dramatic crisis kind we expect to mobilize action."[100] When the CSC did criticize Willis, it was couched as a lapse in professionalism "because of his refusal to provide the board with facts."[101]

Like Cooley, McAndrew, and Hunt before him, Willis also met the Commercial Club's criteria for a good manager. He followed Hunt as a club member and received its members' praise for "efficiency" and his "keen interest in contracting and construction costs."[102] He had many "close personal friends" among the city's corporate leaders and was compensated like a business executive. By 1961 he had been granted one of the country's highest salaries for a public administrator, $48,000.[103] Willis described education as "a big business," a gesture aimed to secure support for his authoritarian management style. He even acknowledged becoming a director of Northwestern Mutual Life Insurance Company because he "wanted to prove that school administrators were well-qualified to serve in positions reserved for businessmen and attorneys."[104]

The traits of efficiency, tirelessness, and superior ability that brought Willis praise from corporate executives and CSC reformers were perceived as rudeness, intolerance, and inaccessibility by the press and as "defensiveness, belligerence, and lack of respect for any person who dares to disagree with him" by those sympathetic to the civil rights struggle.[105] He was unwilling to cede any of his professional authority to parents or to the board of education, which was more polarized over his policies than at any time since the school scandals of 1947.[106] Nor did he ever consider altering his commitment to neighborhood schools. Rather than permitting black students to attend white schools, he vowed to eliminate overcrowding and double shifts by building hundreds of new schools in black neighborhoods and teaching black students in temporary trailers in the meantime. His trailer classrooms, dubbed "Willis Wagons," symbolized Chicago's enforcement of neighborhood segregation.[107]

Defining the Problem

While Willis built schools, civil rights groups prepared a court case documenting de facto segregation. Handicapped by the superintendent's refusal to provide basic data, the NAACP and the Chicago Urban League were forced to estimate that two-thirds of the schools were nearly all white or all black. Reports released in the late 1950s found evidence of resource disparities, including more than three times as many uncertified and inexperienced teachers in the overcrowded black schools. White schools received, on average, $22 more per student per year than black schools, according to one estimate.[108] The NAACP and the Urban League blamed decades of restrictive housing covenants and informal intimidation, but a new U.S. Commission on Civil Rights indicated that the pattern of restrictive transfer policies, resource inequities, and Willis's response to overcrowding in black schools appeared to be intentional. The commission concluded that Willis's central office "suffered . . . the loss of public confidence in its impartiality," but the courts found the evidence "doubtful" and repeatedly asked the litigants to exhaust their administrative remedies before filing suit.[109]

As a result of another out-of-court settlement, the first detailed report on Chicago school segregation was produced in the spring of 1964 by University of Chicago sociologist Phillip Hauser, who was also a consultant to the CSC. It was followed closely by a wide-ranging and tortuously negotiated school survey required by a new Illinois state law and conducted by Hauser's university colleague, Robert Havinghurst, a longtime CSC board member.[110] Hauser described more extreme segregation than civil rights groups had imagined: about 85 percent of all students attended segregated schools. Although Willis had built 266 schools (and additions) in one decade, 40 percent of black schools still had more than 35 students per class, while there was enough excess capacity in the system's white schools for about 17,000 students.[111]

Havinghurst, influenced by the then-popular sociogeography of cities, grouped the schools based on the socioeconomic status of the surrounding neighborhood and discovered that "inner-city" schools, the lowest of four groups, accounted for 53 percent of the elementary schools and 33 percent of the high schools, most of them in black neighborhoods. These schools received large numbers of inexperienced, uncertified (often black) teachers and had high principal turnover.[112] School performance data, revealed for the first time in these studies, also correlated highly with race. On nearly every measure "white schools" fared better than "black schools," and "high-status" schools fared better than "inner-city" schools.[113]

The Hauser report used maps to show that the system's handful of integrated schools were all at the border of black and white neighborhoods, poised to tip into the black category as the ghetto population expanded. Notions of urban life as distorting traditional social relationships influenced the conclusion that "unless the exodus of white population from the public schools and from the City is brought to a halt or reversed, integration may become simply a theoretical matter." But the report also echoed the Democratic machine's long-standing characterization of school problems as being anything but a deliberate injustice to blacks. Havinghurst agreed: "Chicago's chief problem is this: how to keep and attract middle-income people to the central city and how to maintain a substantial white majority in the central city," explaining that elsewhere, integration had been a "failure."[114]

Hauser also insisted on the goal of "maximizing [the] individual's freedom to choose," while Havinghurst created two alternative images of the city's future. One, based on Willis's professional and bureaucratic administration of the schools, he dubbed the "four walls" approach. However, Havinghurst's clear preference was for the other: decentralization through parent and community involvement (the "urban community school"), which was expected to attract and retain the white middle class and permit inner-city schools to be saturated with compensatory services. Special emphasis was put on "the vital factor in every case," the principal.[115]

The same year that the Hauser and Havinghurst reports were released, the CSC also published two reports. One focused on the process of nominating school board candidates from which the mayor might select. The other was the CSC's response to the Hauser report's findings about segregation and resource inequities. Its preference was for a massive dose of compensatory education.[116] The remedies found in all these reports were cautious with respect to integration but nevertheless threatened the school district's centralized governance practice.[117]

Black activists had mixed reactions. White observers at the time represented an older faction that felt that the Hauser report went 90 percent of the way toward meeting civil rights demands, but they were disappointed that its implementation was left in the hands of the school board president, who was also a realtor benefiting from restrictive covenants and a Willis supporter. Many blacks were also displeased with the Havinghurst report. A younger faction was unwilling to accept mere policy statements and sought direct action.[118]

Disillusion abounded in civil rights groups. *Brown v. Board of Education* had promised a legal remedy to segregation, yet judges in Chicago sent the litigants back to seek administrative remedies from the same stonewalling political system.[119] Whites with academic credentials finally certified that black schools were inferior, but their remedies relied on making the city attractive to *white* Chicagoans. It is little wonder that Chicago's impatient black activist Albert A. Raby sought help from the nation's most successful integrationist, Martin Luther King Jr.

Raby, a twenty-nine-year-old "direct, impulsive, and untheoretical" seventh-grade teacher, had helped form the Coordinating Council of Community Organizations (CCCO), a loosely organized interracial civil rights coalition of between twenty and fifty community and religious groups, and was its "convener" by 1964.[120] With encouragement from Raby, his compatriot Lawrence Landry, and the group's younger and more activist faction, the CCCO organized a series of civil rights demonstrations against Chicago's "Jim Crow schools," beginning in 1963 with a stunningly successful school boycott.[121] Half of Chicago's schoolchildren stayed home to protest the board's refusal to accept Superintendent Willis's resignation.[122]

Willis resigned after the board approved the transfer of a handful of black high school students to a nearby white school. He claimed to be protesting "administrative activity of the board," a charge intended to recall the school scandals of the 1940s.[123] Civil rights leaders and the *Chicago Defender* cheered his resignation, but other interests swayed the board. The CSC's ambivalence—the group still praised Willis's efficiency but disliked his intransigent personality—limited its influence. White bigots and real estate executives who approved of segregation, as well as business leaders and educators who approved of his management, won the day. They were backed by hundreds of telegrams sent to city hall and the school board demanding that Willis stay on.

One telegram sent to Mayor Daley and signed by twenty-three businessmen, including many Commercial Club members, was published in the *Chicago Tribune*. Calling Willis "a great superintendent," it urged the board "to meet with Dr. Willis and reconcile your differences" for the sake of "stability and progress."[124] Described by contemporaries and historians alike as very influential in the board's decision to retain Willis, the telegram also marked the beginning of the club's renewed public activism in school affairs, after a hiatus of more than two decades.[125] Officially, Daley stayed out of the discussion but coyly signaled his approval: "Everyone has said [Willis] is doing a good job."[126]

Small demonstrations followed throughout the school year as the city awaited official publication of the Hauser and Havinghurst reports. Their expensive remedies designed to attract and retain whites offended Raby, who replied to Hauser's specter of white flight: "If the white folks want to run from us, we will chase them where ever they go and integrate with them. We will transmit to our children—maybe—segregation. But also self-respect."[127] Raby then called on the CCCO to support another boycott to draw attention to the reports' unsatisfactory remedies. But Daley had already had enough; he "called in all the outstanding IOUs" from every black politician and the city's established black organizations. Black aldermen who had been permitted by Daley to express their tentative support for the first boycott agreed to "work hard" to see the second one fail. The Urban League and the NAACP, in the face of machine pressure, also backed away from the CCCO and Raby. Even so, one-third of the students again boycotted their classes.[128]

Raby concluded from the experience that the "enemy" of decent black schools was Mayor Richard J. Daley, the only person with enough power to control the superintendent as well as most of the city's black leadership. Raby led increasingly disruptive marches on city hall in the summer of 1965, pointedly ignoring the mayor's protestations that he was legally constrained from intervening and asserting instead that "we need to prepare to . . . enter the mayoralty campaign in 1967."[129] The CCCO also claimed that the schools were in violation of Title VI of the Civil Rights Act of 1964 and demanded that U.S. Commissioner of Education Francis Keppel withhold federal funds from Chicago. Daley countered by going directly to President Lyndon Johnson. Within a week the Office of Education reversed its initial agreement to investigate the CCCO's charges, in the process, delaying for the next two years any Department of Health, Education, and Welfare (HEW) investigations or enforcement proceedings.[130] Chicago's black activists had sized up their enemy but could not subdue him.

Raby's emerging prominence as a civil rights activist and the formation of grassroots coalitions like the CCCO were a direct result of the Democratic machine's successful co-optation of more established black organizations and leaders. The local NAACP's commitment to integration had been questioned repeatedly since 1957, when its leadership was silenced by an internal takeover orchestrated by Congressman Dawson. By the late 1960s activists were also questioning Urban League executive director Edwin Berry's commitment to the struggle, demanding that the league embrace Black Power, community control of schools, black history, and poor blacks instead of middle-class "Negroes" and their tactics of backdoor political negotiation. When traditional leaders resisted, they were no longer seen as effective advocates of black frustration. Daley had seeded dissent among black leaders and pushed activists toward direct action by insisting on absolute loyalty. He also made it clear that he would give no hearing to civil rights leaders who could not deliver votes to the machine.[131]

Reverend King and his deputies had been debating whether they should launch a northern campaign when the CCCO turned to them for help.[132] Chicago held several attractions for the Southern Christian Leadership Conference (SCLC): Mayor Daley was a powerful politician with a national reputation; James Bevel and Jesse Jackson, two of King's lieutenants, had already begun work in Chicago; and the CCCO was organized as well as any northern civil rights organization. The SCLC accepted the CCCO's invitation to conduct a nonviolent organizing campaign in 1965, and at first it appeared that the goal would be school integration and Willis's ouster.[133]

By May 1965, however, the superintendent finally agreed to retire. The city's four white newspaper editors, once all his firm supporters, were now evenly divided, and pro- and anti-Willis demonstrations took place almost daily.[134] By this time he had also lost the public endorsement of the Commercial Club. In an open letter printed in the newspaper six months before his retirement was expected, forty-eight executives, most Commercial Club leaders, changed their position on Willis's leadership capabilities, demanding that "the choice of his successor be completed promptly" and asserting "business's responsibility to share in the solving of problems which are ever present in a dynamic, changing city." They insisted that any candidate for his replacement be prepared to consider "equal access to our schools by all races, with a positive policy and program to eliminate segregation."[135]

Reflecting the executives' apparent conversion and his own growing skepticism about personalized targets of direct action, King announced that the "primary objective" of the Chicago Freedom Movement (as the partnership between the CCCO and the SCLC was known) "would be to bring about the unconditional surrender of forces dedicated to the creation and maintenance of slums."[136] Slum housing was not the most salient issue in Chicago, but the SCLC believed that it was less easily manipulated by the behavior of a single political leader and required a broad institutional solution. The Chicago Freedom Movement linked slum housing to economic exploitation, a problem that the newly receptive business leaders might be willing to help resolve.[137] But as Alan Anderson and George Pickering observed, identifying slums as the problem gave Daley's machine a significant organizational and material advantage.

In his characteristically blunt style, popular local columnist Mike Royko immediately identified the movement's dilemma: "One of Mayor Daley's favorite activities is tearing down slums."[138]

The Mayor, the Street, and the Boardroom

On July 10, 1966, after a massive rally at Soldier Field, King taped a list of thirty-five demands on the door of city hall.[139]As planned, nonviolent civil rights marches in white communities followed, calling attention to the extent of housing segregation. Freedom Movement demonstrators, about half of them white and middle class, were shocked at the violent reaction from Chicago's working-class whites, who burned cars, attacked demonstrators, and overwhelmed both the marchers' police escort and their black gang protectors. White violence was preceded that summer by two neighborhood riots, both on the black West Side. To quell the second riot, 4,000 National Guardsmen were required. After responding to black riots with troops, minor concessions, and assistance from the Freedom Movement, Daley desperately wanted the marches on white neighborhoods to stop. He looked to the city's business leaders for help.[140]

Daley called on Ben W. Heineman, chairman and chief executive officer of Chicago and North Western Railroad and a nationally prominent Commercial Club member, to chair a conference with King. In addition to twenty-two civil rights and religious leaders, the invited participants included five top unionists; ten human-relations heads from various agencies; seventeen businessmen, including six club leaders and the city's biggest real estate men; and Daley. Noticeably absent were the city's black elected officials; their participation was deemed "irrelevant." Nor were there any representatives from the school district. Movement leaders realized only in retrospect that their absence meant that the issues of segregated housing and schools would not be considered. Corporate executives played good cop to the real estate brokers' bad cop, while Heineman kept everyone at the table.[141]

The Chicago marches were aimed at "embarrassing the rulers and ultimately creating in them a change of heart," but Daley would not be moved.[142] His press secretary would later explain: "King overestimated Daley's power. Daley did not have the power to make all men brothers, nor was brotherhood necessarily a priority for Daley, who was also concerned about white flight to the suburbs. He saw whites running, and the real issue to him was how to keep them from running."[143]

Nor did the housing conference bring relief to black slum dwellers. Thomas Ayers, Daley's confidant and the father of two anti-establishment radicals, wrote the vaguely worded housing conference agreement.[144] It set up a Leadership

Council for Metropolitan Open Communities to determine how open housing might be pursued and to oversee its implementation by three city agencies: the Chicago Housing Authority, the Commission on Human Relations, and the Department of Urban Renewal.[145] Dependent on the goodwill of business leaders who met regularly with the mayor, the Leadership Council chose to educate the public about the potential good effects of open housing and seek federal injunctions against those (mostly suburbanites) who engaged in discrimination. As Ayers explained twenty years later, "Understand that we were hard-nosed business people, not sociologists." He also described the secret of the group's judicial successes and the subtleties of business–machine interaction: "We would screen [the cases] ourselves so that we aren't picking on some politician who owns a piece of property."[146] From the mayor's perspective, the Leadership Council served a useful function: every announcement it made was met with praise in the city's white dailies for both the mayor's cautious responsiveness and the civic leaders' initiative. Daley was even honored as "Democrat of the Year" by President Johnson for confronting the demonstrators. Many black community leaders, including King himself, felt obliged to praise its efforts, despite meager results.[147]

The riots of the 1960s, however, confounded business's hopes and the mayor's expectations. The Leadership Council, for all its good intentions, was an incremental, ameliorating strategy, unsuited to the crisis of resentment and anger in Chicago's black communities. Black activist leaders felt that the religious and civil rights signatories to the housing conference agreement had sold out their cause. Raby himself resigned in mid-1967, "with little hope of change," to go back to school and "rethink his position."[148] By April 1968 news stories of arson and firebombing in downtown department stores merged in an unsettling pattern with the daily headlines of gang warfare. That fury was to culminate in a full week of mayhem on the West Side following King's assassination.[149] The burning neighborhood symbolized that King's attempt at nonviolent change for blacks in Chicago was in tatters. The mayor was "saddened and depressed," but having engaged corporate executives as his spokespersons, he merely buffered himself from the conflict and made no attempt to remedy it.[150]

In retrospect, Chicago's riots had numerous other flash points. Daley had already been warned by the CSC of a "growing loss of confidence in the school board [nominating] commission" (the same advisory body that Mayor Kelly had agreed to abide by in 1947) when he reappointed two septuagenarian school board members opposed to school integration in 1968.[151] The commission had recommended neither, although its business and labor representatives supported them both. When appointing anti-integrationists in the past, Daley had demurred that he was abiding by the commission's judgment, but after being forced to add civil rights leaders to the advisory group, he no longer felt so constrained.[152]

An even more obvious trigger was Chicago's continuing failure to desegregate its schools. Hired to heal the racial wounds inflicted during Willis's contentious tenure and to rebuild public trust in the schools, James F. Redmond (1966–1975) immediately proposed a desegregation plan so elaborate and costly that no one could foresee how it might be implemented (Redmond expected the federal government to pick up the tab).[153] Nor did it unify the city. Although the CSC praised the plan as visionary and the AFL and CTU endorsed it, the parent-teacher associations equivocated. Chicago's four dailies were evenly split. White aldermen from both parties spoke out against its implementation, and HEW called it a mere "first step." Equally divided school board members accepted the plan only "in principle."[154]

Pressed by HEW for some sign that his plan would be implemented, Redmond suggested starting with its least attractive aspect: busing a few thousand mostly black children. This small gesture toward integration elicited waves of white opposition—petitions, student boycotts, hearings, rallies, and threats of violence. Within six weeks, implementation was reduced to busing a few hundred black student volunteers from two of the system's overcrowded schools to a handful of others. Even this token effort lasted only a year, as the black students involved chose to go back on double shifts.[155]

CCCO leaders had initially supported Redmond when he asked for their help in drafting the plan, but their first sight of his budget left them disillusioned. Funds were allocated for new schools to increase the segregation of neighborhoods in a manner reminiscent of Willis and in violation of the law, and all their recommendations at task force meetings were rejected as fiscally impractical.[156] Recognizing that the Redmond plan supported neither integration nor educational improvements in black schools, they protested both, but to no avail. And the board's adoption of the plan, even in principle, had institutionalized the machine's implicit goal expressed in both Havinghurst's and Hauser's reports: "to anchor whites in the city," while black enrollments were to be "limited and fixed immediately."[157] School board and club member Cyrus Adams III took full advantage of this rationale when he explained his vote against implementation: "If plans intended to retain middle-class people in the city are going to drive a larger number of middle-class people out of the city, they don't make sense."[158]

Meanwhile, Chicago's corporate leaders sought to reorient the school debate from expensive and threatening integration plans to managerial decentralization and cost containment. Writing at the time, Paul Peterson explained their reasoning: property values and tax receipts were expected to decline, and demand for city services was expected to increase, as blacks moved into white neighborhoods. Their presence in the central business district was expected to drive away white shoppers, reduce advertising revenues, and dry up support for cultural institutions.[159] Thus, business leaders reasoned, it was better to focus on making segregated schools more responsive to the parents and families they served. Or, as Daley dryly justified the new approach, "Some try to make this a Negro-white situation, which it is not."[160]

Though Redmond's desegregation plan had little chance of success, his near-simultaneous decentralization plan was instantly implemented. While the board had been searching for Willis's replacement, the consulting firm of Booz, Allen & Hamilton had been hired to write a management audit of the schools.[161] Its strongest recommendation was administrative decentralization—creating another layer of governance between the central office and the school system's twenty-seven existing districts. Three new regions, each as segregated as the schools themselves, were intended to "bring responsibility for decision making closer to the school."[162] At about the same time, the school board asked each subdistrict and school to assemble an advisory citizens council, in the hope of substituting citizen access for racial integration. Neither district councils nor local school councils, as they were known, were uniformly implemented. Many seldom met, and no training was attached to the board's mandate.[163]

Administrative decentralization would become an oft-repeated panacea. As a response to the racial crisis gripping the schools, decentralization delayed integration until it was largely irrelevant. And it reconceptualized the problem of school failure, initiating a wave of management changes that were to engulf the system for decades to come.

A DARING DÉTENTE

Those who argue that business lost its voice in public education policy making between the 1930s and the 1980s are only partly right. The Commercial Club's independent policy voice was subordinated to its partnership with the Democratic machine, but on the issue of race relations in the schools and elsewhere, it felt obliged to reassert its independence.[164] While superintendents Willis and Redmond buffered Daley from much of the civil rights "heat," club leaders were repeatedly asked to serve as the mayor's shadow cabinet, seeking solutions to racial problems where he dared not tread.[165] In effect, the mayor gave the club public policy responsibilities. But earning legitimacy as policy actors in the arena of race relations was something club members had to do without his help.

There were at least two reasons that club members agreed to fill the vacuum in race relations. One was defensive. Some of the Commercial Club's leading companies had been targeted for arson the week of King's assassination. The Loop's flagship Carson Pirie Scott department store sustained $7.5 million in damage, Montgomery Ward was firebombed, and the First National Bank's headquarters was reportedly threatened by black gang members.[166] Daley's stubborn dismissal of black protests had emboldened the more violent activists, black and white alike. So club members felt that it was necessary to defend their interests independently. One white executive likened their efforts to "the fire department, in case we have another explosion."[167] One Latino agreed that business activism was reinvigorated because "the people who were empowered—the white establishment—were afraid."[168]

At the same time, the more farsighted executives anticipated racial succession. Club leader Ben Heineman commented that their responsibility was "to arrange the orderly transfer of power from the white community to the black community."[169] He and a small group of like-minded executives wanted to reach an accommodation with the blacks who might be running the city in the future, just as they sought the immediate safety of their employees, buildings, and wealth.

While white corporate Chicago was beginning its reentry into city governance, black militant Chicago accelerated its rebellion. Neither trusted the traditional avenues of accommodation. The mayor's ability to produce social peace through patronage and symbolic benefits was at a low point. Mainline interracial organizations such as the NAACP and the Urban League had been discredited from below. Black activists once again turned to the business elite who had shown their willingness to listen at the open housing summit.

A handful of Commercial Club leaders also sought a direct dialog. An urban coalition was one idea considered but rejected because club leaders feared that it would raise unreasonable expectations.[170] Instead, Thomas Ayers, Ben Heineman, and Gaylord Freeman Jr., chairman of First National Bank of Chicago and a nationally known advocate of the International Monetary Fund, agreed to find a few grassroots leaders with whom to begin a dialog about the problems of Chicago's black community. They already knew the traditional black leaders; this was an attempt to "reach out to street people, the activist people."[171] One was the Reverend J. Archie Hargraves, an associate professor at the Chicago Theological Seminary and a seasoned CCCO activist who had predicted that the housing summit "will not stop the riots." He and his colleague, business consultant Earl Doty, were willing to oblige, but only on the condition that whites not be the decision makers.[172]

Hargraves and Doty represented the Black Coalition, a loose affiliation of about sixty Black Power organizations, civil rights groups, religious leaders, and "teen nations" (street gangs). The Black Coalition had the goal of building "a new black community that will become self-supporting and strong enough to share in the affairs and the decision making of the larger community." This meant training a group of black "functional" leaders to replace Daley loyalists.[173]

Raby's hope of directly challenging Daley in 1967 had failed. Black voter registration went poorly, and voters concerned about civil rights had only conservative Republicans as alternatives. Daley's huge win was also attributable to club leaders, who formed their usual "non-partisan committee to re-elect Mayor Daley."[174] Black activists now hoped to persuade white corporate executives to support their political development in the same way they supported Jesse Jackson's pressure for black economic development in Operation Breadbasket.[175]

Members of the Black Coalition began meeting with Heineman, Ayers, Freeman, and about a dozen other club leaders in June 1969. The businessmen wanted something to come of their discussions, so at Freeman's urging, they reluctantly raised funds for a Black Strategy Center (BSC) to develop black leaders. The BSC was publicly announced in September 1969, with a two-year proposed budget of $1,624,000. Hargraves was its chairman and C. T. Vivian, a senior leader in the SCLC, its president.[176] Hargraves described the partnership as follows: "The business[es] involved   will help raise funds and insure audit procedures. We see the black community's desire for self-determination as a sign of hope. The day of welfare, the day of paternalism is past; so too, we hope, is the day of violence."[177]

Whereas the BSC was to give blacks "protection, prestige and hope" in place of despair, club leaders wanted the group to develop legitimate black spokesmen who could prevent, or at least dampen, another full-scale race riot.[178] The businessmen had reservations, however, about whether these activists had the "administrative capacity" to oversee the budget and whether they represented enough of the black community and could maintain harmony among themselves. The presence of the Blackstone Rangers street gang at organizational meetings and on the BSC board of directors gave them early reason for doubt.[179] After the December 1969 police raid on Chicago's Black Panther headquarters resulted in its charismatic leader, Fred Hampton, being killed in a hail of bullets, negotiating with Black Power organizations seemed even more risky.[180]

White business leaders were not alone in their anxiety about the BSC. Edwin "Bill" Berry, about to retire as the Urban League's executive director, was skeptical about corporate Chicago's decision to support the upstart group, as was Jesse Jackson. After all, "the Black Strategy Center was funded at a level that probably the Urban League, NAACP and half a dozen other traditional organizations never received."[181] And of course, Mayor Daley did not approve of any effort to replace machine-loyal leaders, black or white.

As some of its Commercial Club sponsors had feared, and as Bill Berry had predicted, the BSC was labeled a failure after little more than a year when an audit could not account for all the corporate leaders' money and found that little of substance had been accomplished. Berry described that year as "the most expensive freshman-year education a group of seasoned businessmen ever had."[182] Nevertheless, white executives had shown that they would invest in projects initiated and run by blacks, and black community activists had achieved a partnership with power that was out of their reach in Daley's machine. A club spokesperson described the lessons of the BSC to the press two years later: "We all learned a lot from the experience and as a result certainly forged all kinds of relationships that have been useful to us . . . relationships we would not have . . . if we hadn't first collaborated on the Strategy Center. . . . The BSC showed us a number of things that don't work, but as a direct result we're now embarked on a project that has a real possibility of doing so."[183]

That project was known only as the Group, and it consisted of twenty-six men—half were the original sponsors of the BSC and their club colleagues, and half were black leaders in Chicago. Despite pulling out of the BSC, club leaders remained committed to an ongoing dialog, but now with established blacks. They were more comfortable dealing with black leaders who embraced middle-class values and sat like "salt and pepper" with them around a corporate boardroom table for breakfast once a month. Choosing to be inconspicuous, the Group took no formal name, remained unincorporated, and was a well-kept secret for nearly two years.[184] In addition to the lingering "feeling that the city would burn again if they didn't do something," white corporate leaders were convinced to join the Group partly because of the business influence of Freeman, Ayers, and Heineman. As one black member put it, "If your banker calls you and asks you to do something, you do it."[185] Black and, later, Latino members had complementary motives for participating. "Majority members got together to *protect* their business interests. The minority members are there to *increase* their participation in the economy."[186] There was also the unusual opportunity to speak to those in power and be taken seriously. As another put it, "I can pick up the phone and call any CEO I want and he will return the call if he's in town."[187]

Although everyone had mixed motives, the whites appeared to be genuinely interested in the concerns of their dialog partners. One manifestation was the agreement that each "side of the aisle" had a veto over the agenda, lowering the risk that whites would dominate by virtue of their superior resources.

When their mutual trust grew sufficient to establish a not-for-profit corporation, optimistically named Chicago United, they established a dues structure that reflected the vast gulf in resources between majority and minority members. Still, influencing the whites remained an ongoing preoccupation of black members.[188] In a speech given at the first meeting of the Group, black founding member and prominent dentist James Buckner challenged those assembled to take risks: "If, gentlemen, we are serious, then the involvement must be a total one, not simply financial. . . . It means [whites] taking some of the hurt, making some of the sacrifices and doing some of the speaking out. The Black members, despite our identification with certain organizations, are committed to joining the crusade, attacking problems of the total community and shedding our pet projects."[189]

The result was uncommon for its era. One newsman noted, "There was no other place in the country where minority leaders had this kind of continuing access to the white power structure."[190] The prize was a group of black leaders and white businessmen who lent each other credibility in their separate worlds.

This new partnership was cautious with respect to the machine. In joining the Group, blacks had rejected the confrontational option of building a separate political base in favor of one emphasizing private economic power. They not only avoided conflict with Daley but also drew on their new web of informal relationships to influence government. Both sides preferred to tackle the exclusion of blacks from "private" leadership, using their informal influence and collective resources in ways that would not challenge the mayor's hold on political institutions.[191]

AVOIDING DESEGREGATION

The Chicago public schools were a topic of discussion beginning with the second meeting of the Group. In 1971 Dr. Charles Hirst Jr., then chairman of its Education Task Force, reported on the first of many Chicago United school studies, concluding that it would be nearly impossible to rebuild Chicago's "wreck" of a school system. He dismissed Superintendent Redmond's efforts to engage businesses in revamping the schools and led a wide-ranging discussion on how the Group might use its resources to create new models for public education.[192]

Such discussions, which were frequent in the 1970s, typically defined school problems in strong terms, but their solutions were old saws taken from business journals or executives' personal experiences in their own enterprises. For instance, widely publicized statistics—a 40 percent dropout rate in 1971; a

70 percent increase in the budget from 1966, accompanied by a $58 million shortfall; and ghetto schools receiving $45 per child per year less than white schools—reinforced in business eyes the need for management "restructuring." Discussions also included support for decentralization, increased attention to district management, and long-term planning.[193] Compared with black demands for political integration, community control, and vastly increased supplemental programs—demands that Daley's machine had shown no willingness to meet—Chicago United's proposals were strikingly modest and ill defined.

Even so, the Group's second report, written with the assistance of Professor Herbert J. Walberg of the University of Illinois, unintentionally thrust it into open conflict with the mayor. Based on a survey conducted among seventeen member companies and intended as an internal document, the report concluded that graduates were not prepared for work and placed the blame on teachers and administrators, who were characterized as lacking accountability for the system's "products." The 1974 study had seven recommendations, including administrative decentralization, greater student and school accountability, and private managerial oversight. The executives proposed to support improved management services in the central office, do the same for career education, and nominate themselves for the school board.[194] Chicago United leaders approached the mayor privately before going to the board of education with their recommendations. Those present at the meeting reported that Daley seemed amenable, agreeing to support decentralization, appoint two businessmen to the school board, and convene a conference on urban education. In return, Daley asked Chicago United not to publicize the report and its recommendations.[195]

Little of this backdoor agreement would ever be implemented, however. Just months before the mayoral election, the report was leaked to the press, giving Daley justification to withdraw his commitments. A subsequent newspaper article ominously claimed that Chicago United was "laying the groundwork for a broad attack on the city's problems."[196] A watered-down version of the report was published later that year in an attempt to save face, but the damage had already been done to relations with the mayor.[197] Daley ignored Chicago United's nominees for the two open school board seats in 1975, claiming that they were less qualified than those he reappointed.[198]

Privately, black members fumed. They recommended abandoning all efforts to assist the schools, including fund-raising, in favor of at least a limited "confrontation" with Daley. It "need not be direct," they argued, "it could involve a process that simply identifies and publicizes significant issues, proposes solutions, and develops sufficient public support to make action politically desirable and necessary."[199] They even briefly debated a role for outsiders in some of their deliberations to instill public confidence in their recommendations. During the 1970s such discussions went no further, but they revealed black members' developing independence from the Democratic machine and their lingering differences with white business executives who firmly backed Daley's control.

During this period of backdoor negotiations among Chicago's black and white private-sector leaders over race relations, Superintendent Redmond and Daley's handpicked school board stalled on the issue of desegregation. By 1975 the public schools were more segregated than when Redmond had arrived—half the high schools were 95 percent white or black, and more than 72 percent of the system's students were black or Latino. HEW was threatening to withhold funds due to Chicago's failure to desegregate its teaching force—a significant risk, since fully half of the system's billion-dollar budget came from state and federal programs. Declining test scores, a $95 million deficit, and another looming teachers' strike were only some of the reasons Chicago's schools were being called the worst in the country by local civil rights activists.[200] Facing an angry community and an increasingly divided board, Redmond resigned after two terms.

The business-oriented Joseph P. Hannon (1975–1979), a former independent school administrator in Europe and Chicago's assistant superintendent in charge of facilities, was Redmond's successor, chosen over the more senior black deputy superintendent, Manfred Byrd. Tipping his hand, Daley had reappointed two board members at the last minute who were pledged to the white candidate. This meant passing over Chicago United's business recommendations for the open slots and again overriding the objections of the nominating committee.[201] Hannon's inauspicious beginnings were never overcome. Like Redmond, he left the system worse than he found it. After four years he was forced to resign over threats of court-ordered desegregation and a worsening fiscal and educational crisis.

Halfhearted desegregation plans, usually involving only a few thousand black students when implemented, shuffled between Chicago, Springfield, and Washington, D.C., for the remainder of the decade and into the 1980s. None ever met the spirit or letter of the civil rights legislation. If delay was the strategy, it succeeded. By 1979 racial inequality would be upstaged, and Chicago would move on to a new school reform agenda. Neither Daley nor his immediate successors, Michael Bilandic and Jane Byrne, endorsed integration, and the same white parents who had violently protested desegregation in King's day held the system hostage again and again.[202] It is no wonder that few black parents agreed to transfer their children to the scattered seats available in white schools.[203]

Illinois found the city schools in nonconformance with its desegregation regulations a total of five times in the 1970s, although Chicago never suffered the prescribed consequences.[204] State Superintendent of Schools Joseph Cronin began the process afresh with Superintendent Hannon. Chicago's response was more of the same: a quota of voluntary black transfers, facility upgrades, and a few programs in black schools. Most conspicuous was a succession of committees to propose better plans, including the City-Wide Advisory Committee (CWAC) on which Chicago United members, both black and white, sat. [205]

Consensus eluded the advisory groups, making it easier for Hannon to reject their recommendations in favor of yet another scheme to attract white students back to the system: targeting those who had fled to the city's private and parochial schools.[206] "Access to Excellence" as he called his plan, created a three-tiered system—academic schools with test-based admission criteria, technical (vocational) schools, and "basic studies" schools for students with poor skills. Whites were expected to be disproportionately represented in the academic schools, a prospect underscored by maintaining the 1957 definition of "integrated," which applied to any school with as few as 10 percent nonwhite students. Fully half of the racial mixing that Hannon projected was to come from voluntary summer school and part-time programs.[207]

Hannon marshaled support by calling on friends in the Council of Great City Schools, who applauded the district's Mastery Learning reading program in its 186 basic studies schools and the new school "profiles" for accountability purposes. Despite these accolades, and even though Chicago's two remaining white dailies endorsed his plans, the situation was grim. Reading proficiency had shown no gains, only about 3 percent (17,000) of the city's black youngsters were voluntarily bused, and only 34 of 600 schools were desegregated.[208] As expected, the U.S. Commission on Civil Rights rejected the plan (and its weak successor, Access to Excellence II), bluntly observing that it "offered more potential for continued segregation than desegregation," and threatened a lawsuit to impose busing in the 1979–1980 school year.[209]

For its part, Chicago United avoided public debate over school integration. Although black deacons drafted a series of statements beginning in the spring of 1977, whites protested that their proper role on this issue was "totally in-house, non-public," at most advisory to the businessmen representing them on the school board and the CWAC. The group even equivocated when it came to a request for financial support of a media campaign encouraging voluntary transfers.[210] Their reluctance was noticed, prompting the normally sympathetic *Chicago Daily News* to chide the "shameful" silence: "Where is that coalition of industrial, commercial, financial, and political leaders famous for keeping Chicago's credit rating high and our tempers cool?"[211] This uncharacteristic rebuke was followed the next day by a lukewarm statement from Chicago United calling Hannon's voluntary desegregation plans a "good faith" gesture and raising the specter of court-ordered busing if it were to fail. But the statement also explicitly acknowledged that the group's members themselves were not in unanimous agreement.[212] Notwithstanding civil rights leaders' hopes or the multiracial Chicago United, Chicago's corporate executives were not leaders on school integration.

For the whites among them, integration was beside the point. Chicago's corporate leaders had already reframed the public school problem and were seeking to convince black members. They believed that the central problem was a lack of consequences for adults when students did not perform well (accountability), rather than the racial bias of a system that routinely gave black and Latino students an inferior education. Lingering inequities in the system were explainable, in the corporate view, as a *consequence* of mismanagement, rather than as the fundamental *cause* of the system's failure. The corporate solution for the accountability problem was to improve the budgetary and delegation skills of board members and the personnel management skills of administrators, including their ability to administer a more decentralized system.[213] Chicago's corporate leaders would soon gain sufficient control of the system to put much of this new agenda into practice. In the meantime, they pursued less central goals: a career education program, for which they hired a full-time manager, and a management and training institute for board personnel, both of which were welcomed by Hannon. And they continued to pursue a few business appointments to the board.[214]

Civil rights leaders grew disenchanted with Chicago United, losing hope that their indirect access to power could influence policy on behalf of black children. However, by the close of the 1970s, Chicago United executives and black civil rights leaders agreed that the Chicago public school system was a recalcitrant organization characterized by poor decision making, responsive only when compelled by a major crisis. A climax was soon to come, but it was not the desegregation confrontation that black leaders hoped for. Instead, with no less effect than the Depression-era crash fifty years earlier, the school system was thrown into financial chaos, a state of affairs that elevated the executives' fiscal expertise and management arguments.

By then, Chicago United had earned a legitimacy in local educational policy making that was equally rooted in its partnership with the Democratic machine and its new role as a conduit to power for black community leaders. More than a decade of quiet engagement—urging recommendations about board reorganization, career education, and administrative management on Daley, Willis, Redmond, and Hannon—made Chicago United members nearly as well recognized in the executive offices of district headquarters as they were in city hall. Solicitations for money and donated executive time identified them with public school issues in the eyes of their peers. Working under the umbrella of a single organization that had become a mouthpiece for corporate views on educational issues gave them a common language in which to voice their concerns.

REFORM POLITICS OF THE MACHINE ERA

The organizational structure and relationships underpinning the 1917 Otis law had finally become institutionalized by 1980. This entrenchment of a hierarchically organized, business-emulating governance structure was a direct reflection of the mayor's consolidation of control, rather than a result of any reform movements. The era's sustained changes merely reinforced this centralized, bureaucratic pattern. Both corporate business associations and unions actively supported increasing centralization because each sought marginal concessions from the schools while accepting economic benefits from city hall. The remaining middle-class professional and good-government groups, although critical of the machine and many of its mayors, were relatively easily ignored or co-opted by the era's mayors.

Unlike their predecessors, machine-era mayors were crucial arbiters of school reform efforts, and as a result, little was changed. A large cadre of custodial and service employees appointed by city hall, a monopoly on information about the schools, and mayoral manipulation of board finances institutionalized and perfected the corrupt routines begun at the turn of the century. Despite decades of censure from good-government groups, the NEA, and the state's school accrediting body, Mayor Kelly lasted three full terms. The School Board Nominating Commission, the sole legacy of those attempts to clean up the schools, would be heeded only when Mayors Kennelly and Daley thought it in their political interests. And Kennelly's brief effort to rein in patronage was more than made up for by Daley's expansion of the practice. Daley subsequently sanctioned the era's biggest governance change, collective bargaining, to secure his personal control over the city's workers. These mayors presided over school politics as they did over city hall, by personally doling out favors, approving deals, and rewarding loyalty.

Dependent on city hall for their political support, the era's superintendents were either dishonorable or autocratic rulers who couched their authority in corporate terms. More than anything, the strong superintendents among them were intent on sustaining the existing system and denying and quashing the civil rights claims of black Chicagoans. Hunt avoided dealing with issues by studying them and producing reports that tackled patronage and overcrowding in black schools, but doing little about either. Willis simply stonewalled, providing no information to black activist organizations, the Civil Rights Commission, or the school board and denying all their charges. Vowing that the system would never change while he was in charge, he expected to dissipate racial tension by building new segregated schools. Although ostensibly hired to undo this legacy, neither James Redmond nor Joseph Hannon was able to make a difference. Both faced a status quo mayor, school board, and business community.

The inclusion of corporate capitalists as a governing partner with city hall was crucial to the politics of schooling in the years 1930 to 1980. Each of the era's four mayors, Cermak through Daley, increased the Democratic machine's ties to Commercial Club executives by reliably providing the underpinnings of corporate economic accumulation. To appeal to the executives' belief that government ran best when headed by people like themselves, each mayor also projected the public image of a competent manager. Moreover, corporate leaders' views on schooling received a private hearing by the mayor, and often by the superintendent as well.

In turn, corporate interests supported machine governance of the city and its parallel system of control over the schools. Business executives centralized their organizational structures to conform to the machine's model of interest-group intermediation. Acknowledging that political influence would depend on a personal and confidential rapport with the mayor, the club's leaders cultivated relationships with mayors and invited them to become club members. They also extended invitations to two school superintendents, signifying their agreement that governing the schools, like governing the city, was expected to be a process of private decision making among like-minded executives. In the process, club leaders lost their Progressive era ability to criticize the school system from outside, but they gained a new backdoor influence that was secure and politically unaccountable.

In return for enjoying influence over local policy, business felt obliged to render assistance to the mayor when his own resources flagged. Although club leaders supported the mayor during the school scandals of the 1940s, at no time was their support more important than when the machine came under direct attack over civil rights. As loyal machine partners, club leaders were authorized to resolve the conflicts he was unwilling to address. As a direct result, the club formed Chicago United, symbolically championing a more inclusive version of elite politics through its half-white, half-black membership. In the process, it helped empower a new group of black elites as a political force in the city and may have inadvertently hastened the demise of the machine. Yet theirs was a cautious response. Once immersed in racial controversy, club leaders sought familiar organizational and managerial solutions. This, in turn, gradually expanded their role in the machine, since their tinkering took place within the framework of its basic logic and legitimacy.

Taking the era as a whole, there is little evidence that corporate executives were unhappy with the state of the schools. Before 1939 they oversaw all major school decisions through the Sargent Committee. During the school scandals of the 1940s they praised the system, suggesting only minor adjustments in its management. By the time debates over Willis were polarizing the community, they sided with the mayor and his man. Some say they exerted more influence over Willis's decision to stay (and then to go) than did years of street demonstrations. When white segregationist inciters, black violence, and Daley's abdication of responsibility threatened the social peace, they agreed to meet with blacks and hear their grievances. Even then, they quickly reached the conclusion that the schools were managerially, but not systemically, flawed.

This does not mean that corporate leaders were oblivious to the rampant corruption in the 1940s or to the inequities underscored by the civil rights protests. But their solutions to these problems were always incremental and corrective, never embracing the democratizing changes that others sought. New leaders, better training, and managerial procedures could solve the problems of the era, they reasoned; the system itself was sound.

Unions, formerly the nemesis of club members in their efforts to shape the city's school system, became their coalition allies during this era. After both were incorporated into the machine, their differences—largely over Depression cutbacks and Daley's wage increases—were publicly voiced by only one business member of the board, Warren Bacon, speaking as a *black* businessman, and then only toward the end of the era.[215] Like businessmen, unionists gained a privileged position after they had consolidated and centralized and began seeking favors from city hall. Each mayor then took responsibility, with varying degrees of success, for negotiating between business and labor. Those mediations gave something to both and stressed the common interests each had in maintaining a governance structure that acknowledged their voices while ignoring those of the strident civil rights reformers.

The largest difference between the two sectors was the much longer time it took for the teachers union to become fully incorporated as part of the machine. The CTU began the machine era as it had ended the Progressive era—fighting for better salaries and schools in coalition with the reformist CSC. But this lingering activism was abandoned when access to city hall proved an easier avenue to wage increases. Daley's granting of collective bargaining cinched the deal.

The CTU did not align with the new civil rights reformers. Whereas Daley clearly wanted to send an assimilating message to blacks, the CTU was little interested in their full union participation. It took blacks refusing to cross the picket lines before the union would bargain for their rights. Nor did the CTU ever ally with either the CCCO or the Chicago Freedom Movement, although other unions joined when King moved to Chicago.[216]

Other civic groups also realized that consolidation and collective action were their only hope of influencing school policy. Starting with a handful of civic groups and the help of teachers, the CSC grew to encompass between seventy and ninety separate women's, professional, and religious organizations, none of which could influence policy alone in Chicago's consolidated political culture. But the CSC never sought incorporation into the machine. Instead, it confronted machine mayors by encouraging nonmachine candidates. Lacking the backdoor influence of business and labor, the CSC continued its earlier practices of publicly demanding change, commissioning reports, writing laws, and lobbying the legislature. Such unilateral activities drained resources, and as the energy of CSC volunteers flagged, its efforts were used to legitimize what the mayor found useful. Thus, for most of the fifty-year period described in this chapter, the CSC's primary influence lay outside Chicago, among likeminded professional groups. But its tactic of reform by shame, which had proved useful in bringing the threat of de-accreditation in the 1940s, soon lost its effectiveness.

Although the CSC did not eschew civil rights activity, its commitments were vague and equivocating. The substance of its critique was a continuation of its earlier good-government preoccupation, focusing on corruption, the restoration and rationalization of services, and efficiency concerns. Briefly acting as the city's conscience with respect to school cutbacks, it lost its moral leadership to local civil rights groups. As Anderson and Pickering astutely note, the dominant credo in Chicago at the time was one of amelioration, resting equally on white "fears of imminent violence" and the conviction that existing institutions of schooling would resolve problems over time with only minor administrative tinkering. Blacks were simply seen as the next ethnic group expected to assimilate.[217] The Democratic machine found it easy to adopt this civic rhetoric, co-opting any reformist impulses it may have had. And the view itself represented a fundamental misunderstanding of the central conflict of the era.

There is no doubt that the most compelling school reform ideas of the era were inspired by moral outrage over the city's racial segregation. Few, if any, of these reforms were seriously tried in Chicago, but they might have included racial integration, community control, experimental or alternative schools, saturated services in poor neighborhoods, choice options such as magnet schools, pedagogical experiments targeted toward specific students, and even the wildly expensive education parks that the CCCO favored in the end. But all three organized political actors—corporate business, unions, and civic good-government groups—kept their distance from the most compelling school reform argument of the era: racial justice.

Instead, machine-era reform was a series of alterations to the governance structure formed decades earlier. The addition in 1947 of the Advisory Commission on School Board Nominations and a general superintendent contributed to the overall consolidation and legitimation of the mayor's governing authority and the superintendent's managerial prerogatives. The creation of a series of midlevel management positions in the form of district, area, and deputy superintendents, along with new functions added to the central offices, furthered the consolidation and centralization, as did the city's authority to finance school buildings. Arguably the most influential reform was the mayor's granting of collective-bargaining rights, which undercut any independent authority the school board once held. Even the administrative decentralization of the 1970s added new layers of bureaucracy, strengthening barriers between those outside the system and the professionals in it. All this reinforced the mayor's power, a seemingly permanent feature of Chicago-style politics by the 1970s.

That status quo governance solutions were the response to equity problems during this era is no accident. Apart from the changes instituted in the 1940s, every subsequent reform idea, whether decentralization or collective bargaining, was predicated on a vision of Chicago as a white, middle-class city that could not sustain a change in its demographics without challenging its basic social structure. The earliest reports of the system's racial inequities were glaring, but they framed the solutions in terms that were amenable to the white middle class, whose schools were already the most privileged. No subsequent response from Chicagoans to the many federal challenges over segregation took a different stance. To ensure that whites did not find Chicago school reform objectionable, they seemed to say, it must sustain a governance structure that separated them from blacks, and especially from poor blacks.

It was not only the machine that defined equity in ways destined to leave blacks unsatisfied. Throughout the 1970s Chicago's corporate elite was determined to reframe the desegregation concerns of black leaders as management issues. Their ability to do so was never more evident than in 1979, when, despite a federal desegregation lawsuit that promised to finally force court-ordered desegregation, the system was brought down once again by a financial crisis.

3

Improvising Decentralization

Uncommon Coalitions and Conflicting Agendas
1980–1990

The decades-long struggle for desegregation had left no discernible residue by the close of the 1970s. Unlike the Depression-spurred and business-led financial retrenchment, desegregation as a strategy of school reform seemed to melt away in the face of new concerns about school efficiency. The loss of civil rights leaders' integrationist dream coincided with a disintegration of the Chicago political machine and a weakening of city hall's custody of the school district.

With the active participation of machine mayors, the school system had become adept at hiding problems through delay and misinformation. A Byzantine central office hierarchy added new barriers to citizen involvement in an effort to deflect civil rights complaints. Patronage employment swelled the ranks of support-service employees, who were unresponsive to school leaders' requests for repairs and service. Deferred maintenance left school buildings dilapidated and unsafe. Teachers discovered that there would be no adverse consequences if they simply closed their classroom doors and avoided drawing attention to the school. This culture demoralized the best teachers and misled the poorly skilled into thinking that they were acceptable. Worst of all, questioning the status quo was judged an act of disloyalty.[1]

Notwithstanding efforts to forestall change by superintendents, a conservative union leadership, and the next two hapless mayors, Michael Bilandic and Jane Byrne, reform came in a few short months on the heels of financial collapse. The Chicago public schools would be declared insolvent by the bond rating agencies, and the city's bankers would seize power over the budget with no less impact than they had during the Depression. The shock initiated a series of reform debates as contentious as any in the past century and eventually blossomed into a citywide movement galvanized by the charismatic and politically astute black mayor, Harold Washington. The result would be the reorganization of control and authority across the entire school system.

There were many reasons for these changes, but Mayor Daley's school leadership was not among them. Daley had represented the views of the most vehemently anti-integrationist white ethnics, a declining minority of the city population by the 1980s. Moreover, he had grown less effective after the racial conflicts of the 1970s, seemingly less certain of his hold on power and incapable of crafting a compromise to keep black resentment within bounds. In his final 1975 primary election he faced an African American challenger for the first time (Richard Newhouse) and black voters cast their ballots for Daley in fewer numbers than ever before. Nor did the increasingly diverse Chicago Teachers Union (CTU) endorse him, despite lending its support during his five prior campaigns.[2]

When Richard J. Daley died in December 1976, less than two years after he had been reelected for a sixth term, few anticipated the political instability that followed. The mantle was quickly passed in a city council session to machine stalwart Michael Bilandic (1976–1979), who handily won a special election called to fill the remainder of Daley's term.[3] But the next decade would bring Chicago four different mayors, a turnover more typical of the fractious decades of the pre-machine era. Adding to the uncertainty, for the first time in a generation the power of the mayor's office was reduced because it no longer controlled the Cook County Democratic Committee. Neither Bilandic nor his successors enjoyed the absolute control over the Democratic Party machine that had permitted Daley's management of the city's finances by accumulating a massive, if largely hidden, debt.[4]

Much of the unsettled era's politics played out in racial terms. Unresolved racial tensions over segregated housing and schools, access to city services, and political favors found their expression in electoral contests. After serving out Daley's unfinished term, Bilandic was soundly defeated by the city's first female candidate, Jane Byrne (1979–1983), on the strength of black voters' anger over his failure to plow snowbound streets and his inexplicable order that commuter trains skip the stops in black wards. Harold Washington's subsequent victory over two white candidates was razor thin, but enough to put him in control of city hall on the strength of an unprecedented grassroots, minority coalition. Like every Chicago mayor before him, his governing style set the stage for school reformers. A well-informed populist intent on redistribution, he governed as if development meant rebuilding neighborhoods and providing access to city hall, in the process enabling a racially integrated cross section of low-income community leaders to become school reformers.[5]

Ironically, much of the demand for change in the school system would harry the district's black employees, because growing numbers of black students, court orders, central office cutbacks, and new African American district and union leaders reshuffled traditional career paths. Already about two-fifths of the system in 1976, black educators would reach parity with their white counterparts a decade later as white professionals increasingly abandoned the city. Eager blacks filled the vacancies, giving the city's black middle class a stronger stake in the survival of the school system and good reason to resist the multicultural coalition's efforts to change the rules of governance.

Washington's empowerment of low-income groups, on the one hand, and black educators' resistance, on the other, would play out in cross-class tensions within the black community. Also, a rift would develop between African Americans and the city's rapidly growing Latino population, whose numbers and cohesiveness gave politicians an opportunity not seen since before the Depression: the ability to play one ethnic group against another. Before 1980 Latinos were represented by only one Chicago elected official and accounted for less than 4 percent of the professional educators. By the close of the decade they were still awaiting the rewards of their activism, having only modestly increased their representation in the school system, holding 6 percent of its professional positions, even as their children accounted for 25 percent of the student population.

In this unsettled political environment, Commercial Club leaders responded to the budget crisis by reverting to an old pattern of civic activism. Financial leaders of the club stepped in, offering a fiscal bailout in exchange for another financial oversight committee. Once again they were intent on restructuring the system by applying management and fiscal controls to stop the flow of red ink. And as they had during the Depression, at least some voices would charge that the financiers had precipitated the crash themselves. True or not, it is indisputable that in each case the corporate executives lost faith in the mayor's office and, by extension, the governance of the schools and were determined to take action. They envisioned a new management structure that would ensure better accountability, fiscal and otherwise. They called this new structure *decentralization.*

FINANCIAL CRISIS AND BUSINESS CONTROL

By fiscal year 1978–1979 the Chicago public schools had accumulated a projected deficit of over half a billion dollars. Only eight years earlier the operating fund had had a surplus of $2.6 million. In the intervening years, ballooning interest rates and constant refinancing had caused deferred interest to soar; it accounted for a quarter of the entire debt. An immediate crisis occurred when $85 million in notes came due on November 26, 1979. Tax receipts were down to only 32 percent of revenue, so refinancing was the only option, but this required asking Commercial Club bankers to purchase school bonds. In the absence of a mayor who would pledge city assets as security against school borrowing, the financial community made an independent business decision about the creditworthiness of the school system. The Chicago schools failed the test.

A Joint Investigation Committee of the Illinois legislature identified several reasons for the system's financial problems. One was insufficient and uncollected local taxes: since 1970 corporate property tax receipts had fallen to 40 percent of what was owed, and in 1977 alone 5,422 local firms simply refused to pay at least $10,000 of their levy. Even as corporate taxes went unpaid, long-term leases on real estate that the school board had rented to corporations were undervalued. CTU argued to the legislative committee that the board's $75-per-foot lease to Inland Steel for the district's Loop property was seriously below market rates, and some school property was still being leased at $1 per year to the parks department.[6]

Costly union settlements negotiated by Mayor Daley were another contributing factor, including ballooning increases in the costs of health care and retirement benefits. Given uncontrolled expenses, the board looked to state and federal grants—mostly targeted toward poor children—to "balance" its budget. Yet these too were being scaled back in the late 1970s.[7] The Joint Investigation Committee reproved: "It was simply expected that somebody would make certain the Chicago public schools survived . . . the Mayor could settle the teacher strikes; the city legislators could make certain changes in the general state aid formula benefiting Chicago; the financial community would be monitoring the Chicago Board's financial well-being."[8]

Daley had kept the schools open by settling the nearly biennial teacher strikes with promises of money that the system did not have.[9] He repeatedly convinced legislators in Springfield to make minor changes in state aid and loosen the legal constraints on school borrowing. He also prevailed upon the city's financiers to ignore the unusual, sometimes technically illegal, but time-honored accounting maneuvers used to keep the district's bond ratings high: interfund borrowing, endless refinancing, the infamous pro rata line pioneered in the 1920s, and the equally commonplace overestimation of anticipated tax revenues.[10]

These questionable practices had facilitated the opening of school each year since the late 1960s. It was simply assumed that the next mayor would continue to use them. When it turned out that Mayor Jane Byrne lacked the authority and the will to do so, club members stepped into the breach. Within days of the disclosure that interfund borrowing would have to be covered by a new bond sale, rather than uncollectable tax receipts, the school system's ratings were slashed.[11] Most citizens were caught off guard; it was "a nightmare that stunned many Chicagoans into total disbelief."[12]

The Illinois legislature also heard testimony on a related theme: "an implicit agreement within the Chicago financial community that the Chicago board would have to suffer a financial crisis in order to trigger a solution to its ongoing fiscal problems." Superintendent Hannon claimed that the cash-flow bind was "exaggerated" because Chicago's bankers wanted a new financial structure for the school system. They had "problems selling school board bonds in the past," and "the investment market was tenuous."[13] John Kotsakis, a union staff member, added, "the business community perceived this as an opportunity to get the board of education to offer higher interest rates."[14] Though it remains uncertain whether any group of Chicago bankers precipitated the collapse, more than one Chicago United member echoed Leon Jackson's sentiments: "It wasn't news to some of us that the system was cannibalizing its future just to stay alive. . . . The late Richard J. Daley . . . just went to the legislature and they would bail him out."[15] State senator Arthur Berman concurred: "During all of those years of Daley's tenure, the bond rating agencies, S&P, Moody's, never really dug into the practices of the school system. As long as he was around, things got by. He passed away, [so] the rating houses blew the whistle."[16]

The assumption that the next mayor could "fix" the budget was naive at best. Mayor Byrne had not been involved in any of the events leading up to the collapse and was powerless to stop receivership. In her memoirs, she recalled first learning about the crisis two days *after* Moody's Investors Service had lowered the bond rating. The revelation occurred when Superintendent Hannon and Donald Perkins, president of Continental Illinois National Bank and Trust Company and the Commercial Club president at the time, met with her to explain the impending collapse, just as it was becoming public knowledge. They asked Mayor Byrne to guarantee a loan with city assets; she refused.[17]

By December the board had failed to meet its payroll, teachers were preparing to strike, and the schools were closed for the holidays with no relief in sight. Club members, concerned about the negotiability of their existing debt notes, went to Republican governor James Thompson, who had already advanced state school aid payments. Notwithstanding a state budget surplus, Governor Thompson declined to sign bailout legislation but agreed to meet with corporate leaders, board of education staff, and CTU representatives.[18]

At a New Year's weekend meeting in the governor's Springfield mansion, a private bailout plan was assembled that offered a multipronged response to the crisis. Legislators gave an emergency loan to the school system, the entire board of education was forced to resign (Hannon, his business managers, and the school board president had stepped down in November), and a Joint House and Senate Investigation Committee was appointed to find an explanation.[19]

The plan's centerpiece was a private School Finance Authority (SFA) insisted on by the bankers. It was handed sweeping powers to oversee school finances and approve all major budgetary decisions. Designed to guarantee the bondholders' interest payments, the plan gave the SFA $600 million of the board's taxing authority to sell new bonds intended to balance the 1979, 1980, and 1981 budgets and the authority to appoint a chief financial officer for the system. It also required school board members to obtain SFA approval of three-year forecasts with every budget after 1982.[20]

Within five days of the enabling legislation's passage, all five members of the SFA were appointed—two by the governor, two by the mayor, and a chairman jointly appointed by both. The four men and one woman were all directors of one or more large Chicago corporations. Commercial Club member Jerome W. Van Gorkom, retired chief executive officer (CEO) of Transunion Corporation and a federal State Department appointee, became the authority's first chairman, a post he would hold for nine years.[21] Encouraging speculation about the timing of the collapse, the *Chicago Sun-Times* reported in an article entitled "Schools Push for Tax Collections" that three of the five members were corporate leaders of companies in arrears on their property tax payments. Their combined share of the outstanding tax debt totaled more than $350,000 for the 1978 levy alone.[22]

As had been the case in the financial crisis of 1931, debt restructuring meant cutting costs. For a start, the SFA demanded a retrenchment of $60 million. Predictably, interim superintendent Angeline Caruso's specific cuts were resisted, as was the SFA itself. Ad hoc citizens groups and the Citizen's Schools Committee (CSC) disrupted board meetings and protested corporate refusal to pay school taxes, and parents expressed widespread concern over "the exclusion of the public from deliberations." Lists of programs and personnel to be eliminated were publicized and then retracted within days, whether because the board had erred in its calculations, the teachers union had protested, or the SFA had refused to accept them.[23]

In the end, much of what had been cobbled together in a decade of half-hearted desegregation and enrichment plans was dismantled. The final list of cuts included enrichment programs, career education and basic skills centers, preschool, textbook purchases, some substitute teachers, teacher aides, and large portions of the English as a second language, intensive reading, and intensive math programs. In addition, the system's twenty-seven districts were reduced to twenty, eliminating seven superintendents, and school district headquarters was moved from high-rent downtown offices on LaSalle Street to an abandoned army distribution center on Pershing Road on the South Side. Three years later, a report identified a total of 8,497 lost positions, including associate principals, counselors, teachers, and classroom and bus aides.[24]

Economizing was accompanied by changes in the school system's governance structure. With broad powers, independently powerful members, and a mobilized corporate community behind it, the SFA began a delegitimation of the school board and a reorientation of authority to the corporate community and the executive offices of the city and state. Chicago United member Henry Mendoza described the changing relationships: "You, in effect, have two boards of education. Who runs the system? It is not the superintendent. Certainly not the board of education. . . . [It's] the School Finance Authority. Who controls the School Finance Authority? The mayor and the governor. Who runs the system? Where's the bottom line? It should be accountability with the mayor and the governor. I'm not saying it is right or wrong, but that's where it is. That's where the ultimate control is."[25]

Few African Americans failed to notice that these changes occurred as blacks were finally beginning to make inroads into employment in the system. Blacks had gradually increased their representation among administrators, teachers, and board appointees since 1968. By 1979 they accounted for 38 percent of the central office staff, 30 percent of principals, 43 percent of teachers, and 60 percent of students (see figures 1–4). The SFA, meanwhile, was a select group of white men and women that "did not look like the Board of Education." This meant that the SFA would come under racial attack whenever the increasing numbers of blacks working for the district resisted its policies.[26]

A POLITICAL VACUUM TO BE FILLED

The SFA was not the only vehicle for corporate oversight of school policy in those years. The SFA enabling legislation also gave Mayor Byrne the historic opportunity to select an entirely new school board and, through it, a new superintendent. She chose to pass those responsibilities on to Chicago United.[27]

Mayor Byrne had been elected by a serendipitous, highly unstable coalition of blacks, lakeshore liberals, and Poles "on the crest of a movement of the moment."[28] Like her predecessors, Byrne soon discovered that she would need the support of a governing coalition as much as an electoral victory. But she alienated every potential governing partner, one by one.

She lost the loyalty of city bureaucrats by firing many of those in top-rank positions and replacing them with less experienced individuals. Fiscal crises and subsequent strikes by city workers—not only teachers but also transit

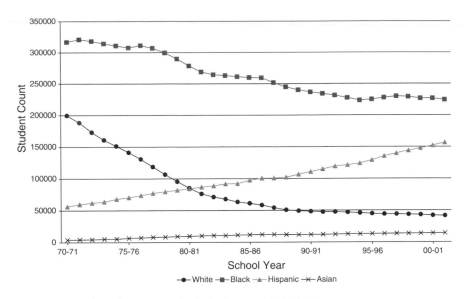

Figure 1. Students by Race and Ethnic Group, 1970–2001

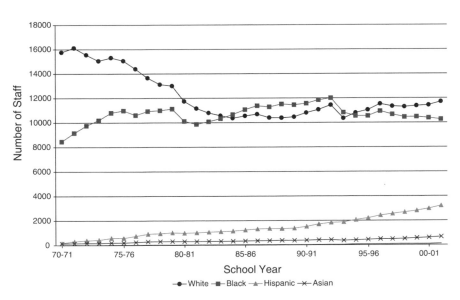

Figure 2. Teachers by Race and Ethnic Group, 1970–2001

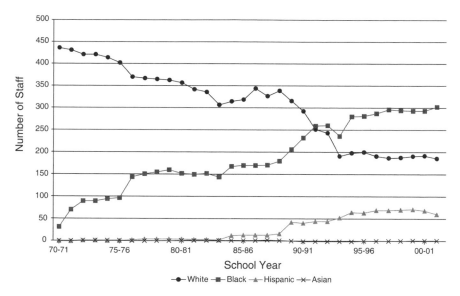

Figure 3. Principals by Race and Ethnic Group, 1970–2001

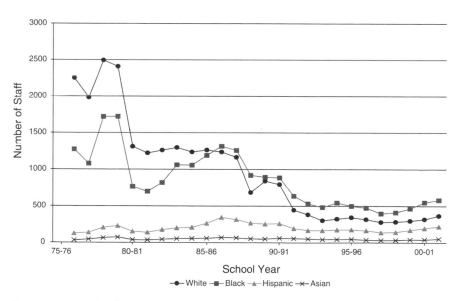

Figure 4. Central Office Staff by Race and Ethnic Group, 1976–2001

Sources of data for figures 1–4: Chicago Public Schools and the Illinois State Board of Education.

workers and firefighters struck in 1979 and 1980—stripped her of the machine's labor allies. She angled for the support of the machine aldermen who had always backed Daley but then lost it by waffling and by announcing that the city was "drowning in its own red ink" from, as she put it, "the hidden deficits" of the Daley and Bilandic years.[29]

After the school fiscal debacle was resolved in the state capital, she reached out to business, hoping to make up for having ignored its warnings. Chicago United president Robert MacGregor became a trusted adviser, and she asked the group to identify candidates for a new school board, "orally dismissing" the president of the Mayor's Advisory Commission of School Board Nominations in order to clear the way.[30]

Chicago United staff members took their new responsibilities seriously. Mindful of criticism over the SFA, the staff made nominations with an eye toward providing a racially balanced group; five of the eleven were black, two were Latino, and four were white.[31] They took the advice of black and Latino members in identifying minority candidates and allowed the labor seat on the school board to be selected by unionists. But there was little other consultation; even Urban League leaders, founding members of the group, felt substantially left out of the decision making.[32] Almost immediately after the board was appointed, racial tension permeated the selection of board president.[33]

Chicago United nominated, and Byrne accepted, Commonwealth Edison CEO Thomas Ayers for the post. The majority of the board, however, was prepared to vote for a black, the Reverend Kenneth Smith, to lead Chicago's schools. Although Ayers was an Urban League board member, league staff agreed with black administrators that "the thinly veiled public and strong private push by Chicago United for Ayers as president has . . . compromised the integrity and independence of the prospective Board members, and has . . . been an insult to the leadership of the Black community."[34] The main argument for Ayers was that the fiscal bonding authorities would not feel comfortable unless a white businessman was at the helm. Byrne also might have hoped that Ayers could provide her with an entrée into the machine's inner circle, since he was well known as a former confidant of Daley's.

Yet Ayers did not even reside within the city limits of Chicago; nor was he eager for the accountability of public office. Provoked by Byrne's attempt to control the board with a man they saw as "establishmentarianism personified," and inspired by Lu Palmer, a longtime black nationalist and community activist in South Chicago, African American grassroots organizations demonstrated in the streets and challenged Ayers's nomination in court.[35] Palmer's Chicago Black United Communities (CBUC) applied pressure sufficient to cause Ayers to withdraw from the board in sixty days.[36]

The mayor further antagonized the black community by removing the appointees representing them. Two black businessmen nominated by Chicago United to the school board, and subsequently appointed by Mayor Byrne, were dismissed within three months. They were replaced with two white women, one of whom had participated in anti-integration demonstrations in the 1970s. Byrne later replaced two blacks on the city housing authority with two whites, triggering a boycott of the 1982 Chicago Fest. These seemingly capricious decisions, and others like them, later contributed to the election of Harold Washington as the first African American mayor of Chicago.[37]

Such warnings of conflict between blacks and city hall notwithstanding, for the next few years corporate Chicago, with Byrne's blessing, led the institutions that governed the schools. Executives had negotiated a financial oversight authority with strong enforcement powers. Then they selected a new, racially balanced school board that they hoped would calm tensions exposed by the SFA. Further, they encouraged their representatives on the board to identify a black for superintendent. With new leadership thus assured, it seemed to them an opportune time to provide specific guidance on how the school system should be run.[38]

ONE OPPORTUNITY, MANY AGENDAS

The Commercial Club and Chicago United joined forces on a blueprint for school system reorganization. In the summer of 1980 the Special Task Force Report was signed by three of the most active and respected of their leaders: Warren Bacon, Chicago United's Education Task Force cochair; Donald Perkins, president of the Commercial Club; and Thomas Ayers.

Bacon, a vice president for public relations at Inland Steel, had been a member of the school board between 1963 and 1973 and Benjamin Willis's most vocal critic. He consistently voted for desegregation plans and against the union contracts that Mayor Daley had negotiated. After being blocked by Daley several times in his efforts to become board president, Bacon resigned, "a quiet warrior." His decades of advocacy for equity and efficiency in the schools— always as an outsider who "knew where the enemies were"—and his role as an intermediary between blacks and whites in Chicago United, of which he was a founding member, had placed him at the center of school reform since the 1960s.[39] It was not surprising, then, that Bacon was appointed administrative head of the Special Task Force of eighty-two executives who worked full time for weeks developing a comprehensive analysis of management and administration in the school system.[40]

Don Perkins was the retired head of Jewel Companies and would soon found the Civic Committee of the Commercial Club. His interest in schooling came through a now-familiar business argument: "You can't facilitate economic development if you don't have trained people coming into the workforce . . . the businessman's pragmatism got us from economic development to schools."[41] Tom Ayers bridged Bacon's equity and efficiency interests and Perkins's economic development rationale with a hard-nosed concern for management and leadership accountability. The Special Task Force Report was intended, he recalled, to function as a sort of "management audit" for the incoming African American superintendent, Ruth Love (1981–1985), "so she would know what she was getting into."[42]

Although constrained by the business executives and their management agenda, the former Oakland, California, schools chief felt welcomed by them. After all, Chicago United had recruited her. The independent-minded Love had negotiated a contract that allowed her to hire a business manager who would report to her rather than to the SFA. Nevertheless, her refusal to work at the Pershing Road district headquarters, as mandated by the SFA—she maintained her office in the Loop—signaled the importance she put on close connections with the city's financial and business leaders. Love met so frequently with Ayers and Perkins that "they seemed almost like family."[43]

The Special Task Force Report was a product of more than fourteen weeks of research into the operations of the school system and also drew on earlier analyses by Chicago United. For instance, when the financial crisis was first revealed to the public in early December 1979, Chicago United had hosted a two-day conference aimed at building a national network of business representatives to influence urban education policy. Conference participants from ten cities agreed to "obtain more education for dollars spent," rather than provide additional funds for financially strapped urban systems. They further sought to "play a watchdog role," which could be facilitated if "many of the management positions [were] filled by persons experienced in . . . finance, management, accounting, transportation."[44]

Their meetings spurred a Chicago United Task Force on Education, which produced a detailed analysis of the school system's management failures. Underlying each of the report's 253 recommendations were the same decentralization and improved management suggestions the business executives had been making for more than a decade. One difference was the daunting level of detail. Recommendations were as diverse as, "Permit principals to suspend individuals for conduct unbecoming a teacher," "Encourage teachers to use greater flexibility in determining class size," "Change the job title of the school maintenance fireman," and "Establish a program to rebind usable books."[45]

The self-assured business leaders thought their hundreds of suggestions "a prudent, thoughtful prescription for something hard to disagree with."[46] After the report was published and promoted, Chicago United took on the task of overseeing its implementation, putting $40,000 into the effort as well as thousands of hours of loaned executive time.[47] Peter Henderson, Chicago United's executive director, who had been recruited from Northwestern University's Kellogg School of Business to replace Robert MacGregor, recalled that fulfilling each of the recommendations constituted "part of my marching orders."[48]

The report also verified a new focus for reform, replacing integration with management efficiency. The business leaders let the unsympathetic Republican White House and its Department of Justice deal with racial disparities and desegregation. The executives' neglect of the system's equity problems—after a decade of encouraging delay and volunteerism—resulted in a court-ordered consent decree in 1980. Typical of its time, the agreement directed the school board to eliminate schools with more than 70 percent "minority" or white students, opened all high schools to voluntary enrollment, authorized magnet schools, stipulated a ratio between white and minority teachers in each school, and suggested that compensatory funding follow schools with high proportions of low-performing students. Yet it was implausible that these remedies could be implemented without the active support of business leaders, the system's new financial overseers and its de facto governors. In nearly every aspect, as it turned out, the consent decree was ignored.[49]

Yet even the executives' narrow attempts to focus on management met with little success. Superintendent Love had appointed Manfred Byrd, her competitor for the top post, to head a newly created and Chicago United–supervised Office of Systemwide Reorganization. Whether as payback for being passed over for the superintendency or because he "took pleasure in being able to say . . . 'It's not going to come of anything,' "[50] Byrd was "very resistant" to the many modifications Chicago United sought and was blamed for the disappointing results. Indeed, Byrd had no heart for the job, describing it as one that "put him in charge of looking out the window." Many Chicagoans later pointed to Byrd as an example of the general principle that change cannot be initiated from within a school system.[51]

Before it was ascertained that its management recommendations for the schools might not be welcomed, the Commercial Club expanded its policy focus beyond education. A year after the Special Task Force Report was released, Don Perkins initiated a longitudinal study of the city's economic health. Entitled "Make No Little Plans," in reference to the club's promotion of its early-twentieth-century Plan of Chicago, it evoked a period when club members had played their most active role in city policy making.[52]

Club executives discovered that job growth in Chicago had been declining ever since Mayor Daley's election. "What we learned was that for thirty consecutive years before we came out with our report in 1984, Chicago had lost its share of the national job market. *Every year!*"[53] Perkins's study began: "For years, Chicago has possessed the appearance and reputation of an economically vital city as public works and private sector construction have reshaped its skyline with gleaming towers of steel, glass and concrete." Then it unmasked these appearances by revealing the costs of doing business in Chicago: high unemployment insurance payments and workers' compensation claims and higher-than-average wages in the industrial sector. By 1983 unemployment stood at 8 percent. Club leaders might have added that the patronage system had used these means to confine private entrepreneurship during those three decades, for they concluded that private-sector high-technology firms should be lured to Chicago, not more quasi-patronage manufacturing and building jobs.[54]

The Special Task Force Report had confirmed what financial oversight and the selection of a school board had begun—a new era of business involvement in school policy making. Like it, "Make No Little Plans" was a largely volunteer effort initiated unilaterally, orchestrated and funded by club members through special tithes, and benefiting from a public consensus among the Chicago business community.[55] Both reports demonstrate how corporate executives developed their policy agenda through the in-kind services of employees hired to research the details; club staff then edited and promoted the final product. In seeking ratification of their ideas by other community groups, they reasserted a political presence that had not been demonstrated since before the Depression.

The change from backdoor influence to public advocacy came partly because new elected officials were not always cooperative. "We started, first of all, to offer our services to the then-governor and the then-mayor . . . [but] we never heard from them."[56] Club members also began to take notice of the underlying costs of remaining behind the scenes for thirty years of machine rule. In the absence of any evidence that city hall was willing to address the region's economic challenges or to create a strategic plan for Chicago's schools, the club again embraced both tasks. And the two were rapidly intertwined in club members' minds: "The failures of Chicago's public schools in previous years have left us with hundreds of thousands of people untrained and ill equipped to fill the jobs of the new economy."[57]

Community Response

The corporate sector was not alone in its desire to influence policy in this volatile era. After half a century of centralized decision making, broken only by protest from those outside the machine, civic dialog became nearly as chaotic as it had been in the early decades of the century. The new fiscal crisis decisively marginalized the civil rights agenda and, in doing so, created an opportunity for all sorts of civic groups to propose their versions of school reform. Whereas corporate leaders had determined that the problem was fiscal and managerial, others were caught up in their own versions of accountability and reform.

Financial crisis spurred the CSC to protest cutbacks, as it had during the Depression. "The lack of school accountability to the public" also led the group to conduct a survey among *Chicago Sun-Times* readers, education leaders, and its own members. An overwhelming majority (84 percent) of the 554 respondents were vexed by the system's apparent inability to remove "ineffective" teachers and principals and by parents' inability to access information on the schools (72 percent).[58]

The CSC's ninety-three recommendations included greater transparency; tighter procedures for dismissal; higher standards for teachers and principals (e.g., "*all* teachers speak, read, and write English at a defensible level"); new hiring, evaluation, and professional development criteria; and school performance testing by which to measure school effectiveness. Although existing assessments had been among the least objectionable (62 percent) items rated, the CSC nevertheless argued that serious consequences (e.g., withholding of diplomas) ought to befall students who failed to meet test-based promotion or graduation standards. On the advice of some school principals, reflecting Robert Havinghurst's "vital factor" of two decades earlier, and in keeping with the general concerns voiced by corporate leaders (Thomas Ayers and Warren Bacon were both on the board of advisers), the CSC also recommended "strengthen[ing] the authority of the local school administrator."[59] But the CSC's commitment to implementation did not match its far-reaching recommendations.

The Chicago Urban League's response to the fiscal crisis and the lack of transparency in school governance was to join with other black, Latino, and Jewish civic, good-government, and activist groups—Chicago United being the only business association among them—to found the Chicago Priorities Panel on School Finance (the Panel). It monitored school funding in light of ongoing budget deficits and publicly reported its findings, which frequently conflicted with announcements made by the SFA. After having built a reputation as a trusted source of financial data, the Panel expanded its research agenda and renamed itself the Chicago Panel for Public School Policy and Finance. Its earliest school study linked the school system's dropout rate of 43 percent to uneven patterns of student retention and reading preparation in elementary schools, both of which were much worse for black students than for whites.[60]

Designs for Change (DFC), a parent advocacy organization founded by Donald Moore in the late 1970s, also took advantage of the new opportunity to influence school policy. A former alternative school organizer with a doctorate in education from Harvard and a background in research on children's advocacy groups, Moore recommended greater citizen oversight and developed a plan for parent and community control of individual schools. DFC's studies of the system's high dropout rate, and the poor reading skills of those who did graduate, convinced him that central office bureaucrats were hiding serious performance deficits. Aware of the reputation for cronyism and corruption earned by district-level community control efforts, the DFC plan sought to avoid both by devolving authority to the much smaller unit of the school itself and ensuring that parents, rather than professionals, would have the lead role.[61]

Moore eventually convinced a coalition of largely white but both left-leaning and conservative community groups, called Chicagoans United to Reform Education (CURE), to adopt a platform of school councils composed equally of parents, teachers, and community representatives. His ideas about popular democracy took shape in the CURE coalition as an alternative governance structure of elected, eighteen-person boards for every school; limits on the mayor's authority to select central school board members; and open enrollment throughout the system. School councils would have the power to hire and fire principals and teachers, set the curriculum, and allocate resources.[62]

A Republican Party–affiliated foundation and a conservative think tank, the Heartland Institute (both CURE organizations), argued that Moore's vision did not go far enough. They saw political decentralization as only the first step toward a citywide choice plan enforced by "education rebates" to subsidize private schools. In their view, every parent, relative, or friend supporting a child who attended a tuition-charging school, as well as businesses that contributed to any public or private school, ought to be eligible for the tax refund. In this way bureaucratic accountability would be replaced with "bottom-line" market accountability to provide incentives for private entrepreneurs to compete with the public schools.[63]

Other school critics found fertile ground as well. By the 1980s Latinos had finally become a political constituency to be reckoned with. Largely ignored for the sixty-plus years they had resided in the city, their proportion of the population had grown to 14 percent by 1980, making them a critical factor in Chicago politics. Research promoted by ASPIRA of Illinois, a Puerto Rican not-for-profit leadership development and advocacy organization, found that the dropout problem was especially salient for Latinos. At least two predominantly Hispanic high schools had four-year dropout rates of 73 percent, significantly higher than the alarming 43 percent systemwide dropout rate decried by the Panel and DFC studies.[64] These disparities infuriated some Latino educator-activists, who also began to wonder aloud why federal and state Title I funds appeared to be earmarked for black children but not for theirs.[65]

The rising criticism of the public schools was not limited to activists. Polled again in 1985, Chicagoans rated their schools lower than other urbanites rated their respective schools. But Chicago residents did not agree that the dropout rate, mismanagement, or an ineffective organizational structure was the system's primary problem. When asked, they identified help for "slow" students, basic skills instruction, better parent-school relations, and stricter enforcement of discipline as their top choices. Closer examination revealed race and class differences. Middle-class, white, city-edge, and lakefront residents were harsher critics of the public schools in general but reported far fewer problems—such as poorly maintained buildings, unequal opportunities, insufficient homework, and gangs, drugs, and overcrowding in their neighborhood schools—than did poor, black, Hispanic, and inner-city residents. Blacks more often supported early childhood education, and Hispanics were more likely to support extending compulsory schooling beyond the age of sixteen.[66]

The groundswell for reform was also boosted by a conservative shift in federal education policy as Ronald Reagan entered the White House. "Block grants" reduced aid to all states and reduced the federal flow of special fund allocations to Chicago, ensuring that the financial crisis would not be resolved by an appeal to Washington, D.C. As important, the Reagan administration came into office with its own education agenda, one that resonated in Chicago. Too much government effort had been spent during the civil rights era, the president argued, in a misguided if well-meaning attempt to use the schools to solve political and social problems. He agreed with his corporate supporters that the public schools should focus on educational goals that fostered economic growth.[67]

The first step in the process was to make explicit the link between the quality of education in the nation and its economic well-being. The case was made in a frequently imitated 1983 call to arms that blamed the public schools for risking the United States' economic future. A Nation at Risk summoned higher standards, greater accountability, and the use of competition and choice to motivate students, teachers, and parents for the hard work that lay ahead.[68] Illinois reacted to the new national mood with legislation in 1985 that raised graduation standards and established mandatory school report cards. A special section of the law applying only to Chicago mandated the elected school advisory councils that some activists sought as an alternative to desegregation. However, in a manner reminiscent of the 1980 desegregation consent decree, the district would also ignore this requirement.[69]

All this school reform activity coalesced around the rhetoric of reform through *decentralization*. Definitions of the term ranged from community control that implied the inclusion of minorities, to administrative decentralization aimed at empowering principals, to the bottom-line accountability of treating parents as customers. The details of each group's vision held different implications for school equity, quality, and efficiency; yet by adopting a common rhetoric, each could hope to garner political allies and increase its influence. Thus, each heard in the decentralization arguments of the others a confirmation of its own desires.[70] Furthermore, the disparate efforts lacked political leadership and a policy arena, a crucial forum within which to act.

Racial Divisions and Electoral Unity

Like most of Chicago, the black activist community was taken by surprise at the fiscal collapse of the schools. For four years the Urban League had been preoccupied with battles over the state's Title I allocation for disadvantaged (low-income) students, insisting that these funds actually reach the neediest schools, rather than be spread throughout the system as Superintendent Hannon and his predecessors had done. League leaders saw their support of the Panel as one way to maintain the pressure. Black politicians, black business leaders, and Black Nationalists remained committed to the civil rights ideal that political representation was a viable means of improving "life conditions among black people." Few were prepared to abandon integration and racial equity for management efficiency.[71]

Black resentment at the lack of tangible support from corporate and political leaders grew stronger as school integration failed to materialize and as Title I funds disappeared into the yawning budget deficit. They chafed at fiscal control imposed by the SFA, noting that it came just as court-ordered affirmative action (and white flight) was putting the system's administration in African American hands. Some critics saw the city's corporate leaders as a cabal plotting to subordinate new black leaders. Lu Palmer's views were extreme, but not unusual: "I don't understand why white guys would want to fix the public schools when their own children go to Catholic schools or the suburbs. I can only think that they want to be able to say 'We tried' [in order] to pave the way for a voucher system."[72]

After it became clear that Mayor Byrne would select a new board and superintendent, both the Urban League and Operation PUSH attempted to influence the process. The hope was that a strategy of political incorporation would make it easier to press their agenda on behalf of black disadvantaged children.[73] They quickly discovered, however, that the only viable avenue for influence was through Chicago United. In spite of their early involvement with the group, their strong preference for superintendent, Manfred Byrd, had been ignored.

The manner of her selection put Superintendent Love in the same category as school chiefs Harold Hunt and Ben Willis, who had been close to business executives. She reinforced the perception by initiating an Adopt-a-School program and a controversial reading method, Mastery Learning, which mandated scripted lessons and a testing regimen reinforced by sanctions such as student retention.[74] Ironically, the Adopt-a-School initiative was not warmly received by Chicago United. Executives warned that "it might be a fund raising program in disguise."[75] Teachers bristled at the limits put on their professional discretion by Mastery Learning, and some questioned the premise that Chicago's underperforming students ought to forgo the literature-rich curriculum taught to high-achieving suburbanites.[76]

Nor did the simple fact that Love was African American ingratiate her with Chicago's black community. "She would kick behind and take names. She didn't mind walking on toes."[77] Although Lu Palmer initially "fought her long and hard," in time he "came to see that if she was not doing a good job she sure in hell was trying." Even so, the early and strong criticism Love received from black activists left its mark.[78]

To Palmer's CBUC, Jesse Jackson's Operation PUSH, and Urban League leaders, among others, Byrd had long been the obvious choice for superintendent. Willie Barnes, president of a mostly black principals association, explained, "He knows the system. He is well qualified. He has the support and respect of the community. We are incensed that Dr. Byrd has been passed over . . . it is an affront to the black people." Barnes was especially galled that the board vote had been split along racial lines, with white and Latino members unwilling to vote for Byrd.[79]

Byrd's assignment as coordinator of the Office of Systemwide Reorganization added insult to injury. It meant that both Love and the business executives who had already rejected him oversaw his work. Angered over the school board selection process and Mayor Byrne's failure to support black candidates, activists in Operation PUSH and the Urban League vigorously took up Byrd's cause. They did not relent until he was appointed superintendent five years later.

Tension and mistrust between corporate leaders and the city's black activists would persist throughout the decade and into the 1990s. Operation PUSH, CBUC, the Chicago Urban League, and South Side neighborhood groups such as The Woodlawn Organization (TWO) and the Kenwood-Oakland Community Organization (KOCO) were noticeably absent from the coalition that drafted and lobbied for a radically decentralizing school reform in 1988; several of those organizations attempted to block it at the last minute.[80] Nor were they supportive of the 1995 legislation that was later layered over the 1988 reform, putting another Mayor Daley in control of the schools.

One measure of the distance between Chicago's black and white business communities was their differing reactions to Harold Washington's 1983 mayoral campaign. When Washington had first run for mayor against Michael Bilandic in 1977, he had won a majority in five middle-class black wards but captured only 11 percent of the citywide vote and virtually no white votes.[81]

This political polarization hastened the establishment of a black political action committee two years later to "gain political control of the city of Chicago," garnering an easy 1980 congressional victory for Washington in the process. Many of the same black business, activist, and civic leaders assisted Washington's campaign for mayor in 1983.[82] His candidacy fulfilled the civil rights dream of black control for a black agenda: "It's our turn" was the mantra. Washington made use of religious and moral symbolism, naming his campaign the Chicago Political Freedom Movement, in an echo of Martin Luther King's Chicago Freedom Movement, and likening it to a "crusade." Fittingly, veteran civil rights leader Al Raby was his campaign manager.[83]

As expected, Washington never won over white voters, except for a few "lakefront liberals," many of whom resided in the Hyde Park section of his congressional district. But Herculean efforts registered four out of every five blacks, and of these, an astonishing 73 percent (both middle class and low income) turned out to vote in the 1983 Democratic primary.[84]

Washington battled two white opponents—incumbent Jane Byrne and heir to the machine Richard M. Daley—who divided the white vote between them in a vitriolic, racially coded campaign. Seventeen black wards went solidly for Washington, giving him the edge. Although only 15 percent of Latinos pulled the lever for him in the primary campaign, 75 percent of them voted for Washington in the general election. Many whites ultimately switched parties to vote for a weak Republican candidate, but Washington's solid black and growing Latino support made the difference.[85]

Chicago United mirrored the city in its racially divided reaction to Washington. Although the group had selected one of the most racially balanced school boards in Chicago history and (indirectly) its first black superintendent, white members were not prepared for the first black mayor of Chicago, especially one who had run without their endorsement. They had instead backed Richard M. Daley, who finished third.[86] The watershed election presaged "a very different ball game, one in which we were on much less familiar ground," Peter Henderson remembered. "There was considerable surprise and some anxiety on the part of the majority members when Harold Washington was first elected."[87] Black Chicago United members, in contrast, worked hard for Washington. His lifelong friend Warren Bacon headed the candidate's citizens committee, and many of Bacon's black colleagues in Chicago United were enlisted as contributors, advisers, or both.[88]

The white executives' anxiety was tempered when they realized that Chicago United's status as the city's only fully integrated business association made it uniquely able to influence this mayor. Black members argued that their participation in his election campaign assured it.[89] Everyone recognized the turnabout: a return to an easy relationship with the new mayor would be dependent on the group's *minority* members. Few were surprised when Bacon replaced Henderson as the organization's chief staff member shortly after Washington won.[90]

Despite his lopsided electoral coalition, Washington knew that he could not govern without broader support. He sought it first among Latinos, particularly the fast-growing Puerto Rican community, and other disadvantaged groups. His administration aimed for a "distinct alternative" to Daley's machine and expanded opportunities for low-income and working-class blacks and Latinos through their incorporation in political processes. He also favored neighborhood economic development over government subsidies.[91] As a state senator and later U.S. congressman, Washington admitted to "strain[ing] the machinery of governance in any way I can to ensure that my community would receive a more equitable share of middle income jobs in both the private and public sectors."[92]

As mayor, he gave collective-bargaining rights and civil-service status to 40,000 (mostly white) municipal employees and instituted affirmative action so that blacks might eventually secure those public-service positions. He separated economic development into two departments: one for downtown development and another focusing exclusively on neighborhood development, an economic objective virtually ignored by his predecessors. He also initiated "delegate agency status," which permitted local community groups to win city contracts for work in their neighborhoods; by 1989 there were 300 such agencies.[93] This redistribution of contracts made corporate leaders "uneasy." Washington's challenge to the machine, including his courageous if debilitating battles with the city council's remaining machine politicians, not only aided blacks and low-income Chicagoans but also gave liberals of any color "more space to influence policy than they had previously enjoyed."[94]

Within two years of his election Washington also sought the advice of white Commercial Club members, independent of their affiliation with Chicago United.[95] Donald Perkins recalled that Washington asked the Civic Committee to look at the city's finances. Washington had inherited financial problems created by the machine, including a deficit of nearly $100 million from Mayor Byrne and the remnants of a "bloated" and mistrustful bureaucracy.[96] The Civic Committee accepted the mayor's offer and formed a Financial Planning Committee (later to become the Financial Research and Advisory Committee [FRAC]), anticipating that it could facilitate city hall support for new downtown development to attract high-technology jobs. Almost as soon as FRAC's first report was completed, the mayor requested that the club collaborate with him on yet another planning group—this time to improve the Chicago public schools.[97]

The Mayor's Challenge

Two city hall staffers approached Larry Howe, president of the Civic Committee, in search of corporate leadership for a proposed education summit the mayor was contemplating. Jacqueline Vaughn, who had replaced Robert Healy in 1984 as CTU's first African American president; Superintendent Byrd; and business leaders were to devise a plan to improve the employment opportunities of high school graduates. The mayor, "raised on the streets of the South Side" by a father he greatly admired, made no secret of having "wended [his] way through the horrible public school system," graduating from all-black DuSable High School. It gave him confidence that Chicago's inner-city schools could be "excellent" if they were given resources, if they were linked to expanded local job opportunities, and if community participation were encouraged.[98]

Although he was no admirer of the SFA, Washington thought that business could play a strong role in providing jobs for high school graduates.[99] Addressing both the widely reported dropout problem and his own interest in employment development, Washington sought a Chicago version of the Boston Compact, which he dubbed the "Learn-Earn Connection."[100]

Chicago United became the lead business organization in the summit, participating through the recently formed Chicago Partnership, a short-lived association of eight powerful business groups. The partnership had been the result of a stinging critique aimed at Chicago's top executives. Described as being "only comfortable with their peers" and, because of their self-imposed isolation, "extremely unsuccessful" at forming coalitions with nonbusiness groups, business leaders were encouraged to communicate better among themselves to "make their point of view understood."[101] Peter Willmott, then CEO of Carson Pirie Scott and cochair of Chicago United, summarized what the executives took away from the scolding: "The business community has not presented any kind of consolidated voice on key issues."[102]

Hardly lacking cohesion in the past, Chicago business became even more centralized. Now Commercial Club leaders—still the most prestigious and influential among corporate executives—could fairly say that they spoke for all Chicago business: the corporate giants represented in the club, black business executives in Chicago United, neighborhood entrepreneurs represented by the Chicago Association of Neighborhood Development Organizations, tax watchdogs in the Civic Federation, and small and midsized businesses in the Chicago Association of Commerce and Industry.[103] When Willmott pronounced the Learn-Earn Summit a failure less than one year into its deliberations because Byrd had "stonewalled us," there was little that city hall, the CTU, or the school board could do about the verdict. All Chicago business had decided.[104]

Notwithstanding its demise, the summit negotiations had been more promising than the business executives admitted. In keeping with their view of accountability, corporate leaders held out for a hard bargain: math and reading test scores raised in three to five years to national levels, dropout levels decreased to the national average in ten years, and their own outside auditor to verify the results. In return, they offered 1,000 jobs to high school graduates, increasing that by 1,000 annually for five years if steady progress were made.[105]

But they were skeptical of the system's willingness to meet the performance goals, recalling that under Byrd the district had not been able to comply with their 253 management recommendations. Superintendent Byrd countered that the initial job offer should be raised to 6,000 and asked for $51.9 million in additional funding to finish implementing Chicago United's 1981 management recommendations, implying that budget cuts were to blame for the failure. Willmott was "appalled by . . . attempts to make the business community responsible for providing resources" and was equally upset that Byrd did not understand who was to be accountable to whom.[106]

Some minority members of Chicago United understood the problem that their friend Manfred Byrd faced: "You wait until we [blacks] get into the game and now you want to change the rules!" Yet as businesspeople, it was hard for them to defend his recalcitrance in the face of criticism. "You would expect the bureaucracy of IBM to begin to change . . . and you would also expect the bureaucracy of the Chicago public schools to change."[107]

Mayor Washington attended every summit meeting and was skeptical of both sides. The sentiments of Ronald Gidwitz (CEO of Helene Curtis) suggest that the mayor was right: "I don't think the Boston Compact [idea] was serious. . . . It was the mayor's initiative." Gidwitz conceded that Washington "had a problem because admittedly the school system in Chicago was inadequate. Then the school strike of 1987 occurred . . . and all of a sudden it got to be not only a latent problem but a real problem."[108]

Business executives saw the "latent problem" in management and organizational terms, and they had a good idea where the blame lay. In their view, CTU's job actions were a long-standing drain on school resources because the board's management team lacked bargaining power, corporate expertise, and was overly bureaucratic. "If there is anything business executives can contribute . . . it is the ability to define the problems, establish priorities, sharpen the focus on a clear solution, build a lean organization, establish accountability for performance and then motivate and support . . . people until the job is done. That's what we're good at."[109] Moreover, they might have added, their new definitions of the problems facing the system—bankruptcy and continuous strike threats— were a good match for the business solutions of management restructuring and administrative decentralization. These solutions were, in fact, much better suited than they had been in the 1970s, when executives had first advocated them as a response to desegregation and school equity debates.[110]

Pressing the management reform agenda, Chicago United president Warren Bacon called many gatherings throughout 1987, often inviting national speakers to describe their own experiences. Encouraged by the accounts of other cities' corporate executives, drawing on his opposition to budget-busting union contracts, and concerned that blacks be seen as credible school decision makers, Bacon spearheaded an effort to mediate discussions between Superintendent Byrd and CTU president Vaughn.

Chicago United and the CTU agreed to cosponsor a conference on site-based management, a plan for devolving authority and responsibility to principals, and shared decision making, in which principals would share their new accountability with teachers. Corporate executives were in ideological agreement with talk about "front-line" leadership and the devolution of accountability to the "shop floor." They also believed that this form of decentralization would help lower administrative costs and might facilitate teacher acceptance of other management changes. But the CTU leadership's tentative embrace of site-based management was unsupported by the rank and file, who remained suspicious. For their part, administrators saw it as a "power grab" by unionists, and Superintendent Byrd refused to attend the conference. Unlike all the other versions of decentralization being promoted at the time, the combination of site-based management and shared decision making died a quiet death.[111]

In another effort to influence school policy, Bacon hired Dr. Terry King, a management consultant who had worked with the Civic Committee, to conduct a reassessment of the 1981 Special Task Force Report. King proved harsh in her judgment of the effort's failure, laying clear blame on the system's central administration, which she characterized as having "swelled to an intolerable degree." In one particularly telling passage, readers were asked to compare the 23 staff members directing the Catholic Archdiocese schools with the 2,950 administrators assigned to Pershing Road. She furthered the business executives' agenda by concluding that real change would require a single, focused lever: administrative decentralization.[112]

Patrick Kelleher, Chicago United's director of public policy, was less impressed. He sought something more radical—perhaps privatization or vouchers—and pressed the issue by convening another Chicago United meeting at which the outspoken conservative secretary of education, William Bennett, addressed the group. It was at this meeting on November 6, 1987, that Bennett famously branded Chicago's schools "the worst schools in the nation."[113]

Bennett's words insulted a city that had just reelected its black mayor for a second term. As in 1983, the 1987 mayoral election had been vigorously contested and the voting racially polarized. Washington received a small plurality, which included only 19 percent of the white vote, despite his having garnered Jane Byrne's endorsement in the general election. Again, large percentages of black and Latino voters swept him to victory. His reelection solidified what looked to be an anti-machine regime in city hall and a realignment of city priorities.[114]

Less propitiously, the city had just weathered the longest teachers strike in its history. Payless paydays brought on by the fiscal crisis had engendered a strike in January 1980, followed by two more in 1983 and 1984, protesting SFA economizing. The fourth since the SFA bailout was also precipitated by a harsh combination of cutbacks from the financiers, the state, and the federal government. Schools remained closed for a month, enraging parents and providing the catalyst for a reform coalition of community groups and Chicago United in the ensuing year.[115]

Washington had hoped to avoid interfering with the labor negotiations between the two African American educational leaders, but associations of blacks, Latinos, and white parent groups held demonstrations and demanded that he settle the strike. As the strike wore on, mainstream civil rights organizations—including TWO, KOCO, Operation PUSH, and the Urban League—joined the protests, ultimately forcing him to intervene. Having taken that step, the mayor took another. As part of the strike settlement for 3 percent raises, he persuaded CTU president Vaughn and Superintendent Byrd to sign an agreement to pursue school reform.[116]

A LEADER FALLS, REFORM STANDS

The strike of 1987 galvanized a citizenry primed to link high dropout rates and low reading scores to the system's financial insolvency and its inability to manage what was by then the largest group of employees in Illinois. Recognizing that the aroused public would no longer accept the status quo, Mayor Washington called a public meeting on Sunday, October 11, at which he reinvigorated his summit. He subsequently appointed fifty-four members to the rechartered summit, among them ten parent and neighborhood representatives, as well as representatives from UNO, the Chicago Urban League, TWO, the Panel, DFC, the Latino Institute, and ASPIRA. As he explained to the press, "in order to run a [school] system, you've got to have the constant oversight of the parents, the citizens, the concerned people."[117]

According to historian Jim Carl, Washington intended for the ten-member Parent Community Council (PCC) to lead the new summit. He appointed the outspoken activist, public school parent, and strike protester James Deanes as its chairman. The mayor had weighted the summit's composition to give the PCC and community-based organizations sufficient votes to rival those held by its business contingent (with eleven members) and made it clear that he expected legislative language for reform that he could champion in the state legislature within 120 days.[118]

Throwing his political muscle behind the PCC in this way reshaped the landscape of school reform organizations. For nearly a century the CSC had spoken on behalf of parents and local residents, as often in concert with the city's teachers unions as with its business associations, but consistently representing middle-class values such as efficiency and meritocracy. By creating the PCC to represent parents, Washington elevated low-income blacks and Latinos to the status of decision makers and ensured that their concepts of educational value and fairness would influence the proposed legislation. The addition of the PCC also made the summit a front-page news story for much of the following year.

Washington knew that he needed to actively guide, not merely attend, the summit's deliberations, or risk losing control of the schools and their reform. Four Chicago school reform bills were already being prepared for the state legislature, none to his liking. Prevailing on his former colleagues in Springfield to delay introduction of the bills until his summit could ready a plan in March 1988, according to Carl, Washington sought three goals: to exclude tax rebates and vouchers, as one faction of CURE had proposed; to protect collective bargaining in response to bills that would have divided the system (and union) into smaller districts; and to sustain mayoral appointments to the board, which several decentralization plans seemed to undermine.[119]

Then came the shock that altered everyone's political calculus. On November 24, 1987, the day before Thanksgiving, Mayor Washington was struck by a fatal heart attack. His death left black middle-class educators "unprotected." The black and Latino parents and neighbors represented by the PCC lost their patron. Both groups had been cornerstones of Washington's cross-class electoral coalition. He had painstakingly adjusted his responses to their competing demands, appointing middle-class blacks as school administrators and upholding their authority to make decisions as professionals, but also creating a forum for grassroots groups of low-income parents and community members who felt "shut out" by those professionals. Now, with his death, school reform was poised to pit the two groups against each other.[120]

Acting mayor Eugene Sawyer was elected to succeed Washington by a divided city council, which also tore apart the black community. Black aldermen split their votes between Sawyer, backed by an odd combination of machine stalwarts and Black Nationalists, and Washington's floor leader, Tim Evans, who was favored by Latinos. Lacking the support enjoyed by Washington, Sawyer became little more than a placeholder, unable to win the 1989 special primary election called to replace the fallen leader. Nor was he supportive of the summit or the PCC. Both were associated with the previous administration, and the summit's deliberations seemed destined to take power from his hands. Summit participants from all factions repaid his distance with predictions that he would bury their recommendations. They were right.[121]

Despite these setbacks, PCC leaders struggled to honor Washington's legacy with a reform law by the deadline he had set for them. Reflecting the broad influence of CURE and DFC and the participants' overlapping memberships in groups represented at the summit, the far-reaching PCC proposal included a new governing council at each school with control over the budget, curriculum, and hiring and firing of the principal. But unlike most of the other decentralization proposals, theirs put parents in a statutory majority on each council. The PCC also included substantial new money for school services; multicultural and bilingual education; remediation procedures for teachers; improved training for teachers, principals, and parents; and more. In the hope of recovering the agenda, the PCC insisted that its proposal become the basis for debate by the full summit.[122]

The summit's other factions also jockeyed for advantage before the window of opportunity closed. Don Moore's strategy was especially bold. With a draft of school reform legislation backed by a faction of CURE in hand, he partnered with Al Raby to secure $250,000 in lobbying support from a wealthy commodities broker. Those funds hired the Haymarket Group, including Raby himself, to promote the CURE-DFC plan in the spring legislative session. Moore thus made use of summit deliberations to promote DFC ideas about political decentralization.[123]

The Chicago Panel readied its own legislation, reflecting a vision of site-based management different from DFC's "parent power." The Panel sought local school councils composed of equal numbers of educators and parents. These councils would have budgetary control over the schools, including control of the proportion of state anti-poverty (Chapter 1) funds that low-income students were due. Although this was considered a radical shift, the plan was careful to call for a phased-in multiyear implementation.[124]

Latinos also announced their intention to make demands on the public schools. Accounting for a relatively small proportion of the population during the 1960s and 1970s, they had been isolated geographically and played only a minor role in civil rights debates. As they grew in numbers (by 1980, doubling their proportion of the population to 14 percent and accounting for 17 percent of schoolchildren), their relatively strong if insular neighborhood organizations demanded more attention from civic and political leaders.[125]

The apparent resurgence of free-for-all pluralism meant that the city's dozens of Mexican American hometown associations and a church-based group of cross-national Latino organizations, United Neighborhood Organizations (UNO), could be organized to deliver votes and demand favors.[126] Given that a sizable number of Latinos were not citizens, their strategy of political incorporation was to draw huge numbers to rallies and organize families to lobby on behalf of legislation, as well as get out the Latino vote.

As was true for black Chicagoans, Latino interests in school reform reflected the broader political issues they faced. They competed among themselves (Puerto Rican and Cuban immigrants were the second and third largest subgroups) and with poor and middle-class blacks for mayoral appointments and policies that favored their neighborhoods. Although Washington had appointed several Latinos to positions in his administration and had supported a few Latino candidates, he had sometimes been forced to back one against another. Mexican Americans in particular felt that they were underrepresented in city hall.[127]

Latinos were also aware that their proportion of the school system's professional employees remained tiny (4 percent), and as a corrective, they sought a greater parental voice in the administration of schools in their neighborhoods. Compensatory funding was also contested. One of the only fourteen Latino principals at the time explained the competition she felt with blacks over categorical and desegregation funding: "The more Hispanic kids the school has, the less money they get from 'deseg.' I also find there is a big discrepancy between what I get for Chapter 1 . . . to what [predominantly black] schools are getting." Latino community organizers such as Peter Martinez, or Danny Solis and Lourdes Monteguedo from UNO, turned their sights toward improved bilingual services, more Latino principals, and greater access to scarce fiscal resources in the Latino neighborhood schools.[128] UNO was also willing to support vouchers, an idea that Kelleher's faction of business executives and some white ethnic parents had proposed as a last resort.[129]

The CTU's relationship to the summit also shifted after Washington's death. Union leaders had cautiously favored decentralization in discussions with

Chicago United over site-based management, and they had briefly promoted a platform consisting of site-based management with greater discretion and professional compensation for teachers, smaller class sizes, improved training, and reduced paperwork. But they became skeptical of what might result from a leaderless summit. Even so, some reformers hoped that the union would side with them in a bid for structural changes, if only to oppose the administration. After all, the recently settled strike had been so acrimonious that Mayor Washington had been forced to call on retired CTU president Robert Healy to bring Vaughn and Byrd to an agreement.[130]

But other reformers put the CTU in the same category as the administration. One education cochair of Chicago United revealed that some business leaders had wanted to "break the back" of the union; other negotiators disagreed, prefiguring another division among executives.[131] Some black activists were equally uncharitable. Sakoni Karanja, one of a few black CURE members, opined, "they don't have any commitment to quality."[132] Among the least critical, UNO representative Danny Solis acknowledged that the unionists had a public-relations problem but were "the most enlightened of all the groups on the other side" and respected adversaries.[133]

Under the onslaught, one might have expected the CTU leadership to fight hard for their own vision of decentralization to professionalize, or at least engage, teachers. At various times Vaughn proposed such a remedy—for instance, professional academies for teachers—only to withdraw it or let it die. At one point a task force of five American Federation of Teachers (AFT) union consultants, including a public-relations executive, was sent to Chicago to promote a union version of reform. National AFT president Albert Shanker made several appearances as well.[134] Despite the prodding, however, the CTU remained "alertly neutral," "sitting it out" during most of the summit process. Vaughn came to life only when the seniority of a few hundred laid-off teachers, a "titular and unimportant" issue to the others, was challenged.[135]

Deborah Lynch Walsh, a national union activist at the time, "wondered why the CTU . . . chose to remain silent, given the implications of the law."[136] But her colleague John Kotsakis, CTU director of field representatives and a summit participant, suggested that anything more than protecting job security would have been opposed by the rank and file. "Our people were leery of SBM [site-based management]; you have to buy into principals' control, and many had bad experiences with principals." As for working with the summit, he said, "we [would] sit with them and go along, and only object when a document went against the union's interests in the executive session." Caught on the horns of a dilemma, in which complaints about the system could jeopardize future money for salaries, their strategy was to keep reform out of the legislature, if possible. Once there, "you can only work to kill a bill or water it down, but not to create something good. . . . Good education should be the goal, not an experiment in democracy." Yet by defensively waiting until several bills had been drafted, the CTU faced unprecedented opposition from all sides.[137]

In the early months of the year, competing proposals were put before the summit. DFC and CURE, the Chicago Panel, and parents groups such as Parents United for Responsible Education (PURE) and Believe in the Public Schools held press conferences before presenting their reform proposals. Some were sent to the voters in the form of referenda, but none could garner consensus. Although Chicago United was late in preparing the business plan, the group stressed business's traditional concerns: tightened management, more authority to principals as school managers, accountability through performance contracts for all employees, and stronger oversight of the board modeled on the SFA. Compromise and common ground became as elusive as they were crucial to the summit's success.[138]

Yet for the business executives who had failed to negotiate an agreement with Byrd in the Learn-Earn Summit, the Reform Summit proved a revelation in the political work of coalition building. At first they were wary; members of the PCC were not the elites they were accustomed to dealing with. As Willmott put it, "Everybody and their brother was included."[139] Ken West, CEO of Harris Bank, described the process from his perspective: "You sit around and here's Coretta McFerren [a black CURE member on the PCC] and Don Moore and the chairman of Amoco and the chairman of First Chicago and me. . . . I'm sure they said, 'What are these rich guys from Winnetka doing here?' Well, it turned out that we found out who the enemy was: the administration. So the coalition of rich folks and poor folks came together."[140]

Coretta McFerren returned the backhanded compliment. "I saw Ken West, a very austere, kind of stuffy guy, turn into the most beautiful, open regular person. I saw Warren Bacon, just stiff, very withdrawn and standoffish, turn into the most warm, fatherly person."[141] Executives were pleased and surprised. "Parents and children and everybody felt like they were shareholders, involved stakeholders in a way that no business is used to."[142] Each faction of parents seemed willing to compromise about most issues arising in the development of their reform agenda—the number of members on each school council or how much emphasis should be put on evaluating principals, for instance.[143]

Corporate executives were alone, however, in insisting on their version of another supraboard oversight group. Not having forgotten their failure to enforce management changes in 1981, some perceived a new attempt to hinder the summit process by the same central administration. As West put it, "The board of education was largely doing the drafting. And it would come back, and it wouldn't be what we said. The staff of the board of education was clearly trying to sabotage this thing, in my opinion."[144] Others acknowledged that business leaders were predisposed to mistrust the administration: "We all agreed that no one from within a bureaucracy had been able to reform it."[145]

When Chicago United representatives announced a reform oversight group as their one nonnegotiable demand to the full summit in May 1988, "All hell broke loose."[146] Middle-class blacks, having just recently gained the district's key administrative and union posts, had never been reconciled to the SFA's control over the district's budget. Now they were being asked to accept a management "overseer" who could determine how they were to interact with schools and one another. Deanes was worried that "a powerful oversight panel to enforce reform was an attempt to rob blacks of power they have achieved in city government and on the school board." "After all," he reasoned, "This system was messed up by them [the city's white leaders] for a long period of time." Black community activists agreed with him, maintaining their resistance until the last moment before a reform bill was signed into law eight months later.[147]

Coalition Building

Before any summit plan was released, Warren Bacon broke the logjam by inviting like-minded groups to join Chicago United in a business–community activist coalition, the Alliance for Better Chicago Schools (ABCs), which met for the purpose of drafting yet another version of reform. Because participants included some of the most powerful civic actors from the official summit, the group became known as the "rump summit." Don Moore, interested in furthering his vision of political decentralization, was among the first to join. After the CURE bill failed to win over enough legislators, he argued his key points in the new forum and redirected DFC's efforts toward an ABCs bill.[148]

According to Danny Solis, UNO was also eager to participate, because Washington's summit had split into two "factions" that foretold a stalemate. Community advocates and corporate executives, he argued, would accept nothing less than structural reform of the schools. On the other side, the board of education, the principals association, city hall, the PCC, the Urban League, and Operation PUSH appeared willing to settle for incremental improvements.[149]

Peter Martinez, a Chicago United deacon representing the Latino Institute, and David Paulus, also a deacon, crafted a meeting process that they thought would avoid the larger summit's difficulties in reaching consensus. Coalition participants would vote on elements of the ABCs agenda separately; those dissenting from the majority would be encouraged to leave, so that cohesion could be maintained. The Chicago Panel, unable to extract agreement from its own board about the ABCs' goals, dropped out to pursue a more moderate agenda. For various other reasons, PCC members and most of the other parent groups left as well. The action-oriented structure thus led to a smaller, more cohesive coalition.[150] Although it was a less inclusive group, the ABCs coalition nevertheless inherited the mantle of Washington's summit by maintaining its cross-sector complexion while consolidating the substantial resources of its powerful corporate sponsors, DFC's policy entrepreneurship, and UNO's grassroots legitimacy.

The ABCs agenda reflected the central focus of nearly all the governance proposals: empowering local school bodies made up of parents, community members, and teachers with substantial decision-making authority. Chicago United made certain that the ABCs bill also authorized a powerful oversight group at the top of the system, installed principals as the middle managers responsible for all school employees, mandated a cut of 25 to 30 percent among central office administrators, and required a spending cap.[151] Equity—meaning that more resources should flow directly to schools with high numbers of low-achieving and low-income students—was another cornerstone. The ABCs coalition avoided mention of a citywide core curriculum or a redesigned student assessment system, both of which had been prominent in the final summit document. Nor did the ABCs agenda embrace the summit's most expensive programs. All-day kindergartens, smaller class sizes, a lengthened school day, and incentive pay for teachers and principals were left out.[152]

Late in the spring of 1988, the ABCs coalition became the core group that drafted a compromise bill on behalf of Democratic legislators. House Speaker Michael Madigan had decreed that no new money would be appropriated in a 1988 school reform law, giving a boost to the coalition's version of structural and governance changes and playing into its insistence on a spending cap. Thus the key features of educational improvement debated in the summit and avoided by the ABCs coalition were now off the table in the legislature as well.[153]

The journey made by corporate executives and a roused Latino community from Chicago's snowbound hotel conference rooms to the Illinois legislature in early summer has become part of Chicago's unique political history. Business members of the summit and their colleagues in the Civic Committee and Chicago United flew their corporate jets to Springfield to spend whole days buttonholing legislators in mid-1988, while hundreds of parents, children, and community members worked the same corridors. UNO had ferried parents down by buses in the sweltering heat for the same purpose, stressing that "you don't have to be an American citizen" to demonstrate on behalf of a school reform law.[154] Flush from their summit encounters, executives took pride in their own civic activism: "All the corporate guys got in their jets and the poor folks who were on our side—we were on their side—got in their buses that they couldn't afford and went to Springfield."[155]

After all the lobbying and negotiating, no bill, including the ABCs version, could garner sufficient votes to pass both houses of the legislature. Speaker Madigan convened a series of marathon meetings in his office, where more than two dozen former summit participants, including representatives of the ABCs coalition and their business- and CURE-backed lobbyists, debated yet another compromise bill, line by line. Because these meetings have also taken on mythic status, it is impossible to know with certainty who attended and for how long. But unquestionably, the level of participation by Latino grassroots activists and corporate business association representatives was extraordinary for a legislative drafting effort. The daily progress of deliberations riveted the attention of all who attended and captured the headlines of Chicago papers. The unusual caucus spawned SB 1839, different from the ABCs bill only in detail.[156] On July 2, 1988, it passed the state senate on the strength of Democratic votes alone, and it passed the Illinois house with only four Republican votes. No new money was allocated for its implementation, nor did the legislation satisfy all the contending parties.[157]

The point of agreement in nearly everyone's reform plan had been that each school should have its own governing body with the power to hire and fire principals and determine the educational direction of the school, as well as sufficient discretionary resources for implementation. Moore was the most vocal advocate of the bill that eventually passed, but it was no coincidence that Madigan had earlier proposed the idea of local school improvement councils in the 1985 Accountability Act. The notion had been born during Superintendent Redmond's tenure, when a Chicago school board resolution had encouraged such advisory groups to help district administrators select principals who would be acceptable to the local community. Yet neither the civil rights version of school councils nor Madigan's law creating local school councils (LSCs) had been implemented to any extent. Long-simmering frustration stirred by broken promises now lent legitimacy to the idea of citizen control of the schools.[158]

Although the decentralizing aspects of LSCs had been expected, if not uniformly welcomed, Chicago's black politicians still hoped to avoid another oversight body. Mayor Sawyer and the Legislative Black Caucus were especially resistant. They knew that a second oversight group with supraboard authority would severely limit the remaining powers of the mayor, the school board, and school administrators. During the summit, when it first became apparent that district control by oversight was a requirement of business support for reform, Sawyer had proposed a seven-person advisory commission, a majority of which he would appoint.[159]

But the business executives' version—more gubernatorial appointees than mayoral ones, and the power to fire recalcitrant administrators—reappeared under the ABCs imprimatur. When that bill failed, Chicago United tried again. Withholding business endorsement of the Democrats' version, which looked more like Sawyer's plan than theirs, the executives conceded only at the last minute. Their aim was to "convince" the governor to use his amendatory veto, and Governor Thompson obliged. He reinserted language in the bill that created a new oversight authority, giving it the power to dismiss or discipline board employees and put school funds in escrow.[160]

The July vote presaged other difficulties as well. The principals association objected to the abrogation of their tenure. They too pressured Governor Thompson to amend the bill, asking him to extend the period of each principal contract from three to five years and to give principals the authority to hire teachers without regard to their tenure status. Thompson compromised with four-year contracts and rewrote the law to give principals the authority to ignore seniority if teachers were already on layoff lists. After having endorsed the Democrats' bill, which did not alter teachers' status, the CTU balked at anyone fiddling with tenure, even for the relatively few "supernumeraries" (about 200 to 300) to which the governor's amendment would apply.[161]

The altered law now faced another uncertain vote. Both the Black Caucus and the Democrats in the legislature seemed ready to scuttle school reform over the governor's changes. Yet by December 1988 a final compromise had been worked out on the oversight issue. The existing SFA would be given reform oversight authority. "That sort of created a victory for the business community," as David Paulus put it, and it resolved the Black Caucus's objection to creating a second body.[162] It did not satisfy Jesse Jackson or Mayor Sawyer, joined in spirit by other local black activists, who continued to object to the entire bill on the grounds that it was a form of "enforced trusteeship," adding that "the problems of the district did not occur overnight and therefore, cannot be resolved via hastily drawn legislation." But by then, African Americans who had lobbied against the bill were being criticized for being more concerned about black educators' job security than about students. Their lobbying was no match for the hard sell of busloads of UNO-organized parents and children and another round of corporate executives in jets.[163]

A New Governance Structure

In all, the 1988 reform act created four new governing bodies, all foreshadowed in the summit's rejected agenda. The law empowered eleven-member LSCs, as had been expected; created weaker subdistrict councils, with the responsibility for selecting district superintendents and providing assistance to LSCs; restructured the central board selection process with a School Board Nominating Committee (SBNC) to be made up of delegates nominated by LSC members; and strengthened the SFA by giving it overall authority to determine whether reform was being implemented in the spirit of the law.[164]

Accountability for results was decentralized to individual schools, and parent-dominated LSCs (parents outnumbered both community members and teachers by three to one) grabbed the headlines. Less often noticed, but just as significant, was the oversight and policy control centralized in an unaccountable group of business and professional appointees.

These changes at the top and bottom of the school system not only restructured governance but also legally empowered two private interests as governors of the public schools: parents and business leaders. Parent representatives were expected to dominate decision making in schools; they were politically accountable to the larger group of parents, who elected LSC representatives every two years. Community members on LSCs had the same political accountability to the neighbors who elected them. At the top of the new governance hierarchy, business leaders were authorized to dominate decision making for the whole system; respond once a year to queries from the legislature, governor, mayor, and city council; and act as "customers" of the system's student output. In between, as black political leaders had feared, the citywide, mayor-appointed school board was squeezed and compromised.

Other parts of the bill gave the new mayor (a special election was scheduled for the spring of 1989 to fill out Washington's term) the opportunity to pick a nine-member interim board. It would set the stage for implementation of the law by beginning a new round of central office downsizing mandated by the budget cap, negotiating the next teachers' contract, and overseeing the first LSC elections. In addition, the bill's dramatic reallocation of state Chapter 1 funds to schools, as the Chicago Panel had proposed, was to be phased in at 20 percent a year, requiring that the interim board plan for a central office phaseout of these dollars.

The credibility that principals and teachers had lost before the summit was codified in the law, although principals would suffer more and sooner. Principals lost their tenure and became appointees of LSCs, in the same manner that most superintendents are appointees of school boards. This left them politically accountable to parents and community members for their very jobs but removed neither the bureaucratic accountability they owed the central office nor their legal responsibility to uphold the school code. Although much lip service was paid to principals' new authority to fill teacher vacancies without regard to seniority, they remained unable to replace nonperforming staff. In another example of giving with one hand and taking with the other, principals were afforded the legal right to make requests of school engineers, but such requests did not have to be obeyed unless the district agreed.

For teachers, too, the results were mixed. Although they were given the right to two seats on LSCs, and therefore some voice in the selection of school principals, they made up only 20 percent of the votes and could easily be ignored. In another half measure, "almost an afterthought," teachers were invited to set up a Professional Personnel Advisory Committee (PPAC) in each school, but these had no statutory authority at all. Salvaging the principle of seniority would be the CTU's only impact on the content of the reform bill.[165]

COALITION PARTNERS IN AN EMPOWERMENT DECADE

Civic actors depended on their relationships with city hall in this decade of postmachine reform. As had been true in the early years of the century, the state courts, legislature, and governor were the final arbiters of school reform laws, while civic actors developed the agenda and sustained governmental interest. What had changed was the importance of mayors in this process. Although postmachine mayors had lost much of the authority that characterized their machine predecessors, the city had also grown accustomed to the centralization of power in city hall and continued to seek leadership there. In this way, each mayor's governing ethos created the context for debates about schooling and its purposes.

Bilandic, Byrne, and Sawyer failed to take the lead, however, emboldening civic groups to engage in civic debate about their visions of schooling as they had not done for fifty years. This alone would not have brought them together into a broad reform coalition. For that, Mayor Washington's populist style of governing was needed—his ultimate, if reluctant, willingness to create an opportunity for reformers to caucus with educators. It also took the skillful use of his office to balance power between poorly resourced low-income community groups and much better resourced business executives.

Washington won the mayoralty by assembling a fragile cross-racial electoral coalition, but his governing coalition would need the participation of the city's powerful business executives, most of whom had not supported his candidacy. Reacting to Commercial Club leaders' apparent interests, as well as to his divided black constituents' deeply felt concerns, he focused on education as a way to bring the two together.

He expected that education would expand social and employment opportunities for his lower-class constituents, just as he believed that neighborhood development would improve a community's economic viability. Political incorporation, a difficult strategy at best, was the primary means to these redistributional goals. When Washington died, the awkward coalition he had created lost the only leader willing to coordinate reform partners with such unequal resources. Nor was his successor committed to Washington's vision of school improvement as a means to neighborhood development. By default, leadership fell to those within the corporate sector.

Warren Bacon assumed the leadership mantle of Chicago United upon Washington's election, as much for the black middle-class community he represented as for corporate advantage. But when the mayor died, Bacon could pull together only some of the summit participants in a narrower coalition that did not include the large majority of black educators in the system. Latino organizers and others insisted on Alinsky-style action-oriented ground rules that facilitated cohesion but tolerated no dissent. This decision-making process narrowed the range of partners that wrote the decentralization law, notwithstanding the historic combination of community-based advocates and corporate leaders that the ABCs coalition represented.

Agreeing on little but their skepticism of educators' willingness and ability to change, corporate executives and white and Latino activists reorganized the system so that educators would be directly accountable to them in the future, legally empowering one another's constituencies as school decision makers. They held the vague expectation that legal authorization—through LSCs and strengthened SFA oversight—would give their fresh ideas a chance to improve teaching and learning over the long run. Although the ABCs coalition appeared to be a pluralist compromise, each partner keeping the others' overly ambitious ideas in check, corporate leaders would soon be in control because power differences between the groups were no longer in balance.

The reasons for corporate dominance were not limited, however, to the accident of a mayor's being struck down in his prime. The corporate sector was unconstrained by a machine mayor for the first time in fifty years, and club leaders and their Chicago United colleagues had little business competition when developing their school reform agenda. During the century's first decades, rival business associations and factions within the club had backed competing school reform plans, diluting business influence and diverting club leaders' attention to internal debates. Corporate leaders' short-term financial bailout in 1979 had emboldened them. Taking advantage of the opportunity of fiscal instability, they sought more thoroughgoing change. Every new shock to the system, especially the 1987 teachers strike, motivated them further. By the mid-1980s Chicago's entire corporate sector seemed to endorse a single plan of action.

Whereas the Commercial Club boasted the city's longest record of engagement in school reform, its Latino partners were among the most recent to enter the fray. By the 1980s Latino communities had grown to a sizable portion of the city and an even bigger proportion of the public schools. Well organized and highly motivated, they shifted their votes among the various mayoral candidates, withholding loyalty to any. They made alliances whenever they could be assured of better Latino employment prospects, as seemed likely with the LSC-based selection of principals, or better benefits for Latino students, including greater access to bilingual education. Confident of their ability to organize the community to affect LCS elections, they insisted that even noncitizen parents should be able to vote.

Reform groups led by white middle-class professionals saw a resurgence in their influence that was far more important than their participation in the long-standing but now relatively moribund umbrella group, the CSC. Whites, like Latinos, now organized their constituents by neighborhood. After being marginalized for much of the past fifty years because they had refused inclusion into the machine's governing coalition, and then sidelined during the civil rights struggles, white reformers were eager to assert an agenda of their own. Rather than embrace the reform language of race, however, white activists adopted a neutral language of democratic empowerment that would have been familiar to their Progressive era counterparts. They accompanied this call to democracy with the anti-bureaucratic rhetoric that had been shaped in the machine era.

What had been a deep fissure marking black-white racial politics during the machine era became more intricate and subtle in the 1980s. The racial complications for African Americans were not limited to competition from Latinos, although they chafed at the grassroots legitimacy that Latinos added to corporate executives' plans. Blacks held most of the system's key decision-making posts, and their numbers had grown to rival those of whites in the system's other professional positions. Like other cities, Chicago had been developing its black middle class largely through civil-service employment, and teachers constituted the largest group of civil servants. Corporate executives, intent on bolstering their legitimacy as fiscal overseers, had also placed an African American in charge of the school system.

As a result, middle-class black organizations and the CTU were wary of the efforts of the summit and the ABCs coalition, suspecting that reformers harbored a hidden motive: to unseat a black middle class just as it was beginning to thrive. By the time decentralization was being called for, African Americans had achieved their plurality in teaching jobs and had held the system's top jobs for only a few short years, during which their decision making had been circumscribed by the SFA's oversight. The new round of mandated downsizing in the 1988 law seemed gratuitous, since it came on top of a full decade of similar cutbacks. Blacks felt betrayed as well by a governance change that lacked support for any specific educational interventions or the funding needed to implement the mandated changes. Moreover, black educators knew that they, rather than the reformers, would be held responsible for any implementation problems.

Even black members of Chicago United were pulled between two poles. On the one hand, decentralization held out a hopeful vision of a system that gave low-income black children a chance to escape poverty and disillusionment. On the other hand, they were offended by being repeatedly told that the African American professionals running the school system did not have the required motivation and skills. They were further unnerved by the contradiction in their public and private roles: arguing for black jobs and dignity in the closed, confidential meetings of the association, while publicly defending a program of reforms and cutbacks backed by Chicago's white elite.[166] Such tensions would limit black business participation in the reform effort and affect African American leaders' perceptions about its value and the motivations of some business executives.

Further complicating the picture was Harold Washington's elevation of low-income communities, still primarily black, to the status of decision makers on reform. One unexpected effect was increased tension between black lower-class reformers and black middle-class educators. Exacerbating this tension were assertions by business leaders and their allies that black educators' resistance to reform was a form of prejudice, indicating that they did not believe that poor black and Latino children could learn at the same high standard as white children.

Low-income blacks, meanwhile, were not easily satisfied. African American parents had been represented by the PCC contingent to the summit and felt that Washington's untimely death had cheated them of their opportunity to lead reform. The costly educational changes they sought for their children— all-day kindergartens, longer school hours, lower teacher-student ratios, and a more reliable curriculum—were not the reforms rallying the ABCs coalition. When faced with a decision to choose reform without resources, the business leaders, white activists, and Latinos were willing to take the risk, but black community groups stood to gain the least.

Educators of all races were marginalized in this reform—something Harold Washington likely would have fought. The school board had been discredited by fiscal collapse and SFA oversight, and the school system's employees felt more besieged than strengthened by the outsider reformers. Few Chicagoans recalled the dynamic role of teachers unions in the early years of the century, whereas all remembered the CTU's contribution to the system's fiscal problems and its relative silence during the civil rights debates. Washington had insisted that CTU president Jacqueline Vaughn participate in the broad, all-embracing summit despite her reluctance, but once it had fallen apart, the ABCs coalition included no school-based educators. Instead of dialog, the ABCs coalition presented proposals that it fully expected union representatives and the school system to oppose in the state capital; it made no early concessions to mollify educators. Nor did CTU representatives seek meaningful participation.

The collective reform agenda crafted by the ABCs coalition partners was an amalgam of the business leaders' definition of bureaucratic inefficiency and the community members' desire to open up the inaccessible system. It promoted a racially neutral, if vehemently anti-bureaucratic, criticism of the schools and offered no substantive changes to the classroom but held out hope that they would come. Resonating with white activists' experience of a school system that withheld information, conducted business through backroom deals, and failed to take responsibility for students' poor performance, it also resounded Latino views of a system skewed toward black concerns. The implications of this agenda would prove crucial to the next reform movement.

The democratic aspects of the 1988 decentralization plan rested on an extremely local vision of representation and voice. LSCs offered thousands of parents and community members access to a legitimate platform where they could speak their minds about their children's school or their neighborhood's school. But the same reform also diminished their voices as citizens with something to say about the patterns of resource inequities *across* schools: common standards for teaching and learning, basic guarantees of school adequacy and appropriate citywide assessment systems, or policies to govern system-level accountability and small, dispersed student populations.

Ironically, the resources eventually delivered to schools (in 1993 the average elementary school received $491,000 in state Chapter 1 funds, and the average high school received $849,000) created an uncommon competition among them for the scarce resources of diagnostic and instructional improvement expertise, the connections and know-how needed to raise additional sums of money from foundations and corporations, and the time to devote to school improvement activities.[167] Community-based organizations pitched in, but they too varied in their capacity to help low-performing schools in poor neighborhoods. Activists responded by narrowing their concerns to the neighborhoods and schools where they might recruit LSC members or gain contracts to support targeted improvements. Sustaining a systemwide vision of improvement would prove to be their most difficult implementation task.

The anticipated benefits of enhanced democracy would eventually be hampered by this narrowly focused view of community. Rejecting the machine era's definition of equity—the central provision of educational services to black children commensurate with those provided to white middle-class children—reformers in the 1980s redefined it as the equal allocation of state Chapter 1 dollars directly to schools. Over the next decade, this emphasis on localism would unintentionally facilitate the gradual elimination of equity as a systemwide concern. Low-income community activists, parents, and principals, working through their LSCs, were now responsible for achieving parity with middle-class schools.

The political premise of this reform also suggested that if their LSCs did not function well, low-income communities could be denounced as inept or corrupt and become further isolated from the resources most needed to turn their schools around. But charges of corruption and ineptness occurred less frequently than critics predicted, if only because LSCs were closely monitored, previously disinterested colleges and universities offered their services in low-income neighborhoods, and everyone was reticent to identify racial disparities.

In accordance with their disproportionate influence, corporate leaders achieved what they had sought: a systemwide veto without public accountability, manifest in the expanded SFA. As in years past, executives relied on a model of reform that reflected their managerial expertise and preoccupation with efficiency. The SFA gave them a rationale and a mechanism for limiting the amount of local and state tax dollars that were spent on education. It also authorized them to specify a set of outcome goals by which to measure schools. And the redefined relationship between the SFA and the district office enabled corporate leaders to hold educators accountable for meeting management as well as fiscal goals, a situation ripe for conflict.[168]

Other unforeseen implementation difficulties would require enormous investments of civic resources to resolve. It would be hard to maintain parent and community involvement in the years to come, although that was the cornerstone of legitimacy for LSCs. The lack of educator support would continue as disgruntled administrators, principals, and teachers raised new hurdles. It would soon become clear that although the final bill signed into law was indeed revolutionary, it had created a governance revolution, not an educational one.

4

Perfecting Management

Standards and Control
1990–2000

As Chicago entered the last decade of the twentieth century, the issues engaging school reformers echoed those of the Progressive era. Local school councils (LSCs) were forums for democratic decision making that resonated with Ella Flagg Young's teachers councils. Civic activism was high: corporate leaders were collaborating with community groups and making public commitments to improve the system's management and efficiency. An ambivalent mayor was constrained by a complicated school governance structure. As they had in the earlier era, growing numbers of immigrants redefined the city's racial politics. A neo-progressive realignment of the city's political fault lines throughout the 1980s resurfaced class cleavages as a defining characteristic of reform battles to come.

But the last decade of the century was not used to perfect the decentralization law passed in 1988. Instead, the city's powerful corporate executives arranged an unprecedented consolidation of authority in the mayor's office, which they justified, ironically, as a way to take politics out of the schools. Reminiscent of the 1917 Otis law, their 1995 sequel adopted the latest management techniques and presumed a causal link between education and the local economy. Within a few years, district leaders—once again, mostly white men—were mandating centrally designed lesson plans. The proportion of students who failed the eighth grade jumped 500 percent, and more than one-fifth of the schools were put on academic probation. Both actions—student retention and school probation—were lauded as victories for accountability.[1]

For the first half of the decade, Chicago was heralded as a model of democratic school reform. Community-oriented service providers blossomed throughout the city and arrived from across the nation, attracted by LSCs' control of state Chapter 1 dollars, foundation-funded partnerships, and the loosening of central office constraints. Meanwhile, corporate leaders made full use of the

School Finance Authority's (SFA's) new management oversight powers to restructure the central office.

The transformation naturally created unanticipated, though not insurmountable, problems. As expected, most of the more than 550 LSCs hired new principals, many of whom reasserted the bureaucratic authority that was to have gone to their employers. Second-generation LSCs revisited their predecessors' choices, slowing progress. Philanthropists discovered hidden training and maintenance costs in LSC governance, and central office administrators resisted SFA mandates. Service providers, often forceful proponents of ideas untested in Chicago, made promises that were difficult to assess. In spite of several attempts to create a citywide forum where activists and educators could agree on a common measurement ruler for judging progress, uncertainty prevailed.

Class reasserted itself as a central cleavage within school politics. Economically struggling parents had to give up more than their middle-class counterparts did to serve on LSCs; their learning curve was steep, and the difficult work was unpaid. Isolated neighborhood schools lacked access to middle-class social capital: in-kind donations from employers, grant writers to keep resources flowing, central office contacts who could circumvent bureaucratic requirements, or advisers to distinguish hucksters from useful consultants. Consequently, parents and community members lost enthusiasm for running the schools. Moreover, accountability sanctions initiated by the mayor after 1996 fell most heavily on low-income African American and Latino students and exaggerated the city's already large socioeconomic disparities.

School politics was also complicated by a wave of immigrants from Mexico and the Caribbean who used the opportunity of LSCs to reshape the principalship and influence city hall. Mayor Richard M. Daley (1989–present) saw in the growing Latino presence a way to craft an electoral coalition without black votes. Latinos were rewarded for their electoral loyalty to Daley, but the benefits were perceived as coming at the expense of African American children. Wary of reformers and preoccupied with recapturing city hall after Harold Washington's death, African Americans lost much of their influence over school policy, and racial mistrust deepened.

The community discord allowed corporate forces to act independently. But as in the era of Edwin Cooley, the executives were divided. Statewide business groups preferred a more vocationally oriented school system that did not tolerate unions, whereas Chicagoans emphasized structural and managerial changes; the former eschewed additional funding, while the latter sought it. They could agree on mayoral control aided by a small advisory board of trustees, expert managers to run the schools like a proper business, and a teacher evaluation system based on standardized and impersonal measures of student performance. As ever, corporate activism was premised on economic grounds: fewer high-skill, high-wage positions and many more service jobs requiring basic skills called for a new sorting mechanism for students.

The cost of education also remained a corporate preoccupation. Although not as desperate as during the Depression or the recession of 1979, rising expenses by the mid-1990s and the SFA's inability to exert fiscal discipline left budget balancing to the mayor. Backdoor negotiations among city hall, the Chicago Teachers Union (CTU), the school board, and the SFA disheartened reformers and encouraged corporate abandonment of its 1988 oversight strategy. Financial accountability was handed to the mayor, whom the executives intended to monitor while they avoided direct responsibility.

In sharp contrast to the Progressive era, however, the 1990s saw no class-based partnership between the teachers union and parents. CTU leaders remained angry at the dismissive treatment they had received from community activists in the summit, and parents remained distrustful of teachers' willingness to listen. Many LSCs were forced to take responsibility for reform efforts without day-to-day professional support: teachers were indifferent to their role as advisers to LSCs, resentful that they were not coequal decision makers, and concerned that their advice was not actively sought.

But only a portion of the responsibility for the increased corporatization of the schools after 1995 came from political wariness, unanticipated implementation problems, or corporate impatience. Deindustrialization and outsourcing during the 1970s and 1980s meant that union solidarity was not an available salve for the mistrust between parents and teachers. National politics shifted to the right as radical conservatives won seats in Congress and in state legislatures, Illinois included. Once elected, these politicians turned to their Republican corporate allies for policy advice, and a wave of market-oriented legislation followed. Welfare reform further diverted low-income parents from volunteer work on LSCs. With a ballooning stock market encouraging gentrification, troubled school systems like Chicago's could take a shortcut to improved performance by attracting middle-class families rather than working with inner-city residents.

Perhaps more than anything else, the loss of its leader presaged the demise of the cross-class reform coalition forged in 1988. After Washington's death, reformers had hoped to maintain momentum by hiring a committed superintendent, but they could find no one to trust. Daley declined to embrace decentralization or coordinate its disparate parts. Using a strategy reminiscent of Progressive era mayors who resisted reform, Daley also refused to appoint new members to the board of education, effectively checkmating reformers. Business groups were free to seize the opportunity of a Republican electoral sweep to design a corporate version of mayoral control, which became Chicago's newest reform model for the nation.

ANOTHER ELECTORAL MACHINE

Richard M. Daley combines a machine mayor's organization with the Progressive era's ethnic politics. He has developed a symbiotic relationship with Washington, D.C., and has shown little enthusiasm for ending graft.[2] Elected in 1989 to complete Harold Washington's term, "Rich" Daley moved quickly to reconstruct his father's electoral coalition: corporate and union financing of white ethnic voters. But in recognition that he was running against Mayor Washington's legacy, he also courted the city's rapidly growing Latino population.

Latinos—overwhelmingly Mexican, but also from Puerto Rico and more recently from Central and South America—became a substantial presence in the city during the 1990s. When Washington first ran for office, whites constituted almost half the city, blacks nearly 40 percent, and Latinos 14 percent. Fifteen years later, whites and blacks both represented about 40 percent, but the Latino population had grown to 20 percent. It would be 26 percent by 2000.[3] Black votes were no longer needed to gain office in Chicago.

Daley's strategy of welding white ethnics to Latino immigrant voters would win a string of electoral victories, but the 1989 election was not a foregone conclusion. That year Latinos split evenly between Daley and his challengers; the high turnout of whites gave him a comfortable but not overwhelming 55 percent majority.[4]

As soon as he was elected, Daley appointed Latinos as aides and officeholders and created organizational ties between the Democratic electoral operation and Latino community activists. Redistricting in 1990 gave Latinos three new wards; by the end of the decade Chicago had seven Latino aldermen, three of them Daley appointees.[5] Danny Solis, the Mexican American reform activist, became one of Daley's first appointed aldermanic allies; he then headed an organization intended to spur naturalization and voter registration. Victor Reyes, Daley's liaison with the city council, spearheaded the Hispanic Democratic Organization (HDO) to "deliver votes for Daley and his handpicked candidates."[6]

The strategy paid off. By 1994 outside observers noted that Latinos had been "conspicuously rewarded" for their loyalty, "taking over several city departments and swelling the ranks of mid-level management" by more than 28 percent.[7] Such inducements delivered over 80 percent of the Latino vote in subsequent elections.

Although Latinos had voted heavily for Washington, the once viable cross-racial coalition of minorities seemed far-fetched in the mid-1990s. Solis believed that Latino interests now supported an alliance reminiscent of an earlier era: "the [Catholic] Church and the immigrant experience have a shared set of values with the Irish, the Polish and the Italians."[8] As John Betancur and Douglas Gills described the tension: "Blacks think Latinos are being incorporated into the government at their expense. Latinos suspect that Blacks will not support their needs and aspirations."[9]

Already well represented in government and civil service, blacks had less to gain by participating in Daley's electoral coalition. Despite inducements to the black establishment and the trouncing of his African American challengers, Daley has only gradually increased his proportion of black votes from less than 10 percent in 1989 to almost 60 percent by 2003.[10] Minority contract set-asides in excess of 40 percent for some years, "unprecedented access," and targeted development projects announced at election time have been repaid with endorsements from key black leaders and institutions, including the *Chicago Defender* and "600 leading blacks."[11] Yet African American voter turnout has remained extremely low during Daley's long tenure, partly because competing black candidates demoralized African American voters.[12]

Indeed, turnouts have been abysmally low overall. Voters lost interest over the decade due to increasingly mismatched campaign finances and, after the 1995 election, a law making all citywide elections in Chicago nonpartisan, passed by a Republican legislature at Daley's urging.[13] Contributions from Daley's corporate and union supporters swamp the campaigns of his challengers, who since 1991 have raised an average of 4 percent of the mayor's multimillion-dollar war chests.[14] Nor do challengers benefit from a party apparatus or poll workers. Without a primary, the entire election cycle culminates at the end of February, when Chicago's infamous weather is often at its worst. In 2003 the 34 percent voter turnout was the lowest recorded in Chicago history.[15] It is little wonder that a succession of black challengers—one of whom ran only to avoid the crowning of "King Richard"—has given him only token opposition.[16]

Like every machine mayor since Anton Cermak, Rich Daley also cultivated the image of a manager, the "chief executive of a nearly $5 billion corporation," and he relies on his corporate supporters for guidance.[17] Daley promoted "privatization" faster than most other mayors, earning him the sobriquet "a great Republican mayor" from both admirers and detractors alike.[18] During his first five years in office he contracted out twenty-six ancillary services (e.g., city hall maintenance, car towing, water bill processing). In his words, privatization "recasts government as more of an overseer than a producer" and helps "reduce public cynicism" about efficiency and effectiveness by shrinking the public sector. Both are crucial for relegitimizing a city government tainted by cronyism, corruption, and patronage.[19]

Whatever its benefits in efficiency, privatization allows him to make no-bid, sole-source agreements with business allies while avoiding the city council's pork-barrel horse trading. Outsourcing ensures that new private-sector jobs can be touted each year.[20]

Like his father, Daley is always proposing new projects as another source of "pinstripe patronage," even if his plans sometimes fail to materialize. His highly successful redevelopment of the lakefront McCormick Place helped Chicago lead the nation as a convention site in 1998, and even his ill-fated downtown trolley circulator still managed to generate $70 million in contracts. Thus, notwithstanding a dearth of official city hall patronage—fewer than 2,000 jobs since the 1983 Shakman decrees outlawed the use of partisan criteria or payments in non-policy-making positions—the mayor has maintained a steady flow of tangible benefits to supporters through the still legal, if often blatantly self-serving, use of quasi-patronage contracts and private-sector jobs for his corporate and community allies. Still unsatisfied, Daley sought to vacate the Shakman limitations in 2002.[21]

Daley has also focused—like manager-mayors before him—on downtown development to the near exclusion of neighborhoods. Ninety-five percent of new development in the 1990s took place in seven of the city's seventy neighborhoods—those in the Loop and surrounding areas. Gentrification has been intensive in West Town and in the Near North Side; to make way for town houses or high-rise and upscale real estate and commercial redevelopment, he demolished three infamous low-income housing projects hemming the Loop.[22]

His reciprocity with the White House never reached the level of his father's with President Johnson, but the younger Daley enjoyed more access to President Clinton than did any other mayor, and Chicago's development projects were partly funded by federal largesse. In 1992 Daley delivered an address on behalf of the Illinois delegation in support of Clinton's nomination at the Democratic National Convention. Three years later Daley garnered one of five $100 million federal Empowerment Zone grants and, shortly thereafter, an additional $50 million in loan guarantees to make "quality of life" improvements throughout the city.[23] Visiting the city in 1997, Clinton commended Daley's efforts to fix the schools as a "model for the nation" and singled him out in both the 1998 and 1999 State of the Union addresses.[24]

Yet the mayor has needed more than friends in the White House to finance his development and privatization agenda. He outpaced all the nation's cities in the use of tax increment financing (TIF): freezing city property taxes in a specified area for twenty-three years, then borrowing against the anticipated taxes from projected growth in real estate value to finance development in the same area.[25] At the century's end, Daley had heavily leveraged the city's future tax income; even some corporate executives thought the strategy "overused" and recognized that TIF districts were skewed toward the downtown business district, which garnered 91 percent of the TIF-leveraged improvements.[26]

This "public sector version of a bottom-line CEO" expressed "skepticism" about the professional expertise found in city agencies, preferring their private-sector counterparts.[27] To determine which city services should be contracted out, and which development projects pursued and tax structures proposed, Daley has consulted the Commercial Club's leaders and its Financial Research and Advisory Committee (FRAC), a group he carried over from Washington's mayoralty, extending its financial audit and restructuring responsibilities to the public schools in 1991.

Daley also maintains close ties to a shrinking unionized labor force through abundant building contracts and higher-than-typical union wages. He also moves gradually when threatening outsourcing—delaying job losses through attrition or simply requiring contractors to hire union labor.[28] Even so, Chicago has shifted from industrial production to a service economy that is dependent on office and tourism workers, of which only about 13 percent are unionized.[29] The CTU is one of the few large public-sector employee groups with which Daley negotiates, and relations with the mayor have become more important for the teachers union than at any time before: with so few parents working in unionized jobs, the teachers cannot expect union solidarity to create many allies should they decide to take on city hall.

Not everyone supports such corporatist priorities. Despite a booming central business district, critics point to low-income black and immigrant Latino neighborhoods that have fared badly and to disproportionate investments in the "toon town glitzy" Near North Side. A 1994 poll about municipal service delivery found white and middle-class residents pleased, while most black and Latino residents rated their services "poor or very poor." African Americans bore the brunt of city hall's emphasis on privatization. Disproportionately represented in the maintenance and service jobs that were privatized, they accounted for 61 percent of the municipal workers laid off in 1992; some said that it was payback for failing to support Daley at the polls.[30] Even former admirers had doubts by the end of the 1990s: the city received below-average marks in "managing for results."[31] Observers also began to question the school turnaround city hall had promised and promoted for half a decade.

Neither the political demands of servicing his electoral coalition nor the development interests of his corporate governing collaborators induced this mayor to take on school reform—certainly not as Harold Washington had envisioned a neighborhood development and low-income empowerment strategy. Although Daley paid lip service to the public schools, the "foundation upon which any city is built," he would not lead the implementation of the 1988 reform. He left that task to his corporate governing partners, whom he called on in his first inaugural address to take even more responsibility for "turning around the system."[32]

IMPLEMENTING (AND ALTERING) DECENTRALIZATION

Daley's reluctance to coordinate a reform he had had no hand in creating was understandable. Business leaders and community activists had won unprecedented influence over the public schools, but with their victory the mayor lost a measure of his control. He had only one opportunity—and eighteen months—to make up his losses: his task was to appoint an interim board to run the system until a School Board Nominating Commission (SBNC) could be formed. After that, each school board appointment would be constrained by LSC nominators. School board members selected by grassroots activists could not be expected to appreciate the political considerations involved in running an ethnically imbalanced electoral machine; nor would they prioritize the management and financial agenda that motivated the mayor's corporate governing partners. Daley's response was to choose an interim board that satisfied his corporate constituents.

Commercial Club members encouraged the mayor to appoint the incoming president of their own newly formed association, Leadership for Quality Education (LQE). Joseph Reed had just taken early retirement as head of AT&T's central region and was able to prevail on his former colleagues to pay for an independent staff, "loyal to the board alone," that would allow them to "throw out the first budget we got and recreate it to our specifications."[33] Then, as vice chairman of the interim board's budget committee, he and its chairman, William S. Singer (a former Democratic alderman and member of the 1979 state task force examining school finances), personally negotiated the first three-year contract between the teachers union and the district. Reed, Singer, and James Compton—Chicago Urban League president, LQE board member, and interim board president—also recruited the first post-reform general superintendent, Ted Kimbrough.[34]

Two months after the reform law passed, LQE had been created by the Civic Committee and Chicago United as "the voice" by which corporate Chicago "intended to impact reform."[35] In addition to about twenty Commercial Club and

Chicago United members, its governing board included ABCs coalition members Danny Solis, Coretta McFerren, and Sakoni Karanja, who served as community representatives. Notwithstanding a vow to "support the new Local School Councils and offer worthwhile professional development to teachers and principals," and a campaign to raise $600,000 for the first LSC elections, the business executives retained their focus on how to manage the $2 billion schooling enterprise.[36]

The executives viewed decentralization as managerial devolution, likening it to customer-oriented business planning. They thought the interim board had two priorities: first, contain the district's fiscal problems; second, develop a long-term union contract to secure labor peace. Many, like LQE chairman Ken West, felt that unions had "the system by the throat."[37] Only with these issues settled could the interim board determine which instructional and resource decisions should be delegated to schools, hold teachers and principals accountable for student performance, and, if necessary, force the central office to provide technical support to the schools. The division of labor had the interim board making these decisions, the SFA enforcing them, and LQE serving as the "monitor."[38]

After its work with the interim board was complete, the LQE board collaborated with FRAC on the Commercial Club's most ambitious management effort. TIME (To Improve Management of Education) was a "re-engineering" of the system's staffing, training, communications, repair, and maintenance capabilities through "re-culturing" and streamlining that sought "big change fast." Each of several areas to be reengineered had its own performance matrices or desired outcomes, plans, and timetables that relied heavily on job standards, office reorganization, increased use of technology, and retraining.[39] It was business's best effort to take on an entrenched bureaucracy.

What might have surprised Daley was the fact that the management recommendations of the Civic Committee and LQE would prove to be contentious among corporate leaders. The SFA, chaired in 1992 by brash venture capitalist Martin "Mike" Koldyke, had commissioned a report explicitly disagreeing with TIME on reengineering. The consultants, relying primarily on "impressionistic" anecdotes, recommended privatizing a large proportion of the system's business functions. In a theme that would be echoed throughout the remainder of the 1990s, they proposed "relying heavily on market incentives." The loss of hundreds of unionized engineer and maintenance jobs to outsourcing would bring $61 million savings, the consultants estimated, and another $27 million could be gained by "aligning incentives": assigning students rather than custodians to take trash to the hallway, or encouraging energy efficiency. Oversight would be left to the press or "outside agencies."[40]

Koldyke attempted to impose a modified version of his plan on the district. Additional state aid should be withheld, he thought, until the central office had been reshaped to serve only four functions: providing services to schools on request, preparing reports for the board, representing the district externally, and managing the board's finances (with SFA oversight). All other responsibilities should be outsourced or given to the schools, including hiring, curriculum development and instruction, training, minor repairs, and the ability to contract with vendors. The district was to be one of those vendors.[41] Koldyke's sweeping plan met with reciprocal opposition from business executives wedded to LQE's managerial changes. Black leaders, including Superintendent Kimbrough, were hostile to both the managerial tinkering and the free-market reforms.[42]

The rift temporarily divided Commercial Club members. In 1993 a son of the retired but still influential Thomas Ayers was appointed LQE's executive director. John Ayers was a former Reed staff member, an LSC member, and a respected reformer—credentials that prepared him to span the gap between the corporate executives and the grassroots activists. But he found himself pulled between two competing business strategies. The club's internal debates sharpened in 1994 when Lawrence Howe retired from his post as head of the Civic Committee and was replaced by Arnold Weber, a former business school professor and president of Northwestern University, who was committed to school reform through competition. Privatization converts were noticeable within three years; by then Ayers had become a champion of charter schools as one of several options (including contract and voucher schools) to infuse competition into the district.[43] The public airing of these debates diminished the credibility of LQE and the club with grassroots activists. Within a few years of the decentralization law's passage, the city's business executives, preoccupied with their own tactical differences, had grown indifferent to other implementation issues.[44]

Competing Agendas

While the mayor's corporate partners were busy restructuring the central office and securing labor peace, Chicago's other reform activists dedicated their energies to developing (and funding) an apparatus for LSC elections.

In 1989 more than 17,000 candidates campaigned to become Chicago's first elected school governors, requiring thousands of volunteers to produce campaign materials, describe the unprecedented voting procedures, and count 300,000 ballots. The democracy-invoking labels attached to this process—social activism and "people power," egalitarian pluralism and democratic localism—stressed that ordinary parents and community members would make crucial fiscal, personnel, and policy decisions. Moreover, LSC members were required to conduct open meetings; hire, fire, and assess principals; analyze budgets; sanction school improvement plans; and evaluate service providers seeking contracts. Such demands called on activists to provide new community resources.[45]

Vital to this aspect of reform was the uncommon "backyard philanthropy" it drew. William S. McKersie concluded that Chicago experienced an explosion in foundation support for new organizations—some created to implement reform, and others attracted to its opportunities. Foundation funding expanded from $2 million in 1987 to $70 million by 1996. McKersie counted 176 groups new to Chicago, including the Comer School Development Program from Yale, or stimulated locally, such as the Citywide Coalition for School Reform.[46]

One inspired Chicagoan was Linda Lenz, a *Chicago Sun-Times* education reporter whose coverage of the 1979 school bankruptcy had made it one of the city's top-ten stories. Frustrated by editors preoccupied with advertising revenues, Lenz wanted to develop a new form of journalism to support school reform. LSCs could prove ineffective, she reasoned, without a source of independent information about how the education system worked and a way to share school improvement models that were "mindful of the complexities."[47] Within three months, she had attracted enough funding to publish *Catalyst: Voices for Chicago School Reform*. Editorially independent and unfettered by the need for advertising, *Catalyst* engaged readers from a cross section of the city by conveying the school law's legislative twists, explaining district policy changes, and reporting the stories of school activists.[48]

Anthony S. Bryk, a sociologist, statistician, and professor at the University of Chicago, contributed two reform-minded proposals. In 1988 he and Sharon Rollow conceived of the Center for School Improvement, whereby they offered a handful of schools their research expertise while learning from the schools' reform experiences. Many other universities followed a similar path.[49] The Consortium on Chicago School Research, formed two years later, made a more unusual contribution. Its investigations were driven by the practical problems of implementing reform systemwide. The consortium's research directors believed that social science methods applied to school assessment could help low-income LSC members; "pluralistic policy research" was intended to compensate for the social capital they lacked.[50] When the first two consortium reports were interpreted and disseminated by *Catalyst*, debating them also became a citywide consensus-building activity.[51] Committed to the value of assessing school outcomes using performance-based measures, Bryk bucked the 1988 law's emphasis on gauging improvements by summary statistics, proposing an alternative modeled on the inspectorate system widely used in Europe.[52]

Lenz's and Bryk's institutions fostered democratic concepts of policy change among residents long accustomed to top-down edicts. *Catalyst* helped rebalance traditionally centralized school decision making by giving parents and community members information useful for making, and defending, tough decisions. In stark contrast to the civil rights era, when activists could only guess at the size of the inequity problems they faced, the consortium put the technical expertise of researchers at the service of a citywide cross section of activists.[53]

But so much sustained philanthropy at the heart of reform implementation also exacerbated the inequalities between communities. Limited resources drove foundation executives to focus on a narrow range of promising projects, leaving most schools without the resources that high-quality service providers could offer. With fewer resources at the central office, reform was increasingly dependent on the services of these civic actors. Moreover, even the dozens of service providers supported were too few for the needs of more than 550 schools, and only a tiny proportion of projects was initiated by black organizations with credentials in Chicago's South Side neighborhoods. Foundation executives were aware that they were pursuing a flawed strategy, but they had a substantial investment in reform by 1988 and envisioned that public funds would eventually become available.[54]

Neither an unprecedented three-year teachers' contract nor the growing number of service providers overcame the mistrust between teachers and parents that had been heightened in the contentious process of drafting the 1988 law. Reformers had hoped that an advisory role for teachers might bridge the gap. But compared to the court-sanctioned authority held by the parent-dominated LSCs, the Professional Personnel Advisory Committee (PPAC) reflected teachers' "powerlessness."[55] When teachers bothered to form a PPAC, it was often led by the school's union representative, had "cordial, but weak" relations with the LSC, and failed to enhance teachers' status; most Chicago elementary school teachers still did not believe that they had parents' support. Nor was there much evidence that teachers collaborated with one another, either in PPACs or in the classroom.[56] LQE's John Ayers explained his disappointment: "We felt like we were running through the schools saying 'you're free!' 'Jailbreak!' 'You can now act differently!' Nobody came out of the cells, because they were very comfortable. I don't think we . . . understood the central forces in a bureaucratic structure and the isolation that has so damaged teaching as a profession."[57]

The 1988 reform law divided union leaders. For most, it curtailed teachers' influence and punished them for a debilitating strike: "It was a terrible experience and political trade-off which didn't include us . . . not much got down to the teachers, outside of pressure."[58] The American Federation of Teachers'

(AFT's) outspoken president Al Shanker partly agreed, but he wanted the CTU to "help shape the reform" rather than resist it.[59] When John Kotsakis, Jacquelyn Vaughn's assistant on educational issues, asked for help in preparing for the new reform, Deborah Walsh, the AFT's assistant director of educational initiatives, responded. Walsh recalls that "tensions emerged" early on between her and CTU staffers, who believed that unions should focus on winning concessions from management, not engage in professional development. Returning to her Chicago home after eight years in Washington, D.C., she became the hardworking "outsider" who accumulated "enemies"—among them Thomas Reese, next in line for CTU president—because she pressed for change and aligned herself with Kotsakis.[60]

A longtime union official who some found intimidating, Kotsakis was perhaps the only union leader who was trusted by reformers; he spoke bluntly of standards, accountability, and "real" change and had been a union critic in his youth. Kotsakis predicted that the 1988 law would fail unless the rules were loosened: permitting school-by-school changes and involving more teachers in the LSCs. To demonstrate this, he and Walsh won a $1 million MacArthur grant to establish a Quest Center that seeded teacher-developed change initiatives in forty-five schools and held citywide conferences for teachers on reform issues. Softening resistance among diehard unionists and bringing a labor voice to the reform table were the main goals—no mean feat for a divided organization facing hostile adversaries. That his efforts persisted past his untimely death in September 1994 (only nine months after Jacqueline Vaughn's death) was testament to Kotsakis's influence, but the school system remained saddled with old problems even as new and unexpected ones were unleashed by reform.[61]

Challenges to the Coalition

The loss of tenure outraged the principals association. Joining other critics of parent dominance in LSCs, they mounted a two-part constitutional challenge based on the denial of principals' contractual property rights and the abridgement of residents' voting rights. In November 1990 the Illinois Supreme Court upheld the principals' new status as fixed-term contract employees, but it struck down the 1988 law in its entirety for violating the U.S. Constitution's equal protection guarantee of one person, one vote. It rejected the practice of parents being the only group voting for parents' seats on the LSCs, because citizens without children in the public schools were "denied an equal voice."[62] Reform was back in the hands of the Illinois legislators.

The unexpected ruling sent reformers scrambling to salvage the 1989 LSC elections, validate principal selections made in spring 1990, and adjust the

LSC voting process before the 1991 elections. But the rewrite resurfaced a "latent mistrust" among community groups.[63] The ABCs coalition wanted every voter to cast a ballot for all ten LSC seats, including the two teachers' slots. Operation PUSH and the Urban League, along with nearly a dozen other groups that temporarily organized as the African-American Educational Reform Institute (AAERI), thought that slate-making would be encouraged if any voter could choose more than three seats. Teachers wanted educators alone to determine their representatives, and parent groups remained unwilling to let teachers select parents. Beleaguered legislators split the difference in July 1991, giving every voter five votes to cast among the eight parent and community seats, and agreeing that only teachers should select teacher representatives.[64]

Community activists had been pleased that the supreme court gave LSCs legal status equivalent to that of the central school board. But corporate leaders sided with the one dissenting justice who said LSCs were "simply to implement in the particular school the district wide policies set by the board."[65] Such disagreements over the meaning of decentralization—community control versus managerial devolution— were fundamentally class based. They reflected different perspectives on who could legitimately make substantive decisions about public schooling, and they would be voiced increasingly over the next four years.

Adding fuel to this debate was a decline in the number of Chicagoans who volunteered to serve on LSCs, giving reform a less democratic footing than community advocates had hoped. There were fewer than half as many candidates running in 1991 as had run in 1989, and this number fell further in successive elections. Voter turnout also declined, from 192,771 in 1989 to 175,845 in 1996, even though the legislature had been persuaded to move the 1995 election forward half a year—to the spring report-card pickup date.

Business leaders felt that the difficulties of the job dampened interest among potential candidates. Ken West summarized the "feedback" he got from Harris Bank employees who had served on an LSC: "The exact role of the LSCs was not clear at the very beginning . . . there was a good deal of scrambling for resources, different points of view. Many of them had to vote to retain or dismiss their principals; that created a lot of tension. A lot of these people had never had *any* kind of experience like that before."[66]

Grassroots activists credited LSCs with renewing community interest in the schools by providing black and Latino city residents a rare opportunity to exercise political authority. But since they fit class-based stereotypes, the 10 to 25 percent of councils that were corrupt or dysfunctional routinely overshadowed the 33 percent operating as participatory democracies. Training and support— the routine prescriptions for such problems—were little more than "haphazard," because "they're doing it with whoever's around, some of them better, some of them worse, some of them not at all." In LQE's survey of the first LSC members, 70 percent said that they had received no training from the central office, and less than 50 percent had received instruction from any source.[67]

The costs of electioneering and LSC training were recurring expenses for which there was no enthusiasm among those concerned with balanced budgets. As a result, LQE dropped out of its fund-raising role by the second LSC election cycle. The district was forced to pick up the slack with funding that varied from year to year, making little impact on the number of candidates or turnout. Foundations, seeing no end in sight, pressed in vain for a dedicated stream of public dollars. Skeptics wondered whether the lack of financial support for training was an attempt to impede the ability of low-income parents to hold middle-class professionals accountable.[68]

At the core of all activists' concerns was the issue of principal accountability. Grassroots activists thought that principals should be politically accountable to LSCs. Conflict and corruption in the bottom quartile of LSCs were linked, they believed, to a revolving door of unprepared principals in a few schools, reinforcing the need for better LSC (and principal) training. A substantial turnover in principals underscored what they meant; according to some estimates, one-half to three-quarters of principals were new by 1995. Their ethnic makeup also changed when UNO and other Latino groups ran slates of LSC candidates, boosting the number of Latino principals from seventeen to forty-three in 1989 and to seventy-two by 2000 (see figure, p. 97).[69]

Corporate activists were more concerned about the principal's bureaucratic accountability. Worried that too much turnover would jeopardize compliance, they preferred more district oversight of the principal selection process. They too had evidence to support their views: principals admitted to spending more time on management and bureaucratic reporting after the 1988 law than before, and according to one survey, principals also dominated one-third to one-half of the councils, as if LSC members were merely advisers.[70]

Compounding these tensions were the underlying inequities of local control in a city of gaping economic and social disparities. The LSCs most likely to be troubled were overseeing predominantly African American schools in low-income neighborhoods.[71] In one set of more advantaged elementary schools, the laudable if relatively rare "professional community" among educators dissolved if the adults in the schools reported racial tension or if there was high principal turnover, both "risk factors" associated with low-income, mixed-race (African American and Latino), and predominantly African American schools. Teachers' reports that reform had no effect on their practice were also worrying; high school teachers, like their students, were the most pessimistic. One-third of the principals said that they had no external organizations assisting them, while another one-third were flush with outside help.[72] New tensions arose between those who wanted a straightforward infusion of new resources into the disadvantaged communities and those who wanted to sanction the troubled schools.

Community perceptions of the central office were uniformly negative. Each administrative change meant reorganizing the entire management staff, leaving "no institutional memory."[73] The law's mandated central office downsizing meant "an inefficient or incompetent group of people [was] . . . burdened with more work."[74] Central administrators failed to provide accurate, timely information and dragged their heels on the release of funds because "there isn't a real philosophical congruence between the central office leadership and the local leadership," one Latina reasoned.[75] An Urban League representative added, "They seem to think that the LSCs are incapable of managing large amounts of money."[76] Others described the central office and the union as "support[ing] one another" in a sort of cabal.[77]

The school board was another focus of these class-based controversies. Daley had made no secret of his objection to the SBNC because it limited his discretion over appointments. Lacking judicial recourse—the supreme court had affirmed that the mayor was obligated to choose from among SBNC candidates—he left nearly half the board's seats empty. His chief of staff lamented, "The choices were . . . structured to screw the mayor," because the SBNC was stacked with "anti-Daley candidates."[78] Joe Reed concluded that the SBNC forced Daley to select a board that was "accountable to no one because it is accountable to everyone."[79] Black leaders held a different opinion: "The mayor . . . has the right to send back all of the people we send him . . . [in effect] the mayor has made the statement, 'These are not *my* people.' "[80]

By 1994 a rash of politically motivated studies claimed that reform had failed to meet its targeted outcome goals. The Heartland Institute, a voucher-promoting conservative think tank, concluded, "Chicago's landmark reform . . . gets mostly failing grades." What mattered were "measurable payoffs" such as aggregate test scores, graduation rates, and attendance numbers, all of which had seen mixed results.[81] A widely read *Chicago Sun-Times* journalist, Maribeth VanderWeele, wrote another condemnation. She described a system that "cries out for leadership," in which unruly children were warehoused in front of "incompetent teachers" guided by "floundering" LSCs, a central office in "chaos," and principals who stole from the till. Students were little better, she asserted, and should be "flunked" for their poor performance. The implication of both reports was that empowering parents and community members to make educational decisions had been a mistake; they lacked the clout or the comprehension or both.[82]

Even as debates over power sharing between the central board and the LSCs divided reformers, widespread dissatisfaction with the new superintendent united them. Only a few months into his 3.5-year, $700,000 contract, Kimbrough was roundly criticized, receiving a grade of D– on an ABCs report card. By 1991 Chicago executives described him as "compliance oriented," a "centrist," and a "defender of the status quo."[83]

Kimbrough had little compensating grassroots support. Like Ruth Love, the last superintendent whom club leaders had recruited, he was an African American without ties to the local black community. One group of black leaders and educators had even sued to block his hiring; remarks by one black activist, labeling him "a tool of the establishment," were typical.[84] Latinos also complained that he deliberately obstructed efforts to improve their schools. Yet Kimbrough served out his term, partly because, as Solis put it, "business wants to support a leader they pick."[85] But every decision he made was met with skepticism, helping to derail efforts to solve the district's chronic fiscal problems.[86]

Besides selecting Kimbrough, the interim board made a second "mistake" that only exacerbated the district's chronic fiscal problems. It signed a three-year teacher contract promising, but not guaranteeing, 7 percent annual raises in exchange for teacher cooperation with other changes. In 1990 the legislature passed a one-time income tax surcharge; Chicago's share paid the first-year increment, but the 7 percent raises could not be sustained thereafter. When the permanent fifteen-member school board took over in 1991, a $315 million shortfall was announced, and a strike was averted only because Daley brokered a settlement that reminded the press of his father's last-minute deals.[87]

In August 1992 Daley again entered budget negotiations, pressing the SFA to ease its hold on revenues that had been sequestered to pay debts. He also prevailed on Governor Edgar to authorize early state aid payments.[88] A similar shortfall and strike threat came again in 1993, accompanied by two system shutdowns, a delayed school opening, and "the typical all night negotiating sessions" involving the union, school board, and mayor's office.[89] A brokered patchwork contract was not signed until three months after the September 1 deadline. Although it reluctantly agreed to the settlement, the SFA predicted that the December fix would leave an estimated $400 million gap by 1995, because the budget problems were "structural."[90] The board's bond ratings were downgraded below investment quality, a rebuke not seen since 1979. Downgraded too were the SFA's ratings for "building a bridge to nowhere."[91] By 1995 even Daley accused the SFA of ineptly "micro-managing" the schools.[92]

Stability appeared to have arrived with Superintendent Argie Johnson, an earnest African American district administrator who succeeded Kimbrough in 1994. She won over reformers and garnered early corporate praise by offering positions on her management team to exemplary principals, business executives, and external researchers. Embracing LQE's TIME project, she added a "three-tiered plan," distinguishing among successful schools to be commended, those in the middle to be supported, and failing ones in which the central office would intervene.[93] When she appeared cavalier about cost cutting, the executives grew more disenchanted. Their intimate involvement in school finances for more than a decade prompted LQE, Chicago United, and the Civic Committee to go along with district requests for a new state funding mechanism—they agreed that the district would not be solvent in the foreseeable future—but they had already convinced themselves that no one from inside the system, no matter how well intentioned, could change it.[94]

MANAGEMENT OR MARKET?

Chicago United's education cochairs thought they were asserting the obvious in 1995: "The economic future of the city, OUR future, depends upon a successful educational system."[95] Even in the booming mid-1990s, corporate leaders agreed that school efficiency and performance affected job growth and business taxes. Yet beneath the consensus, their unanimity had broken down: one group preferred management solutions, and the other wanted an educational marketplace.

By 1990 the Commercial Club, Chicago United, and LQE were committed to improvements in education through the application of modern management techniques. These executives knew that the Chicago public schools had been shaped in the image of the corporation in the Progressive era, and they believed that the school system needed regular updating, much as their own firms did. Aiming to reduce labor conflict between the CTU and the administration, club members sought accountability from principals, teachers, parents, and students for uniform, centrally specified outcomes. The system would be more efficient, they expected, with a modern infrastructure and improved management competence among central office employees and "front-line" school managers.[96] Efforts to upgrade the management expertise of principals in the 1970s, the district's fiscal discipline in the 1980s, the insistence on management oversight in the 1988 reform act, routine cooperation with FRAC to provide audits and donated executives, and the TIME reengineering effort were all manifestations of these commitments.

At the same time, the Illinois Chamber of Commerce, the Illinois Manufacturers Association (IMA), and the recently formed Illinois Business Roundtable challenged the Commercial Club's managerialism with their commitment to entrepreneurial competition.[97] Jeff Mays, lobbyist for the Illinois Chamber of Commerce, explained: "Businesses have to compete or they're not going to be there. They're not in business as a social good, they're in business to sell their wares." So, he implied, were the schools.[98] Reflecting a National Business Roundtable exhortation to Fortune 500 executives that circulated in 1990, these groups sought to deregulate the bureaucratic and inefficient school system, evaluate productivity using a bottom-line measure of student achievement, and create performance incentives.[99]

Like the Progressive era IMA, these statewide business associations were especially concerned about unions. They argued aggressively for undercutting unionism through outsourcing, contract employment, vouchers, and other forms of privatization to break the union's stranglehold on system resources and enable the firing of underperforming teachers. They judged the 1988 decentralization to be "misguided legislation," partly because it merely tinkered with the unions.[100] The "teachers union," Mays declared, "likes the system they've been able to build over the last twenty years. It serves them well. But it doesn't serve the kids. It doesn't serve the parents. It doesn't serve the employer community."[101] Donald C. Ames, the Illinois Roundtable's chief lobbyist, agreed; he was "fighting the teachers union over trying to get Chicago reform."[102]

Such differences needed to be bridged if executives were to sustain their customary influence on politicians. Ron Gidwitz, a Republican committeeman and CEO of Helene Curtis, used his membership in the Civic Committee and the Illinois Roundtable to span the divide with yet another business association. Known for his sharp-tongued wit and lack of sentimentality, he became the point man for the corporate executives' next effort at school reform. The new Illinois Business Education Council (IBEC) intended to rewrite school law for the entire state, fixing Chicago's school problems in the process with "one voice—a unified voice of business," albeit this time a statewide and, theoretically, bipartisan one.[103]

By the fall of 1994, as the IBEC was poised to initiate a new cycle of school reform, national politics intervened. Minority leader Newt Gingrich and his colleagues, under the banner of the socially conservative and antigovernment "Contract with America," not only won the U.S. House of Representatives for the Republicans but also helped their party gain control of nine state legislatures.[104]

Republicans in Springfield, already in control of the senate, took over leadership in the lower chamber and drafted their own sixty-day "Contract with Illinois," signaling their affinity with Gingrich.[105] They also renewed education legislation for Chicago. Republican governor James Edgar, "willing to do to Chicago what he wasn't willing to do for the state," saw an opportunity to impose reform on his Democratic rival in the mayor's office.[106] Only days after the November elections, Illinois senate president James "Pate" Phillips and the new house speaker Lee Daniels made calls to Gidwitz, asking the IBEC for "an educational reform proposal by mid-December and proposed legislation by year-end."[107]

When the legislative target narrowed from the whole state to Chicago, the two business factions became irreconcilable over school funding. While all agreed that the SFA's efforts to balance the school budget had failed, Commercial Club, Chicago United, and LQE leaders supported a change in the state's funding formula, from a reliance on property taxes to a reliance on state income taxes. IBEC groups were more interested in keeping all state taxes low and cutting union-related costs such as pensions and bargained raises.[108]

Club members were not alone in their desire to trade greater accountability and improved management for new and more stable state funding. Noting that more than half of Chicago's public school expenditures came from sources other than the district's general fund, the SFA argued for an end to the "gimmicks" and "one time revenue infusions" that had balanced the budget even under its watch. The club agreed and called for an immediate increase in the state's share of education funding by $350 million.[109]

In exchange for increased resources, club leaders championed unfettered mayoral control to ensure that a politician over whom they had influence would be the ultimate decision maker. They also resurrected their 1940s argument for a CEO led management team, relegating educators to secondary positions. The professional commitments that constrained educators' decisions, they believed, should not trump the CEO's resolve to rewrite labor agreements, outsource even educational services, and overhaul the central office in line with TIME recommendations. Although this did not require abrogating union contracts, it did mean striking from the school code all previously bargained agreements (e.g., class size, seniority privileges, dismissal procedures). Club leaders also thought that the SFA's fiscal and managerial oversight should be eliminated because it was a political target—"a vehicle to blame for lack of funding or difficult decisions." In short, dramatically increased managerial flexibility was expected to lead to cost savings, but only if those in the top posts had the right skills and could be held accountable by corporate leaders.[110]

The Illinois Roundtable was less forgiving, seeing "no reason to throw good money after bad."[111] The IMA briefly revived its Progressive era proposal for a dual system of secondary schooling as a new "school-to-work" concept.[112] The statewide groups also "wanted somebody to take responsibility," but they would tie the mayor's hands by mandating, rather than enabling, outsourcing and privatization.[113] For instance, they would remake unionized teachers into contract employees, hired by principals, with one- to three-year terms and prohibit teacher strikes for at least eighteen months. Although club members cautioned against creating educational "martyrs," the downstate executives were unperturbed about forcing Chicago to dismantle the unions in the mayor's governing coalition.[114]

Despite internal dissension, the IBEC was formidable and united on many particulars. For a start, putting a single politician in charge was ideal, particularly if it was Richard M. Daley.[115] Chicago's Democratic business leaders had backed his candidacy as early as 1983, ensured his election in 1989, and anticipated the favors he would owe them. A local business attorney linked Daley's attractiveness to his patrimony: "Richie . . . was his father's son and, therefore, got to know a lot of [business leaders] as he grew up . . . they feel very comfortable with Richie."[116]

Nor was Daley considered an ideological Democrat. An academic involved in crafting mayoral control explained, "The Republicans are aware of the fact . . . that in another time and another place Richard M. Daley could be a Republican."[117] John Callaway, Chicago's seasoned public television commentator, added, "He's a conservative. The only thing that bespeaks of his old Democratic ties are his necessary, however reluctant, continuing ties to the unions . . . his philosophy is that government should be run more like a business."[118] Moreover, giving the Democratic mayor of Chicago control over the city's schools without new funding carried little risk for downstate Republican politicians. They could be accused of "just wanting to stick an impossible situation on the mayor" and "giving him the noose to hang himself."[119]

A Privileged Process

The corporate groups thus "patched over differences " in a comprehensive "business bill." It included the privatization and strike prohibition clauses that the statewide associations favored, the mayoral control and corporate management structure backed by the Commercial Club, and the administrative authority to sanction failing schools that nearly everyone, including school administrators, seemed to accept.[120]

Early in the spring, Illinois House Speaker Daniels charged the newly seated Republican chairwoman of the House Elementary and Secondary Education Committee with vetting the business leaders' legislative proposal, reconciling it with a slightly more anti-union version from the senate and with Governor Edgar's managerially oriented version.[121] Mary Lou Cowlishaw, a "tough" and "unsentimental" former editor of the *Naperville Sun,* a decade-long member of the Naperville School Board, and a thirteen-year veteran legislator from a suburb thirty miles west of Chicago, embraced the business leaders' radical agenda.[122]

Cowlishaw's Chicago Public Schools Reform Working Group was not well known, attended mostly by those who had routine interaction with Springfield legislators. Interest groups whose staffs were capable of writing legislative language or providing research assistance had special influence, including all the IBEC member associations, whose lobbyists fought out their differences as they helped draft House Bill 206.[123] Lobbyists for the CTU and operating engineers were present but had little impact. Cowlishaw declared that these unions "ran the school system, [but] it had nothing to do with schooling, it had to do with jobs." Giving in to any of their requests would be "backsliding" on the "balance between labor and management" that the business executives and the Republicans jointly sought.[124] Board of education president Sharon Grant and Superintendent Argie Johnson publicly agreed with the corporate leaders, even though it clearly meant that their jobs and authority would be lost.[125]

The only other organizations routinely represented were the Chicago Union League Club (a civic reform group allied with business leaders), the Chicago Urban League, the Mexican American Legal Defense Fund (MALDEF), the Latino Institute, and the Citywide Coalition for School Reform.[126] But according to Cowlishaw, though "very well meaning . . . each one of them has taken [on] some tiny little element . . . and the [grand] vision gets lost."[127]

This handful of civic activists agreed that principals ought to have full responsibility for their staffs, nonperforming teachers should be more easily fired, and contentious principals and LSCs could be better supervised, although none of this was intended to overhaul the system in the way that executives sought. The three groups representing Chicago's "minorities" ignored the executives' more radical proposals, perhaps imagining that Cowlishaw's vetting process, like Speaker Madigan's in 1988, would require consensus before legislation was proposed.[128] But Cowlishaw merely intended them to "feel as though they have a little ownership . . . not [like] somebody imposed something on them that they didn't want."[129]

The IBEC sought bottom-line accountability indicators, clear-cut measures that would identify failing schools, teachers, and students. In this, professor Anthony Bryk, with the help of dean Larry Braskamp and retired professor Bruce McPherson from the University of Illinois at Chicago, hoped to persuade them to accept the idea of an inspectorate rather than the easily gathered but "deeply problematic" single standardized test score.[130]

But Bryk's idea for a quasi-independent accountability agency foundered on the straightforward funding debate between the downstate and Chicago-based business groups. The Commercial Club and Chicago United were willing to support it with "significant new funds," but the remainder of the IBEC would not.[131] The compromise was an accountability council in name only, and—as was true for the bill as a whole—it drew no funding. The downstate business associations prevailed because the club "didn't have the lobbying horsepower" to win resource commitments from Republican legislators or from their entrepreneurially inclined IBEC colleagues.[132]

Daley, running for a second full term, campaigned on the issue of boosting accountability: of principals through uniform performance contracts, of parents through "partnership contracts," and of teachers through peer review. Crucially, he wanted the central school board to be politically accountable to him, which meant dissolving the SBNC. None but the last of Daley's ideas found its way into the final bill.[133] He did not campaign on a platform of mayoral control, perhaps playing a game of cat and mouse with Governor Edgar, with whom he had several high-profile disagreements.[134]

Three weeks after his reelection, Daley met with Edgar to influence the consensus bill; Daley embraced the fiscal flexibility proposed by the governor: collapsing sixteen separate school levies into one fungible source of support and replacing twenty-five state categorical programs (e.g., bilingual education, special education, drivers' education) with two block grants. He also supported abolishing subdistricts and, in principle, adopting bottom-line accountability indicators of school performance, coyly referring to these reforms as "ideas of my own." Agreeing more with the club's managerialism than with the Illinois Roundtable's entrepreneurialism, he offered: "We must reduce the role of the central bureaucracy and give schools resources and the flexibility they need to do their jobs; then and only then can they be held responsible for results."[135]

What he failed to oppose was also telling. By then nearly every position of the business platform had been adopted in the proposed legislation: banning school strikes, cutting all previously bargained language from the school code, eliminating all obstacles to privatization, and installing a corporate-style CEO with a four-person management support team. Some of this worried him, but mostly he held out for increased funding. "Without more money, reform won't come," he announced at a televised standoff with Edgar in May.[136] "They think they're just going to give me the responsibility and walk away? They're greatly mistaken."[137]

When it became obvious that no new funds would arrive, Daley attempted to negotiate the details. He "went down [to Springfield] . . . and asked us to give [him] one of our [club] members so they could ride shotgun."[138] He asked for more flexibility in selecting his own CEO and in parceling responsibilities between that executive and the soon-to-be corporate-style reform board of trustees. Business executives such as Arnold Weber, president of the Civic Committee, "did not see any problem . . . our goals . . . are to make him as accountable as possible."[139]

Jeff Mays took credit for infusing competition into the schools: "When I say 'our law' it's the IBEC group, the Roundtable, IMA, ourselves and several others."[140] But from a Commercial Club leader's point of view, the law was also a reengineered improvement on decentralization: "our balance, [between] those two initiatives [is] moving us in the right direction."[141]

Daley and his corporate management team (CEO, CFO, CPO, COO, CEdO) were given unprecedented fiscal and managerial flexibility. In effect, nearly all state support became part of the district's general fund. The law simply removed the requirement of a balanced budget and SFA oversight. About 20 percent of state Chapter 1 dollars were made available to Daley by redirecting them from schools to the central office, freezing the share given directly to LSCs at 1994 levels. Borrowing from the teachers' pension fund was extended. How this money was spent was now Daley's prerogative, as IBEC executives had hoped.

The schools became a deregulated agency of city hall. The law allowed the board to dismiss employees within fourteen days if privatization or outsourcing made them redundant. Teacher strikes were prohibited for eighteen months. Thirteen previously bargained issues, including class size, teacher assignments, teacher tenure, and the troublesome "supernumeraries," were removed from the school code. Existing educational career ladders were almost completely dismantled; principals had lost theirs in 1988 when they became appointees of LSCs, and now senior members of the school management team no longer needed educational qualifications.

What looked like reengineering to some corporate executives and market competition to others was seen by grassroots activists as recentralization. Nearly all their 1988 governance gains were eroded in 1995. The mayor's selection of the new five-person board of trustees would have no citizen input; the SBNC and the subdistrict councils were both abolished. Responsibility for achievement was not recentralized from the schools to the central office, and principals were still subject to LSC contracts, but the new CEO's powers constrained LSC authority.[142]

The CEO took over the duties of the general superintendent, including responsibility for setting the course of study. Directly below him in a steep hierarchy were the members of his management team, and below them were nearly 600 principals, all charged with carrying out his directives and serving at his pleasure.[143] As managers, they earned some sympathy from the business leaders and were given the ability to evaluate the performance of employees under them and to initiate firing procedures. But principals remained politically accountable to LSCs, even as their bureaucratic accountability to the new CEO was increased. The 1995 law also gave the mayor and the CEO the authority to sanction any Chicago school with "remediation," "probation," "reconstitution," or "intervention." After six years of decentralized accountability, with the LSCs making judgments about school effectiveness, this change promised to standardize the determination of educational performance.[144]

The Modern Corporate Model

Mayor Daley appointed a new school board, a CEO, and his first management team by July. His chief of staff, lawyer Gery Chico, became president of the new reform board of trustees. The other trustee positions went to three business executives and a physician. High-ranking city officials garnered three of four posts on the management team—chief financial officer, chief procurement officer, and chief operations officer. The only educator on the team was the chief education officer, a former principal. To the surprise of some corporate executives, who expected that one of them would be the system's first CEO, Daley tapped one of his own.[145]

Democrat Paul Vallas had been a young legislative assistant investigating the school system's fiscal collapse in 1979. Appointed Daley's first city revenue collector a decade later and promoted in 1994 to budget director, he was known as a hands-on manager averse to delegating, a "no excuses" kind of man. Vallas "yells and screams. He'll ream you," an aide confided to *Catalyst,* but "he also tells you he loves you." To outsiders, he conducted himself like a "ward committeeman," glad-handing everyone and surprising even critics with "legendary" accessibility.[146] In contrast to his strong finance background and proven loyalty, Vallas lacked education credentials. But an aide justified the mayor's choice, saying, it "isn't realistic" to ask an educator to "run a $3 billion operation."[147]

A primary casualty of mayoral control was public education's supposed Progressive era political exceptionalism. Daley demanded that the chronic budget gap be closed and that speculation over the system's financial health end. Vallas complied, providing a balanced budget plan that erased a $150 million shortfall and a projected five-year deficit within three months. In keeping with the TIME and Frykund recommendations, about 1,000 custodial jobs were outsourced in the summer of 1995, saving $35 million. The consolidation of tax levies and block grants "freed up close to $130 million," with long-term savings expected from "renegotiating healthcare contracts and cutting expenditures, and eliminating non-essential positions."[148] The SFA's demise meant that there was no oversight group to challenge the rosy forecasts. One Commercial Club leader allowed, "There might be some smoke and mirrors," but quickly added, "it's just a few puffs and a little shard of a mirror."[149]

Outsourcing, dubbed "more efficient" by Vallas, was also aimed at creating private-sector jobs and contracts in transportation, supplies, food services, and construction. Vallas wondered "if we've saved money on privatization," since the budget grew by $1.5 billion over his tenure, but bankers showed their approval by repeatedly raising the district's bond ratings.[150] Daley, adopting the development strategy he followed in other city hall departments, mounted a school building program that mushroomed to a $2.6 billion initiative for twenty-eight elementary schools and seven college preparatory academies.[151]

This combination of new accounting rules and privatization calmed immediate budgetary fears but could not be sustained. So Daley frequently used the city's "Visa card" TIF deferments to underwrite borrowing for construction, and he raised property taxes five times in six years.[152] His close relationship with the Clinton White House also facilitated federal grants, while his corporate partners, who were invested in the schools through contracts and debt interest, helped pry additional dollars from the legislature.[153]

This new intimacy with city hall led to closer coordination between the Chicago public schools and other city agencies. Public libraries supplemented reading programs, the Park District cleaned playgrounds, the Departments of Human Services and Child and Welfare Services cooperated with the schools, and the police were more responsive. One central office administrator observed, "The most beautiful part of this management team [is] we've had the resources— just almost automatically—that other superintendents did not."[154]

To improve both the schools' image and his own reputation, Daley donned the mantle of "Education Mayor" in 1996 as chair of the U.S. Council of Mayors.[155] He was bolstered by Vallas's relentless good-news media campaign, soon rated the CEO's "greatest contribution." Chicagoans agreed that "there is more political support for the school system now . . . than ever."[156] With support came credibility; in 1997 organizational leaders throughout the city overwhelmingly identified Vallas and his senior staff as the most reliable sources of information about the system: "The mere perception of success is feeding itself."[157]

Vallas hired "very strong school reform promoters . . . so they were no longer outside, able to cause trouble."[158] Among them was school critic and *Chicago Sun-Times* reporter Maribeth VanderWeele. As inspector general, she co-opted external criticism and provided Vallas with a kitchen cabinet member who would discreetly alert him to any wrongdoing.[159] "Before long," commented one *Catalyst* editor, the relationship between the district and the press "was a love fest." But mayoral control and Vallas's media skills also resulted in "very little, if any, skeptical reporting," and when it did happen, Vallas accused the journalists of bias.[160] Even a corporate supporter claimed that he was "not sure that [the media] are sufficiently critical."[161]

Symbols of the old bureaucracy were jettisoned. Closed was the drab South Side Pershing Road barracks, where the central administration had relocated in the 1980s to cut costs. District headquarters moved to a newly renovated Loop building near city hall, signaling the schools' importance to the economy and the close relationship between Vallas and the mayor.[162]

Daley and Vallas were not alone in extolling the Chicago miracle. Corporate executives also promoted mayoral control "as a model for other urban systems that are bankrupt morally and educationally."[163] The positive spin also gave President Clinton a Democratic mayor who had "turned around" a big city school system through "greater accountability."[164]

By 1997 Vallas and his management team had earned high marks for financial management, public-relations savvy, and holding educators, parents, and students accountable.[165] Along with Sunbeam's high-flying CEO Al Dunlap, Vallas was lionized in *Forbes* magazine as "Chain Saw Paul" for his "tough tactics" and "plenty of publicity," largely because he came from "outside the education establishment."[166] *Crain's Chicago Business* made him "Executive of the Year" in 1998.[167] In *Newsweek* he was described as pursuing "accountability and standards" by using "as little democracy as possible," and he was portrayed as the savior of public education, preserving "the high moral ground" by staving off vouchers with a middle path of competition and privatization. Community activists and foundation heads were more reserved, but Vallas dismissed them as "out of touch elitists" who wanted "to celebrate the problems" rather than fix them.[168]

Although not anti-intellectual, Vallas was impatient with educators' research and with their mantra that school improvement required slow, steady work. A Latina community organizer praised his style as a "results-oriented . . . dictatorial leadership."[169] The intuitive Vallas insisted on setting the performance markers that held students back each year, and VanderWeele said that he deliberated all of "60 seconds" before deciding that mandatory summer school would support students who had failed to meet his test score cutoffs. Such hasty hunches often backfired: the first few years of summer school were chaotic, with few teachers knowing what to do, and the cutoff score he set in 1997 was not even calibrated on that year's grade scale. Although frequently forced to change course, Vallas refused to admit mistakes.[170]

Different Versions of Accountability

Daley had been reelected in 1995 promising increased accountability in the schools, and he was determined to test his ideas. Corporate executives also imagined that mayoral control would increase accountability, but they meant that the *mayor* would be politically accountable to *them* for how the schools were run. Concerned that "the superintendent could always blame either the board or the city or some other [group]" and ignore their advice, corporate leaders wanted to put the mayor in the hot seat, because they were confident that they had his ear.[171]

The executives also promoted mayoral control as a way for Chicago voters to hold the mayor accountable for the system's performance. But after he had succeeded in eliminating partisan contests, the possibility of Daley losing an election was remote. Nor could Chicagoans hold the board of trustees accountable. By design, they and Vallas were answerable only to the mayor; consequently, any differences among the school governors were hashed out in private. Meetings that had formerly been hotbeds of citizen discussion and complaint were shortened, and speakers were timed.

Secure from broad accountability himself, Daley envisioned a school system in which he, his CEO, or their managers could hold everyone else accountable. To give this bureaucratic accountability teeth, he made sure to sanction anyone who fell short. It is "a sound business approach: accountability with benchmarks," said one business executive. It also fit corporate notions of accountability: "to find a way to sort the kids."[172] A local radio editor was more blunt: "When people's feet are held to the fire they respond a little bit more than they would otherwise." The consequences were felt first by students, then by educators and eventually by parents.[173]

In spring 1996, eighth-grade students learned that their promotion to high school would be determined by their scores on the reading portion of the norm-referenced, standardized Iowa Test of Basic Skills (ITBS). Those whose scores fell below Vallas's cutoff would be required to attend remedial test-taking instruction in summer school, after which a retest would determine promotion or retention. A year later the same policy was extended to third and sixth graders, and the math portion of the test was added. Each year the cutoff point was raised.

The results were dramatic. About one-quarter of eighth graders failed and were assigned to summer school. From 1996 to 2000 about 7,000 to 10,000 elementary students were retained annually—almost 20 percent of third graders and about 10 percent of sixth and eighth graders. One percent of students attended the same grade three times, and another 20 percent were classified as special education students when their scores did not improve. Most teachers favored the sanctions and adjusted their instruction to include more test-taking skills and basic grade-level math and reading. But students reported feeling no more academically challenged or engaged. Aggregate scores rose significantly in the sixth and eighth grades, although not in the third grade, and the proportion of low-achieving students fell.[174] The accountability-for-kids sanctions appeared sound, and both Vallas and Daley championed them as the end of "social promotion."[175]

But Chicago did not use state tests to determine its sanctions, nor did it compare its students to others in the state. The ITBS, which had "not been validated" for "identifying low-performing schools and students," according to a National Research Council report, was preferred because it had been in place when Vallas arrived, minus the sanctions. A more reliable test, his chief accountability officer explained, "would be viewed with suspicion" and might cause the system to lose credibility. Even after the U.S. Justice Department inquired whether Chicago's sole reliance on the ITBS was discriminatory toward minority children, Vallas did not budge.[176]

Another ad hoc series of test-based accountability sanctions rapidly produced a hierarchy among schools. At the top were college preparatory schools, many of them new, with test-based admission criteria and an accelerated program. The 60 percent of schools just below them were required to respond to district curriculum demands but were otherwise left alone. At the bottom, about one-fifth to one-fourth of the schools were on "probation" because only 15 percent or less of their students (later raised to 20 percent) scored above national norms on the ITBS. The three categories roughly corresponded to the social classes in Chicago, and the implicit goal was to move schools from the lowest category to the middle. About 150 were removed from probation between 1996 and 2001, but some were reassigned a second time, and others languished. Throughout, the relative size of the three layers stayed much the same because new types of low-performing schools were opened for retained eighth graders aged fifteen or older and for disruptive youth.[177]

Schools on probation were targeted for sanctions, which began with LSCs losing their authority and principals being subject to dismissal by Vallas. Schools were next assigned external assistance providers, including a "probation manager," to guide planning and evaluate the principal. These schools were also required to contract with one of eighteen "external partners" for teacher professional development and other instructional services, a costly commitment. Multiple partners and district consultants "almost guarantee[d] fragmentation," according to one assessment, and were unsystematic and "too weak" to change instruction in most of the demoralized, poorly performing schools.[178] In June 1997 seven of the thirty-eight high schools on probation were reconstituted because they failed to improve. Their LSCs were disbanded, and all principals and staff were required to reapply for their jobs.

The pool of applicants for the vacated positions in such troubled schools was to be strengthened with fast-track teacher certification, outsourced management training, screening for principal applicants, and the recruitment of small numbers of nontraditional candidates for both jobs.[179] Shame, less autonomy, a new faculty and staff, and, above all, mandatory district-created lesson plans in four subjects—9,360 plans in all—were expected to turn these troubled schools around. "This is not rocket science," Vallas asserted. "If you're a new teacher, or a weak teacher, or a teacher that doesn't have skills, or if you have a teacher that's burned out . . . if you stick to that curriculum you'll be able to deliver quality instruction."[180]

Aiming to increase the accountability of families with children in pre-kindergarten through third grade, Vallas next initiated parent report cards, an idea that Daley had floated in his 1995 reelection campaign. Twenty-three evaluation marks, including items such as "spends quality time" with the child, were sent home every five weeks beginning in November 2000, because "the school system has got to identify the things that parents are clearly not doing."[181] "Insulted" parent groups called the effort "outrageous," especially because they did not get to grade teachers. Only half the schools agreed to use the device.[182]

PARALLEL REFORMS AND POLICY CHURN

Although it was the dominant one, mayoral control was not the only reform model pursued in the mid-1990s. About twenty-five progressively oriented activists assembled a new reform collaboration focusing on instruction. Hopes of winning a $50 million Annenberg challenge grant provided the stimulus, and the group's proposal bested several others, including city hall's. Perhaps because local foundations committed in advance to the required two-for-one match, the Chicago Annenberg Challenge (CAC) was conceptualized as a regranting institution. It hired Ken Rolling as executive director in October 1995.[183]

Rolling had been the community organizing and school reform program officer for the Woods Fund of Chicago when the foundation put its faith in Designs for Change, the Panel, and UNO to promote community-based school reform. He personified the "dogged determination" with which Woods pursued parent and community reform leadership, "people who usually get left out," and he brought those convictions to the CAC. Rolling assumed that, with the proper help, locally governed schools could motive students and encourage teachers to innovate; improvement would follow.[184]

Even before Rolling arrived, the collaborative wrote a request for proposals and dispensed planning grants to dozens of "external partners," including college-based institutes, reform groups, cultural institutions, and community organizations. Each was to form a network of at least three schools that agreed on a common vision of how altering school time might improve students' experience, how instructional groupings might be made smaller, or how the schools might become less isolated from their communities and from one another.[185]

Despite the huge Annenberg grant, sums available for each school were too little to generate many innovations or services. Between 1996 and 1998 funding was approved for 45 networks with 206 elementary schools, resulting in widespread but thin impact. A rough average per school was $25,000 a year for six years, less than 1 percent of a typical school's budget.[186] Throughout, success was to be measured by "a range of things, everything from test scores [and] looking at student work . . . [to whether] parents say 'Oh *that's* what a good school is' . . . and legislators say 'let's stop dumping on these schools.' "[187]

Reports of disappointing test scores in CAC schools suggested that the mayor's accountability regimen had easily swamped the collaborative's alternative assessment plans. The Consortium on Chicago School Research showed that CAC schools with the same low level of baseline test scores as other Chicago public schools remained indistinguishable six years later. By 1999, 26 percent of CAC schools were on academic probation, compared with 16 percent of the elementary schools systemwide. The CAC had only a vague response to the score gaps between African American and Latino children and their white counterparts. The most prevalent instructional change in Chicago schools was an "increased effort to prepare students for standardized tests," a strategy nearly opposite from the one the CAC sought.[188]

The CAC was also regarded as a problem for the city's politicians. Corporate leaders saw it as resisting the mayor's agenda. One such leader on the CAC board referred to its efforts as "feel-good stuff . . . abstract to the point of irrelevancy."[189]

Most important, the CAC lacked essential teacher support. CAC leaders had hoped that teachers would become engaged through their participation on LSCs and PPACs, but they largely ignored evidence that teachers mistrusted these bodies. By 1994 Quest Center official Walsh (now Deborah Lynch) was carving out instruction as the domain for union influence and expecting reformers to drop hostile rhetoric in order to "reach the teachers."[190] But there was no effort to marry the CAC's emphasis on attitudinal underpinnings of school change to Quest's instructional vision. Although, as a gesture of inclusiveness, the CAC funded one network of three schools guided by the Quest initiative, the CAC's forty-five networks and Quest's forty-five schools functioned in a "parallel universe," according to one critic.[191] Neither proposed realistic alternatives to the city hall governance system or matched the influence of the city's business elite, but each kept alive the prospect that parents and teachers had important roles to play in reform.

Not without the Teachers

The CTU was always divided about the 1995 law. Thomas Reese, the restrained African American leader of the union's United Progressive Caucus (UPC) and Vaughn's successor as CTU president, was delighted to be negotiating directly with a master political bargainer who wanted labor peace. But achieving comity was difficult, since "one of the arguments used early on with the senate was 'This is a great way to stick it to the Chicago Teachers Union.' "[192]

Daley's response was twofold. He asked Reese and other union heads not to fight the law, whose passage was virtually assured, then promised to rescind most of its anti-union restrictions after he gained control. "Every right they took away, Daley gave them back in bargaining, every one," rejoiced a union leader.[193] Following the pattern of his interim board five years earlier, Daley then offered teachers a four-year contract, this time with 3 percent guaranteed raises. One year before it expired, and shortly before Daley ran for a third term, a second four-year contract was ratified with 2 to 3 percent yearly raises. Notwithstanding top salaries that were far below those in suburban districts, Daley's offers improved relations with UPC leaders and "largely co-opted them."[194]

Reese hailed the second contract as "the most positive experience I have ever had" in sixteen years of negotiating.[195] Vallas reciprocated when Reese faced his own election battles, crediting him with taking "union relations out of the Middle Ages." The long-suffering public, accustomed to delayed school openings and strike threats, was also pleased.[196]

With no need for yearly bargaining, the CTU's main role was filing teacher grievances, although it lost most of these disputes to city hall. In June 1997, for instance, 188 of 700 mostly senior African American teachers in the seven reconstituted high schools were told to secure another position or take retirement, a direct challenge to the principle of tenure. A miffed Reese called the move a "serious mistake" but avoided criticizing the mayor personally and negotiated a postponement of the dismissal date.[197] Eventually Daley agreed to an alternative to reconstitution, dubbed "reengineering," whereby teachers could opt for peer review and delay looking for new positions if their school showed reconstitution-level performance.[198]

Some of Daley's flexibility was surely motivated by an attempt to help his bargaining partner stave off a leadership challenge from a union faction led by the less compliant Deborah Lynch. Like Margaret Haley before her, the fiery and persistent Irish American Lynch was unafraid of powerful foes. She found Reese's leadership "stagnant, passive and reactive." Concerned too that mayoral control occasioned a "hysterical emphasis on student test scores," she believed that the results of improved instruction should show first in students' daily progress through the curriculum.[199]

In a witty open letter to Vallas in 1997 that drew favorable but ironic analogies to corporate reengineering, she detailed the failure of any central administration to tackle teaching and learning. She believed that most attempts had actually hindered instructional improvement with useless and demeaning professional development days and staunch resistance to teacher leadership, small schools, joint decision making, or performance-based inspections. Lynch scolded, "You can't change teaching without the teachers," and she challenged Vallas to "co-management of just one school."[200]

While prodding the mayor's new management team, Lynch waged a fierce battle within the CTU. Dismayed by Reese's unwillingness to propose a more equal governing partnership, she left Quest for a teaching position, to "put into practice some of the reforms she had been advocating" and to lead a small group of colleagues in new instructional techniques.[201] Then, confronting Reese and the UPC for allowing the contract to be "gutted" and for putting the union "totally at the mercy of the Board's unilateral decision making," she accused the UPC of having no position on teachers' low status, no strategy to combat privatization, and little interest in school improvement or interventions such as reconstitution: it was "perpetuating the stereotype that the union and its members are part of the problem, not part of the solution."[202]

In October 1995 Lynch audaciously formed a new union faction, ProActive Chicago Teachers (PACT), stressing teachers' responsibility for school improvement and their legitimacy as school reform leaders. After losing two bitter campaigns for CTU president in 1996 and 1998, in May 2001 she was declared victorious by a 14 percent margin, just one week before chief trustee Gery Chico resigned. Perhaps recalling the postscript to her letter warning that he would "pay more attention to [our] views" when PACT headed the union, Vallas resigned just two weeks later.[203]

An Outside Competitive Force

Although it had been their design, corporate executives gradually lost faith that mayoral control alone could reform the schools: "You won't get change of sufficient magnitude unless you have an outside competitive force pressing on the school system . . . vouchers or charters or what have you."[204] Renewed concerns about the system's finances after the boom years of the 1990s gave way to recession in 2000 and heightened their anxiety. Debt payments for the construction and repair of schools cut into dollars intended for instruction. Just before Vallas left, Daley considered school closings while seeking additional state aid and a fifth property tax hike.[205]

Moreover, corporate Chicago had become financially invested in the school system through large no-bid contracts, but accusations of overcharging, poor service delivery, and cronyism left business leaders feeling vulnerable. Some claimed that Chico's law firm had benefited from too many contracts to its clients. Vallas himself called a costly new information management system "over-privatized" when an audit revealed lax financial and contractual safeguards. LQE's John Ayers dismissed such problems as "inevitable" and, in any case, balanced by the private-sector resources that were mobilized. But perceptions were slipping.[206]

The media manipulation that sustained mass support also began to lose its effect. Consortium reports and *Catalyst* investigations encouraged reporters to ask harder questions. The CTU's direct challenge to Vallas seemed to spark public questioning about whether balanced budgets and labor peace were sufficient indicators of school success, and he grew defensive.[207]

Most damaging were recurrent questions about the unfair distribution of benefits. By 2000 a rash of independent reports showed that children in predominantly African American or high-poverty schools still received a substandard education. Schools on probation or reconstituted were disproportionately in the poorest (and most likely to be African American) neighborhoods, where promised magnet and college prep schools were also least likely to be constructed or fully funded when built. After five years, reconstitution was reckoned a failure: test scores in those schools had plunged, as had teacher morale. Vallas had evidently hidden much of the damning evidence.[208]

As early as 1997, elite Chicagoans had begun to doubt Vallas's "weak" educational vision and to criticize him for "sacrificing everything for test scores."[209] According to an African American business leader, his team did "not have the full grasp of the teaching and learning requirement."[210] Another business association leader, commenting on the mayor that he had helped put in control of the schools, said, "I wouldn't classify him right up there with John Dewey."[211]

Nevertheless, the full effects of student retention policies did not become known until well after Vallas had left. Painstaking longitudinal studies by the Consortium on Chicago School Research documented that black students fared worst, and performance gaps were growing. Ninety-seven percent of those retained in grade had been African American or Latino, unsurprising in a system with only 10 percent white students. But retention was not applied equally. About one-third of all students below the cutoff score were "waived" through.

Latino students were exempted from retention for three (later extended to four) years if they were in bilingual education classes. African American students—the group most likely to be retained—may have performed poorly because their schools received by far the slowest instructional pacing.[212]

Retained students did no better than those with the same failing scores who were socially promoted or waived; in fact, by the sixth grade they were doing worse. Those unfortunate enough to be retained more than once or designated special-education students after failing experienced a considerable drop in their performance. Dropouts also increased by 8 to 13 percent among the students retained, and 78 percent of those retained twice dropped out by age nineteen. Mandatory test-prep summer school did not substantially alter the average student's long-term performance, and the tendency of all African American students to drop out more than others was exacerbated.[213]

Mounting evidence of poor performance by sanctioned students and schools was only one of the many reasons Vallas left in mid-2001, in the middle of his second term. The CTU leadership change portended difficult contract negotiations and heavier criticism of central office regulations from teachers. And a legal filing with the U.S. Justice Department had forced the system to broaden its promotion criteria.[214]

After Vallas, polls indicated that 79 percent of Chicagoans were ready for a "career educator."[215] Yet Daley pressed for more, rather than fewer "outside the box" ideas, appointing Vallas's "likeable" and "intelligent" young chief of staff, Arne Duncan, as his next CEO.[216] A Harvard-educated professional athlete, Duncan had worked after college in the district office but otherwise had no training in education and had never balanced a budget or supervised a staff.[217]

Duncan put his own stamp on the system when he was called on to expand the criteria for retention, as required by a consent decree. He also mandated two hours of reading instruction in the elementary schools and provided reading specialists, closed the failed Office of Intervention, moved transition centers for "flunked" eighth graders into high schools, agreed to join the CTU in new turnaround efforts for failing schools, and scrapped the myriad lesson plans designed by Vallas.[218]

Lynch took full advantage of the course corrections, enlisting Daley as an ally. Within one year she persuaded Daley to support a partnership between the CTU and two low-performing schools rather than reconstitution; that number grew to ten schools in three years. With Daley's blessing, she launched the first-ever master's degree in education leadership led by a union, her brainchild while at Quest, and got the mayor's backing for a successful legislative attempt to reinstate the union's legal right to bargain over the class size and tenure consequences of school sanctions.[219] By 2003 it appeared that she enjoyed some of the long-term success of the Progressive era unionists: tempering the excesses of managerialism with a heavy dose of teacher professionalism.

But two new events threw the school system into further uncertainty. First, the Civic Committee, now led by a new group of executives, excoriated the system as a "virtual monopoly." Citing the mayor's "avoiding [of] labor discord and maintaining the political support for teachers" as one of the reasons the school system was "radically dysfunctional,"[220] the executives disavowed any responsibility, claiming that "in the past . . . every idea for reform came from the central district office."[221] Professing a new concern for the performance gap between low-income and middle-class students (test-score comparisons showed that ITBS gains had not translated into improvements on the Illinois Standard Achievement Test), their new prescription unequivocally embraced untried market strategies. They demanded that the mayor close the bottom fifth of schools entirely, reopening them as charter schools or contract schools or, if necessary, adopting a voucher system; they also strengthened their calls for incentive pay. Then they stripped LQE of its school portfolio and created a new organization to represent their interests: New Schools for Chicago. In 2004 Daley acquiesced, on the condition that a business entity raise one-third of the seed money for Renaissance 2010.[222]

That same summer, Lynch lost the CTU leadership in a runoff election following a bitter battle with Reese's UPC faction, a contest filled with allegations of voter fraud. Her African American challenger promised to return to "bread and butter" bargaining and focus on "member services," demonstrating those commitments by summarily firing the Quest Center director and those who had been in charge of Lynch's signature "partnership" schools.[223] Thus, for the Chicago public schools, the twentieth century ended as contentiously as it had begun.

CORPORATIST POLITICS AT CENTURY'S CLOSE

The twentieth century's last decade saw a resurgence of corporate activism in education, but without the multisector coalition of the 1980s. As before, a shift in national politics provided an unexpected opening; the 1994 Republican invitation to remake Chicago's schools would have been unthinkable a few years earlier. Yet corporate leaders had advanced their reform ideas long before and were fully prepared to take advantage of such an opportunity. They swayed legislators, academics, and even some grassroots activists by claiming that the city's economic future was at stake, a belief they shared with Richard M. Daley.[224]

After securing his electoral coalition by outmaneuvering rivals in the city council, constructing a reliable voting bloc of Latinos and whites, and assuring the outcome of future contests by making citywide elections nonpartisan, Daley was free to assemble a separate governing coalition. In contrast to Harold Washington's focus on job creation and skills development for low-income citizens, Daley aimed to please the city's corporate leaders and attract a tax-paying middle class. His city would be measured by physical growth: an expanded downtown with gentrified housing replacing high-rise projects, dozens of beautification initiatives to attract conventions and tourists, and the largest school building agenda since his father's era. Daley also privatized city services and "reinvented" government through large corporate contracts that reproduced his father's pinstripe patronage.

There were risks in this strategy. Daley financed the construction and guaranteed wage hikes for teachers through a combination of noncorporate property taxes and long-term debt, leavened by one-time grants from Washington, D.C., and Springfield. Both forms of financing require growth in real estate values and residents' incomes. Middle-class residents may be willing to pay high property taxes and patronize city services, but they have never formed a cohesive bloc and have always been willing to leave the city if disappointed. For Daley, containing these risks meant relying on his corporate patrons, even when he disagreed with their advice.

Thus dependent on city growth and free of countervailing interests in his governing coalition, Daley has become the quintessential corporatist mayor. Business leaders, confident of his stability in city hall, have returned the compliment by aiding his campaigns and bolstering his reputation.[225] Regarding school reform, his primary challenge has been to bridge the different factions within the corporate sector; pleasing one has not always satisfied the other.

For most of the twentieth century the Commercial Club and its allied associations trusted management techniques to improve the schools. In 1995 club leaders' long-standing vision of the mayor as the chairman of the school board and a noneducator as schools CEO finally became law. In keeping with previous efforts to restructure decision making, the mayor and the CEO were given the management tools that corporate executives take for granted: the ability to reward or sanction performance, the unlimited authority to outsource, and the fiscal flexibility to emphasize some services or clients over others. Notwithstanding claims of originality, mayoral control as envisioned in Chicago was the culmination of prescriptions for managerial reform that club leaders had been developing for more than a hundred years.

In contrast, the Roundtable, the IMA, and statewide chamber leaders have supported a series of competitive markets—for education workers, school operators, and vendors. This business faction has consistently lacked confidence in restructuring; for members of this group, mayoral control is only a small step in the right direction. Without competition, they reason, there is no incentive for highly qualified people to enter and remain in the teaching force, no incentive for students to perform well, and none for the schools to be run efficiently. Stock price increases that accrue to businesses in unfettered markets have a corollary in schooling: test scores will rise by virtue of competitive forces, thus increasing the value of education. Crucial to such market success are deregulation, tangible incentives, and a workforce freed of tenure and collective bargaining. This perspective also dates to the Progressive era, when it was first championed by the IMA. In the course of convincing Daley to privatize 100 of the system's lowest-performing schools in 2004, Civic Committee leaders were also claiming the first victory in a century-long dispute among executives over the proper business model for school reform.

Such policy debates, however, have been minor compared to the class distinctions dividing corporate leaders from their former reform partners. White and Latino activists achieved the power to change their neighborhood schools in 1988, and by the 1990s they were members of Daley's electoral coalition. But they were of less value to him in terms of governing. Each activist group was left to compete for small, often symbolic, benefits: a mayoral appointment, a new elementary school to ease overcrowding, waivers for their children from the accountability sanctions, a few new principals. Community activists' influence on the 1995 law was negligible, and their efforts since then have been mainly defensive.

The coalition between community activists and corporate leaders that created the 1988 law could not survive its implementation. The overwhelming civic resources needed to sustain decentralization taxed even Chicago's generous foundations and energetic volunteers. Reform's political champion was replaced by a mayor with very different interests. Coalition partners could not bridge the gap between themselves and the city's alienated educators or its middle-class blacks. Although some important new civic resources were created—new forms of journalism and independent research institutions helped make this era's reforms the most well documented in a century—the absence of committed leadership, a dearth of dedicated government funding, and the failure to ally with educators doomed the decentralization movement.

Nevertheless, two separate groups proposed alternatives in the 1990s, each garnering significant financial and organizational support. The CAC might have sheltered LSC governance from corporate-style mayoral control and extended it to the classroom, where a progressive community-based pedagogy might have been created. In adopting the controversial Quest agenda that designated teachers the creators of instructional routines, the CTU under Deborah Lynch might have rooted student improvements in educators' expertise. It certainly pointed to a neo-progressive union activism not seen since the earlier era.

But the CTU and the CAC were wary of each other, perhaps because the city's long-standing racial mistrust had been reconceived in 1988 as antagonism between educators and parents. Neither organization seemed to realize that, without the other, it would be nearly impossible to overcome the corporate leaders' inordinate influence on city hall. Nor did they recognize that their substantive agendas depended on the support of the other organization's constituents.

Meanwhile, CEO Paul Vallas, who remained uncommitted to any specific vision of teaching and learning, translated his executive authority into top-down, irreversible decisions. Everyone in the school system was punished when performance targets were not met, and schools suffered a loss of autonomy until performance improved. In the process, educators' expertise was discredited as outdated orthodoxy, replaced with the intuition of politicians, management consultants, academics, advocates, community organizers, and vendors. Even classroom routines became scripted lessons accompanied by improvised, uncoordinated, and sometimes mandated experimental programs. The reliance on accountability sanctions furthered the dismantling of educators' professional career ladders begun in 1988, when principals were reclassified as fixed-term LSC appointees; after 1995 they were also subject to the wishes of the mayor's appointees. Teachers lost tenure if too many of their students failed tests. Consequently, the incentives to work with poorly performing students or schools were weakened, and many teachers and principals embraced scripted lesson plans and mandates, however flawed, as an antidote to failure. By the beginning of the new century, the district was devoting more of its resources than ever before to regulating educators' behavior.

Tensions between the corporate leaders' two versions of reform have also led to significant incoherence in implementation. CEO Vallas won acclaim for balancing the district budget, while Daley let contracts to local firms, raised property taxes, and grappled with deficits as the economy turned down. Vallas insisted on a scripted curriculum and uniform sanctions, earning him approval from some corporate leaders, while Daley supported entrepreneurial charter schools sought by others. Vallas's successor, Arne Duncan, has faced the dual challenges of superseding a commanding CEO with a long shadow and withstanding pressure to adjust policies in the face of legal, moral, and pedagogical objections.

Another round of corporate-led reform appears at the ready in the early twenty-first century. Ironically, corporate leaders apparently do not recognize their own part in the reforms they now judge to be failures, justifying their next reform as if it were an uncommon investment of corporate energy in improving the schools. In any case, Chicago's business executives will be difficult to deny. They have inherited an unmatched capacity to influence school policy, perfected by their predecessors for more than a century.

Notwithstanding successive waves of managerial improvements, persistent attention to cost cutting, and increased reliance on standardized tests, Chicago's schools remain neither fiscally self-sustaining nor high performing. Policies to increase discipline and accountability mask the fact that private providers routinely receive much less scrutiny than do students and educators.[226] Gaps between the majority of low-income African American and Latino students and others—only recently acknowledged by business—are more salient today than ever before. For these reasons, and because one of the two main corporate approaches—competitive entrepreneurialism—has not yet had an impact, this era's reforms are likely unfinished.

If the immediate past is prologue and the political regime remains stable, much of the city's educational future will depend on which faction of corporate leaders is dominant. It is still possible, however, that a coalition absent since the Progressive era could be revived to temper the corporate leaders' reform demands. Alternatives with a broader appeal among Chicago's long-suffering students, parents, teachers, and residents remain options. Such counternarratives, though plausible, face high hurdles: educators and parents must overcome their mutual suspicion, including their reluctance to combine political forces. And, powerful civic leaders must admit the limits of their structural prescriptions for the failures of urban public schools.

5

Powering Reform

Corporate Influence, Civic Coalitions, and the Dynamics of Change

Whether acting in private or using the civic authority delegated to them by politicians, Chicago's executives have exercised enormous power over public education. For more than a century they have doggedly pursued greater systemwide efficiency and improved management, consistently arguing that public schooling should be considered part of the local economy. Yet, despite corporate activism, student performance has remained low. For decades Chicago students' average standardized test scores have ranked below national and, more recently, state averages, and only slightly more than half of the students entering secondary schools have graduated. The gap between black (and now Latino) students and whites remains nearly as large as when it first caught public attention; by some accounts, it is growing. Nor have corporate leaders' preferred management indicators risen. Budgetary shortfalls are routine, and costs continue to rise. The system remains dependent on a large cadre of administrators and still contends with unions.

Explaining this recurrent dynamic of strong influence and poor results involves an understanding of the sources of corporate power and the consistency across time of corporate agendas. In the first section of this chapter I characterize corporate influence as a self-reinforcing, path-dependent process. I then turn to two related questions: What might be a more effective strategy for bringing civic resources to school reform? Can the schools be reformed without corporate actors, powerful though they are?

THE NATURE OF CORPORATE INFLUENCE

Corporate Chicago has benefited from the influence enjoyed by all economic elites in capitalist democracies. Business executives decide where plants will be located, when technology will be substituted for human labor, and what constitutes "investment" in the future of any market. These and other independent economic decisions shape the mix of jobs and taxable assets available to support residents, small firms, and civic organizations that provide city services.[1] Furthermore, corporate leaders are not accountable to any political constituency; rather, politicians attend to *their* wishes. Mayors and city councils, governors and legislators court business executives because they fear losing jobs, contracts, and potential tax revenue to more pliant communities. The globalization of international markets only strengthens the credibility of such threats.[2]

The influence of Chicago's business associations is magnified by extraordinary longevity bolstered by cohesion based on cooperation rather than competition.[3] Progressive era corporate titans founded the Commercial Club and absorbed its rivals. By the Depression, club leaders agreed that having a unified public voice would strengthen their policy influence, so they established rules of secrecy and consensus decision making to contain disagreements. Later, consolidation meant prioritizing and coordinating their policy interests through the Civic Committee. Mandatory corporate dues and voluntary subscriptions gave club leaders substantial flexibility in pursuing their goals: paying for staff, academic policy advice, advocacy campaigns and, as a gesture of goodwill, occasionally supporting a community venture (see the appendix for details). Such organizational resources often shielded the club's activism from public scrutiny, encouraging other school reform actors to overlook or underestimate its influence.[4] At other times, club activities deepened the public's impression of an overwhelming corporate consensus.

A Self-Reinforcing Start

Power and resources are insufficient to make a difference in school policy; they must also be used. This book details the sustained involvement of Chicago's corporate elite, but it was not inevitable; the predisposition toward school reform was inherited from the Progressive era. Nineteenth-century executives believed that a properly organized public school system would improve the local economy through its training of future workers. Their own success in large corporations suggested that other large enterprises, like the public school system, could benefit from modern, business-tested management strategies. They also voiced an overriding concern for efficiency, practiced as cost containment in times of economic distress. The question is how these nineteenth-century purposes and justifications led to the long-term pattern of reform solutions and policy influence we see in contemporary Chicago.

Paul Pierson's synthesis of historical methods and political institutionalism frames my answer.[5] While the Commercial Club was becoming the voice of the city's corporate elite and unions were developing their strongest policy presence, the city's relatively loose collection of schools was also being organized into a system. This pivotal period, 1900 to 1930, was an era of weak governmental authority. Notwithstanding their board appointment and budgetary responsibilities, city politicians were distracted by near constant electioneering and paid little attention to the schools, except to use them for patronage and contracts. One-term mayors lacked consolidated power; their governing coalitions were barely formed before being disbanded. Multiterm mayors (and those elected after terms were extended to four years) assembled governing coalitions that depended on support from either the city's business elite or its unions.

The schools were more vulnerable to social than governmental pressure in this era. Instead of political battles contested by elected officials across party lines, the decisions that would guide the nascent school system for the next century were fought out between labor and capital, with other reform groups typically choosing sides. Coherent reform plans came from these two influential groups, both of which had the resources to assign full-time staff members to the task of developing and promoting their agendas. Business leaders had an edge in status and wealth; women, who accounted for most of the teaching staff, lacked full suffrage for much of the period, and their organizing efforts were dependent on union dues. But teachers were affiliated with vigorous industrial unions. Change prevailed when business leaders initiated it and when teachers unions and their labor allies did not oppose it. Overall, the unions had a moderating effect on corporate reform agendas.

The reform solutions adopted resembled the executives' agenda because it met the perceived needs of the time. Schools of the day were routinely criticized for their inability to "hold" students tempted by work in factories, for corruption, and for failing to meet the varied needs of immigrant children. Manual and vocational schooling was considered a sensible response to the temptations of wages and modernization, even if the curriculum and governance of the system were hotly debated. Managerial efficiency was also a widely accepted antidote to political boodling, since it promised to remove financial, construction, and land-use decisions from political discretion and put them in the hands of a professional bureaucracy. The dispute was over how closely this bureaucracy should be guided by the economic prospects of the city as determined by its bankers. And it was widely believed that a systematic and uniform approach to educational issues such as class size, ancillary school services, and teacher quality would facilitate the assimilation of large numbers of immigrant families. Disagreements centered on who should make such decisions: professional educators or school managers?

Although none of the business leaders' reform agendas were enacted without modification, the ideas they raised created ways of thinking about the schools that have persisted to the present. The Commercial Club was unable to enact a separate vocational school system under its control, but club members' efforts and counterarguments by unionists and others made the public more receptive to the idea of a vocational purpose for the existing schools. Both unionists and club members eventually agreed that *all* schools should accept responsibility for preparing factory, commercial, and scientific workers. Thus, club leaders in the Progressive era lost a reform battle but left a conceptual legacy for their successors.

When the Depression came, the economic reasoning of vocationalism was reversed. Club leaders proposed the controversial idea that the public schools be cut back because the economy had faltered. Unlike businesses forced to constrict labor expenses in a competitive marketplace, they argued, educators unfairly continued to earn the benefits of a system developed for flush times. Bankers convinced politicians that the schools were bankrupt from overspending and that only corporate leaders had the political independence and the fiscal discipline to contain costs. Having laid the conceptual groundwork, they constructed a supraboard to oversee finances, a strategy that was available for use again fifty years later. Corporate leaders' repeated ability to obtain the authority to control school finances clarifies that school vocationalization operates in two ways: business leaders expect taxes to subsidize the expense of developing labor skills during good times, and they demand severe cutbacks in school services when the economy turns down.

Less dramatic, but more complete, have been the Commercial Club's efforts to turn the public schools into a bureaucratic system. Recall that club members played a decisive role in the 1917 Otis law compromise, which set out the system's governing parameters based on a corporate model described in the Harper Commission's 1898 report. A corporate governance structure addressed corruption and patronage, at least in theory, giving it an edge over alternatives that seemed to embed school governance in city hall politics. On paper, the system adopted a functionally defined managerial hierarchy and replaced the political accountability of a large, ward-based school board with an elite-led, bureaucratically accountable hierarchy infused with gendered status differentiations. Teachers lost status to school managers and superintendents, but they were also safeguarded by tenure from the worst excesses of managerial control. Each of several constituencies, among them the mostly male principals and superintendents, the professors in schools of education who taught them, and the appointed school board members, developed a vested interest in the new system and vigorously defended it.

To appreciate the corporate influence, recall how the educator-led alternative fared. The democratically organized professional expression of teachers' expertise through teachers councils was only briefly tried, then abandoned for the rest of the century. When school governance was being reconsidered in the 1980s, adopting a similar educator-led arrangement was considered a dangerous realignment of authority, even though other AFT-affiliated unions were then promoting such models in Dade County, Florida, and Rochester, New York.[6]

Vocational purposes, efficiency criteria, and management orientations embedded in the structure of the system have created a form of path dependency—in Pierson's words, "social processes that exhibit positive feedback."[7] Once the initiating era passed, such self-reinforcing patterns of preference and access were no longer as dependent on logical argument, organizational learning, or the strength of rational evidence.

Business leaders inheriting the legacy of the Progressive era can declare the school system insolvent and earn the right to control the flow of funds, but they need not justify their claim with hard evidence or even past success at the same task. Chicago United could validate its career education reforms in the 1970s by conducting a survey of employers' opinions about high school graduates, even though there was strong evidence that these executives seldom hired anyone without a college diploma. Higher standardized test scores were accepted as indicators of the necessary job skills, even though no evidence was presented that high scores increased students' employment prospects or performance.

Similarly, a new generation of corporate executives has been able to persuade school critics that a retooled management structure (e.g., executive managers in place of education professionals, "reculturing" the bureaucracy, new job descriptions) will improve high-level decisions and therefore the schools, even if the link between management and classroom instruction remains unspecified. Or, they have simply argued that the system was woefully behind state-of-the-art management practices and needed updating. Since management practices change rapidly, this self-reinforcing pattern has produced many alterations in the district's decision-making structure, shifts within the various bureaucratic branches, and efforts to change teacher oversight schemes.

Since the Progressive era, the salience of such corporate arguments has depended on broad political and social acceptance, rather than on their objective merits. The conceptual choices for improvement became narrower over time as politicians, school leaders, and even some community-based reformers grew increasingly invested in the businesslike institutional arrangements negotiated in the earlier period. Newly trained superintendents identified themselves as managers and helped legitimate corporate definitions of school problems and solutions. Successive iterations of management tinkering gave superintendents higher status and more control over their increasingly specialized domains, instilling a shared commitment to the maintenance of narrow bureaucratic definitions of responsibility. Superintendents such as Cooley, Hunt, and Willis flaunted their Commercial Club affiliations with reason. Successive mayors, from Cermak through Daley, have likewise vied to prove their management bona fides.

Even community-based and union reformers found it useful to adopt the rhetoric of managerialism: the muckraking Citizen's Schools Committee and the National Education Association both agreed that corruption and Depression-era cutbacks could be remedied by selecting the right CEO. Decades later, reformers translated the calls for political decentralization and community control as "restructuring." And in 2000, union leader Deborah Lynch claimed a kinship to the latest management techniques in automobile manufacturing to justify teacher empowerment.[8]

The very complexity of education—its multiple goals and the many demands on it from different constituents—has the counterintuitive effect of reinforcing, rather than undermining, managerial solutions to school problems. As political and bureaucratic decision makers filter information to fit their preconceptions, they stick to known strategies perceived to entail little risk.[9] This has meant that various versions of efficiency, hierarchy, and control are prime candidates for school reform agendas; they seem to take advantage of modern technologies and do not challenge the basic structure of the system. Seen in this way, Chicago United's 253-point management audit of 1981 did not threaten to reinvent the school system, as business leaders claimed, but actually reinforced the familiar pattern of managerial tinkering: move some employees from a certain manager's span of control, collect and report data in a new way, redefine some job descriptions.

Hardwired into the new institution were not only business ideas and orientations but also corporate *access,* because corporate leaders first used their power when political authority was highly dependent on social acceptance, well before Chicago had a consolidated machine. Instead of providing political resistance to business leaders' reform plans, most Progressive era mayors acquiesced, and many embraced the corporate executives' education agenda as their own.

After the Progressive era, corporate leaders held a legitimate place in educational debates apart from any solution they offered. If schools were to develop future workers, then employers should be consulted on the technical skills to be emphasized, the appropriate teaching methods, and the proper assessments of graduates expected to enter the labor force. If the schools were criticized for failing to properly manage their finances, politicians took special notice of financial executives' recommendations. If principals were perceived as poorly educated, corporate advice (and perhaps MBA training) was sought, even before it was offered. Guaranteed access to educational policy arenas no longer depended on executives' public visibility: Commercial Club leaders worked behind the scenes for much of the machine era but had little trouble asserting their influence.

Successive generations of CEOs would also remain credible critics—and their recommendations would be taken seriously—because they were believed to possess practical experience in similarly structured organizations. As the professionalization of management progressed, business school sages became secondary sources of corporate solutions for school problems. Reform through managerial adjustment based on corporate and business school advice became routine.[10]

The characterization described here is not unique to Chicago. It has led to a particular political argument about the need for radical governance change. In this view, an "educational cartel" of education school professors, school administrators, and school board members keeps parents as well as other civic actors at bay, and it has forced schooling into a debilitating downward spiral. But if there is truth to the rigidity of these interrelated educational interests, as my research documents, Chicago's corporate leaders have been instrumental in sustaining it.

Strong Consequences, Poor Results

Corporate agendas have also affected how teaching is organized and how educators are chosen, evaluated, and rewarded. For example, the vocational education reform of the Commercial Club helped initiate a noticeable change in content (e.g., reflecting modern technological advances in the workplace) and teaching style (e.g., demonstration and learning by doing) and added new measures of school performance in the form of competency testing.[11] The consequences also affect children directly. In a revival of the club's economic rationale during the 1970s and 1980s, poor test scores were linked to job loss, a stance that has affected how all Chicago children are now promoted.

Much the same is true for corporate efforts to restructure school system management and rein in the system's budget. Managerial changes almost always meant that top school leaders lost their jobs and that the school board was reconfigured, but they also narrowed the criteria for determining school success to aggregated test scores well before the federal "No Child Left

Behind" law made this a national issue. Teachers have seen a similar narrowing in the scope of collective bargaining, while principals' business responsibilities have increased. Efficiency, instilled as a core value and tied to direct corporate oversight, also produced dramatic economic consequences for educators: payless paydays and cutbacks in wages, jobs, and school services. Protests notwithstanding, the cuts usually lingered, as did the sense that school system inefficiency was intractable. Yet the old reform agenda, with its abundance of unintended consequences, would be tried again and again.

The perceived utility of corporate solutions did not require that they actually solve the problems they addressed. By most measures of policy effectiveness—the extent to which the goals of a planned change have been met—the business reform agenda has had a poor record. Vocationalization as well as managerial and efficiency changes have repeatedly failed to provide the economic stability and student performance improvements that business leaders claim are their ultimate objectives.

Data are scant from the early years of the twentieth century, but the evidence suggests that vocational experiments did not keep students in school, prepare demonstrably better workers for the economy, or forestall economic decline. Rather, it seems that students in the few strictly vocational schools and programs were routinely shunted into workplace preparation activities that were poorly matched to available jobs.[12] Poor results were so apparent by the 1980s that Harold Washington sought guaranteed jobs for high school graduates, asking corporate executives to put their money where their reforms were—a request they quickly declined.

Historical evidence also shows that managerial changes did little to deter the corruption and bureaucratic obfuscation that resulted in censure by accrediting associations. For decades, patronage employment and corruption appeared to be tolerated, despite managerial reforms. Corporate efforts to manage the school system's finances in the 1930s were also a demonstrable failure; the Sargent Committee was never able to come up with a sustainable balanced-budget formula or operate high-quality schools with the available funding, while politicians and tax dodgers were let off the hook.

Systematic data have been rigorously collected only since the 1980s, but they point to problems unabated by the executives' solutions, despite typically laudatory initial reports. For example, the Commercial Club emphasized decentralizing management to the school site in its 1981 and 1987 reports but backtracked in 1994, when a new configuration of corporate actors roundly criticized the results in their analyses to the Illinois legislature. After switching the system to a centralized and highly top-down management structure in 1995, corporate leaders changed course once again, with an equally stinging rebuke of the system's flaws in order to promote a more market-oriented management of the schools.

By insisting on a School Finance Authority (SFA) in 1979, club members stalled desegregation and democratic reforms and created a new round of unintended consequences, including the loss of institutional memory in the central office and experienced teachers taking early retirement. Yet, after fifteen years of SFA budgetary oversight, the school system remained in financial turmoil, despite protestations to the contrary, and business leaders were unable to balance the budget without the mayor's assistance. Continuing through the period of mayoral control, when direct corporate oversight was disbanded in favor of indirect guidance, budgetary efficiency has remained elusive.

But perhaps the most serious failing of corporate reform agendas lies in their indirect, even tangential, approach to teaching and learning. Because their generalized models of market production say little about how any particular product should be created or any service delivered—leaving such decisions to the production managers—they are dependent on educators to make substantive decisions about the curriculum, models of instruction, use of time, recipients of ancillary services, and much more. Such tasks cannot be precisely specified without knowing the students, so teachers must fill in the gaps. Yet educators are the very employees that corporate reformers most mistrust. This leaves executives with the classic principal-agent problem: how do they provide guidance that will steer behavior in the direction of their goals when they do not understand the processes involved?

Corporate reformers who have put their faith in management resolve this problem by adopting generic techniques of coordination and control; they use internal hierarchies and bureaucratic rules to monitor the incentives and rewards that shape teachers' behavior. In the heyday of Frederick Winslow Taylor's scientific management mind-set, when the keys to productivity appeared to be a function of time and effort, Chicago's corporate reformers argued for forty-three students in every class as an efficient performance target. Merit pay was to be reserved for those who could produce learning under such circumstances. About fifty years later, after W. Edward Deming and other management gurus developed motivational theories—acknowledging that properly motivated employees could figure out the work processes—executives adopted school reform prescriptions that emphasized outcome-based performance targets, incentives, and rewards. Educators were free to determine instructional routines, but they would be guided by clear production targets and, depending on the results, either rewarded with autonomy or sanctioned by a loss of decision-making authority.[13]

Recently, market-oriented reformers have adopted an even more hands-off approach. They trust competition to spur innovation, some of which they expect to be an improvement. Consumer choice provides the incentive for moving in the right direction. The quality-control information that consumers need is to be coded in a few statistical indicators that distinguish good schools from bad. The success of these corporate reformers is dependent on the adults who establish and maintain schools, although many of them are undoubtedly the very educators whose behavior requires reform. The reformers' faith, however, lies in the market itself rather than in any of its participants, some of whom will be corrupt, incompetent, or overreaching. The education market is expected to weed out the undesirables over the long run.

Thus, for all the sophisticated imagery, corporate leaders' reform agendas are guided by neither students' needs nor the processes of teaching and learning. Children are seldom mentioned. When the curriculum becomes scripted as a way to sanction educators in low-performing schools, its effects on students are a secondary concern. As many have noted, the attention that such reform schemes put on a few aggregate outcome indicators distorts teachers' practices in unknown and sometimes perverse ways and can lead to outright cheating.[14] Equity becomes a relative goal, construed as the statistical reflection of how one group of students compares with another. It is dependent in equal measure on how students are classified and what unknown resources and services they receive. Historical injustice and institutionalized disadvantages are of little concern. This oblique approach to the core work of teaching and learning bears much responsibility for the performance failures documented throughout the preceding chapters.

Yet corporate executives virtually never blame their own solutions for the outcomes produced. Instead, they argue that rampant corruption kept their rational ideas at bay, educators did not faithfully implement their changes, or educator and parent resistance undermined any chance of effectiveness. But such protestations cannot excuse a century of poor results.

This paradox lies at the heart of the Chicago story, and raises questions seldom considered in school reform. If corporate influence has a poor achievement record in the schools, despite its power and consistency, what are the alternatives? And, given business executives' deeply institutionalized legitimacy as reform actors, is reform without them feasible in the twenty-first century?

CIVIC COALITIONS AND REFORM

Even if persistent reform agendas backed by powerful corporate actors have yielded poor results, it is easy to overlook the alternatives. Some observers are so eager to see evidence of renewal that they conflate difference with improvement. Others insist that reformers have been correct in their prescriptions; the education cartel's resistance is to blame for any implementation failure. Still others invoke a systemic critique: something must be perverse in the institution of urban schooling if reforms do not stick; perhaps it is too democratic, too bureaucratic, or both. Yet another view is skeptical about reformers' real commitments. All these answers conflate many agendas and ignore the differential politics of reform that underlies them. But before I propose a method of analyzing reform agendas and coalitions, and therefore a way to examine the alternatives, I return to the premises of regime analysis that began this study.

Urban Regime Analysis Applied to Chicago Schooling

As was presented in the introduction, school reform requires political cultivation: building coalitions, finding resources, and sustaining political momentum. As Clarence Stone and other regime theorists have explained, every viable agenda for urban school system reform depends on a coalition of individuals and groups to develop ideas and press for their acceptance by government authorities. That coalition must also amass sufficient civic resources to sustain the initiative's implementation, sometimes with insufficient government aid. Successful reformers widely promote their ideas and seek partners with complementary resources. At least some of any coalition's resources must be spent on sustaining the coalition itself. Chicago's history illuminates these prescriptions.

Stone and colleagues predict that coalitions will be agenda specific—each requiring a particular configuration of technical expertise, logistical support, organizational capacity, inspiration, and sanctioning authority. Reform coalitions are also dependent on local history and not transferable. Most aspects of agenda specificity are supported by Chicago's school reform history. Corporate executives relied on the competency of donated business managers and their own professional staff in crafting their managerial agendas; their inspiration came from management gurus and macroeconomists. The requisite organizational capacity and logistical support lay within their own business associations. They preferred for city hall allies to sanction their authority— Chicago's mayors have influenced *how* corporate leaders engage in school reform more than *what* they advocate—but when Chicago politicians proved unreliable partners, they sought state allies. And other civic actors who joined them on one issue were unlikely to be partners on the next. Agenda specificity also suggests that corporate leaders would be amenable to joining reform coalitions formed by other civic actors—if not unions, then good-government groups or civil rights activists—but in Chicago, corporate executives almost never supported others' reform ideas.

Yet another distinguishing feature of regime analysis has been the emphasis on partnerships between public and private actors, countering commonsense notions that government insiders are the most prevalent, or even the only, reformers.[15] If anything, Chicago's reform history highlights civic actors' influence; there are remarkably few instances of sustained systemwide change initiated by school boards, superintendents, or educators. For the most part, reform has been an outside activity: conceptualized by coalitions of civic actors, legally imposed on reluctant educators or more directly mandated through uncommon governing institutions such as the SFA, and requiring massive doses of external advice to be sustained. Even so, government actors were always needed to authorize laws and new institutions, raise and allocate tax dollars, and adapt credentialing requirements to the reformers' criteria.

Chicago's reform history confirms another regime analysis premise: core constituents create the agenda and bring essential resources to the project, but other individuals and groups are needed for implementation. Specifically, Stone and colleagues argue that teachers, by virtue of their role in implementation, must be part of the agenda-setting coalition. In this regard I part company with the regime theorists: Chicago's corporate executives clearly regard teachers as workers who lack the "big-picture" perspective of managers and whose activities are to be constrained and guided by incentives. Furthermore, teachers' behavior and their beliefs about students' capabilities are defined as part of the problem to be solved. Such beliefs are reflected in the alliances avoided: virtually every corporate-led reform effort is notable for the absence of teacher influence.

Regime analysis recognizes that coalition members are unequal in the resources they control, but it also insists that those with fewer resources can have their positions considered in a reform coalition. If this were not true, a coalition would be a stand-in for sectoral interests. Too frequently, sectoral interests did guide Chicago's business actors; their coalitions were narrow and aimed at fostering a *business* consensus. But it is also true that a skillful politician or strong opposition could balance corporate advantages. Harold Washington opened up the summit, allowing Latino parents and professional reform groups to modify the corporate agenda, even moving executives in directions that they found unpromising. For example, local school council (LSC) voting would not have been open to noncitizens if Latinos had not been part of the coalition. The strident opposition of the Chicago Teachers Federation (CTF) to the corporate agenda in the Progressive era also forced businessmen to cultivate nonbusiness partners, resulting in a moderated form of managerialism that reinstated tenure and left the door open to collective bargaining.

Perhaps it is obvious that reform agendas are entwined with the coalitions that create and sustain them and that they embody many desires, including accountability assumptions and essential expectations for human relationships. Even so, I underscore this point to unseat the presumption that viable reform agendas arise full blown from partisan think tanks or policy papers. Certainly in Chicago they have been forged in the political cauldron of contention and compromise, the result of messy and unpredictable work that does not always permit logical consistency or moral certainty. Reform has made for uncomfortable, if strategic, partnerships, such as when Margaret Haley's CTF partnered with Big Bill Thompson's school board to sustain teachers councils, or when the Commercial Club backed a succession of racially segregating machine mayors in support of the top-down hierarchy that it thought best for the schools.

The Chicago case also demonstrates that reform coalitions depend on leaders to assemble them, broker compromises when needed, and keep members from losing interest. Although reform can be catalyzed by an unexpected infusion of foundation funding, an economic downturn that affects jobs, or a crisis such as a race riot, some civic or governmental leader must tackle the problems that the external stimulus brought to the fore. In Chicago these individuals have most often been civic leaders: business executives such as Theodore Robinson, Thomas Ayers, Warren Bacon, or Ron Gidwitz; civil rights leaders such as Al Raby; democracy advocates such as Jane Addams, Anita Blaine, or Don Moore; and even unionists such as Margaret Haley, John Kotsakis, and Deborah Lynch. I have already mentioned Harold Washington's politically savvy school reform leadership. Rich Daley, thrust into the role by downstate Republicans with little to lose, has also been a school reform leader, staunchly supporting the business coalition that installed him and funding the school programs that followed. His ambivalence about the reform agenda inspired by Washington is additional testimony that sustained leadership is critical to any reform coalition.

Adapting Regime Analysis to Multiple Agendas

Since every reform must have a viable agenda and a supportive coalition, one way to understand the reform process is to trace the origins and interactions of its animating ideas and political actors. The four preceding chapters approached Chicago's school reform history as narrative. Here, I mine Chicago's story to reveal a series of coalitions and reform agendas that were passed up and the alternative sources of political influence that were available but not used.

Chicago's history suggests three types of reform agendas—market, empowerment, and performance agendas—each with its own distinctive coalitional requirements. Combining the requirements of coalition building and maintenance with the three types of reform agendas creates a typology of possible urban school governing regimes that expands on regime analysis. It more accurately aligns the politics of coalition building with the way reform was conceptualized and pursued in Chicago than does a binary view of reform pitted against the status quo. Exploring the connection between differing reform agendas and their sustaining coalitions also reveals some of the political constraints on each, helping to clarify why some are more difficult to mount or sustain than others.

Table 1 identifies several types of reform agendas pursued in Chicago over the twentieth century, types that are also supported by the literature on school reform.[16] It abstracts a relationship between the politics of coalition building and the development of reform agendas, postulating some of the resources needed to enable and instantiate each agenda as the motivating idea in a school system.

As conceptualized here, every reform aims at one of three broad types of school governing regimes. Conversely, if any one agenda were to be systematically institutionalized, it would create a specific school governing regime. Over the long run, every school governing regime aims to improve one or more public education functions (e.g., social equity, democratic participation, employment efficiency, family choice) while raising student performance, usually measured by test scores, grades, or graduation.[17] I do not distinguish regimes, however, by an ascription of core values or functions. In practice, such long-term goals give way to distinct accountability concerns and indicators.

The three activist regimes are conceptualizations grounded in empirical research on Chicago's reform history, not a comprehensive set of school governing options. They are intended to encourage speculation about how reform agendas and political coalitions interact to create the institutions that currently guide urban school systems and to engender critical reflection that might lead to more promising reforms.

For contrast, I also included the characteristics of an employment regime in Table 1. Stone's conception is adapted here to clarify the opposition or passive resistance that any reform can face from educators; but I also stress the useful buffering role that this opposition can play.

Employment Regimes

Stone and colleagues describe the *employment regime* as intentionally maintaining stable employment opportunities for adults, almost always at the expense of children. In doing so, they create a dualism between reform and the status quo.

An employment regime places undeniable barriers in the way of reformers. Accustomed to bureaucratic accountability, whereby they account for their

Table 1. Four Types of Governing Regimes and Their Coalitions of Political Support

Activist Regimes	Agenda	Accountability	Core and Secondary Constituents	Essential Resources	Essential Relationships
Performance regime	Change the pedagogy and the culture of schools	Professional, possibly moral	Teachers and parents and elected or appointed officials; *professors and researchers*	Teacher and parent commitment, educator technical expertise, intergroup mediation, political legitimacy, funding	Trust between parents and educators across class, race, and ethnic lines
Empowerment regime	Authorize new decision makers to enable better and unprecedented decisions	Political, possibly moral	New decision makers (e.g., parents, teachers, or elites), elected or appointed officials, and complementary interest groups; *professors and researchers*	Implementation by new governors, cohesive group representation, social stability, political legitimacy, redistribution of benefits	Agreement among interest groups to divide decision arenas and share decision making
Market regime	Restructure schooling for efficiency and accountability (corporate) or competition and choice (entrepreneurial)	Market	Business elites and political allies, plus parents, if entrepreneurial; *professors and researchers*	United market-sector approval and financing, relaxed regulations, political legitimacy, public investment in new markets	Consumer and producer roles mediated by contracts and regulations
Employment regime	Buffer existing system from political interference; resist change and stabilize system	Bureaucratic	Teachers, administrators, and school board members; *professors and researchers*	Organized educational groups in mutual support of current distribution of material benefits, habits and shared beliefs	Solidarity among professionals, and skepticism about change

Secondary constituents set in italic.

behavior only to superiors, school employees accept many failings, justifying them as the way things are. Educators often act as if their continuing, unaltered employment is best for children; evidence to the contrary is blamed on intractable class and cultural differences that no other social institution tackles and, often, on insufficient funding. To the extent that educators are dependent on schools of education for credentialing and advancement, professors support their defenses with empirical research and theoretical arguments. School board members, no matter how idealistic, eventually realize that their reputations hinge on changes that they are powerless to effect, and they too learn to make excuses. Because schools are embedded in a network of textbook and test publishers, consultants and research firms, these groups are also potential employment regime supporters; they are invested in the system and in its existing employment opportunities. Unions are presumed to be uniquely perverse; their purpose is to protect teachers' jobs.

A more balanced picture of reform resistance acknowledges the salutary as well as harmful effects. An employment regime contains what all education reformers ultimately seek: the institutionalization of their values and preferred behaviors into the everyday activities of those working in schools—a change in material interests as well as relationships. In this sense, although employment regimes present obstacles to be overcome, they also represent the long periods of stability between waves of school reform. Those employees who resist reform have developed the habits and accepted the institutions realized by the previous successful reform coalition.

Thus, a successful reform alters the relationships among the adults involved in education, the institutions of governance, and the ways that schools function and are rewarded, but it does not change the political mechanisms that ensure long-term stability. I described earlier how managerialism initiated in the Progressive era and subsequently promoted by an activist corporate elite and sympathetic politicians has governed the system for more than 100 years. As managerialism became accepted and institutionalized, it altered the material interests, beliefs, and expectations of all those delivering school services, including private providers, teachers, unions, administrators, school board members, and professors. By the time Ben Willis was criticized for resisting another reform coalition, he was already presiding over a system in which bureaucracy, vocationally sanctioned sorting, and efficiency were assumed to be institutionally sanctioned defenses against inequality. The system as a whole seemed impervious to all but managerial tinkering.

Assume, hypothetically, that a different coalition of reformers had been successful in instituting its agenda. Perhaps the winning coalition would include educators who were part of a broad union movement and ethnic groups with close, patronage-like relationships to a mayor authorized to hire employees. Schools of social work and sociology might then replace business schools as sources of ideas for education professors. Teachers councils and citizen inspectors could displace the appointed board of education. Business associations might supplant union strength as a political counterweight. The material interests and core beliefs of these unionists and ethnic groups would be no less strongly defended than those of the current teachers, professors, superintendents, or boards of education. Nor would the reformers who initiated the changes want it otherwise.

If employment regimes are both the residue of previously successful reformers and the biggest obstacles to new ones, how are the reform options and their supporting coalitions to be understood?

Market Regimes

Market agendas for reform come in two types, corresponding to the divisions among Chicago's corporate leaders. One agenda would improve schooling through better management, steering the behavior of educators and students alike through altered hierarchies and by various coordination and control mechanisms. The *corporate market* model mimics the business school approach to corporate improvement, borrowing new management techniques from the corporate gurus. Although they routinely claim to be seeking radical change, its proponents make essentially incremental changes to an existing model created in the Progressive era and reinforced thereafter. Their retooling of the existing regime partly explains why their reforms are so well received.

The second market agenda imagines that competition and choice will improve schooling even as it forces school systems to be reconfigured as markets with open access to educational suppliers and few barriers to client mobility. Adherents of this *entrepreneurial market* model believe that competition and choice will inexorably force bad schools to close their doors and good ones to proliferate, decreasing the demand for poor teachers and increasing it for good ones. Entrepreneurial reformers require comprehensive changes in the governance structure, institutions, and resource flows between public schools and the private sector.

Although it may not be obvious to all observers, these two views of market reform overlap. The same business actors have sought corporate and entrepreneurial reform agendas at different times, debating only which one would be more efficacious at the moment. They share a common economic perspective on the problems of urban schools, and all market-oriented reformers require educators to take responsibility for meeting targeted outcome goals measured by a small set of indicators—the educational corollaries of profits and stock prices. Those embracing entrepreneurial agendas want additional forms of market accountability: indicators of supply and demand such as school enrollments, waiting lists, and parent satisfaction surveys. Those preferring corporate market agendas borrow additional forms of accountability from contractual language and the internal competition in high-powered firms. But both corporate and entrepreneurial market reformers, despite their differences, make consistent reference to markets as the source of the ideas uniting them. The two factions always agree that either a corporate or an entrepreneurial agenda is preferable to any other alternative.

Business leaders are the core constituents of market regimes for all the reasons just stated. In Chicago, these executives have generalized from their own experience as the leaders of large firms or government agencies, drawing analogies based on size (the school system is a $3 billion enterprise), complexity (half a million customers with different needs), and economic functionalism (educated students are the product, teachers are the workers, principals are the managers) to justify their proposed changes. They are also motivated to expand the market systems to which their material interests are linked.[18] Their active engagement includes calling on market-sector financial resources, but it also requires them to factor public schooling into the economic decisions they routinely make for cities.

Corporate executives must be joined by elected and appointed government officials who will support the use of some version of a revised market model as a legitimate alternative to the existing system. These officials are also needed to relax regulations blocking the privatization of school functions or the reengineering of school management. Without the active participation of Republican governors and legislators, the Commercial Club could not have effected the firing of tenured teachers, increased outsourcing in the system, or commingled categorical funds, all of which club members asserted as perquisites of the CEO. Educational elites—superintendents, professors of education, education pundits, and economists and management gurus—are useful secondary constituents because they provide the intellectual coherence for what might otherwise seem to be an overly risky reform strategy. In addition, these intellectuals provide different arguments to the two factions of market reformers, ensuring a steady debate between them.[19]

Entrepreneurial market regimes also require parents as a core constituent. Parents must trust educational entrepreneurs who are taking inherent market risks, be willing to enroll their children in start-up schools that may not prove viable or stable, and believe that unconventionally trained adults make good teachers. Most susceptible to entrepreneurial market arguments are those who feel permanently disenfranchised in government-run schools and can be convinced that a market of schools will provide them with the limited decision-making authority of a consumer. In cities this often means racial and ethnic minority parents. Yet entrepreneurial regimes also ask middle-class taxpayers to cushion the market risks for individual children. Perhaps for this reason, vouchers and charter schools first became popular in the prosperous 1990s, when new sources of public and private money became available. These innovations also frequently rely on foundation or corporate underwriting, as has recently occurred in Chicago.[20]

Corporate market regimes, in contrast, require few core constituents beyond corporate and political leaders. Therefore, there is much less cross-sector negotiation than in regimes seeking other reform agendas. Both business elites and politicians already have multiple resources to contribute. If these advocates are united and well organized, corporate market regimes can be relatively sustainable, since politicians attend to business leaders because they hold the keys to local economic development and corporate market agendas are predicated on a link to the local economy. For example, politicians are persuaded to go along with managerial agendas such as downsizing and outsourcing because reforming schools in the image of the corporation is one way that they can engage in the stiff competition for job-producing firms. If new jobs promise to increase the tax base or attract (and hold) the middle class, urban mayors find corporate demands nearly irresistible.

Neither teachers nor their unions are a core constituent of market reform regimes. We saw that teachers were opposed to the adoption of management techniques that limited their discretion as professionals in the Progressive era, even though they have since become members of the employment regime that sustains such techniques. Today, they resist reforms that rely on choice and competition just as much. But in order for market regimes to be founded, powerful unions need only be convinced not to oppose enabling legislation; their active support is unnecessary. Daley was aware of this when he bartered for union neutrality before the 1995 law passed, as were Commercial Club members in 1917 when they used the Loeb rule outlawing public-sector unions to gain CTF neutrality on the Otis law. Nevertheless, the institutionalization of either form of market regime can be hindered if it remains vulnerable to organized political opposition or demands from excluded groups.

Empowerment Regimes

Empowerment agendas are expected to spur experimentation by legally altering the background and characteristics of the authorized decision makers, rather than by specifying mechanisms such as competition or management upgrades, as market reformers would do. The new decision makers are trusted to make better choices; the content of their decisions is not prescribed. Decision arenas are divided among them through the construction of new institutions, but they are essentially expected to share authority. This view of reform rests on notions of political representation, but also on moral imperatives about the quality of public life, especially for the disenfranchised and underrepresented.[21]

Empowerment regimes alter the system's political, and possibly moral, accountability. Political authority—the federal and state laws that guide school governance, but also the ways local elected and appointed bodies interact—rests on the concept of responsiveness to local constituents. Political accountability assumes that these laws and governing bodies reflect that responsiveness. A regime designed by an empowerment coalition might measure the level and quality of participation at new decision-making forums, or measure the frequency and quality of decisions from new decision makers. It has a moral dimension when the institutions of accountability are designed to redress previous injustices.

Empowerment agendas come in several variants. Some are democratic in nature, assuming that everyone affected by schooling ought to help make decisions. Others are elitist, presupposing that only a select minority of individuals is capable of making good decisions about education. Democrats believe that decisions will be more effective and equitable if they are based on knowledge derived from a wide range of experiences, representing all constituents. They tend to add varied perspectives to governing bodies and increase the number of forums for debate (e.g., school councils, nominating commissions).[22] For elitists, multiple authorities with varying perspectives merely lead to confusion and indecision, which are especially onerous in times of crisis.[23]

Despite the long causal chain to improved performance, empowerment reform agendas are so common that political scientists and historians typically describe oscillation between political decentralization—in which previously disempowered constituencies are given some authority for educational decisions—and recentralization—in which that authority is taken away and reseated in some (often newly named) executive office such as a general superintendent, CEO, or mayor.[24] Much of the literature on the politics of education is devoted to arguing and researching the merits of the two.[25]

In Chicago, democratic empowerment of parents and community members goes back to the Harper Commission's recommendation that "resident commissioners" represent various communities as lay inspectors. It also includes the CTU's effort to obtain an elected board of education in the Progressive era. Civil rights demands in the 1960s and 1970s represent that era's democratic empowerment; Al Raby's call for community control of black schools, the Urban League's efforts to put more blacks on the board and in other authoritative positions, and Superintendent Joseph Hannon's creation of subdistrict councils are all examples.[26] The most recent manifestation is the concept of LSCs, developed in the mid-1970s and enacted in 1988 as a form of site-based management emphasizing parent empowerment. That LSCs were not disbanded with recentralization in 1995 is testament to the continuing attraction of the empowerment argument and to the democratic ideal underpinning it.[27]

Democratic teacher empowerment also has a long history in Chicago. The Harper Commission's embrace of teachers councils and Ella Flagg Young's subsequent attempt to institutionalize them are Progressive era examples. The ill-fated suggestion that the CTU consider advocating shared decision making in 1988 is another.[28] Efforts by the CTU's Deborah Lynch to comanage schools with the district and to replace Professional Personnel *Advisory* Committees with Professional Personnel *Leadership* Committees are recent examples.

Teacher empowerment is not the same as bureaucratic devolution of authority to the shop floor. When teachers are empowered as governors, they make decisions that affect their own work as well as the work of other educators in different schools. They help set policy agendas, create cross-professional deliberative opportunities, and may also help overcome the trust deficit between educators and the public.

Elite empowerment agendas are harder to find; when elites are empowered, they tend to be corporate leaders whose market agenda is the justification for their new authority. But examples include the elite—but not business-dominated—board of education appointed by reform mayor Edward Dunne and the Chicago Annenberg Challenge (CAC) board, both of which were made up of well-known school reform activists, social advocates, and foundation executives.[29] The empowerment of professors and consultants as arbiters of school performance, as Anthony Bryk's proposed inspectorate would have done, is another example.

The core constituents of empowerment regimes include those groups that represent the newly authorized decision makers. Their indifference or mere acquiescence is insufficient. If reformers authorize a governance role for parents, both parents and the community-based organizations that represent them must actively support the changes. Parents may be less easily convinced to accept their own empowerment, partly because the groups speaking for them are many and fragmented. Governing a school that one's own child attends has obvious attractions, but control over the schooling of others' children is another matter.[30]

Union-organized teachers can be encouraged to support their own empowerment when it advances both their material interests and collaborative decision making. But if reformers hope to sustain teacher empowerment, they must have the active support of teachers and the resources of their unions, a lesson recently learned by Deborah Lynch.[31] Similarly, if reform empowers a city's social and professional elite to govern schools, they must be unified behind the effort and proffer their time and professional resources, a Rubicon that few elite empowerment efforts have crossed.

Also needed is political approval. Even with formal authorization, however, new decision makers are susceptible to legal and moral challenges, including favoritism, corruption, and incompetence, especially from those whose authority is being reduced. Groups seeking greater decision-making power need a range of coalition partners both inside and outside government to buffer them from such criticism. Professional and intellectual elites can provide the social support and moral suasion needed when low-ranking professionals are empowered, as the CTF and Ella Flagg Young did for teachers councils. Similarly, grassroots groups can provide credibility to elites seeking formal authority as educational governors, as when black activists reluctantly agreed to accept Chicago United's leadership in the civil rights era. Educational elites are useful, if secondary, constituents because they provide the intellectual coherence for what will be construed as either a centralization or a decentralization from existing practice.

If the school system's legitimacy has fallen low enough to harm the image of the entire city—not uncommon in urban districts—politicians and civic elites, including business leaders, may be inclined to support a reorganization of school decision making and the possible redistribution of political benefits. This is especially true if they judge a new empowerment regime to be capable of relegitimizing the schools and enhancing the city's image or its development prospects and do not see negative implications for the city's image or class relations. But politicians are likely to change their minds if they become wary of spillover political competition from an empowered teachers union or parents group. They may step back, too, when party dominance, main street–city hall alliances, or race relations threaten to become destabilized, all concerns that Daley faced during the civil rights era.

Empowerment regimes have a mixed record on student performance, as the experiments with LSC governance in 1988 demonstrated.[32] Patterns of change are not easily attributable to the new governance arrangements; the causes are hotly debated and seldom settled. Only a few researchers, such as Bryk, have attempted to trace the pathways from empowerment to performance.[33] Nor are equity problems solved by localism alone. Chicago saw instances of LSCs that were dysfunctional because of internal conflict, with educators using their professional status to reassert control in some cases.[34]

Many parents simply abandoned the effort. Teacher governance has had less opportunity to demonstrate effectiveness; teachers councils lasted only a few short years, and at a time when systemwide statistics were unheard of. Elite governance has had an even shorter life span. Thus, the core problems remain relational and conceptual; too little research and too few prototypes demonstrate that empowerment regimes meet their expectations of greater equity, political responsiveness, experimentation, or long-term performance goals.

Performance Regimes Redefined

I reinterpret Stone's performance regime to encompass only those agendas, coalitions, and political arrangements conducive to changing school cultures and pedagogy in order to improve urban student performance. This includes a district's curriculum and instruction as well as its educational culture. It may begin by altering policies believed to be preconditions for instantiating preferred pedagogies, but the goal remains a simultaneous change in hundreds or thousands of urban classrooms.

Pedagogical reformers seek professional (possibly moral) means of holding educators accountable. Professional accountability comes from consensus among educational leaders about effective practice, sometimes enforced through accreditation processes, but also subject to peer pressure and prior training or experience. It is demonstrated in the alignment of educators' actions with the reform agenda's avowed expectations. This involves establishing a regime that tracks whether the preferred teaching methods have become routine and that adopts indicators to determine whether teacher and student performance gaps are closing.[35]

A performance agenda attempts to change the interaction between students and teachers, the "technical core" of education, and assumes that all other relationships—between lay governors and educators, or managers and workers—are secondary. Competing variants occur here as well. Some are tightly scripted; others are closer to philosophical arguments. Although research on models of teaching and learning constitutes a massive database from which these reformers draw inspiration and justification, it has not improved the sustainability of performance reform. Few performance reforms are attempted systemwide in urban districts, and Chicago saw only a handful of successes in the twentieth century.

Performance reformers rely on inductive evidence to convince others that changing time-tested routines is worth the expense, disruption, and uncertainty. This puts them at a disadvantage relative to empowerment reformers, who can promise political side benefits, and market reformers, who can attract adherents with compelling analogies to the business world and opportunities for profit. Research evidence develops slowly, and debates among researchers raise doubts that often undermine initiatives. Choosing the proper pedagogical change is a process even more contentious than deciding between democratic or elitist political premises.

Two categories of assumptions guide the principal combatants: a more or less regimented orientation toward the curriculum and teachers' classroom responsibilities, and a pedagogical argument based on children's readiness and interests that tends to encourage classroom experimentation. The former, often referred to as the *traditional* approach to schooling, asserts the existence of a formal body of knowledge that should be mastered by every student, including the disadvantaged in urban schools. The latter, typically associated with *progressive* schooling, argues that some students are in greater need of proficiency in deductive or inductive thinking; written, oral, and artistic communication; or social skills.[36]

In recent decades, "effective schools" research has spurred an interest in performance changing agendas. The research paradigm identified inner-city elementary schools with higher test scores than their demographics would predict and found among them a common set of organizational characteristics and behaviors.[37] These generally included "strong" school leadership, a clear vision, high expectations for student learning and discipline, and regular monitoring of student progress, as well as either a basic skills emphasis or a more broadly construed focus on intellectual work,[38] but also attention to a school's culture or ethos.[39] Reform agendas based on such findings proliferated; common to them was the importance of "whole school reform" rather than targeted programs or add-on courses.[40] In Chicago, Bryk and his colleagues outlined "five essential supports" that were postulated to help all elementary schools improve.[41] These stressed the importance of *authentic instruction,* a term closely aligned with the progressive performance agenda promoted in the district office when Bryk agreed to serve as a consulting director.[42]

Bryk's performance agenda was in conflict, however, with the traditional approach of the district, which typically targeted one or more characteristics of effectiveness that were thought to jump-start other changes. Superintendents Hannon in the 1970s and Love in the 1980s both adopted one version: Mastery Learning, based on Benjamin Bloom's ideas about "automasticity."[43] Typical among pedagogical experiments, it was repudiated and resurrected twice before Paul Vallas extrapolated the idea to produce more than 9,000 scripted lesson plans—an extreme application supported by no research.

But performance agendas are difficult to use as a popular rallying cry for a political coalition, partly because they are based on a research literature created and read by specialists. Although Vallas publicly criticized the Consortium on Chicago School Research, among other reform groups, for producing "tree-hugging" curriculum suggestions, the import of his protests was lost in the metaphor. The subtleties of Bryk's objections to overreliance on single indicators of learning and scripted lessons were equally difficult to transmit to parents and community members. Strenuous efforts to engage the public and implement pedagogical changes were conducted by a number of reform organizations in the 1990s, including Designs for Change and the CAC. Most saw success in a few schools but not systemwide. Heated rhetoric from the mayor's office also discouraged public dialog, confining pedagogical debate to professional forums.

LSCs were designed to support an empowerment agenda, but some hoped to redirect them as institutions of a performance regime. To serve this new purpose, they needed a great deal of external professional advice. Tapping the performance agendas of professors and researcher-activists was one way to obtain it.[44] But researchers and professors created those agendas in advance, and they were not typically open to public debate and compromise. In Chicago, whether the advocate's agenda was progressive or traditional, LSCs were *told* what makes a good school. Individual schools could choose to adapt what they were told, of course, and most of them did, but each school's adaptations amounted to unique, localized decisions, not a systemwide change.[45] And if there was conflict with the system's CEO, LSC decisions bore unforeseeable risks.[46] The CAC encountered the inverse problem in fostering its performance agenda: a lack of teacher autonomy—indeed, a central office mandate to use a scripted curriculum in most of its partnering schools—which gave educators little incentive to join the coalition.[47] Both these efforts to foster performance agendas lacked a coalition of political support with the requisite resources to ensure institutionalization.

The natural allies of any performance agenda are the teachers, who have daily contact with students and often communicate with parents. Teachers who back a performance agenda are also able to directly initiate change in their classroom practices. LSCs (or other empowered groups) must first learn about the performance agenda, adapt it to their school's circumstances, convey their wishes to teachers, and hope that the teachers will comply. Empowered parents and community members have the same principal-agent problem that confounds business executives: how do they get teachers to perform as they would like without direct control over their behavior? The answer is for the two groups to collaborate from the beginning in a common coalition on behalf of a mutually agreed-on performance agenda.

The task is not impossible. Recall that in the Progressive era the Commercial Club's effort to divide students into two distinct classes for separate schooling failed because of a vocational alternative fiercely backed by unions and social reform groups. Unionists and social activists won a partial victory because their long and bitter public debate with the club convinced most Chicagoans that all students should have a chance at both vocational and academic studies. This broad view of equitable curricular opportunities has become so embedded in expectations of public schooling that when the Illinois Manufacturers Association (IMA) resurrected the old market-based, dual system in the mid-1990s, it was abruptly rejected by all but the most radical ideologues.

The union–social reformer's version of manual training and vocational education, though disdained as "cultural work" by business executives at the time, was an amalgam of practical efforts to increase the holding power of schools and John Dewey's philosophy of child centeredness. These options remain, just as corporate views of schooling's economic functionalism do, in a handful of progressive schools and some schools of education. Because the compromise simultaneously opened the door to corporate tinkering, as described earlier, it has led to modern high school tracking, as well as to an emphasis on various combinations of manual, intellectual, and experiential learning. Many of these changes would have dismayed the Progressive era reformers, just as others would have delighted them, but the incremental alterations in vocational education since it was initiated are signals of the stability of this compromise.

Examples of less persistent Progressive era performance agendas abound. These were the efforts of a few professional educators who lacked the political backing of any sustaining coalition. For example, Superintendent William McAndrew brought the junior high school and platoon experiments to Chicago. Each was a performance reform supported by a range of national educators, and each had a few local community backers, but both were quickly eliminated. The after-the-fact efforts of the Citizen's Schools Committee (CSC) to resist the Sargent Committee's cuts were less a coalition of support for the junior high school idea than an understandable reaction to the assertion of corporate power. Platoon schooling not only lacked a sustaining coalition; the very teachers who would have had to implement the reform distrusted the idea.

Thus, the core constituents of performance regimes necessarily include teachers and the unions that represent them. Teachers bring the will to change their own classroom behavior, experiment with new techniques, and reorganize their use of time and space in schools, as well as indispensable technical skill, daily contact with students, and trusted mechanisms for professional growth. Unions are needed to sanction new forms of professional development and perhaps altered tenure and reward structures. Without teachers, any performance reform will founder.

Performance regimes also require that parents and community members have the opportunity to help formulate the agenda; they must have enough trust in its efficacy to let teachers experiment with their children. Beyond the generalities, parents tend to be skeptical of unfamiliar or counterintuitive innovations in pedagogy. Many such innovations take years to bear fruit, if at all. Some performance agendas challenge widely held beliefs about what makes a good school, such as those altering the amount of time spent in classes.[48] It is no easy task to encourage parents to embrace the changes that professional educators want in pedagogy or in school culture; it requires active, not merely passive, engagemen. But this does not mean that parents will always be resistant. Two surveys of Chicagoans in the 1980s, for example, revealed deep dissatisfaction with the schools, which did not lead them to ask for more market or empowerment changes. Instead, they wanted stricter enforcement of discipline, more help for struggling students, an emphasis on basic skills instruction, and better parent-school relationships, all potential aspects of a performance agenda.

Producing a performance coalition may require community-based organizations to mediate between teachers and low-income parents. Working-class or poor parents often mistrust educators' motives, suspecting that their children are being experimented with when pedagogies change. Middle-class parents, whose social standing lends credibility to pedagogical and cultural change, are other core constituents, and they may need backing from middle-class professional organizations that can validate the usefulness of the new skills, attitudes, and knowledge being sought. In Chicago, the associations of lawyers and other professionals in the CSC brought credibility to the child-centered vocational education agenda they pursued with the CTF and the city's working-class unions. CSC approval signaled that the new curriculum was one the middle class would accept even for its own children.

Core constituents in a performance regime also include elected officials, who supply legitimacy and function as political buffers. But providing the material resources needed to conduct ongoing professional development and curriculum enhancement—aspects of any performance regime—requires a deep commitment and often considerable economic resources. Thus, elected officials may be drawn toward less expensive alternatives. Other useful constituents of a performance regime include researchers, who can initiate agenda templates and provide technical expertise by collaborating with teachers to develop and refine new pedagogies or modes of instruction.

Business actors are less important to performance regimes than most regime analysts would admit. The arguments for their centrality are empirically suspect, and corporate executives have almost no interest in pursuing agendas that they do not formulate. When confronted with a competing school reform agenda, business leaders have used their influence and resources to recast it in market-friendly terms.

Two arguments undergird the credence that regime analysts give to local business elites. Each is said to make school reform structurally dependent on corporate support and predispose business leaders to schooling's substantive improvement. Yet neither is supported by evidence when a performance agenda has been the policy goal. One argument claims that schools are crucial infrastructure in local economic development, providing the human capital for productivity.[49] Yet when schools manifest performance changes, there is virtually no evidence that increased economic activity results.[50] Even the successful vocational education agenda, now deeply embedded in the current school governing regime, has not discernibly altered Chicago's economic circumstances: neither the decades-long loss of manufacturing jobs nor the unconscionably high unemployment rate among Chicago's blacks and Latinos has been ameliorated. Support for the management agenda of corporate leaders has more directly affected business profits by lowering taxes and improving perceptions of the city's business climate.[51]

The second argument, reflecting mainstream economic theory as understood by most mayors and city officials, is that corporate participation is essential to any reform coalition because schools rely on business (and middle-class) taxes to survive.[52] But the evidence is mixed.[53] When business leaders join a reform coalition, they can veto increases in school funding, as did Commercial Club members in 1988 and the Illinois Roundtable in 1995. Or they may demand that any new funding come from state and federal sources to ease the local business tax burden, as did the Commercial Club in 1995.

By failing to distinguish the characteristics of a coalition needed to advance performance reform, urban regime analysts have, in effect, reinforced a view of school reform as a dubious type of economic development. In my reformulation, I accept a much broader range of inspirations for performance change, including increased equity, knowledgeable and active citizens, and other humanistic values. Thus redefined, performance regimes are less obviously attractive to corporate leaders than they are to teachers, parents, and politicians. Of course, the corporate elite can usefully contribute to a performance regime by encouraging otherwise reluctant public officials to raise taxes or provide legitimacy for difficult adjustments in the curriculum, but such behavior is not predictable. And if their impatience for quick results demoralizes others, as has repeatedly happened in Chicago, corporate leaders may actually hinder an emerging performance regime.

Even without business's opposition, performance regimes are difficult to build and sustain because they require parents and teachers to unite. Larry

Cuban has documented how crucial and difficult it is to persuade teachers to change their practice.[54] Many others have demonstrated the ineffectiveness of asking parents to support pedagogical reforms with which they are uncomfortable.[55] Nor is the difficult path of collaboration between parents and teachers eased by decades of finger-pointing, much of it by academics, about the relative contributions of family background and school factors to student achievement. We lack research on the political processes of creating a reform coalition that combines both actors. Political leaders, too, may be reluctant to support reform that adds taxes, provides no immediate salutary spillover to other urban problems, or cannot be explained in a sound bite.

The Prevalence of Market Reform

Examining reform agendas and coalitional politics at the same time clarifies that some agendas need only narrow coalitions made up of core constituents who already trust one another. Robert Putnam describes the constituents that make up a narrow coalition as "bonding" social capital organizations.[56] They consolidate their resources and reinforce members' identities. Individual members learn to conceptualize social problems and solutions in ways that are acceptable to the organization as a whole. Coalitions of such organizations are both self-regulatory and self-promoting.

The Commercial Club is a particularly good example of a bonding organization; it has membership and induction procedures designed to weed out diversity and to socialize members in the accepted ways of viewing Chicago's school system and its economy. Since the 1930s the club has spoken with a single voice. In addition, the other groups it has formed—the Financial Research and Advisory Committee (FRAC), Chicago United, and Leadership for Quality Education (LQE)—are dependent on the Commercial Club, both financially and for their leaders. Accordingly, any coalition among them represents an especially parochial set of interests. But even when the club forms a coalition with statewide organizations such as the IMA and the Illinois Roundtable, the bonds between them as similarly educated business elites ensure that narrow, sectoral interests dominate.

Research in decision making by James March, Herbert Simon, and others demonstrates that solutions to problems rarely arise rationally—that is, from a thorough examination of all potential options. Rather, solutions exist in the minds of participants before the problems themselves are crystallized. Chicago's corporate leaders bring uncommon market experience and management training to their decision making about education. This expertise guides the solutions they propose for schools and frames the way they formulate educational problems. Their bonding organizations nurture such predilections. School reform examples abound: the school system *lacks* corporate accountability, a bottom-line indicator of student performance, or competition among teachers and schools. When a narrow coalition of business groups accepts such statements as self-evident problems, its members are seldom called on to convince one another of the solution. Instead, they need only privately debate the details and then promote a consensus agreement. Secondary coalition members, if any, are needed only to provide additional intellectual or political support. The business coalition behind the formation of the 1995 school reform agenda is a case in point.

Such narrow coalitions are easier to assemble and maintain than those bridging classes, races, or social groups. Status within the business sector draws corporate leaders to the Commercial Club and provides them career-enhancing benefits. Politicians are drawn to club members' resources and are predisposed to listen to their governing suggestions because of corporate leaders' extraordinary influence over the local economy. The political favors needed to keep a narrow coalition of constituents satisfied are predictable, if not always easily delivered. Moreover, nominal or passive membership, a problem for all activist groups, is less important in narrow coalitions, to the extent that the bonds among member organizations encourage deference to coalition leaders.

Conversely, civic activism by coalitions that bridge constituencies have the political benefit of representing a broad spectrum of the city. When political leaders seek guidance about their constituents' preferences, broad coalitions are said to provide more reliable information than do narrow coalitions of bonding associations. But this benefit depends on the disposition of political leaders— in Chicago's case, the mayor's responsiveness to his excluded or disaffected constituents. We saw that Dick Daley had little interest in understanding the demands of the broad-based civil rights coalition, since he perceived its gains as his loss. Reanalyzing data collected in the turbulent 1970s, political scientists have similarly discovered that bridging organizations did not have the anticipated salutary effect on leaders' democratic responsiveness; in fact, many politicians, like Daley, seemed to reject the views of such coalitions.[57]

In contrast, Harold Washington was vitally interested in forming a regime that encompassed diverse constituencies, and he deliberately constructed his governing coalition to do so. Moreover, he skillfully balanced the composition of the school reform summit ensuring that parents and community members could outvote business leaders, and he required the two groups to develop a consensus plan as equal members of the executive committee. The ensuing bridging coalition encompassed Latino activists, white professional reformers, a handful of grassroots black leaders, and business executives. But it barely survived Washington's death. Absent his leadership, it broke down before the 1988 reforms could be institutionalized, confirming the importance of political leadership to broad cross-sector coalitions.

Putnam has also argued that bridging organizations enhance the expectation that the benefits of membership will be shared, and he suspects that they may build intergroup trust as well. The ABCs coalition certainly brought the expectation of selective benefits to the Latino and black community organizers who participated: they were funded by LQE for their organizing work and sat on its board, where they were privy to the deliberations of powerful executives and had the ear of the mayor. Some were eventually appointed to public office or employed by the school district.

But such payoffs miss the main point. Because the activists gave popular legitimacy to corporate decisions on the interim board and the SFA, they had the opportunity to affect the business reform agenda. At the time, Ken West and other executives noted the influence "poor folks" had on their conceptions of reform, persuading them to empower parents when many executives thought the strategy ill-advised. For more than a decade executives also eschewed vouchers because Commercial Club leaders were persuaded that privatization could not be initiated "without further injuring the very people that a broad-based educational reform effort ought to be helping."[58]

Yet activists in 1988 also wore blinders. Low-income Latino and African American community leaders were accustomed to being dismissed by professionals in city hall and the schools. Decades of thwarted community organizing had left a mistrust so deep that, when given the chance, activists demanded political power over the schools and sought to control educators' work. Although straightforward from a political organizing perspective, the gains they sought and won did not flow from an analysis of the school problem any more than did the corporate leaders' management approach.

When in a coalition with business leaders, these activists were forced to compromise. Corporate executives wanted a continuing role in school governance and to ensure that future decisions would bear *their* stamp. And because they were executives, accustomed to seeing the big picture, they compromised by temporarily ceding control of the individual schools to activists—a tactic intended to help shake up the status quo—while keeping governance of the system's centralized functions for themselves.

The ABCs coalition was politically useful to corporate executives and community activists because each group was unhappy with the schools, albeit for different reasons, and sought new institutions to replace the existing governance structure. Both sides agreed that the administration was their common enemy. But any new governing institution would be perceived by corporate executives as an improvement if it merely denied educators the decision-making authority they had in the past. Community activists had more at stake: the opportunity handed to them by Harold Washington would not arise again anytime soon. Their institutional preference for parent-dominated school boards at every school could be enacted only with corporate support, and they would have to accept significant corporate oversight authority in the bargain. The broad coalition between community activists and corporate leaders required active participation to bridge the resource and experiential differences between them, making their negotiated empowerment agenda more fragile than the market agenda supported by a narrow, self-referential business coalition.[59]

Broad coalitions are thus harder to construct and sustain than narrow ones. The former lack the bonding advantages of the latter and must compensate by expending personal and financial resources on coalition maintenance. Yet cross-sector coalitions also create the conditions for reciprocal benefits if their leadership is strongly committed and provides the opportunity to envision uncommon reform agendas. Figure 5 captures these differences graphically, suggesting that performance agendas—requiring the broadest coalition—are the most difficult to mount and maintain.

POLITICAL DYNAMICS OF SCHOOL IMPROVEMENT

Chicago's story also offers some answers to the question: how might the schools be reformed without business leaders? My answer begins with a reconsideration of teachers unions.

By most accounts, teachers unions are powerful political actors with a demonstrated potential to influence reform; the CTU is no exception.[60] Union resources rival, and in some areas exceed, those of business associations: a large, stable membership; a ready-made organization and experienced, knowledgeable staff; access to member dues; legitimacy conferred by the state; the ability to speak publicly with a single voice; and a small army of foot soldiers to rally voters and demonstrators alike.[61] Yet since the Depression, teachers unions have rarely championed reform. Instead they have been preoccupied with maintaining and extending teacher benefits to the near exclusion of the broader purposes of education, and they have seldom participated in sustained cross-sector coalitions.

One of the reasons has been collective bargaining. It strengthened teachers' organizational resources and influence by conferring state legitimacy on unions: teachers could count on a hearing from school system managers each time a contract was being negotiated. But collective bargaining is a ritualized, adversarial process in which the union makes demands for benefit expansion and

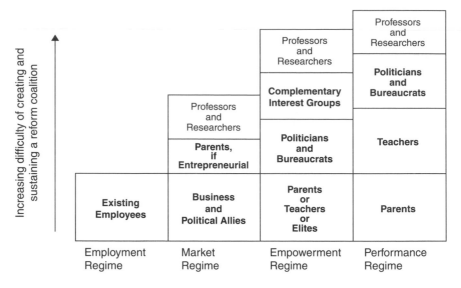

Figure 5. Mobilizing For Regime Change

salary increases, managers rebuff their demands, and each holds out for concessions from the other. The common goal is a standard contract for all schools, which is not expected to address reform issues or pedagogical concerns.[62]

Collective bargaining also reinforces the centralized and hierarchical nature of managerial decision making.[63] Negotiating sessions take place in publicly inaccessible arenas where teachers have more in common with managers than they do with community activists and their concerns. And the effects can be disconcerting: evaluation processes that are not serious, inflexible compensation schemes, seniority provisions that place the least experienced teachers in the hardest posts, and the perception that tenure is a "lifetime employment sinecure."[64] Such agreements can be construed as unfairly benefiting senior teachers over newcomers or as favoring teachers over other workers and parents. In these ways, collective bargaining has discouraged solidarity between teachers and other nonunionized workers, while strengthening the bonds between teachers union leaders and school system managers.

Strikes increased everywhere after collective bargaining was attained.[65] In Chicago teachers struck eight times between 1969 and 1987 for higher wages and more expansive health and pension benefits, but also for smaller class sizes and for preparation periods, over assignment and transfer rules, and when bargained agreements were violated.[66] Parents' and community members' lives were disrupted each time, encouraging opposition to teachers. The local media typically portrayed the job actions as illegitimate, siding with school board members across the nation who agreed that collective bargaining would "force a disproportionate share of school funds into salaries and benefits" as opposed to other school services.[67]

The decline in the national unionized workforce—union membership in 2000 was about 12 percent, down sharply from 30 percent in 1950—has also hampered the efficacy of teachers unions.[68] Teachers in Chicago, as elsewhere, have been deprived of one source of like-minded partners in the debate over the future of public schooling; they no longer have union membership in common with the parents of their students.

There are other reasons for the CTU's failure to collaborate with community groups in a reform agenda. When the CTU gained access to the mayor's office as part of his electoral coalition, the union kept its bargaining power only if it toed the mayor's line. This ensured that bargaining would be limited to items that the mayor was willing to deliver, typically short-term material benefits. Yearly bargaining was a reliable means of securing material benefits and was not altered until the 1989 interim board offered a three-year contract in exchange for calmer public relations. But neither the interim board and its successor nor the mayor could deliver on that contract, creating more reform cynics than advocates among educators.

Private bargaining sessions, strikes, and isolation from other workers made it easy to brand union officials as corrupt and wasteful; infighting among Chicago's union factions furthered such speculation. By the 1980s the CTU was routinely labeled a tax-eating dinosaur; it was accused of holding back the types of innovation that kept the increasingly nonunion private sector competitive and was largely held responsible for the rise in local taxes. Solidifying this perception was Daley's practice of settling strikes with raises that his appointed school board disavowed. By the time the CTU struck in 1987, it had already dug a deep well of resentment among parents and community members.

The Effects of a Weakened Teachers Union

The CTU was so weak in 1995 that it failed to contest its most significant loss of influence and professionalism in a century. In order to deliver a compliant workforce to the board, Rich Daley returned the CTU's lost bargaining rights. This was small compensation, however, since it put unionists in the position of acknowledging that their workplace conditions were management prerogatives, not professional privileges. Their acquiescence would mean the loss of bargaining authority over layoffs, class size, and even tenure.

With the elevation of managerialism that accompanied mayoral control, hitherto uncontested professional discretion over lesson plans, teaching strategies, and student assessment became incentives to be earned. Teachers of low-performing students were soon directed to put aside their training and to adopt standardized (and occasionally inaccurate) curricula because it was assumed that their discretion had caused the poor performance. Emboldened by the widespread use of standardized tests, managers adopted the simplistic assumption that student performance was both quantifiable and capable of being sorted on a single scale, which in turn would reveal a parallel alignment of teachers. This kind of thinking took teaching one step closer to piecework labor.

That the CTU encouraged its members to fall in line is the result of the politically isolated position it found itself in by the mid-1990s. Taking the small raises offered but ignoring the other losses, it seemed to prove the perception that a union's only role is to "selfishly" bargain for financial gain at the expense of students. This helped substantiate the business view of teachers as interchangeable, even expendable, workers. As Al Shanker had put it in 1983: "Those [union] organizations that are mired in what seems to the public to be petty interests are going to be swept away."[69]

Responding to the erosion of union influence, some reform-oriented union leaders have adopted a professional stance to collective bargaining characterized by joint labor-management committees that make binding decisions about issues such as class size, peer evaluation, or the comanagement of individual schools.[70] Professional bargaining changes the content of the issues debated, but not the arena; it "bends" industrial unionism to "professional purposes."[71] Bargaining for professionalism assumes that both labor and management are prepared to forgo their adversarial ways and honor the collaborative agreements made by their predecessors. Other cities' unions seeking professional changes have been routinely rebuffed, if not initially, then by a new manager or board.[72] Notwithstanding Deborah Lynch's hard-won deal to comanage a limited number of chronically failing schools, the CTU has mostly avoided professional bargaining; Chicago teachers appear reluctant to trust managers to implement such agreements fairly. After only three years at the helm, Lynch narrowly lost a leadership contest to a candidate who argued that reform was the responsibility of the district office, not the unions.

Unions as Coalition Partners

Securing teachers' *material* interests stands in stark contrast to the public image of union leaders in the Progressive era, when they devoted substantial resources to organizing broad coalitions for the democratic purposes of public education and the proper means of teaching working-class children. Collective bargaining began a long period of union insularity; but the CTU, guided by its own history, can be a vital partner in reform again. Early in the century the CTF, the Chicago Federation of Labor, the International Federation of Labor, and the Men's and Women's High School Federations participated in mass organizing campaigns with churches, women's organizations, and civic groups to obtain democratically elected school boards, the restoration of services to immigrant and poor children, and a single system of schooling. Although teachers stood to benefit materially from each of these positions, they earned political legitimacy by casting their agenda in social welfare terms, reminding the public of their concern for children above and beyond the schools. Even when they lost battles, they won the political legitimacy that came from furthering the causes of their coalition partners and especially the working poor.

Just as every viable reform agenda requires a sustaining coalition, teachers need reliable civic partners from which to obtain the resources and legitimacy they currently lack, and with which they are willing to compromise. Some have suggested that an alliance with corporate executives might benefit the CTU. In fact, corporate associations and unions are the two most powerful reform actors in Chicago, and any collaboration between them would be politically difficult to resist. But a business-union coalition is unlikely, given the ideological and practical differences between them. For a start, any such coalition would have to overcome the entrenched resistance to unions among corporate groups such as the IMA. Although some Commercial Club members understand that good schools depend on teachers who ignore managers when they hamper students' learning,[73] the club has recently accepted the IMA stance, either convinced by the anti-unionists or in an effort to maintain corporate unity.

To make matters worse, corporate leaders have adopted the strategy of separating teachers from their unions. The turn-of-the-century image of (female) teachers was of "docile, obedient and self-sacrificing servants," whereas union members were portrayed as radicals prone to violence and anarchy.[74] Such images remain in the contemporary imagination, available for manipulation. The updated version identifies teachers as caring, intrinsically motivated, and self-sacrificing, whereas their union leaders are interested only in promoting their own influence. The lesson is that "attacking teachers as a profession is a loser. Confronting teachers as a labor union, however, can produce political returns . . . portraying their opposition to [reform] . . . as nothing more than the defense of the status quo."[75] Both the Citywide Coalition for School Reform and the CAC were persuaded by this argument; each sponsored small groups of teachers as a substitute for union support of their performance-based reforms. These organizations seemed to say that teachers are necessary to the solution, but their unions are part of the problem. Chicago's history shows that antipathy to unions is long-standing, not situational.

A business-union reform coalition would be one-sided, with teachers required to cast their professionalism in market terms. It would also be precarious, abandoned by executives if management fashions, fiscal crises, or sectoral solidarity persuaded executives that a narrow coalition of market actors could better serve their purposes.

More plausible is union opposition to corporate plans with the hope of mitigating the excesses of market reforms. This would entail augmenting criticism with reform alternatives that contend with market approaches and require collaboration with parent and community groups. Such a strategy could give the CTU a policy arena that is not limited to the opaque venue of collective bargaining, professional or otherwise. It could also augment state legitimacy, demonstrated in collective bargaining, with public legitimacy. For both to occur, teachers unions need stronger relationships with other school reform actors.

Public Trust and Legitimacy

The CTU has squandered several opportunities to collaborate with other civic groups. Rather than seek coalition partners and address their concerns through compromise and debate, union officials have addressed reform only when it reached the legislative phase. By preferring backdoor negotiations to public forums, union leaders have failed to promote teachers' indispensable contributions to school reform, allowing others' negative perceptions to dominate reform debates.

Nor has the CTU expended much effort to earn public trust since the Depression. Recall that unionists did not wage a public campaign for collective bargaining, receiving a backdoor political deal instead. Chicagoans never learned why teachers needed the security of contracts to work effectively. More importantly, by accepting Dick Daley as its patron, the CTU struck a bargain that included quiescence on the desegregation and community control reforms that he opposed, a stance that precluded any possibility of a coalition with the machine era's black activists.[76] The union also shunned opportunities to join (or lead) decentralizing reform coalitions in the 1980s, forgoing any influence that teachers might have had on that far-reaching empowerment agenda. Union leaders focused instead on the broken promise of raises every year. By 1995 the CTU was in a weak position to seek community support for teachers' professional discretion, and its leaders never even tried, acting as though the union's future were unrelated to its public acceptance.

Gary Chaison and Barbara Bigelow remind us that unions require legitimacy to be effective. External groups of several types—employers, nonunionized workers, the general pubic, and potential coalition partners—have essential resources and support with which to reward unions if they conform to expected practices and values. Two crucial forms of legitimacy are conferred from outside: "pragmatic" legitimacy granted by employers (and members) when unions bargain effectively for workers' economic interests and welfare, and "moral" legitimacy bestowed by external organizations and the public at large.[77]

In terms of my regime analysis framework, pragmatic legitimacy is *bureaucratic* legitimacy, reinforced by collective bargaining with management. It is necessary but "weak and transitory," requiring continual advances for members and dependent on managers' and union leaders' calculations of the "net value" of maintaining existing relationships. Relying on bureaucratic legitimacy can backfire when members who have never worked without union protection, nor been involved in union organizing, judge their union to be merely "an insurance policy or a service to be purchased."[78] And bureaucratic legitimacy can be effectively challenged by market legitimacy, which sees unions as an unalloyed obstacle to progress. Moral legitimacy is the belief that unions serve a purpose beyond their members' interests. It is achieved only through coalitional activity and by taking stands in support of values that are accepted by the public at large. These two forms of legitimacy—bureaucratic and moral—compete with each other in times of reform because bureaucratic legitimacy supports the status quo and moral legitimacy is active.[79] This dichotomy is at the heart of the classification of unions into two kinds: bread-and-butter and reform-minded.

In the context of a one-sided pursuit of bureaucratic legitimacy through collective bargaining, the CTU can fairly be categorized as part of an employment regime for much of the post–World War II era. The CTU agreed to a bargain that elevated the authority of managers over that of teachers in exchange for the job security, regular pay, and benefits afforded functionaries, and for the legitimacy enjoyed by state bureaucrats. This has been union leaders' strategy even though teachers' work routinely requires that they behave as moral exemplars, political negotiators, independent professionals, and even managers of scarce classroom resources.

Despite its failure to reach out to the public over the last fifty years, there are many pressures on the CTU that could spur a new alliance with community actors on behalf of school reform. Research shows that traditional collective-bargaining contracts are becoming more restrictive for teachers and increasingly favor managerial prerogatives, highlighting the limitations of seeking stability through bureaucratic legitimacy.[80] Union officials now realize the folly of waiting for legislation before acting on reform; doing so brought wrath and retaliation from the Republicans when they took over legislatures and state houses in the 1990s, not only in Illinois but also in other industrial states.[81] The strong pressure from the corporate sector to eliminate unions from schooling requires a response as well. Each of these constitutes a spur to action for teachers unions.

There are also positive reasons for taking action. In rebuilding private-sector unions, organizers have learned how to take their case to the public more effectively, tactics that the CTU can borrow. Organizers have learned that their own union strategy is at least as important in determining success as the character of the opposition from employers or a hostile economic and political climate. Important too are the demographics of the union; having at least 60 percent women or people of color is an advantage, and many urban teachers unions fit this profile.[82] Moreover, unions have begun to attract a group of social reformers and community leaders nurtured in the 1970s who move back and forth between union organizing and their social concerns without losing sympathy for either, creating and nurturing bridging organizations in the process.[83] The CTU has itself recently nurtured some reformist leaders, albeit with a professional rather than a democratic bent. If these national lessons apply to Chicago, then cross-class and cross-race coalitions may be more viable options for reform than they once were.

The union also holds powerful political resources that are unrivaled outside of the corporate sector: the keys to implementing successful reform. Their members' firsthand knowledge of students and the learning process and unions' repeatedly demonstrated concern for teachers' professional growth should make them attractive partners for community groups that are willing to consider the difficult work of developing a performance agenda.

Teachers' Empowerment Options

Chicago's reform history highlights several "existence proofs" for different forms of teacher activism. In addition to teachers unions, Chicago's Progressive era gave us another option: teachers councils. The CTF and the other teachers unions were freer to focus on coalition building and on broad social issues when teachers councils could address the problems of professional practice in each school and the district as a whole.[84] Teachers councils were democratically organized legislative bodies present in every school, but they also operated on the district and system level, and each voted independently on unrestricted issues: textbooks, curriculum, and discipline; the nomination or removal of district superintendents; and reform issues such as platoon schooling.[85] Although only advisory, their votes were a public demonstration of teacher sentiments and provided the CTF with strong backing that could be used to address citywide issues. When in agreement, civic groups could be supportive advocates for the teachers' concerns. This strategy resonates with recent research, which demonstrates that "an active representative committee" and active union volunteers can be two of the most important ways to revitalize the movement.[86]

Progressive era Chicago reveals another path to reform: good-government groups, elite women's clubs, and unionists united in a cross-class coalition on behalf of a democratic version of vocational education. Later, under the banner of the CSC, many of the same groups joined in an even broader coalition to ameliorate the effects of the Sargent Committee's drastic funding cuts and to expose corruption. Both examples suggest that unions can be a crucial bridging form of teacher organization, catalysts for creating cross-sector groups and even alternative forms of organization among the teachers' ranks. The legitimacy of these two Progressive era options rested on broad public support, not state sanction.

It is also possible to speculate about the results if the CTU had engaged in the public activity of school reform organizing in recent decades. Had the CTU vigorously fought for equal numbers of teachers, parents, and community members on LSCs, teachers would have had a stronger voice in each school's reform plan and in the selection of principals. With the CTU fully committed to LSCs, it would have been much harder for the corporate reformers to circumvent their power so thoroughly in 1995. Moreover, the falling turnout among parents and community members in LSC elections would have had less impact, since teacher turnout never dropped significantly.

As recently as 1994 the CTU and the Annenberg project might have collaborated to sustain a vision of schooling that did not rely on the top-down homogenizing effects of mayoral control, each bringing its own resources—including Quest and CAC funding—to the coalition. Parents and community-based organizations were the core constituents of the CAC coalition, but no matter how pedagogically sophisticated they were, many lost interest as their children progressed through the schools. Teachers remain in the same general school setting; any change in their practice necessarily leaves a longer-lasting residue in the schools. Beyond the moral legitimacy it would have gained with a CAC partnership, the CTU would have had the opportunity to temper the extremes of the CAC's progressive agenda with the realities of day-to-day teaching.

Either of these two scenarios would have required an extraordinary willingness to bridge long-standing mistrust between low-income parents and middle-class teachers. Also necessary would have been committed leadership and additional resources to stimulate the difficult work of negotiation between the two groups. Yet either would have also strengthened the foundation for future trust between them.

Notwithstanding such missed opportunities, the current era of reform offers one of the most fluid openings to change the structure of public education in

100 years. The privatization and outsourcing now being envisioned by a narrow coalition of corporate leaders pose such major problems for both teachers and parents that their collaboration may be the only viable alternative.

Parents and Unions as Reform Partners

Chicago history documents a wide array of organizations with important assets needed to accomplish a school reform agenda. Foundations can provide an early infusion of funding. Neighborhood organizations may encourage parents and other concerned citizens to change their views of schools and educators. Civil rights and religious groups can use their elevated moral standing to press for commitments to disadvantaged urban children. Limited assets, however, can make each of these groups fickle reform partners, distracted as soon as a law is passed or a battle is won. But properly motivated, they can provide public or moral legitimacy for either of two powerful economic actors in the school reform arena. In the Progressive era such civic groups lent crucial public legitimacy to teachers unions, demonstrating that a coalition of unionists and community organizations can be politically strong enough to mobilize change without the business sector, and even in opposition to a corporate agenda.

An alliance of parents and teachers has what every corporate-community coalition lacks: the key support of the professionals who must embrace, adapt, and implement any reform before it can affect students' learning. This prerequisite for a performance agenda does not mean that reform depends on teacher or union acquiescence. But reform without teachers, as we have seen, is almost without exception a change by market or empowerment mechanisms, none of which can create a direct or systemic path to improvements in student performance. Such reforms can affect a few schools deeply, or trickle down in small ways to many classrooms, but they have failed to close the performance gap in urban schools or to relegitimize the many other democratic purposes of schooling that engage the public. For either of those goals to be met, teachers and parents must agree to join forces, knowing that corporate leaders, with their current ideological preoccupations, are more likely to oppose them than to join them.

The last decades of the twentieth century saw many missed opportunities to unite in opposition to managerialism, but opportunities to collaborate on a new performance agenda were also passed up, with students, families, and teachers each suffering in their own way. It is this common plight that provides the strongest reason for a new coalition, perhaps the surest way to lasting educational change in our urban school systems.

Appendix:
Characteristics of the Commercial Club of Chicago and Its Network of Associated Organizations

Chicago's uncommon capacity for school reform rests on the organizational and political resources of its civic groups, and no sector has been more consistently engaged than business. Among the city's many business groups, the most influential is an elite network of associations known as the Commercial Club of Chicago, including since 1982 its public policy arm, the Civic Committee, and two of its affiliates, Chicago United and Leadership for Quality Education (LQE). Working through these associations, corporate Chicago has been involved in nearly every attempt at school reform since the late nineteenth century.

Membership in the Commercial Club is by invitation only, and it is an induction into public activism, binding corporate leaders to a common vision of civic life. Operating procedures stress member discipline and control, while decision-making patterns and interlinked funding encourage cohesion and consensus. Members enjoy social standing and easy access to corporate wealth and local politicians. Few of the city's other civic organizations, including its other business associations, can match these advantages.[1]

Chicago's other business associations—the Chicago Association of Commerce and Industry (CACI), the Cosmopolitan Chamber of Commerce (primarily serving Chicago's "minority" businesses), and the Illinois Manufacturers Association (IMA)—are voluntary associations, accepting members from both large and small, central and marginal firms.[2] These groups' policy decisions are typically made by their officers and paid professionals on behalf of mostly passive members.[3]

By contrast, the Commercial Club's size is relatively small, reflecting its elitism and cohesion. In 1901 the membership of the IMA already included 250 of Illinois' largest manufacturers, 175 of which were Chicago based, whereas Commercial Club membership was limited to 60. By 1928 the Chicago Association of Commerce (later CACI) numbered 6,500 members, compared with the club's 90. Business leaders acting through such large and diverse organizations have not been able to rely on member consensus to guide decision making, as has been the case in the Commercial Club.

Studies of corporate influence on the policy process usually assume that the primary purpose of business groups is to win legislative battles over profitability-related issues such as taxation, consumer protection, environmental safety, and labor relations. These are the foremost concerns of Chicago's chambers of commerce and industry-specific associations. Like their counterparts in cities throughout the United States, and in striking contrast to the Commercial Club network, these groups engage in school policy making only when it suits their immediate business interests. A diverse range of scholars has noted the emphasis on vocational schooling in the CACI and the anti-union stance toward regular schooling taken by the IMA during the early years of the twentieth century.[4] Such biases remain in the successor organizations. But these business groups have generally ended their efforts when the law they sought was passed, each returning to its core concerns of taxation and regulation. Compared with the Commercial Club's activism, their influence has been ephemeral.[5]

The Commercial Club's activities go well beyond lobbying or philanthropy. In the arena of schooling, the club has often initiated reform, creating and then promoting (sometimes for decades) plans for the efficient organization of school resources or the ideal district governance structure. In turn, state or local political officials have invited the club to craft policy or oversee the implementation of school laws. These roles—reform initiator, policy maker, and implementation overseer—also set the Commercial Club network apart from other business associations.

ORGANIZATIONAL TIES AND STRUCTURAL SIMILARITIES

The Commercial Club of Chicago was founded in 1877. It merged twenty-eight years later with the Merchant's Club, a younger generation of business titans similarly bent on reorganizing the city's social and political life.[6] The partnership began a decades-long process of consolidation among Chicago's elite business associations and a consistent focus on education policy. Club members' contemporary interests reflect this legacy of educational activism, even as they are conditioned by a modern view of the global economy.

Chicago United was initiated in 1968, during an era when business leaders were widely expected to help solve urban problems in reaction to the "deterioration of the inner cities and the exclusion of blacks from the economic mainstream."[7] It began as a secret union between black community leaders and the Commercial Club's white leadership that focused on race relations and schooling.

The Civic Committee was formed in 1982 to focus on metropolitan economic development. Club members were concerned about the loss of manufacturing jobs throughout the 1970s and the "rust belt" predictions being made for the region.

The impetus for LQE was a school reform law in 1988 restructuring school governance. Chicago United and the Civic Committee created LQE to monitor and promote the law's implementation in line with business expectations.

Often in response to changes in the city's governing regime, these groups have reshuffled responsibilities on such issues as school reform; for example, there was nearly unanimous agreement that LQE should replace Chicago United as the "lead" business association on school policy in 1991. Such coordinated deliberations are facilitated by the many structural similarities among these organizations: selecting and inducting members, raising funds, sustaining operations, making decisions, and informing civic actors and the public.[8] These commonalities create the initial conditions for organizational stability, social cohesion, and comprehensive scope, all traits required for the effective long-term representation of business interests.[9] Table 2 itemizes the essential organizational underpinnings of the Commercial Club. The more prestigious inner-circle Civic Committee wholly reflects the club's characteristics because, for the most part, its fifty to seventy-five members are nominated from among those who have served on the Commercial Club's Executive Committee.[10] A description of the unique aspects of Chicago United and LQE follows the outline of club characteristics provided below.

MEMBERSHIP

Each association in the network is a "closed club" of the city's most powerful corporate leaders. Commercial Club members informally vet the qualifications of potential nominees and obtain seconds from at least six other members. After the membership committee's screening process, each nominee is voted on by the entire membership. Ratification requires virtual unanimity.[11]

A prospective member is expected to be the principal leader of his or her organization with full authority to act on its behalf. Thus, decisions can be reached quickly in either closed or open meetings, adding to the effectiveness of negotiations with politicians.

A second membership criterion is a background in local public service. This ensures that members have developed personal relationships with Chicago's elected and appointed officials and with one another. They can thus address civic concerns from a base of common experience that facilitates like-mindedness.

Mergers and acquisitions have increased the number of transient executives unfamiliar with Chicago and have occasioned periodic hand-wringing in the local business press, which is aware that impermanence, global consciousness, and even financial fragility can diminish corporate commitment to local civic affairs and reduce the effectiveness of business activism.[12] The distinction between the civic activism demonstrated by local corporations and the relative disinterest displayed by national or multinational corporations is a primary analytic tool for understanding business involvement in public schooling. It is an observed difference that reflects environments where the primary business actors are individual corporations.[13] But in Chicago, corporate activism arises out of associational activity; the civic activism of nonlocal corporations is mediated by associational rules. In particular, the club's membership and induction criteria socialize newcomers; even those with temporary appointments grasp civic issues, encouraging less separation between local firms and global corporations in Chicago than has been observed in other cities.

Club membership also enhances the executives' national influence. Since their membership need not expire when they leave the region or retire, business leaders often promote locally successful club initiatives across the country.

A select few nonbusiness civic elites and politicians are invited to join the Commercial Club, providing informal opportunities for corporate leaders to influence them, and vice versa.[14] The club extended membership to the first president of the University of Chicago, William Rainey Harper (1891–1906), and nearly every one of his successors has joined, which required gender integration in 1978 when Hannah Gray accepted

Table 2. Commercial Club Characteristics in Three Reform Eras

	1880–1939	1940–1979	1980–2000
Members	60 (1901) 90 (1930)	90	250 (1980) 350 (2004)
"No" Votes Permitted for Membership	N/A	3	15
Boundary-Spanning Members	University presidents: University of Chicago University of Illinois, Northwestern University, Illinois Institute of Technology (Chicago City Colleges followed in 1940s)	Mayor: Martin Kennelly (1942) Senator: Charles Percy (1951) Superintendent: Harold Hunt (1951) Black: George E. Johnson (1971) Civic organizations: presidents of Field Museum and Hospitals (1960s) Female: Hannah Gray, University of Chicago president (1978) Governor: James Thompson (1979)	Civic organizations: (e.g., Chicago Opera, Chicago Symphony, YMCA)
Dues	$40 (1881) (CPI adjusted 2000 = $670)	$680 (1978) (CPI adjusted 2000 = $1795)	$1800 (2000)
Educational Subscriptions/ Grants	Chicago Manual Training School (1882) $130,000 (CPI adjusted 2000 = $2.2 million)	N/A	LSC electioneering (1989) $600,000 (CPI adjusted 2000 = $833,000)

Committees	Standing committees: executive, reception, and nominating committees and 1–16 topical committees (e.g., Education, Sargent's Citizen's Committee, Plan of Chicago)	Committees associated with mayoral commissions: Housing Commission, City Planning Commission, and "catalyzed" civic bodies (e.g., Leadership Council for Metropolitan Open Communities)	Civic Committee of the Commercial Club (1982) Leadership for Quality Education (1988) City commissions (e.g., Metropolitan Planning Commission, Chicago Metropolis 2020)
Professional Staff	Club secretary	Club secretary	Executive director of the Civic Committee (1982) President of the Civic Committee
Publications	*Year Book of the Commercial Club of Chicago* (1911–1982) Plan for Chicago	*History of the Commercial Club of Chicago* "Central Areas Plan"	*Chicago Enterprise* (until 1994) Economic reports Public school studies
Decision Making	Consensus based on committee recommendations	Consensus based on Executive Committee decisions	Consensus based on cross-organizational deliberations
Cross-Business Alliances	N/A	N/A	Chicago Partnership (1986) Illinois Business Education Coalition (1994)

CPI, consumer price index; LSC, local school council; N/A, not available.

membership.[15] Two years after beginning the biracial dialog that became Chicago United, the club accepted its first African American businessman, George E. Johnson. In 1942 club members nominated former businessman Martin Kennelly, the first of a succession of Chicago mayors to hold honorary (non-dues-paying) membership in the club. In 1951 U.S. Senator Charles Percy joined, followed in 1979 by James Thompson, the first sitting Illinois governor to accept the club's nomination. In 1951 Superintendent Harold Hunt became the first schoolman elected to the Commercial Club.

DUES AND SUBSCRIPTIONS

Members of the club pay a considerable amount in mandatory membership dues and additional sums for special projects.[16] One of the earlie·t subscriptions built and staffed the private, fee-charging Chicago Manual Training School, an 1882 venture financed with $130,000 raised from club members. Another, in 1909, paid half of Edwin Cooley's expenses while he surveyed the vocational schools of Europe.[17] The member businesses are also expected to donate executive time, office space, and support services. Increasingly, projects are partially sustained by foundation grants and state or federal funds, requiring support staff to secure and maintain them.

Club members who are asked to become part of the inner circle of the Civic Committee pay additional dues for the privilege and are tithed additional sums (or engage in fund-raising) when a project requires resources. This combination of subscription and personal solicitation raised the corporate funds that supported the grassroots organizing effort during the first local school council elections in 1989.[18] In the late 1990s member corporations paid nearly 95 percent of the operating expenses of Chicago United.[19] LQE receives nearly all its operating funds from the Civic Committee; members of its board do not pay additional dues.[20] Thus, access to new members and external funding for subsidiary associations are tied to club relationships.

COMMITTEES AND PROFESSIONAL STAFF

Active participation by the heads of member corporations is embedded in the Commercial Club's earliest articles of confederation. To ensure top-level involvement, there is a "no substitute" rule: chief executives are the working members of the organization. Accustomed to acting as the primary decision makers in their own firms, officers and Executive Committee members have greatly overshadowed the club's professional staffers. Membership committees did the club's civic work during its first half century, and assignments served as a kind of policy apprenticeship for members. As the Commercial Club absorbed one similar club after another, membership grew, along with the number and breadth of its committees. In 1910 sixteen separate committees represented a high point in the club's Progressive era activism. Serving as long as they desired, committee chairpersons came to be identified with specific club initiatives.[21]

After the club invited Mayor Kennelly to become an honorary member, committee service ensured appointments on city commissions. To cite one example, four of the six members of the short-lived Committee on Slum Clearance (established after World War II) simultaneously served as chairmen, vice chairmen, or coordinators of mayoral commissions on housing, land clearance, and city planning. One committee member also lent his executive assistant to the mayor, who described him as an "alter ego," to coordinate the work of all three commissions.[22]

Two decades later, cooperation between city hall and the Commercial Club advanced further. About halfway into Richard J. Daley's tenure, the club began a pattern of seeding new organizations to preserve its projects instead of asking committee chairmen to sustain them.[23] This allowed club leaders who preferred confidentiality in their dealings with city hall to work behind the scenes, while a subsidiary organization became the public advocate.[24]

Chicago United falls into the category of organizations founded by the Commercial Club, as does the Financial Research and Advisory Committee (renamed Chicago Consulting Alliance—CCA), which helped design the management reforms that executives would seek for the school system in the 1990s. This seeding process, referred to by members as "catalyzing," also describes the relationship between the older associations and LQE.[25]

Each association has a respected, if small, professional staff. Executives know that a relatively large staff might relieve some of the burden on members, but it would also dilute the club's influence. Professional employees of the Commercial Club were, until recently, insignificant in decision making, with only one employee for about every 140 members. The executive directors (or presidents) of Chicago United and LQE had a more elevated status than the club's professional secretary and significantly more professional support, although none had the civic influence of the corporate executives who serve as the lay leaders of the club and its Civic Committee.

DECISION MAKING AND ALLIANCES

Executives understand that when all three organizations speak with one voice about education (or another social issue), their already strong influence is amplified. When they coordinate resources to persuade politicians in multiple and reinforcing ways (e.g., pilot programs, managerial audits, public surveys, personal favors), their preferences are more likely to be enacted.

To reach consensus, negotiations typically occur among the Executive Committee members and other officers of each association, many of whom sit on several of these groups. Agreements among them are sent to the full membership for ratification, if necessary. Every full member has a vote of equal weight. Although differences of opinion are common, most votes are expected to be unanimous, or nearly so. Therefore, a vote is rarely called until the discussions within the Executive Committee and inquiries among the membership—often the result of extensive internal lobbying—have reached the point of consensus.[26]

Confidentiality safeguards the decision-making processes, no matter how heated the discussions. Without it, highly visible elites would be unwilling to discuss their views for fear of jeopardizing their corporate reputations or committing organizational resources too hastily. Since the Depression, this policy has kept the club network safe from public scrutiny. Nor are individual association members held publicly accountable for their internal decisions and agreements. For example, until the late 1970s, few citizens even knew of the existence of Chicago United, and club members wanted it that way: "We didn't want to try a case on the ten o'clock news. . . . We didn't entirely escape taking a public position, but we felt we were vulnerable because so many of the white (member) CEOs lived in the suburbs. [People might think,] 'Who the hell are these suburban fat cats telling us what to do?' "[27]

Interorganizational coordination is evident when the business leaders who simultaneously sit on several of the executive committees decide that the network should examine its division of labor. One such realignment in the early 1990s saw each of the three associations restate its core mission and, acknowledging redundancy, restructure their work. Chicago United decided to emphasize its unique race relations mission and focus on advocacy and demonstration projects: dual boards of twelve to fifteen members were selected to lead the two functional areas, and a narrow set of committees was formed for economic development and education. The number of professional employees declined as some programs were "spun off."[28]

The Commercial Club and the Civic Committee underwent a parallel restructuring, also decreasing staff and focusing on activities related to the metropolitan region's economic future. Their work in education became more firmly tied to economic development. The executive director of the Civic Committee (with the new title of president) assumed the responsibilities of the retiring club secretary, and the chairmen of both the Civic Committee and the Commercial Club were expected to collaborate more often. The Civic Committee and LQE were also brought into closer coordination, as LQE moved away from its role as a support system for managerial reform in the district office to focus on alternatives to neighborhood schooling, including vouchers and charters.[29] These changes attracted the city's new (and retiring) business leaders by opening previously unexplored opportunities for civic activism and shaking up the network's leadership.

Such internal reorganization also responds to changes in the governing arrangements of the city. Like a similar rearrangement in the early 1980s, the reshuffling in the mid-1990s occurred after the club network had achieved a major restructuring of the school governance system, and after a new mayoral regime was firmly in place. In the mid-1990s Mayor Richard M. Daley was newly in charge of a school system organized around the principles of centralization and accountability, which had been conceived and promoted by these business leaders. With mayoral control, the club network reordered its priorities and operations, until then heavily tilted toward sustaining a decentralizing school reform agenda.

Notwithstanding many debates over the vitality of corporate interest in school reform, Chicago's Commercial Club continues to adjust its organizational capacity to reflect its changing school reform priorities. In 2005 the Civic Committee formed another group to take the lead in its effort to privatize 100 Chicago schools through charters, contracts, or vouchers. New Schools for Chicago replaced LQE as the club's lead school reform organization.[30]

Although the Commercial Club network is cohesive and well coordinated, its relationship to other Illinois and Chicago-based business associations cannot be taken for granted. Chambers of commerce and industry-specific and statewide business associations all have some membership overlap with the club, but this, by itself, is not sufficient to forestall rivalry among them when the policy agenda is of broad interest.

To facilitate cross-network collaboration among the city's business associations and present a united business voice, well-connected club members have twice formed temporary umbrella coalitions of business groups. The first occurred when Chicago United and the Civic Committee prepared to offer school decentralization legislation. They formed the Chicago Partnership, which included representatives from each of the city's interested business associations and some statewide groups. The Partnership's only substantive activity was to designate Chicago United as business's lead organization in school reform in 1988, enabling its president, Warren Bacon, to speak to Illinois legislators as the corporate spokesman on school issues.[31]

In 1994 the Illinois Business Education Council (IBEC) was inaugurated to represent business in deliberations about the law that gave Mayor Daley control of the school system. IBEC met with legislative success, even though members of the short-lived group did not reach consensus; statewide groups and the Commercial Club network parted ways over the Chicago school system's revenue needs. Even so, the fundamental differences between the groups were not apparent to the public, and concealing those differences under a cloak of consensus remained an important tactic.[32]

UNIQUE CHARACTERISTICS OF CHICAGO UNITED

Chicago United has a modified version of the "principals only" membership rule. Full voting members of Chicago United—referred to as "principals"—are all CEOs, directors, or presidents of their organizations, and each nomination for a new principal is vetted in a manner similar to that used by the Commercial Club. One difference is that each principal appoints a "deacon," who serves as a primary staff person to one or more of the association's committees and acts as his or her principal's representative, helping to set the group's agenda by deliberating with the other deacons and drafting proposals for consideration by the principals.

In its early years, half of Chicago United's principal membership was white, and the other half was black. More recently, Hispanic and Asian members have filled some of the "minority" positions.[33] Of the ninety-five deacons listed in the 1991 roster, approximately 33 percent were African American, and about 15 percent were Latino. Chicago United has also been gender integrated. Although there were few female principals in its first twenty years, by 1991 more than a third of the deacons were women, and by 1995 the president was a woman. More recently, the distinctions among members have been formally based on company size rather than race or ethnic status, aiming for a sixty-forty ratio of large corporations to small firms, which are typically minority owned.[34]

Like the requirement of local service, the process of selecting minority members has been important to the civic education of white principals and reflects their social development. In the 1970s white corporate executives were unlikely to know African American and other minority leaders living and working in unfamiliar sections of the city; this social distance resulted in a longer vetting process for minority nominees. For example, the inclusion of the first Latino principal started with a list of more than twenty-five Mexican American and Puerto Rican leaders who were vetted for months before one was invited to join. Now that corporate Chicago is more integrated, and community leaders are no longer inducted as new members, the vetting process is similar for all.

The status distinctions between white and minority members reflect their changing relationship with corporate Chicago and city hall. For much of Chicago United's first two decades, minority principals represented the city's most influential civil rights groups or were African American or Latino entrepreneurs, whereas white principals represented the city's most powerful corporations. Accordingly, dues were assessed on a sliding scale, based on six categories that took into account the member organization's "profits" and number of employees. The largest corporate members could be assessed as much as 150 times the nominal dues paid by nonprofit member organizations. In 1975 the dues schedule ranged from $15,000 to $100 ($48,040 to $932 in 2000 dollars). Twelve "white" corporations, all of whose principals were Commercial Club members, paid dues in the highest category.[35] As recently as 1990, all white principals were also members of the Commercial Club, but only a handful of minority members held that honor. Yet by 2000 the corporate ranks in the city had become sufficiently integrated to permit the selection of a minority CEO as cochair of the organization.[36]

One consistent feature of Chicago United had been the cochairing of every committee by a majority and a minority member. Uncommon access to mainstream corporate leaders accrues to minority members, and they learn how and when to use this influence.[37] Minority members can also disarm their political opposition when it becomes known that the city's white corporate elite has approved their civic proposals.[38]

Benefits also accrue in the other direction. Biracial decision making proved crucial in the mid-1980s when the mayor, superintendent of schools, and teachers union head were all African Americans. They were wary of the Commercial Club because of its indifference during civil rights struggles and because white corporate members had backed Rich Daley over Harold Washington for mayor. When Warren Bacon, a longtime friend of Washington's, founding minority member of Chicago United, and Education Task Force cochair, was made Chicago United president, the group was afforded instant access to an unfamiliar and suspicious city hall. As president, Bacon had the opportunity to link business reform ideas to a mayoral regime focused primarily on neighborhood development, influencing both in the process.[39]

These complex distinctions periodically produced tension, further complicated by the city's changing social geography. In the first decade of Chicago United's existence, deacons appointed by white principals were typically vice presidents in the same corporation with responsibility for community affairs or personnel. By contrast, deacons chosen by minority principals were typically grassroots community leaders who were thought to have firsthand knowledge about the potential for racial unrest in the city.[40] In 1974 an informal organization of black deacons proposed that, as a condition of Chicago United membership, its corporate affiliates must refuse to reimburse executives for enrollment fees in discriminatory private clubs. Black and white deacons were divided about whether they had the "right" to raise the issue with principals. The African Americans reluctantly accepted a procedural twist, which they perceived to be an avoidance tactic: the issue would first go to the deacons as a whole, and only if they reached a consensus would it pass to the principals' Executive Committee.[41] This circuitous route avoided any decision, since neither side could convince the other.

By the 1990s members were again divided over deacons' influence. White principals felt that the group was "adrift and diffuse," while black and Latino principals and deacons were torn by internal dissension.[42] In response, deacons were briefly abandoned as a category of membership, only to be quickly reinstated when their contributions were missed. But their return came after a reorganization that no longer permitted community leaders, whatever their race or ethnicity, to become deacons. Chicago United's desire to maintain an authentic minority presence remains strong, but since the number of minority business leaders is now deemed sufficient, and women are routinely included, all new members—principals and deacons alike—are expected to be businesspeople.[43]

UNIQUE CHARACTERISTICS OF LEADERSHIP FOR QUALITY EDUCATION

LQE began as a board of twenty-eight directors, not as a membership organization.[44] The large majority of board members were also members of the Commercial Club, its Civic Committee, Chicago United, or all three. A small number of vice presidents were appointed to the LQE board after 1995, a breach of the principals-only rule that reflected LQE's subordination to the Civic Committee.

LQE's noncorporate directors have always included both minorities and women; leaders of the minority community groups that participated with Chicago United in its ABCs coalition to lobby for the 1988 law were the first members. However, they did not sit on the Executive Committee of LQE or participate as equals on issues of staffing or organizational direction. Nor did they provide financial or in-kind resources to the organization; on the contrary, they were often beneficiaries of LQE support.[45]

A structural shift that paralleled Chicago United's decision to abandon its institutional bridging function in favor of business-only membership also occurred in LQE. By 1998 all but one of these community leaders had left LQE, replaced by corporate vice presidents, a business professor, and a black Illinois legislator. Gender integration among business members was never an issue: the chairperson of LQE was female as early as 1993, and in 1998 the board included three businesswomen.[46]

LQE is more staff driven than the other groups in the network. Its initial staff members were highly qualified in school finance and the politics of advocacy, and they encouraged the directors to focus on those issues in LQE's early years. Directors, in turn, charged staff with initiating reports, making policy suggestions, and representing them in public. For example, Joseph Reed, LQE's first president, a Commercial Club member, and a principal at Chicago United, was appointed by Mayor Rich Daley to serve on the eight-member interim board of education installed in 1989. Under his leadership LQE's professional staff served as consultants to the interim board, helping to shape the early implementation of the reform law.[47]

These overlapping avenues of influence eventually led to staff-driven initiatives, occasionally undermining the corporate directors' commitment to the organization. In 1991 the problem drove the Executive Committee to seek a new senior staff member, one more closely attuned to the expectations of the board. But after only three years, executive director Diane Nelson was replaced for essentially the same reason: her commitment to community-based school reform activists hemmed in the board of directors' decision-making authority. Activists publicly criticized LQE for backtracking, but the organization was simply asserting its essential business nature.[48] The next executive director of LQE, John Ayers, was one of only a few Civic Committee employees reporting directly to *its* executive director, Larry Howe. His role symbolized the links between the two groups and the interest that Commercial Club members had in asserting control over the organization they had founded and still funded. When Ayers left LQE in 2005, the head of FRAC was tapped as the lead staff person for LQE's successor organization, New Schools for Chicago.[49]

Notes

Documents referenced in the Chicago Urban League Archives are from the Special Collections of the Richard M. Daley Library at the University of Illinois at Chicago. Documents referenced in the Presidents' Papers are from the Special Collections Research Center of the Joseph Regenstein Library of the University of Chicago. Documents referenced in the Cowlishaw Papers were provided by the Honorable Mary Lou Cowlishaw to the author and are in the possession of the author. Interviews were conducted by the author, her assistants, or other employees of the Consortium on Chicago School Research, where the author was employed as a director and principal investigator between 1996 and 1999. All were tape-recorded and transcribed and are used here with permission. Informants were offered anonymity on request.

INTRODUCTION

1. James G. Cibulka and William Lowe Boyd, eds., *A Race against Time: The Crisis in Urban Schooling* (Westport, Conn.: Praeger, 2003); Larry Cuban and Michael Usdan, eds., *Powerful Reforms with Shallow Roots: Getting Good Schools in Six Cities* (New York: Teachers College Press, 2002); Jeffrey Henig and Wilbur Rich, eds., *Mayors in the Middle: The Politics of Governance and Urban School Reform* (Princeton, N.J.: Princeton University Press, 2003).

2. Lizabeth Cohen, *Making a New Deal: Industrial Workers in Chicago, 1919–1939* (New York: Cambridge University Press, 1990); Janet L. Abu-Lughod, *New York, Chicago, Los Angeles: America's Global Cities* (Minneapolis: University of Minnesota Press, 1999), 79–84, 212.

3. Abu-Lughod, *New York, Chicago, Los Angeles,* 124–126.

4. U.S. Census Bureau, *Mapping Census 2000: The Geography of U.S. Diversity, Census 2000, Hispanic or Latino Origin Data* (December 7, 2001), http://factfinder.census.gov/servlet (accessed September 2003).

5. John J. Attinasi, "Hispanic Educational Research in View of Chicago Education Reform" (paper presented at the Assessing School Reform in Chicago conference, Consortium on Chicago School Research, Chicago, 1991); Latino Institute, *A Profile of Nine Latino Groups in Chicago* (Chicago: Latino Institute, 1994).

6. James B. Conant, *Slums and Suburbs: A Commentary on Schools in Metropolitan Areas* (New York: McGraw-Hill, 1961); Robert J. Havinghurst, *Education in Metropolitan Areas* (Boston: Allyn and Bacon, 1966); John Rury, "Race, Space and

Politics of Chicago's Public Schools: Benjamin Willis and the Tragedy of Urban Education," *History of Education Quarterly* 39, no. 2 (1999).

7. National Center for Educational Statistics, *Characteristics of the Largest 100 Elementary and Secondary School Districts in the United States* (Washington, D.C.: U.S. Department of Education, Office of Educational Research and Improvement, 1991–1999).

8. Ibid.

9. Elaine Allensworth and John Q. Easton, *Calculating a Cohort Dropout for the Chicago Public Schools* (Consortium on Chicago School Research, 2001); National Center for Educational Statistics, *Characteristics.*

10. Allensworth and Easton, *Calculating a Cohort Dropout;* John Q. Easton, T. Rosenkranz, and Anthony S. Bryk, *Annual CPS Test Trend Review, 2000* (Consortium on Chicago School Research, 2001); G Alfred Hess Jr. and Christina Warden, "Who Benefits from Desegregation Now?" *Journal of Negro Education* 57, no. 4 (1988).

11. Abu-Lughod, *New York, Chicago, Los Angeles,* 216.

12. David B. Tyack, Robert Lowe, and Elisabeth Hansot, *Public Schools in Hard Times: The Great Depression and Recent Years* (Cambridge: Harvard University Press, 1984), 35–41.

13. David B. Tyack and Larry Cuban, *Tinkering toward Utopia: A Century of Public School Reform* (Cambridge: Harvard University Press, 1995), 4.

14. David B. Tyack, *One Best System: A History of American Urban Education* (Cambridge: Harvard University Press, 1974); David B. Tyack and Elisabeth Hansot, *Managers of Virtue: Public School Leadership in America 1920–1980* (New York: Basic Books, 1982); Diane Ravitch, *The Great School Wars,* vol. 2 (New York: Basic Books, 1988); Jeffrey Mirel, *The Rise and Fall of an Urban School System: Detroit, 1907–1981* (Ann Arbor: University of Michigan Press, 1993).

15. Quoted in Michael B. Katz, *Class, Bureaucracy and the Schools: The Illusion of Educational Change in America* (New York: Praeger, 1971): 2; John E. Chubb and Terry M. Moe, *Politics, Markets and America's Schools* (Washington, D.C.: Brookings Institution, 1990); David K. Cohen, "Reforming School Politics," *Harvard Education Review* 48, no. 4 (1978); Frederick Hess, *Spinning Wheels: The Politics of Urban School Reform* (Washington, D.C.: Brookings Institution, 1999); Paul T. Hill, Lawrence C. Pierce, and James W. Guthrie, *Reinventing Public Education* (Chicago: University of Chicago Press, 1997); Harvey Kantor and Robert Lowe, "Bureaucracy Left and Right: Thinking about the One Best System," in *Reconstructing the Common Good in Education: Coping with Intractable American Dilemmas,* ed. Larry Cuban and Dorothy Shipps (Stanford, Calif.: Stanford University Press, 2000); Wilbur Rich, *Black Mayors and School Politics: The Failure of Reform in Detroit, Gary and Newark* (New York: Garland, 1996); David Rogers, *110 Livingston Street: Politics and Bureaucracy in the New York City School System* (Lexington, Mass.: Lexington Books, 1967).

16. G. Alfred Hess Jr., *School Restructuring, Chicago Style* (Newbury Park, Calif.: Corwin Press, 1991); Dan A. Lewis and Katherine Nakagawa, *Race and Educational Reform in the American Metropolis: A Study of Decentralization* (Albany: State University of New York Press, 1995); Anthony S. Bryk et al., *Charting Chicago School Reform: Democratic Localism as a Lever for Change* (Boulder, Colo.: Westview Press, 1998); David B. Tyack, "School Governance in the United States: Historical Puzzles and Anomalies," in *Decentralization and School Improvement: Can We Fulfill the*

Promise? ed. Jane Hannaway and Martin Carnoy (San Francisco: Jossey-Bass, 1993); Kenneth K. Wong et al., *Integrated Governance as a Reform Strategy in Chicago Public Schools* (Philadelphia: National Center on Education in the Inner Cities, 1997).

17. Jennifer L. Hochchild, *The New American Dilemma: Liberal Democracy and School Desegregation* (New Haven, Conn.: Yale University Press, 1984); Gary Orfield and Susan Eaton, *Dismantling Desegregation* (New York: New Press, 1996); Amy Stuart Wells and Robert L. Crain, *Stepping over the Color Line* (New Haven, Conn.: Yale University Press, 1997).

18. Frank W. Lutz, and Laurence Iannaconne, *Public Participation in Local School Districts: The Dissatisfaction Theory of American Democracy* (Lexington, Mass.: D. C. Heath, 1978); Fredrick Wirt and Michael W. Kirst, *Schools in Conflict,* 3rd ed. (Berkeley, Calif.: McCutchen, 1992); L. Harmon Zeigler, M. Kent Jennings, and G. Wayne Peak, *Governing American Schools: Political Interaction in Local School Districts* (North Scituate, Mass.: Duxbury Press, 1974); Laurence Iannaconne and Frank W. Lutz, "The Crucible of Democracy: The Local Arena," in *The Study of Educational Politics: The Politics of Education Association Yearbook,* ed. Jay D. Scribner and Donald H. Layton (Washington, D.C.: Falmer Press, 1994).

19. Jeffrey Henig et al., *Building Civic Capacity for School Reform: Race, Politics and the Challenge of Urban Education* (Princeton, N.J.: Princeton University Press, 2001); John Portz, Lana Stein, and Robin R. Jones, *City Schools and City Politics: Institutions and Leadership in Pittsburgh, Boston and St. Louis* (Lawrence: University Press of Kansas, 2001); Clarence N. Stone et al., *Building Civic Capacity: The Politics of Reforming Urban Schools* (Lawrence: University Press of Kansas, 2001).

20. Clarence N. Stone, "Civic Capacity and Urban School Reform," in *Changing Urban Education,* ed. Clarence N. Stone (Lawrence: University Press of Kansas, 1998), 263.

21. Ibid., 254.

22. Charles E. Lindblom, *Politics and Markets: The World's Political Economic Systems* (New York: Basic Books, 1977); Wolfgang Streeck and Philippe Schmitter, eds., *Private Interest Government: Beyond Market and State* (Beverly Hills, Calif.: Sage Press, 1985).

23. Charles E. Lindblom and Edward J. Woodhouse, *The Policy Making Process,* 3rd ed. (Englewood Cliffs, N.J.: Prentice Hall, 1993).

24. John W. Kingdon, *Agendas, Alternatives and Public Policies,* 2nd ed. (New York: HarperCollins College, 1995).

25. Clarence N. Stone, "Urban Regimes and the Capacity to Govern," *Journal of Urban Affairs* 15, no. 1 (1993): 11; Stone, "Civic Capacity and Urban School Reform," 267.

26. Stone, "Civic Capacity and Urban School Reform."

27. Stone, "Urban Regime and Capacity," 15–16.

28. Ibid., 22–26.

29. Tyack and Cuban, *Tinkering toward Utopia;* Dorothy Shipps, Joseph Kahne, and Mark A. Smylie, "The Politics of Urban School Reform: Legitimacy, Urban Growth and School Improvement in Chicago," *Educational Policy* 13, no. 4 (1999).

30. Mickey Lauria, ed., *Reconstructing Urban Regime Theory: Regulating Urban Politics in a Global Economy* (Thousand Oaks, Calif.: Sage Publications, 1997); Stone, "Civic Capacity and Urban School Reform," 250–273.

31. Paul E. Peterson, *School Politics, Chicago Style* (Chicago: University of Chicago Press, 1976), 252; Paul E. Peterson, *City Limits* (Chicago: University of Chicago Press, 1981), 6.

32. Ira Katznelson and Margaret Weir, *Schooling for All: Class, Race and the Decline of the Democratic Ideal* (New York: Basic Books, 1985), 213.

33. Barbara Ferman, *Challenging the Growth Machine: Neighborhood Politics in Chicago and Pittsburgh* (Lawrence: University Press of Kansas, 1996).

34. Katherine M. Doherty, "Changing Urban Education: Defining the Issues," in *Changing Urban Education,* ed. Clarence N. Stone (Lawrence University Press of Kansas, 1998): 240.

35. Ibid.

36. Stone et al., *Building Civic Capacity.*

37. Hess, *Spinning Wheels,* 127–150.

38. Stone, "Civic Capacity and Urban School Reform," 255–259.

39. Charles E. Lindblom, *Democracy and the Market System* (Oslo: Norwegian University Press, 1988); Cathie Jo Martin, *Stuck in Neutral: Business and the Politics of Human Capital Investment* (Princeton, N.J.: Princeton University Press, 2000); Streeck and Schmitter, *Private Interest Government.*

40. Mark A. Smith, *American Business and Political Power: Public Opinion, Elections and Democracy* (Chicago: University of Chicago Press, 2000), 165, ch. 8.

41. Katz, *Class, Bureaucracy and the Schools;* Joel H. Spring, *Education and the Rise of the Corporate State* (Boston: Beacon Press, 1972); Samuel Bowles and Herbert Gintis, *Schooling in Capitalist America* (New York: Basic Books, 1976).

42. Paul E. Peterson, *The Politics of School Reform 1870–1940* (Chicago: University of Chicago Press, 1985).

43. David J. Hogan, *Class and Reform: School and Society in Chicago: 1880–1930* (Philadelphia: University of Pennsylvania, 1985).

44. Julia Wrigley, *Class Politics and Public Schools: Chicago 1900–1950* (New Brunswick, N.J.: Rutgers University Press, 1982).

45. William Simon, *A Time for Truth* (New York: Berkley, 1978); David Vogel, *Fluctuating Fortunes: The Political Power of Business in America* (New York: Basic Books, 1998).

46. Peterson, *Politics of School Reform;* Stephen D. London, "Business and Chicago Public Schools: 1890–1966" (Ph.D. diss., University of Chicago, 1968); Stephen Lewis Garay, "Business Influences in the Formation of Educational Policy: A Case Study of Chicago United Initiatives" (Ph.D. diss., University of Illinois at Chicago, 1982).

47. Robert L. Crain, *The Politics of School Desegregation* (Chicago: Aldine Publishing Co., 1968); Kathryn A. McDermott, *Controlling Public Education: Localism vs. Equity* (Lawrence: University Press of Kansas, 1999).

48. Roslyn Arlyn Mickelson, "International Business Machinations: A Case Study of Corporate Involvement in Local Educational Reform," *Teachers College Record* 100, no. 3 (1999); Carol A. Ray and Roslyn A. Mickelson, "Corporate Leaders, Resistant Youth and School Reform in Sunbelt City: The Political Economy of Education," *Social Problems* 37, no. 2 (1990).

49. Kathryn Borman, Louis Costnell, and Karen Gallagher, "Business Involvement in School Reform: The Rise of the Business Roundtable," in *The New Politics of Race and Gender: The Politics of Education Association Yearbook,* ed. Catherine Marshall

(Washington, D.C.: Falmer Press, 1993); Dorothy Shipps, "The Invisible Hand: Big Business and Chicago School Reform," *Teachers College Record* 99, no. 1 (1997); Thomas Longoria Jr., "School Politics in Houston: The Impact of Business Involvement," in Stone, *Changing Urban Education;* Steven S. Smith, "Education and Regime Change in Charlotte," in ibid.

50. Cohen, "Reforming School Politics;" Alex Molnar, *Giving Kids the Business: The Commercialization of America's Schools* (Boulder, Colo.: Westview Press, 1996).

51. Henig et al., *Building Civic Capacity;* Portz, Stein, and Jones, *City Schools;* Stone et al., *Building Civic Capacity.*

1. SHAPING THE MODERN SYSTEM

1. Frederic Cople Jaher, *The Urban Establishment: Upper Strata in Boston, New York, Charleston, Chicago and Los Angeles* (Urbana: University of Illinois Press, 1982), 494–498, 537.

2. Janet L. Abu-Lughod, *New York, Chicago, Los Angeles: America's Global Cities* (Minneapolis: University of Minnesota Press, 1999), 6, 101.

3. William Cronon, *Nature's Metropolis: Chicago and the Great West* (New York: W. W. Norton, 1991); Emmett Dedmon, *Fabulous Chicago* (New York: Atheneum, 1981); Jaher, *The Urban Establishment,* 455; Vilas Johnson, *A History of the Commercial Club of Chicago: Including the First History of the Club by John J. Glessner* (Chicago: Commercial Club of Chicago, 1977).

4. Mary Herrick, *The Chicago Schools: A Social and Political History* (Beverly Hills, Calif.: Sage Publications, 1971); Kate Rousmanicre, *Citizen Teacher: The Life and Leadership of Margaret Haley* (Albany: State University of New York Press, 2005); David B. Tyack, *One Best System: A History of American Urban Education* (Cambridge: Harvard University Press, 1974); Julia Wrigley, *Class Politics and Public Schools: Chicago 1900–1950* (New Brunswick, N.J.: Rutgers University Press, 1982).

5. Herrick, *The Chicago Schools;* Ira Katznelson and Margaret Weir, *Schooling for All: Class, Race and the Decline of the Democratic Ideal* (New York: Basic Books, 1985); Bessie Louise Pierce, *A History of Chicago, 1871–1893: The Rise of a Modern City,* vol. 3 (New York: Alfred A. Knopf, 1957); George Counts, *School and Society in Chicago* (New York: Harcourt, Brace, 1928); Michael B. Katz, *Reconstructing American Education* (Cambridge: Harvard University Press, 1987); Paul E. Peterson, *School Politics, Chicago Style* (Chicago: University of Chicago, 1976).

6. Counts, *School and Society;* Katznelson and Weir, *Schooling for All;* David J. Hogan, *Class and Reform: School and Society in Chicago: 1880–1930* (Philadelphia: University of Pennsylvania, 1985); Paul E. Peterson, *The Politics of School Reform 1870–1940* (Chicago: University of Chicago Press, 1985).

7. William T. Stead, *If Christ Came to Chicago! A Plea for the Union of All Who Love in the Service of All Who Suffer* (Chicago: Laird and Lee, 1894), 455–461; Jaher, *The Urban Establishment,* 475, 502–504.

8. Stead, *If Christ Came to Chicago,* 99–121.

9. Ibid., 174–175; see also Wrigley, *Class Politics and Public Schools.*

10. Counts, *School and Society,* 22.

11. Jaher, *The Urban Establishment;* Stead, *If Christ Came to Chicago;* Peterson, *Politics of School Reform;* Alan Ryan, *John Dewey: The High Tide of American Liberalism* (New York: W. W. Norton, 1995).

12. Abu-Lughod, *New York, Chicago, Los Angeles;* Thomas Lee Philpott, *The Slum and the Ghetto: Immigrants, Blacks and Reformers in Chicago, 1880–1930* (Belmont, Calif.: Wadsworth, 1975–1991); Pierce, *A History of Chicago;* Allan H. Spear, *Black Chicago: The Making of a Negro Ghetto, 1890–1920* (Chicago: University of Chicago Press, 1967).

13. Jaher, *The Urban Establishment,* 471; Johnson, *A History.*

14. Jaher, *The Urban Establishment,* 493–494.

15. Abu-Lughod, *New York, Chicago, Los Angeles,* 102–106. See Wilbert R. Hasbrouck's introduction to Daniel H. Burnham and Edward H. Bennett, *Plan of Chicago* (New York: Da Capo Press, 1970).

16. Jaher, *The Urban Establishment,* 473.

17. Cronon, *Nature's Metropolis.*

18. Ibid., 292–295; Jaher, *The Urban Establishment,* 496; Johnson, *A History.*

19. Johnson, *A History,* 13; Jaher, *The Urban Establishment,* 456.

20. Stead, *If Christ Came to Chicago,* 69–97.

21. Frank Norris used Joseph Leiter, Levi's son, as the model for the self-destructive character in his fictionalized account of Chicago's wheat speculation. Frank Norris, *The Pit: A Story of Chicago* (1903; reprint, New York: Grove Press, 1956).

22. Dedmon, *Fabulous Chicago,* 18; Jaher, *The Urban Establishment;* Johnson, *A History;* June Skinner Sawyers, *Chicago Portraits: Biographies of 250 Chicagoans* (Chicago: Loyola University Press, 1991).

23. Dedmon, *Fabulous Chicago,* 114; Jaher, *The Urban Establishment.*

24. Johnson, *A History,* 21.

25. The list of meeting agendas and speakers provided in the Commercial Club's official history covering the years 1877 to 1977 reveals the following topics, in order of frequency: education (35); municipal and state reform (34); sewers, streets, water, transportation, and other urban infrastructure (25); workers, labor, and immigration (21); taxation (18); Plan of Chicago (11).

26. National and international issues discussed in its first fifty years included market-making activities such as trade policy, industry regulation, and new scientific discoveries (72); international affairs (37); war (23); and broad political discussions (16).

27. Ralph, as cited in Cronon, *Nature's Metropolis,* 293.

28. Johnson, *A History,* 12, 47–58.

29. Harvey Kantor and David B. Tyack, eds., *Work, Youth and Schooling: Historical Perspectives and Vocationalism in Education* (Stanford, Calif.: Stanford University Press, 1982); Commercial Club of Chicago, *Year Book, 1912–1913;* Stephen D. London, "Business and Chicago Public Schools: 1890–1966" (Ph.D. diss., University of Chicago, 1968).

30. Raymond E. Callahan, *Education and the Cult of Efficiency: A Study of the Social Forces that Have Shaped the Administration of the Public Schools* (Chicago: University of Chicago Press, 1962); Tyack, *One Best System;* David B. Tyack and Elisabeth Hansot, *Managers of Virtue: Public School Leadership in America 1920–1980* (New York: Basic Books, 1982).

31. David B. Tyack, Robert Lowe, and Elisabeth Hansot, *Public Schools in Hard*

Times: The Great Depression and Recent Years (Cambridge: Harvard University Press, 1984). Herrick, *The Chicago Schools.*

32. Commercial Club of Chicago, *Year Books of the Commercial Club of Chicago* (1911–1982).

33. Commercial Club of Chicago, *Year Book, 1914–1915,* 195.

34. Hogan, *Class and Reform,* 152–160; Pierce, *A History of Chicago,* 383–389, 394; Herrick, *The Chicago Schools,* 52–59; Herbert Kliebard, *The Struggle for the American Curriculum, 1893–1958* (New York: Routledge and Kegan Paul, 1987); London, "Business and Chicago Public Schools," 28; Wrigley, *Class Politics and Public Schools,* 50.

35. London, "Business and Chicago Public Schools," 34.

36. Ryan, *John Dewey,* 138; William B. Owen to William Rainey Harper, March 11, 1901, University of Chicago Presidents' Papers, 1889–1925, box 25.

37. Edward O. Brown to William Rainey Harper, April 17, 1901, University of Chicago Presidents' Papers, 1889–1925, box 19; Manual Training School Director Belfield to William Rainey Harper, June 19, 1902, ibid.; Commercial Club of Chicago, *Year Book, 1912–1913,* 155; *Year Book, 1929–1930,* 83.

38. Commercial Club of Chicago, *Year Book, 1912–1913,* 158–162; *Year Book 1913–1914,* 197–200, 248–255.

39. Edwin C. Cooley quoted in Commercial Club of Chicago, *Year Book, 1912–1913,* 154, 158–159.

40. Quoted in Theodore W. Robinson, "Industrial Education in Our Public Schools," in *Addresses and Proceedings* (National Education Association, 1910), 368–375; Chairman of the Subcommittee on Vocational Education to Chairman of the Executive Committee of the Chicago Association of Commerce (Elmer Adams), December 31, 1912, University of Chicago Presidents' Papers, 1889–1925, box 67; Henry Pratt Judson to Nicholas M. Butler, January 4, 1913, ibid.

41. London, "Business and Chicago Public Schools," 38; Wrigley, *Class Politics and Public Schools,* 110–113, 210. Tyack, *One Best System,* 170–171; Hogan, *Class and Reform,* 160.

42. Edwin G. Cooley, "Vocational Education in Europe: Report to the Commercial Club of Chicago" (1912), 67–68; Herrick, *The Chicago Schools,* 81; Peterson, *Politics of School Reform,* 160–161; Tyack and Hansot, *Managers of Virtue;* Wrigley, *Class Politics and Public Schools.*

43. John D. Buenker, "Edward F. Dunne: The Limits of Municipal Reform," in *The Mayors: The Chicago Political Tradition,* ed. Paul M. Green and Melvin Holli (Carbondale: Southern Illinois University Press, 1987), 35.

44. Ibid., 43.

45. Quoted in ibid., 48; Dominic Candeloro, "The Chicago School Board Crisis of 1907," *Journal of the Illinois State Historical Society* 68, no. 5 (1975); Rousmaniere, *Citizen Teacher,* 139–142, 146.

46. Jane Addams and Anita McCormick Blaine were not removed. Maureen A. Flanagan, "Fred A. Busse: A Silent Mayor in Turbulent Times," in Green and Holli, *The Mayors;* Rousmaniere, *Citizen Teacher,* 149.

47. Commercial Club of Chicago, *Year Book, 1911–1912,* 277.

48. Wrigley, *Class Politics and Public Schools,* 69–70.

49. Commercial Club of Chicago, *Year Book, 1912–1913,* 227.

50. Commercial Club of Chicago, *Year Book, 1911–1912,* 135–153.

51. Ibid., 154.

52. Ibid., 160, 349–350; Cooley, "Vocational Education"; Wrigley, *Class Politics and Public Schools;* Tyack, *One Best System;* Johnson, *A History.*

53. Commercial Club of Chicago, *Year Book, 1912–1913,* 259–266; Thomas Bender, *New York Intellect: A History of the Intellectual Life in New York City from 1750 to the Beginnings of Our Own Time* (Baltimore: Johns Hopkins University Press, 1988), 286; Kliebard, *The Struggle,* 113; David Snedden, "Vocational Education," *New Republic,* May 15 1915; see also John Dewey's response in the same issue.

54. Quoted in London, "Business and Chicago Public Schools," 55; see also Peterson, *Politics of School Reform,* 163.

55. Counts, *School and Society,* 210; Hogan, *Class and Reform,* 160.

56. Hogan, *Class and Reform,* 167.

57. John Dewey, "Splitting up the School System," *New Republic,* April 17, 1915.

58. John Dewey, "Education vs. Trade-Training—Dr. Dewey's Reply," *New Republic,* May 15, 1915.

59. Hogan, *Class and Reform,* 163.

60. Professor Nicholas Murray Butler to President Judson, January 1913, University of Chicago Presidents' Papers, 1889–1925, box 67.

61. Wrigley, *Class Politics and Public Schools,* 17.

62. Katznelson and Weir, *Schooling for All,* 89–93.

63. Commercial Club of Chicago, *Year Books of the Commercial Club of Chicago* (1911–1982); Johnson, *A History.*

64. Abu-Lughod, *New York, Chicago, Los Angeles,* 113–114; Commercial Club of Chicago, "Plan of Chicago" (1909).

65. Quoted in Wrigley, *Class Politics and Public Schools,* 60–81; Herrick, *The Chicago Schools;* Rousmaniere, *Citizen Teacher,* 50.

66. Theodore Robinson and Clayton Mark quoted in Commercial Club of Chicago, *Year Book 1914–1915,* 199, 252, 274–276.

67. Commercial Club of Chicago, *Year Book 1927–1928,* 70–77.

68. Quoted in London, "Business and Chicago Public Schools," 50; see also Wrigley, *Class Politics and Public Schools,* 86–90.

69. Hogan, *Class and Reform,* 168–172; London, "Business and Chicago Public Schools," 77–78.

70. Quoted in Commercial Club of Chicago, *Year Book, 1911–1912,* 298.

71. Tyack, *One Best System,* pt. 4; Tyack and Hansot, *Managers of Virtue,* 105–114; Callahan, *Education and the Cult of Efficiency.*

72. Johnson, *A History,* 194.

73. Edward R. Kantowicz, "Carter Harrison III: The Politics of Balance," in Green and Holli, *The Mayors.*

74. Education Commission of the City of Chicago (University of Chicago, 1900), xiii; Tyack, *One Best System,* 169; Wrigley, *Class Politics and Public Schools,* 92–98.

75. *Who's Who in Chicago and Vicinity,* 4th ed. (Chicago: A. N. Marquis, 1926).

76. *The Book of Chicagoans: A Bibliographic Dictionary of the Leading Men of the City of Chicago, 1905–1911,* 2nd ed. (Chicago: A. N. Marquis, 1911); Tyack and Hansot, *Managers of Virtue.*

77. Education Commission of the City of Chicago, article 1.

78. Ibid., xiv–xvii.

79. Ibid., xviii, 139–144, 167–168.

80. Hogan, *Class and Reform.*

81. Wrigley, *Class Politics and Public Schools,* 97–98.

82. Rousmaniere, *Citizen Teacher,* 89, 110.

83. Aaron Gove quoted in Tyack, *One Best System,* 257.

84. Rousmaniere, *Citizen Teacher,* 212.

85. Ibid., 120.

86. Education Commission of the City of Chicago, appendix K.

87. Hogan, *Class and Reform,* 196–197, 200–202; Wrigley, *Class Politics and Public Schools,* 94–95. Rousmaniere, *Citizen Teacher,* 34.

88.Quoted in Hogan, *Class and Reform,* 197.

89. Herrick, *The Chicago Schools,* 103; Wrigley, *Class Politics and Public Schools;* Peterson, *Politics of School Reform.*

90. Rousmaniere, *Citizen Teacher,* 94.

91. Ibid., 100.

92. Wrigley, *Class Politics and Public Schools,* 102–104.

93. Hogan, *Class and Reform,* 202.

94. Wrigley, *Class Politics and Public Schools,* 104.

95. Hogan, *Class and Reform,* 40–42, 218.

96. Flanagan, "Fred A. Busse," 50–60; Hogan, *Class and Reform,* 206–207; Counts, *School and Society;* John W. Leonard, ed., *The Book of Chicagoans* (Chicago: A. N. Marquis, 1905); Albert N. Marquis, ed., *The Book of Chicagoans* (Chicago: A. N. Marquis, 1911); Chicago Public Schools, *School Report,* vols. 52–57 (Chicago: Board of Education, 1906–1911).

97. Quoted in Hogan, *Class and Reform,* 207; Wrigley, *Class Politics and Public Schools,* 106–110.

98. Ella Flagg Young, *Isolation in the Schools* (Chicago: University of Chicago Press, 1900).

99. Rousmaniere, *Citizen Teacher,* 157.

100. Quoted in Hogan, *Class and Reform,* 176–177. Tyack and Hansot, *Managers of Virtue,* 194–200.

101. Tyack and Hansot, *Managers of Virtue,* 180–187.

102. Hogan, *Class and Reform,* 208–209; Wrigley, *Class Politics and Public Schools,* 120–132.

103. Commercial Club of Chicago, *Year Book, 1921–1922,* 15–22; Public Education Association of Chicago, *Bulletin,* nos. 1–4 (1916).

104. Public Education Association of Chicago, *Bulletin,* no. 1 (1916): 1–12.

105. Ibid., no. 2, 10–12.

106. The legacy left by the CTF is in dispute. See Hogan, *Class and Reform;* Peterson, *Politics of School Reform;* Wrigley, *Class Politics and Public Schools.*

107. Quoted in Hogan, *Class and Reform,* 209.

108. Peterson, *Politics of School Reform,* 143; Wrigley, *Class Politics and Public Schools,* 132–135.

109. Quoted in Counts, *School and Society,* 53; Hogan, *Class and Reform,* 211; Rousmaniere, *Citizen Teacher,* 173.

110. Rousmaniere, *Citizen Teacher*, 39, 173–174.

111. Peterson, *Politics of School Reform*, 145–152; Public Education Association of Chicago, *Bulletin*, no. 2 (1916); Counts, *School and Society*, 38; Wrigley, *Class Politics and Public Schools*, 137–139.

112. Hogan, *Class and Reform*, 217–219; Peterson, *Politics of School Reform*, 141–142.

113. Peterson, *Politics of School Reform*, 144–150; Wrigley, *Class Politics and Public Schools*, 141.

114. Wrigley, *Class Politics and Public Schools*, 135–136; Hogan, *Class and Reform*, 210.

115. Peterson, *Politics of School Reform*, 144–150.

116. Commercial Club of Chicago, *Year Book, 1916–1917*, 196–207; *Year Book, 1921–1922*, 188–190.

117. Commercial Club of Chicago, *Year Book 1927–1928*, 70–77; Johnson, *A History*, 193; Rousmaniere, *Citizen Teacher*.

118. Herrick, *The Chicago Schools*, 95–96.

119. Ibid., 101; Rousmaniere, *Citizen Teacher*, 61.

120. Herrick, *The Chicago Schools*, 102; Counts, *School and Society*, 93.

121. The 1926 assessments were $1,760,000, whereas the Federation of Men's Teachers of High School claimed that $132,359,987 was a more realistic assessment.

122. London, "Business and Chicago Public Schools," 68; Herrick, *The Chicago Schools*.

123. Johnson, *A History*, 132–138.

124. Herrick, *The Chicago Schools*, 190; London, "Business and Chicago Public Schools," 110–120; Peterson, *Politics of School Reform*.

125. Herrick, *The Chicago Schools*, 140, 406.

126. Robert L. Ruffus, "Big Billism Again Sets Chicago Agog," *New York Times*, November 6, 1927; Douglas Bukowski, "Big Bill Thompson: The 'Model' Politician," in Green and Holli, *The Mayors;* Lloyd Wendt and Herman Kagan, *Big Bill of Chicago* (Indianapolis, Ind.: Bobbs-Merrill, 1953).

127. Bukowski, "Big Bill Thompson," 65.

128. Philpott, *The Slum and the Ghetto*, 137–162; Abu-Lughod, *New York, Chicago, Los Angeles*, 124–126.

129. Philpott, *The Slum and the Ghetto*, 168, 178–180.

130. Ibid., 160; Wrigley, *Class Politics and Public Schools*, 141–151; Hogan, *Class and Reform*, 211; Herrick, *The Chicago Schools*, 142, 180–181.

131. John Shoop (1915–1918) was ill for almost his entire superintendency and died before his four-year term was complete. Thompson illegally ousted Charles Chadsey (1919–1922) after winning a second term as mayor. Although reinstated by the courts, Chadsey then resigned. Peter Mortensen (1920–1924), the Thompson board's choice in 1919, took his place and sought teachers' support by reinstituting teachers councils. Herrick, *The Chicago Schools*, 138–141; Rousmaniere, *Citizen Teacher*, 185–189, 197.

132. Bukowski, "Big Bill Thompson," 64.

133. London, "Business and Chicago Public Schools."

134. Quoted in John R. Schmidt, "William E. Dever: A Chicago Political Fable," in Green and Holli, *The Mayors*, 86; Wendt and Kagan, *Big Bill*, 201–214.

135. Wendt and Kagan, *Big Bill*, 234.

136. Counts, *School and Society*, 114–116; Schmidt, "William E. Dever," 86–92; Tyack, *One Best System*.

137. Counts, *School and Society,* 169–191; Schmidt, "William E. Dever," 92.

138. Quoted in Wrigley, *Class Politics and Public Schools,* 157.

139. Ruffus, "Big Billism."

140. Herrick, *The Chicago Schools,* 179–180; London, "Business and Chicago Public Schools," 81–82; Peterson, *Politics of School Reform,* 157–158; Wrigley, *Class Politics and Public Schools,* 209–210.

141. Herrick, *The Chicago Schools,* 184.

142. Ibid., 186–187.

143. Silas Strawn quoted in Commercial Club of Chicago, *Year Book, 1929–1930,* 186–200; Wendt and Kagan, *Big Bill,* 314.

144. Roger Biles, "Edward J. Kelly: New Deal Machine Builder," in Green and Holli, *The Mayors,* 112.

145. Strawn quoted in Commercial Club of Chicago, *Year Book, 1929–1930,* 186–200; second quote in Commercial Club of Chicago, *Year Book, 1932–1933,* 169.

146. Wendt and Kagan, *Big Bill,* 314–315.

147. Ibid., 277; Herrick, *The Chicago Schools,* 188–190; Peterson, *Politics of School Reform,* 175–176.

148. Commercial Club of Chicago, *Year Book, 1929–1930,* 190–192.

149. Peterson, *Politics of School Reform,* 175.

150. Herrick, *The Chicago Schools,* 187, 189–195.

151. Ibid., 193; London, "Business and Chicago Public Schools," 86–89.

152. Herrick, *The Chicago Schools,* 194–195; Johnson, *A History,* 155; Wendt and Kagan, *Big Bill.*

153. Herrick, *The Chicago Schools,* 205.

154. Fred Sargent, "The Taxpayer Takes Charge," *Saturday Evening Post,* January 11, 1933, 21, 76.

155. Quoted in Wrigley, *Class Politics and Public Schools,* 215.

156. Herrick, *The Chicago Schools,* 199; Wrigley, *Class Politics and Public Schools,* 213; London, "Business and Chicago Public Schools," 84–90.

157. Sargent quoted in London, "Business and Chicago Public Schools," 103.

158. Herrick, *The Chicago Schools,* 200–220.

159. London, "Business and Chicago Public Schools," 104.

160. Wrigley, *Class Politics and Public Schools,* 218–220; London, "Business and Chicago Public Schools," 107–108.

161. London, "Business and Chicago Public Schools," 112–113.

162. Biles, "Edward J. Kelly."

163. Ibid., 113–115.

164. Commercial Club of Chicago, *Year Book, 1932–1933,* 103.

165. Sargent, "The Taxpayer Takes Charge," 80.

166. Ibid., 82.

167. London, "Business and Chicago Public Schools," 115–116; Wrigley, *Class Politics and Public Schools,* 225.

168. Sargent, "The Taxpayer Takes Charge," 82.

169. Commercial Club of Chicago, *Year Book, 1938–1939,* 256.

170. Omitted are Carter Harrison I (1893), fatally shot just after he was sworn into office; George Swift (1893), who briefly replaced him; and Frank Corr (1933), who briefly filled in after Anton Cermak (1931–1933) was fatally shot. Schmidt, "William E. Dever," 8.

171. Rousmaniere, *Citizen Teacher,* 87.
172. Wrigley, *Class Politics and Public Schools.*

2. CONFRONTING RACE

1. For an account of these events in Detroit, see Jeffrey Mirel, *The Rise and Fall of an Urban School System: Detroit, 1907–1981* (Ann Arbor: University of Michigan Press, 1993).

2. David J. Greenfield and Paul E. Peterson, *Race and Authority in Urban Politics* (New York: Russell Sage Foundation, 1973); Mike Royko, *Boss, Richard J. Daley of Chicago* (New York: Penguin Books, 1971); Howard Biles, *Big City Boss in Depression and War: Mayor Edward J. Kelly of Chicago* (De Kalb: Northern Illinois University Press, 1984); Stephen P. Erie, *Rainbow's End: Irish-Americans and the Dilemmas of Urban Machine Politics* (Berkeley: University of California Press, 1988); Samuel K. Gove and Louis H. Massotti, eds., *After Daley: Chicago Politics in Transition* (Urbana: University of Illinois Press, 1988); William A. Grimshaw, *Bitter Fruit: Black Politics and the Chicago Machine: 1931–1991* (Chicago: University of Chicago Press, 1992); Len O'Connor, *Clout: Mayor Daley and His City* (Chicago: Henry Regnery, 1975).

3. Paul M. Green, "Anton Cermak: 1931–1933," in *The Mayors: The Chicago Political Tradition,* ed. Paul M. Green and Melvin Holli (Carbondale: Southern Illinois University Press, 1987), 101.

4. Lloyd Wendt and Herman Kagan, *Big Bill of Chicago* (Indianapolis, Ind.: Bobbs-Merrill, 1953); Howard Gosnell, *Machine Politics: Chicago Model* (Urbana, Ill.: University of Chicago Press, 1937); Howard Gosnell, *Negro Politicians: The Rise of Negro Politics in Chicago* (Urbana, Ill.: University of Chicago Press, 1935); Grimshaw, *Bitter Fruit.*

5. Green, "Anton Cermak."

6. Ibid., 104; Gosnell, *Machine Politics,* 167; Stephen D. London, "Business and Chicago Public Schools: 1890–1966" (Ph.D. diss., University of Chicago, 1968); Julia Wrigley, *Class Politics and Public Schools: Chicago 1900–1950* (New Brunswick, N.J.: Rutgers University Press, 1982).

7. Adam Cohen and Elisabeth Taylor, *American Pharaoh: Mayor Richard M. Daley* (Boston: Little, Brown, 2000), 54–55.

8. "Policy" was a technically illegal but tolerated form of lottery run in the black belt by men who often owned legitimate businesses. It provided the police with boodling opportunities and local politicians with a form of "protection" financing. Dempsey Travis estimates that between 1920 and 1940, 15,000 blacks were employed annually in the South Side policy houses. Dempsey Travis, *An Autobiography of Black Politics* (Chicago: Urban Research Press, 1987), 174; Biles, *Big City Boss;* Grimshaw, *Bitter Fruit.*

9. Biles, *Big City Boss,* 89–90; Travis, *An Autobiography,* 107.

10. Cohen and Taylor, *American Pharaoh,* 56.

11. Grimshaw, *Bitter Fruit.*

12. The black belt was a four- to five-block strip of primarily slum housing west of State Street. In the mid-1920s it was bounded by Sixteenth Street on the north and Fifty-fifth Street on the south, hemmed in by working-class immigrant whites to the

east and by the mansions of native-born Protestant merchants and industrialists on the west. Whites owned 70 percent of the approximately 500 establishments in the State Street and Thirty-fifth Street commercial center. St. Clair Drake and Horace R. Cayton, *Black Metropolis: Study of Negro Life in a Northern City,* vols. 1 and 2 (New York: Harcourt, Brace and World, 1970), 184; Gosnell, *Negro Politicians;* Glen E. Holt and Dominic A. Pacyga, *Chicago: A Historical Guide to the Neighborhoods: The Loop and South Side* (Chicago: Chicago Historical Society, 1979), 52; Allan H. Spear, *Black Chicago: The Making of a Negro Ghetto, 1890–1920* (Chicago: University of Chicago Press, 1967).

13. Restrictive covenants were created when 95 percent of property owners in a neighborhood signed a document indicating that their property could not be sold to Negroes. Covenants were not declared unconstitutional until 1948. Drake and Cayton, *Black Metropolis,* 182–190; Spear, *Black Chicago,* 142–150.

14. Gosnell, *Machine Politics;* Spear, *Black Chicago,* 212–216; Arvarh E Strickland, *History of the Chicago Urban League* (Urbana: University of Illinois Press, 1966), 59–60; Wendt and Kagan, *Big Bill.*

15. Under the system of cumulative voting in Illinois before the Depression, each voter had three votes to spread among candidates or concentrate on one candidate, as he or she chose. It gave Chicago one black member of the state legislature in every session since 1878. Gosnell, *Negro Politicians,* 55–57, 65–69, 157–159, 204–240; Drake and Cayton, *Black Metropolis;* Wendt and Kagan, *Big Bill.*

16. Roger Biles, "Edward J. Kelly: New Deal Machine Builder," in Green and Holli, *The Mayors,* 116–117; Cohen and Taylor, *American Pharaoh,* 60.

17. Biles, *Big City Boss,* 90–137; Arnold R. Hirsch, "The Black Struggle for Integrated Housing in Chicago," in *Ethnic Chicago,* ed. Peter d'Almoy Jones and Melvin G. Holli (Grand Rapids, Mich.: W. B. Eerdmans, 1984), 380–411; Strickland, *History of CUL,* 231; Travis, *An Autobiography,* 123; Gosnell, *Machine Politics,* 19; Grimshaw, *Bitter Fruit,* 55–56.

18. Commercial Club of Chicago, *Year Book, 1942–1943,* 151.

19. Commercial Club of Chicago, *Year Book, 1938–1939,* 222.

20. See the appendix of this book.

21. Biles, "Edward J. Kelly."

22. Quoted in Biles, "Edward J. Kelly," 114, see also 118–121.

23. Ibid.

24. Ibid., 115–121; Erie, *Rainbow's End,* 115.

25. Citizen's Schools Committee, *Chicago Schools* 1, no. 1 (1934); *Chicago's Schools* 2, no. 8 (1935).

26. Citizen's Schools Committee, *Chicago's Schools* 1, no. 2 (1934); Citizen's Schools Committee, "A Call to Arms," *Chicago's Schools* 1, no. 1 (1934).

27. Quoted in John A. Lapp, "Unfinished Business," *Chicago's Schools* 10, no. 2 (1944); Paul E. Peterson, *School Politics, Chicago Style* (Chicago: University of Chicago, 1976), 19–24.

28. Citizen's Schools Committee, *Chicago Schools* 1, no. 1 (1934).

29. *Chicago Schools* 1, no. 3 (1934).

30. Lapp, "Unfinished Business" (emphasis added).

31. Citizen's Schools Committee, "School Board Is Not Asked to Reappoint Johnson," *Chicago's Schools* 10, no. 3 (1944).

32. Quoted in National Commission for the Defense of Democracy through Education, *Certain Personnel Practices in the Chicago Public Schools* (Washington, D.C.: National Education Association, 1945), 37–52, 61; Citizen's Schools Committee, *Chicago's Schools* 11, no. 2 (1945).

33. National Commission, *Certain Personnel Practices,* 44.

34. Administrative Survey Commission, *Report on the Administrative Organization and Business Procedures of the Board of Education of the City of Chicago* (Chicago: Chicago Association of Commerce and Civic Federation, 1943).

35. Ibid., 30–66.

36. Ibid., 9, appendix; National Commission, *Certain Personnel Practices,* 49.

37. Citizen's Schools Committee, *Chicago's Schools* 14, no. 1 (1947).

38. Citizen's Schools Committee, *Chicago's Schools* 16, no. 3 (1950).

39. Biles, "Edward J. Kelly," 129.

40. Arnold R. Hirsch, "Martin H. Kennelly: The Mugwump and the Machine," in Green and Holli, *The Mayors,* 129.

41. Ibid., 136.

42. Citizen's Schools Committee *Chicago's Schools* 16, no. 3 (1950); Hirsch, "Martin H. Kennelly."

43. Quoted in Citizen's Schools Committee *Chicago's Schools* 14, No. 1 (1947); Alan B. Anderson and George W. Pickering, *Confronting the Color Line: The Broken Promise of Civil Rights in Chicago* (Athens: University of Georgia Press, 1986), 60–70; Hirsch, "Martin H. Kennelly," 130–133.

44. William Reeves, "Harold C. Hunt," *Chicago's Schools* 14, no. 1 (1947).

45. William J. Grimshaw, *Union Rule in the Schools: Big City Politics in Transformation* (Toronto: Lexington Books, 1979), 35–40.

46. Anderson and Pickering, *Confronting the Color Line,* 61.

47. Chicago Public Schools, *Facts and Figures* (Chicago: Chicago Public Schools, 1950).

48. James R. Ralph, *Northern Protest: Martin Luther King Jr., Chicago, and the Civil Rights Movement* (Cambridge: Harvard University Press, 1993).

49. Biles, *Big City Boss,* 156.

50. Janet L. Abu-Lughod, *New York, Chicago, Los Angeles: America's Global Cities* (Minneapolis: University of Minnesota Press, 1999), 218–223; Grimshaw, *Bitter Fruit,* 96–97.

51. Wood quoted in Travis, *An Autobiography,* 199; Hirsch, "The Black Struggle," 407–411; Erie, *Rainbow's End.*

52. Abu-Lughod, *New York, Chicago, Los Angeles,* 128.

53. Erie, *Rainbow's End,* 150–156; Hirsch, "Martin H. Kennelly," 140.

54. Hirsch, "Martin H. Kennelly," 138–140.

55. Quoted in Travis, *An Autobiography,* 215; Anderson and Pickering, *Confronting the Color Line,* 53; Grimshaw, *Bitter Fruit;* Hirsch, "Martin H. Kennelly"; O'Connor, *Clout;* Royko, *Boss.*

56. Cohen and Taylor, *American Pharaoh,* 311; John M. Allswanger, "Richard J. Daley: America's Last Boss," in Green and Holli, *The Mayors.*

57. Grimshaw, *Bitter Fruit,* 94–95; Royko, *Boss,* 68–71; Allswanger, "Richard J. Daley," 159.

58. Allswanger, "Richard J. Daley"; Cohen and Taylor, *American Pharaoh;* Peterson, *School Politics,* 9–10.

59. Cohen and Taylor, *American Pharaoh*, 438.

60. First quote by Richard J. Daley in Citizen's Schools Committee, *Chicago's Schools* 21, no. 4 (1955); second quote in Allswanger, "Richard J. Daley," 162.

61. Vilas Johnson, *A History of the Commercial Club of Chicago: Including the First History of the Club by John J. Glessner* (Chicago: Commercial Club of Chicago, 1977).

62. Charles Davis, interview with author, October 24, 1991.

63. Allswanger, "Richard J. Daley," 146.

64. Peterson, *School Politics*, 17.

65. Abu-Lughod, *New York, Chicago, Los Angeles*, 230; Erie, *Rainbow's End*, 162.

66. Wendt and Kagan, *Big Bill;* Wrigley, *Class Politics and Public Schools*.

67. Biles, *Big City Boss*, 19; Travis, *An Autobiography*, 108, 141.

68. Michael Kilian, Connie Fletcher, and F. Richard Ciccone, *Who Runs Chicago?* (New York: St. Martin's Press, 1979), 342; Johnson, *A History*.

69. Thomas Ayers, interview with author, October 18, 1991.

70. John Kretzmann, "The Affirmative Action Policy: Opening up a Closed City," in *Harold Washington and the Neighborhoods: Progressive City Government in Chicago 1983–1987*, ed. Pierre Clavel and Wim Wiewel (New Brunswick, N.J.: Rutgers University Press, 1991).

71. Erie, *Rainbow's End*, 157–161.

72. Thomas Ayers interview.

73. Erie, *Rainbow's End*, 252.

74. Ibid., 217; William J. Grimshaw, "The Daley Legacy: A Declining Politics of Party, Race and Public Unions," in *After Daley: Chicago Politics in Transition*, ed. Samuel K. Gove and Louis H. Massotti (Urbana: University of Illinois Press, 1988), 64; Clavel and Wiewel, *Harold Washington and the Neighborhoods;* Peterson, *School Politics*, 11.

75. Grimshaw, *Union Rule;* Mary Herrick, *The Chicago Schools: A Social and Political History* (Beverly Hills, Calif.: Sage, 1971).

76. The new CTU took the old CTF's designation as AFT #1. Kate Rousmaniere, *Citizen Teacher: The Life and Leadership of Margaret Haley* (Albany: State University of New York Press, 2005), 198–204.

77. Ibid., 210.

78. Grimshaw, *Union Rule*, 41.

79. Quote from board member Warren Bacon in ibid., 68; Thomas Foster Koerner, "Benjamin C. Willis and the Chicago Press" (Ph.D. diss., Northwestern University, 1968), 181–184, 268, 400–403.

80. Peterson, *School Politics*, 213.

81. The 1969 settlement, which was preceded by a one-day strike, brought the union a 13 percent raise and other benefits. The 1971 strike brought a two-year contract and 8 percent raises for each year, although the 1972 increase was reduced to 5.5 percent. In 1973 a three-week strike brought the union a 2.4 percent increase and a week's vacation with pay. The 1975 strike lasted eleven days and was settled only when Daley interrupted the school board's welcoming party for Superintendent Hannon to dictate the terms of the settlement—a cost-of-living increase and a reduction in class sizes. Grimshaw, *Union Rule*, 8; Peterson, *School Politics*, 194–213.

82. Peterson, *School Politics*, 193–194.

83. Grimshaw, *Union Rule*, 80–82.

84. Ibid.

85. Erie, *Rainbow's End.*

86. Allswanger, "Richard J. Daley," 151.

87. Peterson, *School Politics,* 194–197.

88. Anderson and Pickering, *Confronting the Color Line,* 63; Erie, *Rainbow's End,* 156, 165; Grimshaw, *Bitter Fruit,* 93–107.

89. Allswanger, "Richard J. Daley."

90. Ibid., 156.

91. Arthur M. Brazier, *Black Self-Determination: The Story of the Woodlawn Organization* (Grand Rapids, Mich.: William B. Eerdmans, 1969), 49; Travis, *An Autobiography,* 222–235, 356–357; Allswanger, "Richard J. Daley," 155–158.

92. Anderson and Pickering, *Confronting the Color Line.*

93. U.S. Commission on Civil Rights, *Civil Rights USA: Public Schools, Cities in the North and West* (Washington, D.C.: U.S. Government Printing Office, 1962), 185–248; Abu-Lughod, *New York, Chicago, Los Angeles,* 218–226; London, "Business and Chicago Public Schools," 127; Ralph, *Northern Protest.*

94. U.S. Commission on Civil Rights, *Civil Rights USA,* 216.

95. Koerner, "Benjamin Willis," 44; London, "Business and Chicago Public Schools," 126; Ralph, *Northern Protest,* 14; Grimshaw, *Bitter Fruit.*

96. The formula used identified a "Negro school" as one with less than 10 percent white students, and a "white school" as one with less than 10 percent Negroes. Advisory Panel on Integration of the Public Schools, *Report to the Board of Education* (City of Chicago, 1964); Robert Havinghurst, *The Public Schools of Chicago: A Survey for the Board of Education of Chicago* (Chicago: Board of Education, 1964); U.S. Commission on Civil Rights, *Civil Rights USA.*

97. U.S. Commission on Civil Rights, *Civil Rights USA,* 185.

98. *Chicago Defender* quoted in Ralph, *Northern Protest,* 20; Anderson and Pickering, *Confronting the Color Line,* 124.

99. Koerner, "Benjamin Willis," 3–6; John Rury, "Race, Space and Politics of Chicago's Public Schools: Benjamin Willis and the Tragedy of Urban Education," *History of Education Quarterly* 39, no. 2 (1999); Michael Usdan and Lee Anderson, "Anatomy of a Compromise: The Chicago School Board's Decision in 1965 on Superintendent Willis' Contract" (n.p.: n.d.), 1–6.

100. First quote in Citizen's Schools Committee, *Chicago's Schools* 28, no. 2 (1962); second quote in Citizen's Schools Committee, *Chicago's Schools* 27, no. 3 (1961). See also Citizen's Schools Committee, *Chicago's Schools* 21, no. 1 (1954); Citizen's Schools Committee, *Chicago's Schools* 20, no. 1 (1953); Koerner, "Benjamin Willis," 75–79.

101. "School Board Void Shifts: Order that Irked Willis Is Rescinded," *Chicago Tribune,* October 10, 1963; Joseph Pois, *The School Board Crisis: A Chicago Case Study* (Chicago: Educational Methods, 1964).

102. Koerner, "Benjamin Willis," 20–32.

103. Ibid.

104. Willis quoted in Citizen's Schools Committee, *Chicago's Schools* 22, no. 2 (1956); second quote from *Chicago Tribune,* February 14, 1961, in Koerner, "Benjamin Willis," 68.

105. Quote from resignation letter by board member James W. Clement to Mayor Richard J. Daley, February 24, 1966, cited in Koerner, "Benjamin Willis" addendum; Larry Cuban, *Urban School Chiefs under Fire* (Chicago: University of Chicago Press, 1976).

106. Grimshaw, *Union Rule,* 39. Peterson, *School Politics,* 68–71.

107. Cuban, *Urban School Chiefs*, 11–12; London, "Business and Chicago Public Schools."

108. Anderson and Pickering, *Confronting the Color Line*, 76; U.S. Commission on Civil Rights, *Civil Rights USA*, 185; Travis, *An Autobiography*, 260–261.

109. First quote in U.S. Commission on Civil Rights, *Civil Rights USA*, 232 (see also 210–215); second quote in *Webb v. Board of Education*, 61C11569 Civ (1961). Subsequent cases dismissed on the same grounds include *Burroughs v. Board of Education*, 62C206 Civ (1962); *Webb v. Board of Education of Chicago*, 6510 LEXUS 223, supp 466 (1963).

110. Cuban, *Urban School Chiefs*, 21–26.

111. Anderson and Pickering, *Confronting the Color Line*, 58; Advisory Panel on Integration, *Report to the Board of Education*, 14–19, 21, 52–53, 59.

112. Havinghurst, *The Public Schools*, 57–78, 143–175, 203–239, 372–373; see also John L. Rury and Jeffrey E. Mirel, "The Political Economy of Urban Education," in *Review of Research in Education*, ed. Michael W. Apple (Washington, D.C.: American Educational Research Association, 1997).

113. Advisory Panel on Integration, *Report to the Board of Education*, 14–21; Havinghurst, *The Public Schools*, 337.

114. Advisory Panel on Integration, *Report to the Board of Education*, 12; Havinghurst, *The Public Schools*, 26, 374.

115. Advisory Panel on Integration, *Report to the Board of Education*, 27; Havinghurst, *The Public Schools*, 28–30, 67, 370–374.

116. Citizen's Schools Committee, *Steps Toward Compensatory Education in Chicago Public Schools* (Chicago: Citizen's Schools Committee, 1964).

117. Advisory Panel on Integration, *Report to the Board of Education*, 27–38; Havinghurst, *The Public Schools;* Citizen's Schools Committee, *Steps Toward Compensatory Education*.

118. Koerner, "Benjamin Willis," 268, 270–277; Usdan and Anderson, "Anatomy of a Compromise," 38–56.

119. *Webb v. Board of Education of Chicago*.

120. Anderson and Pickering, *Confronting the Color Line*, 87, 121, 128; Kathleen Connolly, "The Chicago Open Housing Conference," in *Chicago 1966*, ed. David J. Garrow (Brooklyn, N.Y.: Carlson, 1989), 49–53; David Garrow, *Bearing the Cross: Martin Luther King Jr. and the Southern Christian Leadership Conference* (New York: William Morrow, 1986); Travis, *An Autobiography*, 304.

121. Anderson and Pickering, *Confronting the Color Line*, 89–92, 118; Cuban, *Urban School Chiefs*, 8–13; John McKnight, "The Summit Negotiations: Chicago August 17, 1966–August 26, 1966," in Garrow, *Chicago 1966;* Ralph, *Northern Protest*, 17–19; Strickland, *History of CUL*, 232.

122. Brazier, *Black Self-Determination;* Ralph, *Northern Protest*, 17–21.

123. Usdan and Anderson, "Anatomy of a Compromise," 22; Koerner, "Benjamin Willis," 240–242; Cuban, *Urban School Chiefs*, 18.

124. "Appeals for Superintendent Willis Flood School Board and Mayor Daley," *Chicago Tribune*, October 8, 1963.

125. London, "Business and Chicago Public Schools," 134, 152.

126. "Daley Hopes Willis Remains: Mayor Discusses Many Issues on TV Interview," *Chicago Tribune*, October 10, 1963.

127. Quoted in Anderson and Pickering, *Confronting the Color Line*, 135.

128. First quote in Travis, *An Autobiography,* 335 (see also 317–335); second quote in Cohen and Taylor, *American Pharaoh,* 309–314; Koerner, "Benjamin Willis," 257–261.

129. First quote in Connolly, "Open Housing Conference," 53; second quote in Anderson and Pickering, *Confronting the Color Line,* 143.

130. Albert A. Raby, "The Facts of the Chicago Federal Aid Controversy" (n.p., 1965); Charles Nicodemus, "School Fund Thaw: The Inside Story," *Chicago Daily News,* October 6, 1965; Anderson and Pickering, *Confronting the Color Line,* 181; Cohen and Taylor, *American Pharaoh,* 334–353; Garrow, *Bearing the Cross,* 433.

131. Casey Banas, "Edwin Berry Quits as Urban League Chief: He Calls for Strong Young Successor," *Chicago Tribune,* June 19, 1969; Anderson and Pickering, *Confronting the Color Line,* 284–285.

132. Garrow, *Bearing the Cross,* 343–349.

133. Mary Lou Finley, "The Open Housing Marches: Chicago Summer, '66," in Garrow, *Chicago 1966,* 6–8; Anderson and Pickering, *Confronting the Color Line,* 160–161; Garrow, *Bearing the Cross,* 431–434.

134. The school board crafted a compromise, giving Willis a face-saving contract on the condition that he agree to retire in spite of it, and he wavered for months. Koerner, "Benjamin Willis," 352–359; London, "Business and Chicago Public Schools"; Peterson, *School Politics,* 60; Usdan and Anderson, "Anatomy of a Compromise"; Cuban, *Urban School Chiefs.*

135. *Chicago Sun-Times,* July 13, 1965, cited in London, "Business and Chicago Public Schools," 139 (see also 147–150); Usdan and Anderson, "Anatomy of a Compromise," 54; Ralph, *Northern Protest,* 26.

136. Garrow, *Bearing the Cross,* 457; Ralph, *Northern Protest.*

137. Hirsch, "The Black Struggle," 383–385.

138. Quoted in Anderson and Pickering, *Confronting the Color Line,* 192.

139. Chicago Freedom Movement, "Program of the Chicago Freedom Movement," in Garrow, *Chicago, 1966.*

140. Connolly, "Open Housing Conference," 50–88; Finley, "Open Housing Marches," 19; Ralph, *Northern Protest.*

141. Quote in McKnight, "The Summit Negotiations," 112; Connolly, "Open Housing Conference," 93–94, appendixes; Ralph, *Northern Protest,* 152; Anderson and Pickering, *Confronting the Color Line,* 230–231; Grimshaw, *Bitter Fruit,* 95–112.

142. Finley, "Open Housing Marches," 38–39.

143. Earl Bush quoted in Travis, *An Autobiography,* 345.

144. McKnight, "The Summit Negotiations," 141; Bill Ayers, *Fugitive Days* (Boston: Beacon, 2001).

145. Anderson and Pickering, *Confronting the Color Line,* ch. 9; Garrow, *Chicago, 1966,* 271; Ralph, *Northern Protest.*

146. Quote from Thomas Ayers interview with author; Ralph, *Northern Protest,* 206–228.

147. Anderson and Pickering, *Confronting the Color Line,* 361; Cohen and Taylor, *American Pharaoh,* 436–438.

148. Anderson and Pickering, *Confronting the Color Line,* 336.

149. "Troops Curb Violence, 1,200 GIs Patrol Southside Streets," *Chicago Tribune,* April 8, 1968; "The Week that Was, and What a Week!" *Chicago Tribune,* April 7, 1968; Ralph, *Northern Protest.*

150. "Daley Makes Air Survey of Riot Area, Saddened and Depressed," *Chicago Tribune,* April 8, 1968.

151. Quoted in Citizen's Schools Committee, *Report on Nominating Process,* 1.

152. Peterson, *School Politics,* 90–106.

153. Christina Hawkins Stringfellow, "Desegregation Policies and Practices in Chicago during the Superintendencies of James Redmond and Joseph Hannon" (Ed.D. diss., Teachers College, Columbia University, 1991), 35–38; Peterson, *School Politics,* 143–156.

154. Peterson, *School Politics,* 151–157.

155. Ibid., 143–185; Stringfellow, "Desegregation Policies," 42–45.

156. Anderson and Pickering, *Confronting the Color Line,* 288–312.

157. Quoted in Peterson, *School Politics,* 174–175; Stringfellow, "Desegregation Policies," 25–34.

158. Peterson, *School Politics,* 158.

159. Ibid., 176.

160. Ibid., 194.

161. Ibid., 217–218.

162. Stringfellow, "Desegregation Policies," 39–41.

163. Peterson, *School Politics,* 217–218; Stringfellow, "Desegregation Policies," 39–41, 191.

164. Peterson, *School Politics,* 22–26; Wrigley, *Class Politics and Public Schools.*

165. Rury, "Race, Space and Politics," 136.

166. Charles Davis, interview with author, November 24, 1991; Dan Rottenberg, "The Healers," *Chicago Guide,* December 1973.

167. David Paulus, interview with author, September 30, 1991.

168. Henry Mendoza, interview with author, November 26, 1991.

169. Rottenberg, "The Healers," 81.

170. Warren Bacon, "Business and the Big City Schools" (speech to Illinois Association of Big City Schools, January 26, 1984); Stephen Lewis Garay, "Business Influences in the Formation of Educational Policy: A Case Study of Chicago United Initiatives" (Ph.D. diss., University of Illinois at Chicago, 1982); Rottenberg, "The Healers."

171. Quoted in Norman Ross, interview with author, November 15, 1991; Thomas Ayers interview; Bacon, "Business and the Big City Schools"; "World Money Rate Proposed," *Chicago Tribune,* June 30, 1969.

172. Hargraves quoted in Anderson and Pickering, *Confronting the Color Line,* 296. Ross interview; Rottenberg, "The Healers"; Garay, "Business Influences"; Ralph, *Northern Protest.*

173. Archie Hargraves and C. T. Vivian, "Black Strategy Center Proposal" (June 1969).

174. Quoted in Cohen and Taylor, *American Pharaoh,* 434; Anderson and Pickering, *Confronting the Color Line,* 323–324.

175. Garrow, *Bearing the Cross,* 462; Garrow, *Chicago, 1966.*

176. Rottenberg, "The Healers," 79.

177. "Businessmen to Aid Blacks in Job Search," *Chicago Tribune,* September 20, 1969.

178. Brazier, *Black Self-Determination,* 70.

179. Ibid.; Cohen and Taylor, *American Pharaoh,* 440; Ralph, *Northern Protest.*

180. Travis, *An Autobiography,* 434, 446–458.

181. Davis interview.

182. Quoted in Warren Bacon, "Keynote Address" (speech given at Principals' Retreat of Chicago United, April 14, 1985), 4; Rottenberg, "The Healers."

183. Norman Ross, "Open Letter to Ms. Cornelai Honchu," *Chicago Tribune,* August 2, 1972.

184. Ross interview; Thomas Ayers interview.

185. Minority member of Chicago United, interview with author, November 22, 1991; Rottenberg, "The Healers," 80.

186. Minority member of Chicago United interview.

187. Mendoza interview.

188. Ross interview.

189. Quoted in Bacon, "Keynote Address."

190. Rottenberg, "The Healers," 81.

191. Ibid., 78–81.

192. Garay, "Business Influences."

193. Ibid.; Joel Havemann and Douglas P. Woodlock, "Viewpoint: Schools, Bureaucracy, Lack of Funds Impede Needed Changes," *Chicago Sun-Times,* March 22 1971; Ross interview.

194. Garay, "Business Influences," 68–69; Herbert Walberg and Jeanne Sigler, "Business Views Education in Chicago," *Phi Delta Kappan* (1975).

195. Garay, "Business Influences," 66–68.

196. Quoted in "A Secret Report Flunks Schools," *Chicago Sun-Times,* January 7, 1975; "City Business Chiefs Move to Aid Schools," *Chicago Tribune,* January 8, 1975; Garay, "Business Influences."

197. Garay, "Business Influences"; Walberg and Sigler, "Business Views Education in Chicago."

198. Casey Banas, "School Board Got Best for Job: Daley," *Chicago Tribune,* July 18, 1975; Casey Banas, "Malis Appointment Rocked the Boat," *Chicago Tribune,* July 17, 1975; "Daley Deserves Schools," *Chicago Sun-Times,* July 17, 1975; "Daley Blows a Chance for Change," *Chicago Tribune,* July 8, 1975.

199. Chicago United, "Deacon's Retreat Recommendations on Chicago United Identity" (n.p., n.d.).

200. Stringfellow, "Desegregation Policies," 47–50.

201. Seth S. King, "Chicago Seeking New School Head," *New York Times,* July 6, 1975.

202. See, for instance, Jim Casey, " 'Paper' Bomb Explodes: South Sider Loses Hand," *Chicago Sun-Times,* August 25, 1977; Phyllis Hudson, "Interracial Group to Boycott Schools," *Chicago Defender,* August 19, 1977; Lawrence Muhammad, "Beaten, Dumped in Street by White Mob," *Chicago Defender,* August 25, 1977.

203. Jan Faller, "Blacks Fearful, Shun Transfer Plan," *Chicago Defender,* August 19, 1977; Harry Golden Jr. and Robert Suro, "Full Pupil Protection Pledged," *Chicago Sun-Times,* September 1, 1977.

204. The years of noncompliance were 1972, 1976, 1977, 1978, and 1979. Chicago Lawyers Committee for Civil Rights under Law Inc., Draft Class Action Complaint, August 29, 1979.

205. City of Chicago Board of Education, *Equalizing Educational Opportunity in*

the New Chicago (Chicago Public Schools, February 1977); Geof Dobson, "Mobile Units Shutdown Eyed," *Chicago Sun Times,* May 10, 1977.

206. Board of Education, *Equalizing Educational Opportunity;* Rury, "Race, Space and Politics," especially James Lewis citation.

207. Board of Education for the City of Chicago, "Access to Excellence: Recommendations for Equalizing Educational Opportunity Adopted by the Board of Education April 12, 1978"; Anderson and Pickering, *Confronting the Color Line,* 76; Stringfellow, "Desegregation Policies," 57–60, appendix.

208. Casey Banas, "Study Hails Progress of the City: Work with Minorities Praised," *Chicago Tribune,* July 24, 1979; Casey Banas, "School Reading Plan Failing: Study," *Chicago Tribune,* July 25, 1979; Rury, "Race, Space and Politics," 138; Midwestern Regional Office, U.S. Commission on Civil Rights, "Access to Excellence: A Review," April 28 1978; Linda Wertsch, "City Schools Program Rated High," *Chicago Sun-Times,* July 24, 1979; Linda Wertsch, "Reading Program Shows No Gains," *Chicago Sun-Times,* July 25, 1979; Rury, "Race, Space, and Politics," 138.

209. Stringfellow, "Desegregation Policies," 57–75, appendix; U.S. Commission on Civil Rights, "Access to Excellence."

210. Quoted in Judson Hixson to James W. Compton, September 1, 1977, on Chicago United Meeting, August 30, 1997, Chicago Urban League Archives 1984, acquisition box 16, file 3; Casey Banas, "Banks Busing Promo Strikes Out," *Chicago Tribune,* August 7, 1977; "Banks Thrown a Curve on TV Ad," *Chicago Defender,* August 11, 1977.

211. "The Silence Is Shameful," *Chicago Daily News,* September 1, 1977.

212. Dennis Byrne, "Execs Here Speak Out: Back School Transfers," *Chicago Daily News,* September 2, 1977.

213. Gerald L. Sbarboro, *Eleven in the Wind: A View of the Chicago Public Schools in the Early 1970s* (Chicago: Tallman Robbins, 1974).

214. Garay, "Business Influences," 75–76, ch. 5.

215. For a different view of Bacon, see Peterson, *School Politics,* ch. 8.

216. Anderson and Pickering, *Confronting the Color Line,* 99, 127, 174, 193.

217. Ibid., 63–68.

3. IMPROVISING DECENTRALIZATION

1. Anthony S. Bryk et al., *Charting School Reform: Democratic Localism as a Lever for Change* (Boulder Colo.: Westview Press, 1998); *Chicago Tribune, Chicago Schools "Worst in America:" An Examination of the Public Schools that Failed Chicago* (Chicago: R. R. Donnelley and Sons, 1988); Studs Turkel, ed., *Race: How Blacks and Whites Think and Feel about the American Obsession* (New York: Anchor Books, 1992), 179–202.

2. William J. Grimshaw, *Union Rule in the Schools: Big City Politics in Transformation* (Toronto: Lexington Books, 1979), 109; Diane M. Pinderhughes, "An Examination of Chicago Politics for Evidence of Political Incorporation and Representation," in *Racial Politics in American Cities,* ed. R. P. Browning, D. R. Marshall, and D. H. Tabb (New York: Longman, 1997), 123–124.

3. Pinderhughes, "An Examination"; Milton L. Rakove, "Jane Byrne and the New Chicago Politics," in *After Daley: Chicago Politics in Transition,* ed. Samuel K. Gove and Louis H. Massotti (Chicago: University of Illinois Press, 1988); Gary Rivlin, *Fire*

on the Prairie: Chicago's Harold Washington and the Politics of Race (New York: Henry Holt, 1992).

4. For a more sympathetic discussion of Daley's fiscal decision making, see Esther R. Fuchs, *Mayors and Money: Fiscal Policy in New York and Chicago* (Chicago: University of Chicago Press, 1992).

5. Paul M. Green, "Michael Bilandic: The Last of the Machine Regulars," in *The Mayors: The Chicago Political Tradition,* ed. Paul M. Green and Melvin Holli (Carbondale: Southern Illinois University Press, 1987); Pinderhughes, "An Examination."

6. Joint House and Senate Chicago Board of Education Investigation Committee, "The Chicago Board of Education's 1979 Financial Crisis and Its Implications on Other Illinois School Districts: Final Report," ed. Illinois General Assembly (State of Illinois, 81st Illinois General Assembly, January 13, 1981); David Moberg, "Bankers, Businessmen and Bankruptcy," *Chicago Reader,* February 1, 1980; Jim Carl, "Harold Washington and Chicago's Schools: Between Civil Rights and the Decline of the New Deal Consensus, 1955–1987," *History of Education Quarterly* 41, no. 3 (2001).

7. Carl, "Harold Washington"; Joint House and Senate Committee, "The 1979 Financial Crisis," 57–69; President of the Chicago Region PTA, Mrs. Steve Leftakes, to Mayor Richard Daley, September 20, 1975, Chicago Urban League Archives, 1984 acquisition, box 16, file 35; State Representative Barbara Flynn Curie, "Real School Crisis Goes On," *Hyde Park Herald,* February 6, 1980.

8. Joint House and Senate Committee, "The 1979 Financial Crisis," 43; Chicago Urban League, *Urban Times* (draft, March 7, 1980), Chicago Urban League Archives, acquisition 1984, box 16, file 16.

9. Grimshaw, *Union Rule.*

10. A pro rata line was simply a transmittal letter from the district to itself saying how much the board expected to fall short of the legally mandated balanced budget. Casey Banas and Meg O'Connor, "Breaks His Silence, School Crisis Exaggerated: Hannon," *Chicago Tribune,* January 31, 1980; Joint House and Senate Committee, "The 1979 Financial Crisis," 70–77.

11. Joint House and Senate Committee, "The 1979 Financial Crisis"; Grimshaw, *Union Rule;* Charles L. Kyle and E. R. Kantowitz, *Kids First—Primero Los Ninos: Chicago School Reform in the 1980s* (Springfield: Illinois Issues, 1992).

12. James Compton quoted in Chicago Urban League, *Urban Times* (draft).

13. First quote in Joint House and Senate Committee, "The 1979 Financial Crisis," 43; second and third quotes in Banas and O'Connor, "Breaks His Silence."

14. John Kotsakis, interview with author, December 12, 1991.

15. Leon Jackson, interview with author, October 28, 1991.

16. Arthur Berman, interview with author, December 11, 1991.

17. Jane Byrne, *My Chicago* (New York: W. W. Norton, 1992), 286–298; Judson Hixson, "A Chronology of the Chaos: The Chicago Public Schools Fiscal Fiasco" in Chicago Urban League, *Urban Times* (draft).

18. Joint House and Senate Committee, "The 1979 Financial Crisis," 55; G. Alfred Hess Jr., *School Restructuring, Chicago Style* (Newbury Park, Calif.: Corwin Press, 1991); Kyle and Kantowitz, *Kids First,* 33–34.

19. Joint House and Senate Committee, "The 1979 Financial Crisis," 83.

20. Hess, *School Restructuring;* Kyle and Kantowitz, *Kids First,* 34; Legislative Committee of the Board of Education, "Report of the June 6 Meeting to the Members

of the Board of Education," June 11 1980, Chicago Urban League Archives, acquisition 1984, box 16, file 55.

21. The SFA was modeled after the 1975 Finance Authority of New York City. School Finance Authority, "Fourth Report to the Governor of the City of Chicago, the Illinois General Assembly, the Mayor of the City of Chicago, and the Chicago City Council Pursuant to Section 606 of the Chicago School Finance Authority Act, 1982–1983 Data" (n.d.); School Finance Authority, "Seventh Report to the Governor of the City of Chicago, the Illinois General Assembly, the Mayor of the City of Chicago, and the Chicago City Council Pursuant to Section 606 of the Chicago School Finance Authority Act, 1984–1985 Data" (n.d.); School Finance Authority, "Eleventh Report to the Illinois Governor, the Mayor of the City of Chicago, the Illinois General Assembly and the Chicago City Council Pursuant to Section 606 of the Chicago School Finance Authority Act, 1989–1990 Data" (May 7, 1993).

22. Citizen's Schools Committee, "Report III" (Chicago, 1980); Michael Zielenziger and Jonathan Landman, "Schools Push for Tax Collections," *Chicago Sun-Times,* February 28, 1980.

23. Citizen's Schools Committee, "Report III," 2–3.

24. Hess, *School Restructuring,* 24–25; Citizen's Schools Committee, "Report III," 5–6; Chicago Region PTA, "A Conversation with Harriet and Doris," *Chicago Region PTA News,* March 1980; Michael Martinez, "Daley Pushes Traffic Court for School Headquarters," *Chicago Tribune,* August 8, 1991; memo from Marilyn Epps to James W. Compton, "Meeting of the Board of Education, July 16, 1980," July 17 1980, Chicago Urban League Archives, acquisition 1984, box 16, file 55; Stephen Lewis Garay, "Business Influences in the Formation of Educational Policy: A Case Study of Chicago United Initiatives" (Ph.D. diss., University of Illinois at Chicago, 1982).

25. Henry Mendoza, interview with author, November 26, 1991.

26. Quoted in Mendoza interview; Hess, *School Restructuring,* 27; see also Douglas Gills, "Chicago Politics and Community Development: A Social Movement Perspective," in *Harold Washington and the Neighborhoods: Progressive City Government in Chicago, 1983–1987,* ed. Pierre Clavel and Wim Wiewel (New Brunswick, N.J.: Rutgers University Press, 1991).

27. Chicago United, "Chicago's Public School System: A Chicago United Response," July 1979, Chicago Urban League Archives, acquisition 1984, box 16, file 41; Citizen's Schools Committee, "Report III," 2; Peter Henderson, interview with author, November 7, 1991; Margaret Blanford, interview with author, October 23, 1991.

28. Charles Davis, interview with author, November 24, 1991.

29. Quoted in Melvin G. Holli, "Jane Byrne: To Think the Unthinkable and Do the Undoable," in Green and Holli, *The Mayors,* 175, 177; Byrne, *My Chicago;* Clavel and Wiewel, *Harold Washington and the Neighborhoods,* 213–232; Bill Granger and Lori Granger, *Fighting Jane: Mayor Jane Byrne and the Chicago Machine* (New York: Dial Press, 1980); Paul Kleppner, *Chicago Divided: The Making of a Black Mayor* (De Kalb: Northern Illinois University Press, 1985), 118–124; Rakove, "Jane Byrne."

30. Quoted in Advisory Commission on School Board Nominations, "Minutes of February 5 Meeting," 1980, Chicago Urban League Archives, acquisition 1984, box 16, file 74; memo to Members of the School Board Candidates Search Committee from James Compton, March 18, 1989, box 16, file 76; Blanford interview, October 23;

Garay, "Business Influences"; Henderson interview; Norman Ross, interview with author, November 15, 1991.

31. Kleppner, *Chicago Divided,* 60; Kyle and Kantowitz, *Kids First,* 34.

32. Memo from Judson Hixson to James Compton, "Thomas Ayers and the Chicago Board of Education," April 24, 1980, Chicago Urban League Archives, acquisition 1984, box 16, file 55; memo from Judson Hixson to James Compton, "Update on the School Board," April 23, 1980, box 16, file 75.

33. Margaret Blanford, interview with author, September 25, 1991; Blanford, interview, October 23.

34. Memo from Judson Hixson to James Compton, "Thomas Ayers and the Chicago Board of Education."

35. Lu Palmer, interview with author, November 20, 1991.

36. Thomas Ayers, interview with author, October 18, 1991; Blanford, interview, October 23; Palmer interview; Kleppner, *Chicago Divided;* Rivlin, *Fire on the Prairie,* 33–34.

37. Gills, "Chicago Politics and Community Development," 50; Jeffrey Mirel, "School Reform, Chicago Style: Educational Innovation in a Changing Urban Context, 1976–1991," *Urban Education* 28, no. 2 (1993). Davis interview; Palmer interview. Thomas Ayers interview; Jackson interview.

38. Blanford interview, October 23.

39. First quote in Palmer interview; second quote in Sakoni Karanja, interview with author, December 4, 1991; Paul E. Peterson, *The Politics of School Reform 1870–1940* (Chicago: University of Chicago Press, 1985); Grimshaw, *Union Rule;* "Chicago Loses a Leader," *Chicago Sun-Times,* May 31, 1991; Karen M. Thomas, "Warren Bacon, Education Crusader," *Chicago Tribune,* May 31, 1991; Jacoby Dickins, interview with author, November 25, 1991; Chicago-based white CEO, interview with author, November 11, 1991; Blanford interview, September 25; Davis interview.

40. Warren Bacon, "Keynote Address" (speech given at the Principals' Retreat of Chicago United, April 14, 1985).

41. Donald Perkins, interview with author, October 21, 1991.

42. Thomas Ayers interview.

43. African American Chicago school leader, telephone interview with author, June 6, 1993.

44. Chicago United, "Report of the Conference on Business and Public Education Held at the University Club, Chicago Ill., December 10–11" (1979).

45. Chicago United, "Special Task Force on Education: Chicago School System" (1981).

46. Henderson interview.

47. Garay, "Business Influences," 122.

48. Henderson interview.

49. The stipulated ratio for teachers was not to deviate from the systemwide percentage by more than 15 percent. G. Alfred Hess Jr. and Christina Warden, "Who Benefits from Desegregation Now?" *Journal of Negro Education* 57, no. 4 (1988); Chicago United, "Special Task Force"; Loraine Forte, "Faculty Segregation Increases since Reform," *Catalyst; Voices of Chicago School Reform* 5, no. 4 (1993); G. Alfred Hess Jr. and James L. Greer, *Bending the Twig: The Elementary Years and Dropout Rates in the Chicago Public Schools* (Chicago Panel on Public School Policy and Finance, 1987); Michael Timpane, *Corporations and Public Education in the City* (New York:

Carnegie Corporation of New York, 1982); Blanford interview, October 23; Perkins interview.

50. Henderson interview.

51. Quoted in Peter Willmott, interview with author, October 25, 1991; Dickins interview; Henderson interview; Martin Koldyke, interview with author, November 2, 1991; Palmer interview; David Paulus, interview with author, September 30, 1991; B. Kenneth West, interview with author, November 14, 1991; African American Chicago corporate executive, interview with author, November 21, 1991; Jean Franczk, "School Reform Pressure Continues; Competing Plans Vie for Support," *Chicago Reporter,* January 1988.

52. Commercial Club of Chicago, *Make No Little Plans: Jobs for Metropolitan Chicago* (Commercial Club, 1984).

53. Perkins interview.

54. Quoted in Commercial Club of Chicago, *Make No Little Plans,* 5; see also John Betancur and Douglas Gills, eds., *The Collaborative City: Opportunities and Struggles for Blacks and Latinos in U.S. Cities* (New York: Garland, 2000), 27–28.

55. Commercial Club of Chicago, *Make No Little Plans.*

56. Perkins interview.

57. Quoted in Civic Committee of the Commercial Club, *Jobs for Metropolitan Chicago: An Update* (Commercial Club of Chicago, 1990), 4; see also Civic Committee of the Commercial Club, *Jobs for Metropolitan Chicago: A Two Year Report* (Commercial Club of Chicago, 1987); Elizabeth Hollander, "The Department of Planning under Harold Washington," in Clavel and Wiewel, *Harold Washington and the Neighborhoods.*

58. Citizen's Schools Committee, *Better Schools for All Chicago: A School Accountability Study* (Chicago: Citizen's Schools Committee, 1982), vi–vii, appendix.

59. Ibid., 1–2, 16, appendix.

60. Marilyn Epps, "Quarterly Report, Education Department," fourth quarter 1981, Chicago Urban League Archives, acquisition 1984, box 16, file 74; G. Alfred Hess Jr., interview with author, November 13, 1991; G. Alfred Hess Jr. and Diana Lauber, *Dropouts from the Chicago Public Schools* (Chicago Panel on Public School Policy and Finance, 1985); Hess, *School Restructuring.*

61. Donald R. Moore, "After the Vote: Improving Children's Lives in the Restructured Chicago School System" (paper presented at the Catherine Malony Memorial Lecture, City University of New York, School of Education, April 28, 1990); Donald R. Moore, "Voice and Choice in Chicago," in *Choice and Control in American Education: The Practice of Choice, Decentralization and School Restructuring,* ed. William Clune and John Witte (San Francisco: Falmer Press, 1992); Designs for Change, *The Bottom Line: Chicago's Failing Schools and How to Save Them* (Chicago: Designs for Change, 1985).

62. Mary O'Connell, "School Reform Chicago Style: How Citizens Organized to Change Public Policy," *Neighborhood Works,* spring 1991; Herbert J. Walberg et al., *We Can Rescue Our Children: The Cure for Chicago's Public School Crisis—with Lessons for the Rest of America* (Chicago: Heartland Institute, 1988), 126. For a view of CURE coalition members that suggests that they were primarily interested in avoiding integration with blacks, see Manning Marable, *Black Leadership* (New York: Columbia University Press, 1988), 140.

63. Quoted in Walberg et al., *We Can Rescue,* 65, 141.

64. Charles L. Kyle, *Los Preciosos: The Magnitude of and the Reasons for the Hispanic Dropout Problem* (Chicago: Aspira Inc. of Illinois, 1984); Hess and Lauber, *Dropouts;* Designs for Change, *The Bottom Line.*

65. Latina principal, interview with Consortium on Chicago School Research, February 14, 1994.

66. Herbert J. Walberg and G. Alfred Hess Jr., *Chicagoans View Their Public Schools: A Public Opinion Survey* (Chicago Panel on Public School Finances, 1985).

67. D. T. Stallings, "A Brief History of the U.S. Department of Education, 1979–2002," *Phi Delta Kappan* (2002): 679; see also Terrel H. Bell, "Education Policy Development in the Reagan Administration," *Phi Delta Kappan* (1986).

68. National Commission on Excellence in Education, *A Nation at Risk: The Imperative for Educational Reform* (Washington, D.C.: U.S. Department of Education, 1983).

69. Hess, *School Restructuring*, 3–4.

70. For an alternative view, see Moore, "After the Vote."

71. Quote in Bill Berry, Interim Chairman of Political Action Conference of Illinois, to multiple individuals, December 8, 1979, Chicago Urban League Archives, acquisition 1984, box 16, file 75; Chicago Urban League, "Controversy over State Aid to Chicago District Schools" (press release), December 30, 1979, box 16, file 41; James Compton, "Statement of the Executive Director of the Chicago Urban League to the State Board of Education," March 10, 1977, ibid.; Chicago Urban League, "Statement to the Education and Appropriations Sub-Committees of the General Assembly in Support of House Bill 2619," May 9, 1978, ibid.; memo from Roger Fox to James Compton, "Title 1 Situation," November 9, 1979, ibid.; Peggy Blanford, Luis Salces, and Elmer Washington, *A Report on Citizen Involvement in Education* (Chicago United, 1979); Chicago Urban League, "Quarterly Report, Second Quarter of FY '80," 1980, Chicago Urban League Archives, acquisition 1984, box 16, file 27.

72. Palmer interview. Moderate opposition was represented in Dickins interview.

73. Rufus P. Browning, Dale Rogers Marshall, and David H. Tabb, *Racial Politics in American Cities,* 2nd ed. (New York: Longman, 1997). For a critique of incorporation theory, see Jeffrey Edwards, "Theorizing Race in Urban Political Analysis" (paper presented at the annual meeting of the American Political Science Association, San Francisco, August 29–September 1, 1996).

74. M. Katims and B. F. Jones, "Chicago Mastery Learning Reading: Mastery Learning Instruction and the Assessment of Inner-City Schools," *Journal of Negro Education* 54, no. 3 (1985).

75. Memo from Pete Henderson to Chicago United Principals and Deacons, "Adopt-a-School Program," July 8, 1981, Chicago Urban League Archives, acquisition 1984, box 16, file 85.

76. Deborah Lynch Walsh, *Labor of Love: One Chicago Teacher's Experience* (Lincoln, Neb.: Writers Club Press, 2000), 30; Moore, "After the Vote."

77. Karanja interview.

78. Palmer interview; James W. Compton, "Speech: Tribute to Dr. Ruth Love," March 20, 1985, Chicago Urban League Archives, acquisition 1987, box 34, file 2.

79. Quoted in Nate Clay and Michelle Young, "Will History Repeat Itself Today?" *Chicago Defender,* December 10, 1980; Norman Jenkins, "Rally 'Round Byrd: 300 March in the Cold," *Chicago Defender,* December 12, 1980.

80. O'Connell, "School Reform," 22.

81. Paul M. Green, "The Primary, Some New Players, Same Old Rules," in *The Making of the Mayor: Chicago 1983, The Primary,* ed. Melvin Holli and Paul M. Green (Grand Rapids, Mich.: Eerdmans, 1984); Robert McClury, "Up from Obscurity: Harold Washington," in ibid.

82. Quoted in Political Action Conference of Illinois, "Minutes of the (First) Meeting of the PAC Illinois," November 17, 1979, Chicago Urban League Archives, acquisition 1984, box 16, file 75; Pinderhughes, "An Examination," 126.

83. Quoted in William J. Grimshaw, "Harold Washington: The Enigma of the Black Political Tradition," in Green and Holli, *The Mayors,* 183, 201; Carl, "Harold Washington."

84. Gills, "Chicago Politics and Community Development"; Holli and Green, *The Making of the Mayor;* Rivlin, *Fire on the Prairie.*

85. Holli and Green, *The Making of the Mayor;* Pinderhughes, "An Examination"; Katherine Tate, "Racial Politics Is Not Dead in American Cities," *Urban News* 9, no. 3 (1995).

86. Rivlin, *Fire on the Prairie,* 122–123.

87. Henderson interview.

88. McClury, "Up from Obscurity," 4–6; Davis interview; Dickins interview; African American Chicago corporate executive interview; Rivlin, *Fire on the Prairie.*

89. Gills, "Chicago Politics and Community Development," 58; Hollander, "The Department of Planning," 122; Marable, *Black Leadership,* 130.

90. Henderson interview; Paulus interview; Hollander, "The Department of Planning," 132; Holli and Green, *The Making of the Mayor;* Kyle and Kantowitz, *Kids First;* Rivlin, *Fire on the Prairie.*

91. Pinderhughes, "An Examination," 118.

92. Quoted in Carl, "Harold Washington," 317; Marable, *Black Leadership,* 137–138.

93. Carl, "Harold Washington," 332.

94. Quoted in Pinderhughes, "An Examination," 130; see also S. Alexander, "Black and Latino Coalitions: Means to Greater Budget Resources for Their Communities?" in Betancur and Gills, *The Collaborative City;* Clavel and Wiewel, *Harold Washington and the Neighborhoods.*

95. Rivlin, *Fire on the Prairie;* Betancur and Gills, *The Collaborative City,* 86, n. 19; Kyle and Kantowitz, *Kids First.*

96. Quoted in Hollander, "The Department of Planning," 124; Perkins interview.

97. Civic Committee of the Commercial Club, *Jobs: An Update;* Perkins interview.

98. Quote from Washington in McClury, "Up from Obscurity," 4; Carl, "Harold Washington," 313.

99. Carl, "Harold Washington," 329–330.

100. The Boston Compact was a 1982 pact between the public schools and Boston's powerful financiers, involving a promise of jobs for graduates in exchange for better rates of high school graduation. Eleanor Farrar and Anthony Cipollone, "After the Signing: The Boston Compact 1982–1985," in *American Business and the Public School: Case Studies of Corporate Involvement in Public Education,* ed. Marsha Levine and Roberta Trachtman (New York: Teachers College Press, 1988); Carl, "Harold Washington," 330.

101. Pastora San Juan Cafferty, *The Chicago Project: A Report on Civic Life in Chicago* (Chicago: Central Areas Committee, 1986), 2–5.

102. Quoted in Linda Lenz, "City Summit Raises Hopes for Schools," *Chicago Sun-Times,* May 1, 1988.

103. Chicago Partnership, "The Chicago Partnership Position on Educational Reform in Chicago" (1988); Paulus interview.

104. Willmott interview.

105. Steering Committee of the Mayor's Education Summit, *An Agenda for Education and Employment in Chicago: A Report to the Mayor's Education Summit of the Work Groups* (City of Chicago, 1988).

106. Quote in Carl, "Harold Washington," 332–333; Steering Committee of the Summit, *An Agenda for Education.*

107. Davis interview. Byrd engendered many such complex reactions, as in Karanja interview; Franczk, "School Reform"; Kotsakis interview.

108. Ronald Gidwitz, interview with author, October 29, 1991; Business Work Group of the Mayor's Education Summit, *Business Support Options Work Group* (City of Chicago, 1987).

109. CEO of IC Industries Karl D. Bays, "No More Business Coalitions!" *Crain's Chicago Business,* August 29, 1988.

110. John W. Kingdon, *Agendas, Alternatives and Public Policies,* 2nd ed. (New York: HarperCollins College, 1995).

111. David Peterson quoted in Kyle and Kantowitz, *Kids First,* 261; Hess, *School Restructuring,* 62, 71, 120; O'Connell, "School Reform," 10. On school-based management, see Peter Cistone, Joseph Fernandez, and Pat Tornillo Jr., "School-Based Management/Shared Decision Making in Dade County (Miami)," *Education and Urban Society* 21, no. 3 (1989).

112. Chicago United, "Reassessment of the Report on the 1981 Special Task Force on Education" (1987), 10; Henderson interview; Terry King, interview with author, November 12, 1991; Gidwitz interview; Loren Smith, telephone interview with author, September 23, 1991.

113. Quoted in "Reforming the Nation's Worst Schools," *Chicago Tribune,* May 15, 1988; see also Carl, "Harold Washington," 339; Hess, *School Restructuring,* 6; Kyle and Kantowitz, *Kids First,* 2, 192; O'Connell, "School Reform," 8; King interview.

114. Betancur and Gills, *The Collaborative City,* 67; Pinderhughes, "An Examination," 124–131.

115. Carl, "Harold Washington," 335; Hess, *School Restructuring;* Moore, "Voice and Choice"; Kyle and Kantowitz, *Kids First;* O'Connell, "School Reform."

116. Gwendolyn LaRoche, interview with author, November 25, 1991; Carl, "Harold Washington," 335–336; Kyle and Kantowitz, *Kids First,* 180–185; O'Connell, "School Reform," 1–4.

117. Quoted in Kyle and Kantowitz, *Kids First,* 186 (see also 178); City of Chicago, *The Mayor's Education Summit: An Agenda for the Reform of the Chicago Public Schools* (Office of the Mayor, City of Chicago, May 19, 1988); Hess, *School Restructuring;* Carl, "Harold Washington"; Moore, "Voice and Choice"; O'Connell, "School Reform."

118. Carl, "Harold Washington," 338; Hess. *School Restructuring;* Kyle and Kantowitz, *Kids First,* 191; Moore, "Voice and Choice"; O'Connell, "School Reform," 18.

119. Carl, "Harold Washington," 337–339, n. 56; see also Hess interview; Diana Lauber, interview with author, November 3, 1991; Linda Lenz, "Mayor Vows Unified Reform Plan," *Chicago Sun-Times,* October 12, 1987.

120. Quoted in Carl, "Harold Washington," 326, 341 (see also 329).

121. John J. Betancur and Douglas C. Gills, "The African American and Latino Experience in Chicago under Mayor Harold Washington," in *The Collaborative City,* 74; Carl, "Harold Washington"; Franczk, "School Reform"; Hess, *School Restructuring,* 69–72; O'Connell, "School Reform"; Joseph Reed, interview with author, October 1, 1991.

122. Carl, "Harold Washington"; O'Connell, "School Reform," 12.

123. The broker was Richard Dennis, who frequently bankrolled liberal causes, including Washington's reelection campaign. Kyle and Kantowitz, *Kids First,* 144–155, 212–215; O'Connell, "School Reform," 15; Marable, *Black Leadership;* Moore, "Voice and Choice."

124. Quoted in Moore, "After the Vote"; Hess interview; Hess, *School Restructuring;* Lauber interview.

125. Betancur and Gills, *The Collaborative City;* Gustavo Cavo, "Political Mobilization of Mexican Immigrants in Chicago and Houston" (paper presented at the Urban Policy Workshops, School of International Policy Analysis, Columbia University, New York, spring 2002); Kyle and Kantowitz, *Kids First;* Pinderhughes, "An Examination"; O'Connell, "School Reform," 3.

126. By 1990 Chicago had 160 hometown associations linking Mexican Americans to Mexico and passing on the Mexican cultural heritage. Cavo, "Political Mobilization"; Danny Solis, interview with author, November 21, 1991; Peter Martinez, telephone interview with author, December 13, 1991.

127. Marable, *Black Leadership,* 137–138, 141–144; Betancur and Gills, "The African American and Latino," 71–81.

128. Quote in Latina principal interview. For an earlier mention of Latino concern for better parent-school relations, see memo from Judson Hixson to James Taylor, "Deacon's Retreat 11/28/78," December 6, 1978, Chicago Urban League Archives, acquisition 1984, box 16, file 80.

129. Blanford interviews, September 25, October 23; King interview; Martinez interview; Solis interview.

130. Hess, *School Restructuring,* 70; Walberg et al., *We Can Rescue,* 176–177; Kotsakis interview; O'Connell, "School Reform."

131. Smith interview. For differing views, see Gidwitz interview; Reed interview.

132. Karanja interview.

133. Solis interview.

134. Jean Latz Griffin, "Two Issues at Stake in Legislative Debate over Education," *Chicago Tribune,* June 12, 1988.

135. First quote in Davis interview; second quote in Joe Washington, telephone interview with author, November 3, 1991; third quote in Paulus interview. See also Linda Lenz, "Union Urges Pilot School Reform Plan," *Chicago Sun-Times,* April 29, 1988; Martinez interview; Theodore Wright, interview with author, October 20, 1991; Mary Dempsey, interview with author, November 12, 1991; Kyle and Kantowitz, *Kids First,* 259–262; Hess, *School Restructuring,* 70.

136. Walsh, *Labor of Love,* 98.

137. Kotsakis interview; see also Washington interview; CTU official, interview with Consortium on Chicago School Research, March 5, 1994.

138. Franczk, "School Reform"; Kyle and Kantowitz, *Kids First;* Linda Lenz, "Education Summit Groups Reject Elected School Board," *Chicago Sun-Times,* March 15,

1988; Linda Lenz, "Local Control Gets Boost from Voters," *Chicago Sun-Times*, March 17, 1988; Linda Lenz, "School Summit Has Blow-up," *Chicago Sun-Times*, April 8, 1988; Moore, "Voice and Choice."

139. Willmott interview.

140. B. Kenneth West, interview with author, October 18, 1991.

141. Corretta McFerren quoted in Barbara Marsh, "Small School Wins Leave Reformers with Tough Job," *Crain's Chicago Business*, July 11, 1988.

142. Paulus interview.

143. The final summit plan was very much a compromise document. See Acting Mayor Eugene Sawyer, *The Mayor's Education Summit: An Agenda for the Reform of the Chicago Public Schools, Adopted April 28, 1988* (City of Chicago, 1988).

144. West interview, October 18.

145. Paulus interview.

146. Willmott interview; see also Kyle and Kantowitz, *Kids First*, 244–245; Paulus interview; West interview, October 18.

147. Quoted in Linda Lenz, "School Summit Wants Outsiders Kept Out," *Chicago Sun-Times*, April 29, 1988; see also Kyle and Kantowitz, *Kids First*, 245.

148. At its peak, the ABCs coalition also included representatives of about ten other neighborhood organizations and all eight member business organizations in the Chicago Partnership. Chicago United, "Don't Come Home without It" (informational flyer, ABCs coalition, n.d.); Hess, *School Restructuring;* Kyle and Kantowitz, *Kids First*, 244; Moore, "Voice and Choice"; Joseph Reed, telephone interview with author, January 3, 1992; West interviews, October 18, November 14.

149. Solis interview.

150. Martinez interview; Solis interview; Paulus interview; see also Lauber interview; O'Connell, "School Reform," 16–18.

151. Juanita Bratcher, "School Improvement Eyed: CTU, Others Give Reform Ideas," *Chicago Defender*, June 15, 1988; Jean Latz Griffin and Karen M. Thomas, "Democrats Offer School Plan: Proposal Slashed Bureaucracy 25%," *Chicago Tribune*, June 24, 1988.

152. Chicago United, "Don't Come Home without It"; Sawyer, "The Mayor's Education Summit."

153. "Why School Reform Is Key to Tax Hike," *Crain's Business*, June 20, 1988; Lynn Sweet, "School Bill Faces Tough Senate Sell," *Chicago Sun-Times*, June 30, 1988. For a comparison, see James Brice, "Report of the Education Task Force, a Speech Delivered at the Chicago United Principals' Retreat," August 14, 1985; Sawyer, "The Mayor's Education Summit."

154. Solis interview.

155. West interview, October 18. Chicago United paid for many of the buses that were used to transport parents. Hess, *School Restructuring*, 70; Moore, "Voice and Choice," 13; O'Connell, "School Reform," 21.

156. SB 1839, sponsored by Senator Arthur Berman, had already passed the Illinois senate when it became the shell for the plan crafted in the house. O'Connell, "School Reform," 20.

157. Ibid., 22; Kyle and Kantowitz, *Kids First*, 217–272; Hess, *School Restructuring;* Dempsey interview; Moore, "Voice and Choice," 14.

158. "How They Voted on School Reform," *Chicago Sun-Times*, July 3, 1988; Hess,

School Restructuring; Kyle and Kantowitz, *Kids First;* Moore, "Voice and Choice"; O'Connell, "School Reform," 19–26.

159. Cheryl Deval and Karen M. Thomas, "Oversight Board Urged for Schools," *Chicago Tribune,* June 7, 1988.

160. In Illinois, the governor has the authority to change portions of a law passed by the legislature before signing it. Lynn Sweet, "School Bill OKed: Dems Push Reform Packages through; Legislation's Effects Delayed for a Year," *Chicago Sun-Times,* July 3, 1988; Karen M. Thomas, "School Reform Signed; Battle Seems Certain," *Chicago Tribune,* September 27, 1988; Rob Karwath, "School Law Deal Must Be Near," *Chicago Tribune,* November 24, 1988; Kyle and Kantowitz, *Kids First,* 279.

161. Leslie Balducci, "Backers Urge School Reform OK: Jobs Depend on It; Thompson Warned," *Chicago Sun-Times,* August 22, 1988; "School Bill Changes Should Be Passed," *Chicago Tribune,* September 2, 1988; Lynn Sweet and Linda Lenz, "Thompson Alters and Inks School Reform Bill," *Chicago Sun-Times,* September 27, 1988; Karen M. Thomas, "Thompson Flirts with Fire on School Bill," *Chicago Tribune,* September 1, 1988.

162. Paulus interview.

163. First quote in Kyle and Kantowitz, *Kids First,* 283; second quote in Karen M. Thomas and Daniel Egler, "Job Security Stalls School Reform Deal," *Chicago Tribune,* November 20, 1988. See also Moore, "Voice and Choice"; Daniel Egler and Joan Crawford, "School Reform Bill Approved," *Chicago Tribune,* December 2, 1988; Patricia Smith, "Kids Lobby for School Reform," *Chicago Sun-Times,* November 29, 1988; Solis interview; Karen M. Thomas, "School Reform Bill Signed into Law," *Chicago Tribune,* December 13, 1988.

164. Dorothy Shipps, "The Invisible Hand: Big Business and Chicago School Reform," *Teachers College Record* 99, no. 1 (1997).

165. Quote in O'Connell, "School Reform," 23.

166. Davis interview; Dickins interview; African American Chicago businessman, telephone interview with author, December 12, 1991; African American Chicago corporate executive interview; Leon Jackson, telephone interview with author, January 3, 1992.

167. Todd Rosenkranz, "Reallocating Resources: Discretionary Funds Provide Engine for Change," *Education and Urban Society* 26, no. 3 (1994): 264–284.

168. Shipps, "The Invisible Hand."

4. PERFECTING MANAGEMENT

1. Dorothy Shipps, Joseph Kahne, and Mark A. Smylie, "The Politics of Urban School Reform: Legitimacy, Urban Growth and School Improvement in Chicago," *Educational Policy* 13, no. 4 (1999).

2. James L. Merriner Jr. and Mike Cramer, "The Stealth Boss," *Illinois Issues,* March 1998; Robert Davis, "The Bully Gets Some Class," *Illinois Issues,* October 1999.

3. John J. Attinasi, "Hispanic Educational Research in View of Chicago Education Reform" (paper presented at the Assessing School Reform in Chicago conference, Consortium on Chicago School Research, Chicago, 1991); Latino Institute, *A Profile of Nine Latino Groups in Chicago* (Chicago: Latino Institute, 1994).

4. Diane M. Pinderhughes, "An Examination of Chicago Politics for Evidence of Political Incorporation and Representation," in *Racial Politics in American Cities*, ed. R. P. Browning, D. R. Marshall, and D. H. Tabb (New York: Longman, 1997).

5. Scott Fornek, "The Chicago City Council," *Chicago Sun-Times*, May 6, 2003; Pinderhughes, "An Examination."

6. Quoted in "Victor Reyes: Coalition Man," *Governing*, October 1995; "Reinventing Tammany Hall," *Government Executive*, January 1997; Fran Spielman and Robert Herguth, "Daley Protégé Packing Clout," *Chicago Sun-Times*, April 13, 2003.

7. Charles Mahtesian, "Taking Chicago Private," *Governing*, April 1994.

8. Danny Solis quoted in John Oclander, "Latinos Credit Daley for Clout," *Chicago Sun-Times*, February 3, 1995.

9. John Betancur and Douglas Gills, eds., *The Collaborative City: Opportunities and Struggles for Blacks and Latinos in U.S. Cities* (New York: Garland, 2000), 34.

10. Fran Spielman, "Mayor Wins Nearly 60% of Black Vote," *Chicago Sun-Times*, February 26, 2003.

11. First quote in Fran Spielman, "Black Ministers Get Behind Daley," *Chicago Sun-Times*, February 4, 2003; second quote in Paul M. Green, "Chicago's 1991 Elections; Richard M. Daley Wins Second Term," *Illinois Issues*, June 1991; Steven Alexander, "Black and Latino Coalitions: Means to Greater Budget Resources for Their Communities?" in Betancur and Gills, *The Collaborative City;* Paul M. Green, "Check the Numbers: Daley Could Beat Dad's Record," *Crain's Chicago Business*, January 13, 2003; Jesse L. Jackson Jr., "With Mandate in Hand; Daley Faces Future," *Chicago Sun-Times*, February 28, 1999; Fran Spielman, "After Years of Struggle, Daley Is Enjoying Life," *Chicago Sun-Times*, February 21, 1999.

12. Pinderhughes, "An Examination," 125; Rob Gurwitt, "Collision in Brown and Black," *Governing*, January 1993; Steve Neal, "Washington and Daley: Builders of Coalitions," *Chicago Sun-Times*, April 4, 1995.

13. The 1991 turnout (45 percent) was lower than it had been in any election since 1947. Green, "Check the Numbers"; Green, "Chicago's 1991 Elections"; Spielman, "Mayor Wins."

14. Green, "Chicago's 1991 Elections"; Mary A. Johnson, "Fighting the Odds: Gardner Stays Focused in Race against Daley," *Chicago Sun-Times*, February 15, 1995; Alexander, "Black and Latino"; Scott Fornek, "Mayor's War Chest at $4.2 Million," *Chicago Sun-Times*, February 23, 2003; Green, "Check the Numbers."

15. Scott Fornek, "Daley Wins Big," *Chicago Sun-Times*, February 23, 2003.

16. Quote from the Reverend Paul Jakes in Spielman, "Mayor Wins."

17. Quoted in Merriner and Cramer, "The Stealth Boss"; Richard M. Daley, "Chicago City Government: Smaller in Size, but Greater in Performance," *Business Forum*, winter/spring 1994.

18. Quoted in John Callaway, interview with author, July 24, 1997; Ralph Reed Jr., "Rise of the Republicrats," *Village Voice*, September 3, 1996.

19. Quoted in Daley, "Chicago City Government"; Betancur and Gills, *The Collaborative City*, 34.

20. Daley, "Chicago City Government"; Mahtesian, "Taking Chicago Private."

21. Quoted in Merriner and Cramer, "The Stealth Boss," 17; Richard M. Daley, inaugural address (Chicago Public Library, May 6, 1991), http://www.chipublib.org/ 004chicago/mayors/speeches/daley91.html (accessed July 1, 2004); D. O. Simpson

et al., "Chicago since September 11, 2001: An Uncertain Future" (paper presented at the Resurgence of America's Great Cities: Lanier Public Policy Conference, Houston, April 26, 2002); order appointing court monitor and counsel, *Shakman v. Democratic Org. of Cook Co.,* No. 69C2145 (N.D. Ill., August 2, 2005); application to hold the city of Chicago and its mayor in civil contempt for violation of the court orders, *Shakman v. Democratic Org. of Cook Co.,* No. 69C2145 (N.D. Ill., July 26, 2005).

22. Betancur and Gills, *The Collaborative City;* Alan Ehrenhalt, "Pleasure and Guilt on Michigan Avenue," *Governing,* July 1999; Pauline Lipman, *High Stakes Education: Inequality, Globalization and Urban School Reform* (New York: Routledge Falmer, 2004); Kim Phillips-Fein, "The Still Industrial City: Why Cities Shouldn't Just Let Manufacturing Go," *American Prospect,* September–October 1998.

23. Mary A. Johnson, "City Gets $50 Million to Push Development," *Chicago Sun-Times,* February 10, 1995; Charles Mahtesian, "Showdown on E-Z Street," *Governing,* October 1995; Steve Neal, "Snub of Daley Could Cost Clinton," *Chicago Sun-Times,* February 27, 1995.

24. William J. Clinton, "State of the Union Address by the President" (White House Office of the Press Secretary, January 27, 1998); Federal News Service, "Full Text of President Clinton's State of the Union Address as Delivered on January 19, 1999," *Washington Post,* January 20, 1999; Scott Fornek, "President Hails Chicago Schools: Reform Efforts Cited as a Model," *Chicago Sun-Times,* October 29, 1997.

25. Paul M. Green, "Mayor Richard M. Daley: His Views of the City and State," *Illinois Issues,* August–September 1991.

26. Donald Ames, interview with author, July 24, 1997; Eli Lehrer, "The Town that Loves to TIF," *Governing,* September 1999; Phillips-Fein, "The Still Industrial City"; Peggy Boyer Long, "TIFs," *Illinois Issues,* October 1999; Burney Simpson, "The Trouble with TIFs," *Illinois Issues,* October 1999.

27. Steven R. Strahler, "Daley Had Dreams of Going Corporate; Looking Ahead, Mayor Fancies a CEO Career," *Crain's Chicago Business,* March 1, 1995; Janet Ward, "Chicago's Richard Daley: 1997 Municipal Leaders of the Year," *American City and County,* December 1997; Alan Ehrenhalt, "Leading in Good Times and Bad," *Governing,* December 1997.

28. Alexander, "Black and Latino," 206; Daley, "Chicago City Government."

29. Phillips-Fein, "The Still Industrial City."

30. Alexander, "Black and Latino," 197; Simpson et al., "Chicago since September 11."

31. "The Government Performance Project: Report Card, Chicago," *Governing,* February 2000.

32. Richard M. Daley, inaugural address (Chicago Public Library, April 24, 1989), http://chipublib.org/oo4chicago/mayors/speeches/daley89.htl (accessed July 1, 2004).

33. Joseph Reed, interview with author, October 1, 1991.

34. Charles L. Kyle and E. R. Kantowitz, *Kids First—Primero Los Ninos: Chicago School Reform in the 1980s* (Springfield: Illinois Issues, 1992), 293–296, n. 5; Peter Martinez, interview with author, December 13, 1991; Reed interview; B. Kenneth West, interview with author, November 14, 1991.

35. First quote in Leadership for Quality Education, *LQE: Leadership for Quality Education* (Chicago, 1991); second quote in Lawrence Howe, interview with author, November 9, 1991.

36. Quoted in Lawrence Howe, "Reviving the Zeal for School Reform," *Chicago Enterprise*, December 1991; Leadership for Quality Education, "Board of Directors" (1989–1993); Kyle and Kantowitz, *Kids First*, 296–300; William S. McKersie, "Strategic Philanthropy and Local Public Policy: Lessons from Chicago School Reform, 1987–1993" (Ph.D. diss., University of Chicago, 1998), 272–274; Kenneth K. Wong and Gail L. Sunderman, "Redesigning Accountability at the System-Wide Level: The Politics of School Reform in Chicago," in *Advances in Educational Policy: Rethinking School Reform in Chicago*, ed. Kenneth K. Wong (Greenwich, Conn.: JAI Press, 1996).

37. Quoted in Howe, "Reviving the Zeal," 4; Shipps, Kahne, and Smylie, "The Politics of Urban School Reform."

38. West interview.

39. Chicago Board of Education, "Its About T.I.M.E.: To Improve Management of Education" (n.d.); Chicago Board of Education, *TIMEOUT*, November 1994.

40. Quoted in Fryklund Consulting, "Chicago Public Schools Management Information Systems, Submitted to the Chicago School Finance Authority" (1994), 3, 17, 31 (see also 12, 21–30); Rosalind Rossi, "Finance Authority Taps Consultants: School Board Irate," *Chicago Sun-Times*, May 19, 1994.

41. Mark Hornung, "School Panel Bids for Radical Reform," *Crain's Chicago Business*, June 22, 1992; Martin Koldyke, interview with author, June 23, 1997; Martin Koldyke, "Memo from the Chicago School Finance Committee to the Governor of the State of Illinois, the Leadership of the General Assembly, and the Mayor of the City of Chicago" (April 17, 1995); Maribeth VanderWeele, "Panel Puts Schools in a Vice Grip: Hiring of Ex May Signal Move to Policy-Shaping Role," *Chicago Sun-Times*, July 4, 1992; Chicago Public Schools, "Systemwide Educational Reform Goals and Objectives Plan, 1993–1995, Adopted by the Board of Education and Approved by the School Finance Authority" (August 1992), 110, 126–130; Mary A. Johnson, "School Board Plan Rejected: President Says 'Task Borders on Impossible,'" *Chicago Sun-Times*, August 13, 1992.

42. Brian Jackson, "School Reformers Back Board, Fix Finance Panel," *Chicago Sun-Times*, July 28, 1992; North Central Regional Educational Laboratory, "Chicago School Reform Study Project" (1992).

43. John Ayers, interview with author, December 15, 1997.

44. Jahahara Armstrong et al., "Open Letter to Ms. Diana Nelson, President of LQE" (December 13, 1993); Civic Committee officer, interview with author, June 18, 1997; Barbara Rose, "School Watchdog Loses Some Bark," *Crain's Chicago Business*, November 29, 1993; William Gruber, "NU President Gets Ready to Take a Swing at Civic Challenge," *Chicago Tribune*, December 23, 1994; Francine Knowles, "City at Center Marks Shift in Civic Committee's Focus," *Chicago Sun-Times*, September 10, 1995; Steve R. Strawler, "Commercial Club Awaiting Overhaul," *Crain's Chicago Business*, April 27, 1996.

45. Anthony S. Bryk et al., *Charting Chicago School Reform: Democratic Localism as a Lever for Change* (Boulder, Colo.: Westview Press, 1998); Michael M. Katz, Michele Fine, and Elaine Simon, "Poking Around: Outsiders View Chicago School Reform," *Teachers College Record* 99, no. 1 (1997); Linda Lenz and Frank Burgos, "Elections Hailed as Success: But Will There Be Real Reform?" *Chicago Sun-Times*, October 13, 1989; Sharon Rollow and Anthony S. Bryk, "Democratic Politics and School Improvement: The Potential of Chicago School Reform," in *The New Politics*

of Race and Gender: The 1992 Yearbook of the Politics of Education Association, ed. Catherine Marshall (San Francisco: Falmer Press, 1993); William Snider, "Chicago Elections Usher in New Era of Reform," *Education Week,* October 18, 1989.

46. Quoted in William S. McKersie, "The Brash View—Local Philanthropy Matters: Lessons from Chicago School Reform, 1987–1993" (paper presented at the Philanthropic Foundations in History: Needs and Opportunities for Study, New York University, November 14–15, 1996); William S. McKersie, "Philanthropy's Paradox: Chicago School Reform," *Educational Evaluation and Policy Analysis* 15, no. 2 (1993). See charts of grant-making activity available in McKersie, "Strategic Philanthropy."

47. Linda Lenz, interview with author, December 12, 2003.

48. Dorothy Shipps, Elisabeth Fowlkes, and Alissa Peltzman, "Journalism and Urban School Reform: Versions of Democratic Decision Making in Two American Cities," *American Journal of Education* (forthcoming, spring 2006).

49. McKersie, "Strategic Philanthropy," 107–111.

50. Quoted in Anthony S. Bryk and Kim L. Hermanson, "Educational Indicator Systems: Observations of Their Structure, Interpretation and Use" (paper presented at the Conference on the Research Agenda for Assessing School Reform in Chicago, March 8, 1991).

51. Penny Bender Sebring and Anthony S. Bryk, "Charting Reform in Chicago Schools: Pluralistic Policy Research," *New Directions in Program Evaluation* 59 (1993).

52. Anthony S. Bryk, "A New Accountability and Quality Assurance System for the CPS; Draft for Discussion Purposes" (January 23, 1995); Albert L. Bennett and Ruben Carriedo, *Restructuring Research, Evaluation and Analysis Functions of the Chicago Public Schools* (Consortium on Chicago School Research, 1995).

53. Sebring and Bryk, "Charting Reform in Chicago Schools," 20.

54. William S. McKersie, "Grant Data Abstract: Funding by Selected Chicago Foundations for Chicago School Reform, 1987–1993" (December 1996); McKersie, "The Brash View."

55. Deborah Lynch Walsh, *Labor of Love: One Chicago Teacher's Experience* (Lincoln, Neb.: Writers Club Press, 2000), 98.

56. Quoted in Albert Bennett et al., *Charting Reform, the Principals' Perspective: Report on a Survey of Chicago Public School Principals* (Consortium on Chicago School Research, 1992), 7; Penny B. Sebring et al., *Charting Reform: Chicago Teachers Take Stock* (Consortium on Chicago School Research, 1995), 60–61; Betty Malen, "Enacting Site Based Management: A Political Utilities Analysis," *Educational Evaluation and Policy Analysis* 16, no. 3 (1994).

57. Quoted in John Ayers interview; Allen Beardon, interview with Karin Sconzert, August 25, 1997.

58. Senior union leader, interview with author, September 9, 1997.

59. Shanker quoted in Walsh, *Labor of Love,* 60.

60. Quoted in Walsh, *Labor of Love,* 103–107; Beardon interview; John Kotsakis, interview with author, December 12, 1991; senior union official, interview with Consortium on Chicago School Research, October 11, 1994.

61. Beardon interview; Kotsakis interview; "A Quest for Change: The Teachers Union Has Emerged as an Unlikely Advocate for School Reform," *Education Week,* June 22, 1994; "Jonathan G. Kotsakis, Teachers Union Voice of Reform," *Chicago Sun-Times,* September 5, 1994.

62. Quoted in *Arthur Fumarolo et al. v. the Chicago Board of Education et al.,* 142 Ill. 2nd 54, 566 N.E. 2nd 1283, 1990 Ill. LEXUS 136, 153 Ill. Dec 177, 217, 10, 13 (1990); William S. McKersie, "Chicago School Reform's Latest Challenge," *SchoolWatch* (n.d.).

63. Henry Mendoza, interview with author, November 26, 1991.

64. Kyle and Kantowitz, *Kids First,* 316–327; Donald Ames, interview with author, October 21, 1991; John J. Lane and Edgar G. Epps, "Site-Based Management: Disconcerting Policy Issues, Critical Policy Choices," in *Restructuring the Schools: Problems and Prospects,* ed. John J. Lane and Edgar G. Epps (Berkeley, Calif.: McCutchan Publishing, 1992), 192.

65. *Arthur Fumarolo et al. v. the Chicago Board of Education et al.,* 10–11.

66. West interview; Richard Day Research Inc., *A Survey of Members of Local School Councils* (Chicago: Leadership for Quality Education, October 25, 1990); Susan Ryan et al., *Charting Reform: LSCs—Local Leadership at Work* (Consortium on Chicago School Research, 1997).

67. Quoted in Latina activist, interview with Consortium on Chicago School Research, February 14, 1994; Anthony S. Bryk et al., *A View from the Elementary Schools: The State of Reform in Chicago* (Consortium on Chicago School Research, 1993); Ryan et al., *Charting Reform: LSCs.*

68. See *Catalyst* 15, no. 6 (2004) for subsequent changes; McKersie, "Strategic Philanthropy"; Ryan et al., *Charting Reform.*

69. The Chicago Public Schools Office of Standards, Assessment, and Research provided racial and ethnic survey numbers; calculations are the author's. Estimates of turnover come from Daniel D. Polsby, *Chicago School Reform: First Annual Evaluation* (Chicago: Heartland Institute, 1994), and Bennett et al., *Charting Reform: Principals.* See also Bryk et al., *A View;* Sebring et al., *Charting Reform: Teachers.*

70. Bennett et al., *Charting Reform: Principals;* Dorothy Shipps, Karin Sconzert, and Holly Swyers, *The Chicago Annenberg Challenge: The First Three Years* (Consortium on Chicago School Research, 1999).

71. Penny B. Sebring et al., *Charting Reform: The Students Speak* (Consortium on Chicago School Research, 1996).

72. Sebring et al., *Charting Reform: Teachers.*

73. CTU Quest leader, interview with Consortium on Chicago School Research, March 9, 1994.

74. Cross-city campaign activist, interview with Consortium on Chicago School Research, October 19, 1994.

75. Latina activist.

76. Quoted in Urban League representative, interview with Consortium on Chicago School Research, August 11 and 12, 1994; North Central Regional Educational Laboratory, "School Reform Study Project".

77. Sakoni Karanja, interview with author, December 4, 1991.

78. Mayor's chief of staff, interview with author, June 25, 1997; "Get Moving Mayor: Fill out the School Bd.," *Chicago Sun-Times,* August 26, 1994; John Kass, "Daley Appoints 4 to School Board: Mayor Shuts Door on Foe, Making No Decision on 3 Spots," *Chicago Tribune,* August 27, 1994.

79. Reed interview.

80. Jacoby Dickins, interview with author, November 25, 1991.

81. Polsby, *Chicago School Reform: First Annual Evaluation.*

82. Quoted in Maribeth VanderWeele, *Reclaiming Our Schools: The Struggle for Chicago School Reform* (Chicago: Loyola University Press, 1994), xx, xxiii, 25, 29, 92. See also "Reform Data Book," *Catalyst* 6, no. 5 (1994).

83. Of the twenty-six comments made about Kimbrough by business executives in interviews conducted in 1991, 80 percent were negative. Quotes in Reed interview; Thomas Ayers, interview with author, October 18, 1991; Peter Willmott, interview with author, October 25, 1991. See also Tracy Robinson, "Kimbrough Gets Poor 'Report Card,' " *Chicago Sun-Times,* June 23, 1990.

84. Lu Palmer, interview with author, November 20, 1991.

85. Danny Solis, interview with author, November 13, 1991.

86. Charles Mount and Jack Houston, "School Council Sues to Ward Off Superintendent," *Chicago Tribune,* January 13, 1990.

87. Dickins interview; Arthur Berman, interview with author, December 11, 1991; G. Alfred Hess Jr., interview with author, November 13, 1991; Lou Ortiz and Maureen O'Donnell, "School's In! Teachers Union OKs Two Step Pay Hike," *Chicago Sun-Times,* November 18, 1991; Maribeth VanderWeele, "Schools Hoping to Bag $1 Billion: Board Asks Big Hike in Property Taxes," *Chicago Tribune,* December 9, 1991; Illinois Business Roundtable, *Current Activity, Education Task Force; Prepared for David T. Kearns, U.S. Deputy Secretary of Education* (Chicago, 1991); Kyle and Kantowitz, *Kids First,* 330.

88. Maribeth VanderWeele, "Annual School Crisis Over: Panel OKs Budget, Reform Plan," *Chicago Sun-Times,* September 1, 1992; Mary A. Johnson, "Daley Enters School Budget Fray," *Chicago Sun-Times,* August 29, 1992.

89. Mary Sue Barrett, interview with author, June 25, 1997.

90. Chicago United, *Building towards Better Performance* (Chicago, n.d.); James L. Greer and G. Alfred Hess Jr., *Revenue Shortfalls at Chicago Board of Education* (Chicago Panel on Public School Finances, 1984), i–vi, 37–40; Christina Warden, Diana Lauber, and G. Alfred Hess Jr., *1987–1988 Assessment of School Site Budgetary Practices of the Chicago Public Schools* (Chicago Panel on Public School Policy and Finance, 1988).

91. Paul Devine, from Moody's Public Finance Department, quoted in Rosalind Rossi, "School Bond Ratings Lowered: Moody's Edict Makes Borrowing More Expensive," *Chicago Sun-Times,* December 21, 1993.

92. Daley quoted in Fran Spielman, "Daley Assails School Finance Authority," *Chicago Sun-Times,* February 22, 1995; see also Maribeth VanderWeele, "Panel Regains Broad Powers over the System," *Chicago Sun-Times,* September 2, 1993; Chicago Public Schools, "Role Modification as a Result of Public Act 88-511 and the Failure to Have a Balanced Budget by 9/1/83" (n.d.); Rosalind Rossi, "Schools Face New Crisis in 1995, Authority Says," *Chicago Sun-Times,* December 9, 1993.

93. City of Chicago Board of Education, "The Three-Tiered Process for School Improvement" (May 25, 1994); Jacquelyn Heard, "City Schools Plan Is Softened," *Chicago Tribune,* June 23, 1994; John Simmons, *Evaluation of the Self-Analysis Process, Pathways to Success* (Chicago: Participation Associates, 1995).

94. Chicago Public Schools, "Chicago Public Schools Transformation Design: Working Draft" (February 28, 1995); Urban League representative interview.

95. Quoted in Thomas Reynolds, Lester McKeever, and Raul Villalobos, Education Co-Chairs of Chicago United, to Gery Chico, President of the Board of Education, September 5, 1995, Cowlishaw Papers.

96. Janet Froetcher, interview with author, December 11, 1997; Carolyn Nordstrom, interview with author, June 30, 1997; Ray O'Connell, interview with author, September 12, 1997. For a detailed description of the origins of this "modern" management view, see Stephen P. Waring, *Taylorism Transformed: Scientific Management Theory since 1945* (Chapel Hill: University of North Carolina Press, 1991), 187.

97. The Illinois Business Roundtable was formed in 1989. Ames interview.

98. Quoted in Jeff Mays, interview with author, September 5, 1997; Ames interview.

99. Business Roundtable Public Policy Committee, "Essential Components of a Successful Education System" (September 11, 1990); Scott R. Fowler, *The Business Role in State Education Reform: Report Prepared of the Business Roundtable* (Washington, D.C.: Committee on Economic Development, 1990); Kathryn Borman, Louis Costnell, and Karen Gallagher, "Business Involvement in School Reform: The Rise of the Business Roundtable," in *The New Politics of Race and Gender: The Politics of Education Association Yearbook,* ed. Catherine Marshall (Washington, D.C.: Falmer Press, 1993). The best-known intellectual proponents of this argument at the time were John E. Chubb and Terry M. Moe, *Politics, Markets and America's Schools* (Washington, D.C.: Brookings Institution, 1990).

100. Ronald Gidwitz, interview with author, July 8, 1997.

101. Mays interview.

102. Ames interview.

103. Illinois Business Roundtable, *One Vision, One Voice: Coordinated Action; Report of the 1999 Business Leaders Education Summit* (n.d.), http://www.ilbusinessroundtable.com/education/onevision2.pdf (accessed June 8, 2003).

104. Republican Members of the House of Representatives, "Contract with America" (1994), http://www.townhall.com/documents/contract.html (accessed June 2, 2003); Howard Fineman, "Revenge of the Right," *Newsweek,* November 21, 1994.

105. Fran Spielman, "GOP Initiatives Draw Daley's Praise," *Chicago Sun-Times,* January 7, 1995.

106. Gidwitz interview.

107. Memo from Chairman and CEO of Carus Corporation to the Illinois Business Education Council, "Agenda Change in November 28, 1994 Meeting," 1994, Cowlishaw Papers.

108. Chicago United, *Building towards Better Performance.*

109. Quoted in School Finance Authority to the Governor of the State of Illinois, the Leadership of the General Assembly and the Mayor of Chicago, April 17, 1995, Cowlishaw Papers; Civic Committee of the Commercial Club, "Business Leaders: Education Is Our Top Priority" (press release), March 20, 1995.

110. Gidwitz interview; Civic Committee of the Commercial Club, press release; "Business Weighs in on Education," *Chicago Tribune,* March 22, 1995.

111. Quoted in Gidwitz interview.

112. The dual system was to start at age sixteen, after which students would go to either an international baccalaureate track or a vocational track to be overseen by a state Youth Apprentice Council. Illinois Manufacturers Association, "Draft Legislation for School-to-Careers" (1995).

113. Mays interview.

114. Quoted in Civic Committee Associate Director Cordelia Meyer to the Honor-

able Mary Lou Cowlishaw, May 2, 1995, Cowlishaw Papers; Chicago Public Schools Reform Working Group (Don Ames, comp.), "Accountability, Remediation and Governance Subcommittee" (1995); Chicago Public Schools Reform Working Group (Pat Harvey, comp.), "Innovations Subcommittee" (1995); Illinois Business Education Council, "Proposal to the Illinois General Assembly" (February 9, 1995).

115. Of seventy-two interviews conducted in 1997, the largest number of positive comments made about Richard M. Daley's contribution to school reform dealt with his capacity to bring public and private resources to the schools. Informants gave him especially high marks for collaborating with the business community.

116. Local business lawyer, interview with author, November 5, 1991.

117. Bruce McPherson, interview with author, July 21, 1997.

118. Callaway interview.

119. First quote in Mays interview; second quote in Callaway interview.

120. Senior club leader, interview with author, June 16, 1997; Chicago Public Schools Reform Working Group, "Accountability, Remediation and Governance Subcommittee"; Chicago Public Schools Reform Working Group, "Innovations Subcommittee."

121. Governor Edgar to Mary Lou Cowlishaw, "Chicago School Reform Proposal," April 26, 1995, Cowlishaw Papers.

122. McPherson interview.

123. Mary Lou Cowlishaw, list of Chicago Public Schools Reform Working Group (n.d.), provided to author.

124. Mary Lou Cowlishaw, interview with author, June 6, 1997; see also David Peterson, interview with author, September 18, 1997.

125. City of Chicago Board of Education President Sharon Grant and General Superintendent Argie Johnson to the Honorable Mary Lou Cowlishaw, fax, April 7, 1995, Cowlishaw Papers.

126. Other individuals and organizations showed up on Cowlishaw's list, but there was no corroborating evidence of active participation.

127. Cowlishaw interview.

128. James Compton to the Honorable Mary Lou Cowlishaw, fax, April 10, 1997; James Isaacs, MALDEF, to the Honorable Mary Lou Cowlishaw, fax, April 7, 1995; Sylvia Puente, Latino Institute, to Representative Cowlishaw, fax, May 4, 1997, all in Cowlishaw Papers.

129. Cowlishaw interview.

130. Quoted in Bryk et al., *Charting School Reform,* 294. Larry Braskamp, "The Second Stage of School Reform," April 7, 1995, Cowlishaw Papers.

131. Bryk et al., *Charting School Reform,* 291–302.

132. Gidwitz interview; Ames interview.

133. Gidwitz interview; McPherson interview.

134. Fran Spielman, "Daley Offers School Agenda: Seeks Reforms Based on Accountability," *Chicago Sun-Times,* January 19, 1995; Fran Spielman, "Daley Seeks Tighter Grip on School Bd; Rips Size, Selection Process," *Chicago Sun-Times,* April 1, 1995; Fran Spielman, "Despite Mandate, Daley Likely to Make Changes: Mayor to Start His New Terms with Renewed Chances for Pet Projects," *Chicago Sun-Times,* April 5, 1995.

135. Mayor of Chicago Richard M. Daley, "Speech to the Civic Federation of Chicagoans and Press Release" (April 26, 1995).

136. Daley quoted in Charles Nicodemus, "Solutions? Summit on Schools Sunk by Squabbles," *Chicago Sun-Times,* May 7, 1995.

137. Daley quoted in Fran Spielman, "Daley Left Out; Calls Off Trip," *Chicago Sun-Times,* May 11, 1995; see also Michael Gillis, "GOP Sets Course to Fix City's Schools; Sweeping Plan Weakens Union, Empowers Daley," *Chicago Sun-Times,* May 11, 1995; Michael Gillis and John Oclander, "Edgar: Ban School Strikes; His Chicago Plan Would Give Daley Key Education Role," *Chicago Sun-Times,* April 26, 1995.

138. Commercial Club executive, interview with author, June 18, 1997.

139. Arnold Weber, President of the Civic Committee, to the Honorable Mary Lou Cowlishaw, May 18, 1997, Cowlishaw Papers.

140. Ames interview; Mays interview.

141. Commercial Club leader, interview with author, June 23, 1997.

142. Shipps, Kahne, and Smylie, "The Politics of Urban School Reform."

143. *Amendatory Act to the Illinois School Code and Other Statutes,* 1995.

144. In 1999 another sanction, "reengineering," was added to the list. It gave a school's teachers a greater role in determining which changes follow from intervention.

145. Mark Miller, "A CEO Superintendent? Interesting, but Unlikely," *Crain's Chicago Business,* December 7, 1992.

146. Quoted in Grant Pick, "What Makes Vallas Run?" *Catalyst,* December 1996. For a more critical view, see Sharon Schmidt, "Lies in Vallas' Vitae" (March 2002), http://www.substancenews.com/march02/vallas/html (accessed July 19, 2004).

147. Barrett interview.

148. Paul Vallas, telephone interview with author, September 3, 1997; John Ayers, "Business and Civic Leadership for Change: The Houston Experience" (paper presented at Making the Grade: Assessing the Reform of Houston's Public Schools, University of Houston, October 23, 2000); Lorraine Forte, "New Law Lets Board Shift Money to Balance Budget," *Catalyst,* September 1995; Ann Scott Tyson, "New Schools of Thought," *Christian Science Monitor,* September 7, 1995.

149. Commercial Club executive interview.

150. Vallas interview; Chicago Public Schools Office of Communications, "CPS Receives 5th Straight Bond Rating Increase" (press release, May 23, 2000).

151. Brett Schaeffer, "Watchdog Group: CPS Capital Plan a Project Wish List," *Catalyst,* April 2001.

152. John Ayers inerview; Rosalind Rossi, "Board OKs $48 Million Tax Levy for Schools," *Chicago Sun-Times,* December 18, 1997; Kenneth K. Wong et al., *Integrated Governance as a Reform Strategy in Chicago Public Schools* (Philadelphia: National Center on Education in the Inner Cities, 1997); Rosalind Rossi and Fran Spielman, "School Tax Hike on the Table," *Chicago Sun-Times,* May 23, 2001.

153. Dave McKinney, "153 School Districts Come out Winners; but Tax Package Not a Boon to All," *Chicago Sun-Times,* December 10, 1997; Tyson, "New Schools of Thought"; Joe Ruklick, "New $5.7 Million Grant to Help Poor-Performing Chicago Schools," *Chicago Defender,* March 6, 2000; Sheila Washington, "Ryan Announces $400 Million in School Grants," *Chicago Defender,* July 12, 1999.

154. Cozette Buckney, interview with author, August 25, 1997; see also Shipps, Kahne, and Smylie, "The Politics of Urban School Reform."

155. F. James, "Daley Lectures on Schools: If Chicago Can Turn Around, Others Can, Mayor Says," *Chicago Tribune,* June 6, 1997.

156. Patricia Graham, interview with author, July 16, 1997; Nordstrom interview.

157. Greg Hinz, "Executive of the Year: Schools CEO Vallas Goes to the Head of the Class," *Crain's Chicago Business,* June 8, 1998.

158. Shipps, Fowlkes, and Peltzman, "Journalism and Urban School Reform."

159. Maribeth VanderWeele, interview with author, June 26, 1997.

160. Shipps, Fowlkes, and Peltzman, "Journalism and Urban School Reform."

161. Gidwitz interview; Alexander Russo, "Political Educator" (*Education Next*, winter 2003), http://www.educationnext.org/20031/38.html (accessed July 2004); Kenneth K. Wong and P. Jain, "Newspapers as Policy Actors in Urban School Systems" (paper presented at the American Political Science Association, Washington, D.C., August 1997).

162. Barrett interview; Tom Sharpe, "Costly Move Downtown Called into Question by Recent Innovations at Pershing Road" (Substance Online, March 2002), http://www.substancenews.com/March02/musicalchairs.html (accessed July 19, 2004).

163. Mays interview.

164. Clinton, "State of the Union Address"; Fornek, "President Hails."

165. Praise for Vallas came from seventy-two interviews of Chicago community leaders conducted by the author in 1997. Business and union leaders had nearly identical amounts of praise for Vallas and his team; only the media had higher praise. Community activists and foundation executives were more reserved.

166. Bruce Upbin, "Chain Saw Paul," *Forbes,* April 6, 1998, 66.

167. Hinz, "Executive of the Year."

168. Quoted in Jonathan Alter, *Newsweek,* June 22, 1998, 30; Pick, "What Makes Vallas Run?"

169. Latina community organizer, interview with author, July 2, 1997; see also O'Connell interview.

170. VanderWeele quoted in Pick, "What Makes Vallas Run?"

171. Diane Donavan, interview with Karin Sconzert, July 10, 1997.

172. First quote in Pick, "What Makes Vallas Run?"; second quote in Commercial Club executive interview.

173. David Schaper, interview with Karin Sconzert, July 16, 1997.

174. Robin Tepper Jacob, Susan Stone, and Melissa Roderick, *Ending Social Promotion: Responses of Teachers and Students* (Consortium on Chicago School Research, 2004); Melissa Roderick, Brian A. Jacob, and Anthony S. Bryk, "The Impact of High Stakes Testing on Student Achievement in Promotional Gate Grades," *Educational Evaluation and Policy Analysis* 24 (2002); Donald Moore, *Chicago's Grade Retention Program Fails to Help Retained Students* (Chicago: Designs for Change, 2000); Melissa Roderick et al., *Ending Social Promotion* (Consortium on Chicago School Research, 1999); Melissa Roderick et al., *Update: Ending Social Promotion: Passing, Retention and Achievement Trends among Promoted and Retained Students 1995–1999* (Consortium on Chicago School Research, 2000). See also Chicago Public Schools Office of Communications, "CPS Promotes Retained Students: Promotion Policy Helps Students Catch Up" (press release, January 22, 1999).

175. Rosalind Rossi and Fran Spielman, "Daley Backs Board: Mayor Opposes Sham Graduation for 8th Graders," *Chicago Sun-Times,* June 5, 1997.

176. Quoted in Jay P. Heubert and Robert M. Hauser, *High Stakes: Testing for Tracking, Promotion and Graduation* (Washington, D.C.: National Academy Press, 1998), 31; "High School Accountability Strategies 1996–2000: A Scorecard, Web Extra" (Catalyst

Online, August 1, 2000), http://www.catalyst-chicago.org (accessed August 10, 2003); Chicago Public Schools, "Intervention Status (02-P36-C)" (2000), http://www.CPS.k-12 .il.us (accessed August 2002); Chicago Public Schools Office of Communications, "Vallas Responds to Allegation of Discrimination in CPS Promotion Policies" (press release, October 21, 1999); Joe Rucklick, "Watchdog Group Hits CPS with Law Suit," *Chicago Defender,* October 26, 1999.

177. There were 109 schools on probation in 1996; the number dropped, then rose to a high of 212 in 2004. "School Reform Timeline 2004" (Catalyst Online, 2004), http://www.catalyst-chicago.org/timeline/time04.htm (accessed June 20, 2005).

178. Kara Finnegan and Jennifer O' Day, *External Supports to Schools on Probation* (Consortium on Chicago School Research and Consortium on Policy Research in Education, 2003), viii, 43.

179. "Staff Development a Low Priority" (Catalyst Online, 1998), http://www .catalyst-chicago.org/02-98/o28wmmo4.htm (accessed August 12, 2003); Mandy Burrell, "Teachers for Chicago Out, Fast Track Certification In," *Catalyst,* March 2001; Alexander Russo, "Chicago, NY Welcome a New Breed of Principals," *Catalyst,* April 2001; Faye A. Silas, "Principal Training Program Scores Average in Placements," *Catalyst,* February 2003.

180. Vallas interview.

181. Vallas quoted in Amanda Paulson, "In an Era of 'Accountability,' Parents Get Report Cards Too," *Christian Science Monitor,* July 18, 2000.

182. Rosalind Rossi, "Parents to Get Grades: Chicago Schools Chief, Paul Vallas Wants to Issue Report Cards to Tell Mom and Dad How They Are Performing Too," *Chicago Sun-Times,* May 18, 2000; Rosalind Rossi, "Reaction Mixed to School Parent Report Card," *Chicago Sun-Times,* November 30, 2000.

183. Foundation executive, interview with author, September 15, 1997; Foundation officer, interview with Karin Sconzert, August 4, 1997; Kenneth Rolling, interview with author, July 30, 1997; Kenneth Rolling, "Reflections on the Chicago Annenberg Challenge," in *School Reform in Chicago: Lessons in Policy and Practice,* ed. Alexander Russo (Cambridge: Harvard Education Press, 2004); Shipps, Sconzert, and Swyers, "Chicago Annenberg Challenge."

184. First quote in McKersie, "The Brash View," 28; second quote in McKersie, "Strategic Philanthropy," 330.

185. Mark A. Smylie et al., *The Annenberg Challenge: Successes, Failures and Lessons for the Future* (Consortium on Chicago School Research, 2003); see also Mark A. Smylie et al., *Getting Started: A First Look at Chicago Annenberg Schools and Networks* (Consortium on Chicago School Research, 1998); Stacey A. Wenzel et al., *Development of Chicago Annenberg Schools: 1996–1999* (Consortium on Chicago School Research, 2001); Walsh, *Labor of Love.*

186. By 1999 Rolling had switched gears, doubling funding to eighteen "breakthrough" schools and assisting the others through a series of systemwide professional development opportunities.

187. Rolling interview; Smylie et al., *The Annenberg Challenge.*

188. Quoted in Smylie et al., *The Annenberg Challenge,* 43 (see also 84–85); Fred Newmann and Karin Sconzert, *School Improvement with External Partners* (Consortium on Chicago School Research, 2000); Wenzel et al., *Development of Chicago Annenberg Schools;* Rolling, "Reflections."

189. Commercial Club executive interview.

190. Senior union official interview.

191. Commercial Club executive interview.

192. Koldyke interview.

193. Margaret Blackshire, interview with author, October 27, 1997.

194. VanderWeele interview.

195. C. Lawrence, "Delegates Approve Teachers Contract," *Chicago Sun-Times,* October 13, 1998.

196. Vallas quoted in Greg Hinz, "Teachers Union's Leadership Fight: Record of Schools Chief Will Be Central Issues in May Election," *Crain's Chicago Business,* April 30, 2001; Rosalind Rossi, "Teachers Pact Vote Won't Be Itemized," *Chicago Sun-Times,* December 10, 1998.

197. Michael Martinez and Juanita Poe, "CTU, Board at War over Reserve Teachers," *Chicago Tribune,* July 24, 1997.

198. Michael Martinez, "Schools Still Slow to Fire Teachers," *Chicago Tribune,* October 20, 1997; Juanita Poe, "Dismissal Notices Are Sent to 188 Teachers: Troubled Schools Lose Third of Staffs," *Chicago Tribune,* July 29, 1997; Patricia Monsoon, "Law Revamping City Teachers Tenure Upheld," *Chicago Daily Law Bulletin,* July 19, 1999.

199. Walsh, *Labor of Love,* 115, 132.

200. "CTU Backs Strong Role for Teachers," *Catalyst,* March 2002; "A New CTU Drummer," *Catalyst,* September 2001; Walsh, *Labor of Love,* 166, 175.

201. Walsh, *Labor of Love,* 115.

202. Ibid., 147–148; Julie Blair, "Long Passage," *Education Week,* June 5, 2002.

203. Walsh, *Labor of Love,* 176.

204. Commercial Club executive interview.

205. Daniel C. Vock, "CPS Fares Well in General Assembly Despite Record State Budget Shortfall," *Catalyst,* July 2003; Leo Gorenstein, "The Legacy of Vallas Financial Manipulations: Feast or Famine?" (Substance Online, March 2002), http://www.substancenews.com/March02/phoneydeficits/html (accessed July 29, 2004).

206. Upbin, "Chain Saw Paul," 66; Greg Hinz, "Surprise! City Deal for Comedy: Before Outages, Schools Enter 8-Year Pact," *Crain's Chicago Business,* August 23, 1999; Jorge Oclander, "Firm to Charge Schools More for Supplies," *Chicago Sun-Times,* May 24, 1996; Rosalind Rossi, "School's Chief Information Officer Ousted," *Chicago Sun-Times,* February 11, 2000; Chinta Strausberg, "Vallas Denied Claims He Sat on Data about Phony Firm," *Chicago Defender,* April 29, 2000; David Mendell, "Proud of 'Battle Scars,' Chico Still in Fight," *Chicago Tribune,* March 7, 2001.

207. "Board Keeps Test Data under Wraps," *Catalyst,* November 1998; "Ex-Superintendent Becomes Consultant for Chicago Schools," *Telegraph Herald,* January 16, 1999.

208. Elaine Allensworth and Todd Rosenkranz, *Access to Magnet Schools in Chicago* (Consortium on Chicago School Research, 2000); Hinz, "Executive of the Year"; David Weissman, "Everyone Wins, Some Win More," *Catalyst,* November 1998; Rosalind Rossi and Fran Spielman, "Hunger-Strikers Demand Little Village High School," *Chicago Sun-Times,* May 22, 2001; D. Newbart and Rosalind Rossi, "Scores Drop at Schools under Tightest Rein," *Chicago Sun-Times,* June 6, 2001; Rosalind Rossi, "Study Faults Low Scoring High Schools," *Chicago Sun-Times,* March 11, 2001.

209. Barrett interview; Suzanne Kerbow, interview with Karin Sconzert, July 10, 1997.

210. Leon Jackson, interview with author, June 24, 1997.

211. Commercial Club executive interview; summary data from seventy-two interviews conducted in 1997 by author.

212. Julia B. Smith, Valerie E. Lee, and Frank M. Newmann, *Instruction and Achievement in Chicago Elementary Schools* (Consortium on Chicago School Research, 2001); Julia B. Smith, Betsann Smith, and Anthony S. Bryk, *Setting the Pace: Opportunities to Learn in Chicago's Elementary Schools* (Consortium on Chicago School Research, 1998).

213. Elaine Allensworth, *Ending Social Promotion: Dropout Rates in Chicago after Implementation of the Eighth Grade Promotional Gates* (Consortium on Chicago School Research, 2004), 28; Jenny Nagoaka and Melissa Roderick, *Ending Social Promotion: The Effects of Retention* (Consortium on Chicago School Research, 2004); Melissa Roderick and Mimi Engel, "The Grasshopper and the Ant: Motivational Responses of Low Achieving Students to High Stakes Testing," *Educational Evaluation and Policy Analysis* 23, no. 4 (2001); Melissa Roderick, Mimi Engel, and Jenny Nogaoka, *Ending Social Promotion: Results from Summer Bridge* (Consortium on Chicago School Research, 2004); Moore, *Chicago's Grade Retention Program Fails.*

214. "School Reform Timeline" (Catalyst Online, 2000), http://www.catalyst-chicago.org/timeline/time00.htm (accessed July 28, 2004); Anna Mendota, "Schools Aim to Toughen Standards, 8th Grade Bar May Be Raised," *Chicago Sun-Times,* June 27, 2000; Rosalind Rossi, "Public School Test Policy Hit; Too Much Riding on Tests," *Chicago Sun-Times,* January 28, 1999.

215. Lynn Guerrero, "Public Favors Picking an Educator," *Chicago Sun-Times,* June 27, 2001.

216. Daley quoted in Rosalind Rossi and Fran Spielman, "Daley Demands School Reform: Mayor Says Educators Must Focus on Improving Student Reading," *Chicago Sun-Times,* February 16, 1999.

217. "Chicago Public Schools, Fall 2001: An Organization Chart" (Catalyst Online, 2001), http://www.catalyst-chicago.org/11-01/orgchart/Duncan.htm (accessed July 29, 2004); Fran Spielman and Rosalind Rossi, "Aide Move to the Head of the Class: Vallas Deputy in Running for Schools CEO," *Chicago Sun-Times,* June 13, 2001; Fran Spielman and Rosalind Rossi, "New Chief: Untested, Unblemished, Unfazed," *Chicago Sun-Times,* June 27, 2001.

218. "Duncan Charts a New Path for Chicago Public Schools," *Catalyst,* September 2001.

219. Blair, "Long Passage."

220. Civic Committee of the Commercial Club, "Left Behind" (2003), 51.

221. Amanda Paulson, "Chicago Hope: Maybe *This* Will Work," *Christian Science Monitor,* September 21, 2004.

222. Maureen Kelleher, "First Renaissance Schools Chosen as Charter Leaders Depart," *Catalyst,* February 2005.

223. Quoted in John Myers, " 'Bread and Butter' v. Reform Agenda," *Catalyst,* May 2004; John Myers, "New Leadership Shifts Union Focus," *Catalyst,* September 2004; John Myers, "Votes Cast Months Ago, but Election Still Not Over," *Catalyst,* July 2004.

224. John W. Kingdon, *Agendas, Alternatives and Public Policies,* 2nd ed. (New York: HarperCollins College, 1995).

225. For more on the symbiotic relationship between corporate leaders and mayors, see Dorothy Shipps, "Echoes of Corporate Influence: Managing Away Urban School

Troubles," in *Reconstructing the Common Good: Coping with Intractable Dilemmas,* ed. Larry Cuban and Dorothy Shipps (Stanford, Calif.: Stanford University Press, 2000).

226. David K. Cohen, "Reforming School Politics," *Harvard Education Review* 48, no. 4 (1978).

5. POWERING REFORM

1. Charles E. Lindblom, *Politics and Markets: The World's Political Economic Systems* (New York: Basic Books, 1977); Paul E. Peterson, *City Limits* (Chicago: University of Chicago Press, 1981).

2. Charles E. Lindblom and Edward J. Woodhouse, *The Policy Making Process,* 3rd ed. (Englewood Cliffs, N.J.: Prentice Hall, 1993); Robert B. Reich, *The Work of Nations: Preparing Ourselves for the 21st Century* (New York: Alfred A. Knopf, 1991).

3. Michael Howlett and M. Ramlesh, *Studying Public Policy: Policy Cycles and Policy Subsystems* (Toronto: Oxford University Press, 1995).

4. G. Alfred Hess Jr., *School Restructuring, Chicago Style* (Newbury Park, Calif.: Corwin Press, 1991); Mary O'Connell, "School Reform Chicago Style: How Citizens Organized to Change Public Policy," *Neighborhood Works,* spring 1991.

5. Paul Pierson, *Politics in Time: History, Institutions and Social Analysis* (Princeton, N.J.: Princeton University Press, 2004).

6. Peter Cistone, Joseph Fernandez, and Pat Tornillo Jr., "School-Based Management/Shared Decision Making in Dade County (Miami)," *Education and Urban Society* 21, no. 3 (1989); Christine Murray, "Teaching as a Profession: The Rochester Case in Historical Perspective," *Harvard Education Review* 62, no. 4 (1992).

7. Pierson, *Politics in Time,* 21.

8. Hess, *School Restructuring;* Charles E. Reeves, *School Boards: Their Status, Functions and Activities* (Westport, Conn.: Greenwood Press, 1969); Deborah Lynch Walsh, *Labor of Love: One Chicago Teacher's Experience* (Lincoln, Neb.: Writers Club Press, 2000), 168–169.

9. Michael T. Hannon and John Freeman, *Organizational Ecology* (Cambridge: Harvard University Press, 1989); Pierson, *Politics in Time,* 126.

10. Richard E. Callahan, *Education and the Cult of Efficiency: A Study of the Social Forces that Have Shaped the Administration of the Public Schools* (Chicago: University of Chicago Press, 1962); Dorothy Shipps, "Echoes of Corporate Influence: Managing away Urban School Troubles," in *Reconstructing the Common Good: Coping with Intractable Dilemmas,* ed. Larry Cuban and Dorothy Shipps (Stanford, Calif.: Stanford University Press, 2000).

11. Larry Cuban, *The Blackboard and the Bottom Line: Why Schools Can't Be Businesses* (Cambridge: Harvard University Press, 2005).

12. Marsha Silverberg et al., *National Assessment of Vocational Education: Final Report to Congress* (Washington, D.C.: U.S. Department of Education, 2004).

13. For a fuller discussion of this argument, see W. Edward Deming, *The New Economics* (1993; reprint, Cambridge, Mass.: MIT Press, 2000); Robert Kanigel, *The One Best Way: Frederick Winslow Taylor and the Enigma of Efficiency* (New York: Viking, 1997); Dorothy Shipps, "The Science and Politics of Urban Education Leadership: Toward a Reorienting Narrative," in *New Foundations for Knowledge for Education*

Policy, Politics and Administration: Science and Sensationalism, ed. Douglas E. Mitchell (Mahwah, N.J.: Laurence Erlbaum Associates, in press); Stephen P. Waring, *Taylorism Transformed: Scientific Management Theory since 1945* (Chapel Hill: University of North Carolina Press, 1991).

14. Jay P. Heubert and Robert M. Hauser, *High Stakes: Testing for Tracking, Promotion and Graduation* (Washington, D.C.: National Academy Press, 1998); Linda M. McNeil, *Contradictions of School Reform: Educational Consequences of Standardized Testing* (New York: Routledge, 2000); Melissa Roderick, Brian A. Jacob, and Anthony S. Bryk, "The Impact of High Stakes Testing on Student Achievement in Promotional Gate Grades," *Educational Evaluation and Policy Analysis* 24 (2002).

15. Civic Committee of the Commercial Club, "Left Behind: A Report of the Education Committee" (2003); Frederick Hess, *Spinning Wheels: The Politics of Urban School Reform* (Washington, D.C.: Brookings Institution, 1999).

16. For a fuller discussion of how the reform literature can be categorized, see Dorothy Shipps, "Pulling Together: Civic Capacity and Urban School Reform," *American Educational Research Journal* 40, no. 4 (2003).

17. Fredrick Wirt and Michael W. Kirst, *Schools in Conflict,* 3rd. ed. (Berkeley, Calif.: McCutchan, 1992); Laurence Iannaccone, "Excellence: An Emergent Educational Issue," *Politics of Education Bulletin* 13, no. 3 (1985); Robert T. Stout, Marilyn Tallerico, and Kent P. Scribner, "Values: The What of the Politics of Education," in *The Study of Educational Politics: The Politics of Education Association Yearbook,* ed. Jay D. Scribner and Donald H. Layton (Washington, D.C.: Falmer, 1994).

18. Alex Molnar, *Giving Kids the Business: The Commercialization of America's Schools* (Boulder, Colo.: Westview Press, 1996); Craig Richards, Rima Shore, and Max B. Sawicky, *Risky Business: Private Management of the Public Schools* (Washington, D.C.: Economic Policy Institute, 1996).

19. John E. Chubb and Terry M. Moe, *Politics, Markets and America's Schools* (Washington, D.C.: Brookings Institution, 1990); Peter Drucker, *Management Tasks, Perspectives and Practices* (New York: Harper and Row, 1973); William G. Howell and Paul E. Peterson, *The Education Gap: Vouchers and Urban Schools* (Washington, D.C.: Brookings Institution, 2002); Stephen Murgatroyd and Colin Morgen, *Total Quality Management and the School* (Philadelphia: Open University Press, 1993).

20. Steve Farkas, Jean Johnson, and Anthony Foleno, *On Thin Ice: How Advocates and Opponents Could Misread the Public's Views on Vouchers and Charter Schools* (New York: Public Agenda, 1999); Karla S. Reid, "Poll Finds Support for Vouchers Wanes If Public Schools Affected," *Education Week,* October 3, 2001.

21. John Dewey, *The Public and Its Problems* (1927; reprint, Athens: Swallow/Ohio University Press, 1954); Robert Putnam, *Bowling Alone* (New York: Simon and Schuster, 2000).

22. Dewey, *The Public and Its Problems;* Lindblom and Woodhouse, *The Policy Making Process.*

23. John W. Kingdon, *Agendas, Alternatives and Public Policies,* 2nd ed. (New York: HarperCollins College, 1995); Walter Lippmann, *Public Opinion* (New York: Macmillan, 1922).

24. David B. Tyack, "School Governance in the United States: Historical Puzzles and Anomalies," in *Decentralization and School Improvement: Can We Fulfill the*

Promise? ed. Jane Hannaway and Martin Carnoy (San Francisco: Jossey-Bass, 1993); Hans Weiler, "Control versus Legitimation: The Politics of Ambivalence," in ibid.

25. Anthony S. Bryk, Dorothy Shipps, and Paul T. Hill, *Decentralization in Practice: Towards a System of Schools* (Consortium on Chicago School Research, 1998); Kenneth K. Wong et al., *Integrated Governance as a Reform Strategy in Chicago Public Schools* (Philadelphia: National Center on Education in the Inner Cities, 1997).

26. William Boyd and David W. O'Shea, "Theoretical Perspectives on School District Decentralization," *Education and Urban Society* 7, no. 4 (1975); Leonard J. Fine, *The Ecology of Public Schools* (New York: Pegasus, 1971); Allan Ornstein, *Metropolitan Schools: Administrative Decentralization vs. Community Control* (Metuchen, N.J.: Scarecrow Press, 1974); Melvin Zimet, *Decentralization and School Effectiveness: A Case Study of the 1969 Decentralization Law in New York City* (New York: Teachers College Press, 1973); Hannaway and Carnoy, *Decentralization and School Improvement.*

27. Archon Fong, *Empowered Participation: Reinventing Participatory Democracy* (Princeton, N.J.: Princeton University Press, 2004).

28. Charles T. Kerchner and Julia E. Koppich, eds., *A Union of Professionals: Labor Relations and Educational Reform* (New York: Teachers College Press, 1993); Myron Lieberman, *The Teachers Unions: How the NEA and the AFT Sabotage Reform and Hold Students, Parents, Teachers and Taxpayers Hostage to Bureaucracy* (New York: Free Press, 1997); Tom Loveless, ed., *Conflicting Missions? Teachers Unions and Educational Reform* (Washington, D.C.: Brookings Institution, 2000); Lorraine M. McDonnell and Anthony Pascal, *Teacher Unions and Educational Reform* (Santa Monica, Calif.: Center for Policy Research in Education, Rand Corp., 1988); Marjory Murphy, *Blackboard Unions: The AFT and the NEA, 1900–1980* (Ithaca, N.Y.: Cornell University Press, 1990).

29. George S. Counts, *The Social Composition of Boards of Education: A Study in the Social Control of Public Education* (Chicago: University of Chicago Press, 1927); Joseph M. Cronin, *The Control of Urban Schools; Perspectives on the Power of Educational Reformers* (New York: Free Press, 1973); Jacqueline Danzberger, Michael W. Kirst, and Michael Usdan, *A Framework for Redefining the Role and Responsibilities of Local School Boards* (Washington, D.C.: Institute for Educational Leadership, 1993); Reeves, *School Boards.*

30. Bryk, Shipps, and Hill, *Decentralization in Practice;* Betty Malen, "Enacting Site Based Management: A Political Utilities Analysis," *Educational Evaluation and Policy Analysis* 16, no. 3 (1994).

31. Linda Darling-Hammond, "Teacher Professionalism: Why and How?" in *Schools as Collaborative Cultures: Creating the Future Now,* ed. Ann Lieberman (Bristol, Pa.: Falmer Press, 1996); Kerchner and Koppich, *A Union of Professionals;* Anthony S. Bryk and Barbara Schneider, *Trust in Schools: A Core Resource for Improvement* (New York: Russell Sage Foundation, 2002).

32. "Reform Data Book," *Catalyst* 6, no. 5 (1994); John Q. Easton, T. Rosenkranz, and Anthony S. Bryk, *Annual CPS Test Trend Review, 2000* (Consortium on Chicago School Research, 2001); Penny B. Sebring et al., *Charting Reform: Chicago Teachers Take Stock* (Consortium on Chicago School Research, 1995); Penny B. Sebring et al., *Charting Reform: School Learning Climate, Student Engagement and Effort* (Consortium on Chicago School Research, 1996).

33. Anthony S.Bryk et al., *Charting Chicago School Reform: Democratic Localism and a Lever of Change* (Boulder, Colo.: Westview Press, 1998).

34. William H. Clune and P. A. White, *School-Based Management: Institutional Variation, Implementation and Issues of Future Research* (New Brunswick, N.J.: Rutgers University, Center for Policy Research in Education, 1988); William H. Clune and John Witte, *Choice and Control in American Education,* vols. 1 and 2 (San Francisco: Falmer Press, 1992); Betty Malen and Rodney T. Ogawa, "Professional-Patron Influence in Site-Based Governance Councils: A Confounding Case Study," *Educational Evaluation and Policy Analysis* 10, no. 4 (1988); Susan Ryan et al., *Charting Reform: LSCs—Local Leadership at Work* (Consortium on Chicago School Research, 1997); Susan A. Mohrman and Pricilla Wohlstetter, *School-Based Management* (San Francisco: Jossey-Bass, 1994); Joseph Murphy and Lynn G. Beck, *School-Based Management as School Reform* (Thousand Oaks, Calif.: Corwin Press, 1995).

35. William A. Firestone and Dorothy Shipps, "How Do Leaders Interpret Conflicting Accountabilities to Improve Student Learning?" in *A New Agenda: Directions for Research in Educational Leadership,* ed. William A. Firestone and Carolyn Rhiel (New York: Teachers College Press, 2005).

36. Larry Cuban, "Why Is It So Hard to Get Good Schools?" in Cuban and Shipps, *Reconstructing the Common Good.*

37. Daniel Levine and Lawrence Lezotte, *Unusually Effective Schools: A Review and Analysis of Research and Practice* (Madison, Wis.: National Center for Effective Schools Research and Development, 1990); Stuart Purkey and Marshall S. Smith, "Effective Schools: A Review," *Elementary School Journal* 83, no. 4 (1983); Jane Hannaway and Joan E. Talbert, "Bringing Context into Effective School Research: Urban-Suburban Differences," *Educational Administration Quarterly* 29, no. 2 (1993).

38. Ronald R. Edmonds, "Effective Schools for the Urban Poor," *Educational Leadership* 37, no. 10 (1979); John Witte and Daniel Walsh, "A Systemic Test of the Effective Schools Model," *Educational Evaluation and Policy Analysis* 12 (1990): 190.

39. James Comer et al., eds., *Rallying the Whole Village: The Comer Process for Reforming Education* (New York: Teachers College Press, 1996); Henry Levin, "Accelerating Schools for Disadvantage Students," *Educational Leadership* 44, no. 6 (1989).

40. Anthony S. Bryk, Valerie E. Lee, and Peter B. Holland, *Catholic Schools and the Common Good* (Cambridge: Harvard University Press, 1993); Leslie S. Siskin and Judith Warren Little, *The Subjects in Question: Departmental Organization and the High School, the Series on School Reform* (New York: Teachers College Press, 1995); Theodore Sizer, "Essential Schools: A First Look," *NASSP Bulletin* 67, no. 465 (1983); Witte and Walsh, "A Systemic Test."

41. Anthony S. Bryk et al., *A View from the Elementary Schools: The State of Reform in Chicago* (Consortium on Chicago School Research, 1993); Susan E. Sparke, Stuart Luppescu, and Kumail Nanjani, "Key Measures of School Development" (Consortium on Chicago School Research, January 2004), www.consortium-chicago.org (accessed September 1, 2004).

42. Julia B. Smith, Valerie E. Lee, and Frank M. Newmann, *Instruction and Achievement in Chicago Elementary Schools* (Consortium on Chicago School Research, 2001).

43. M. Katims and B. F. Jones, "Chicago Mastery Learning Reading: Mastery Learning Instruction and the Assessment of Inner-City Schools," *Journal of Negro Education* 54, no. 3 (1985).

44. Fong, *Empowered Participation*.

45. Richard F. Elmore, "Getting to Scale with Good Educational Practices," *Harvard Educational Review* 66, no. 1 (1996).

46. David K. Cohen and Deborah L. Ball, "Relations between Policy and Practice: A Commentary," *Educational Evaluation and Policy Analysis* 12, no. 3 (1990); Barbara Ferman, *Challenging the Growth Machine: Neighborhood Politics in Chicago and Pittsburgh* (Lawrence: University Press of Kansas, 1996); Marshall S. Smith and Jennifer O'Day, "Systemic School Reform," in *Politics of Curriculum and Testing*, ed. Susan Fuhrman and Betty Malen (Bristol, Pa.: Falmer Press, 1991).

47. Bryk and Schneider, *Trust in Schools*.

48. David B. Tyack and Larry Cuban, *Tinkering toward Utopia: A Century of Public School Reform* (Cambridge: Harvard University Press, 1995).

49. Shipps, "Echoes of Corporate Influence."

50. Andrew Hacker, *Money: Who Has How Much and Why* (New York: Scribner, 1997); Henry M. Levin, "Educational Performance Standards and the Economy," *Educational Researcher* 27, no. 4 (1998); Thomas I. Palley, *Plenty of Nothing: The Downsizing of the American Dream and the Case of Structural Keynesianism* (Princeton, N.J.: Princeton University Press, 1998).

51. Lane Pritchett, *Where Has All the Education Gone?* (Washington, D.C.: World Bank, Poverty and Human Resources Division, 1996); Jonathan D. Weiss, *Public Schools and Economic Development: What the Research Shows* (Cincinnati, Ohio: Knowledge Works Foundation, 2004); Eric A. Hanushek, "The Importance of School Quality," in *Our Schools and Our Future: Are We Still at Risk?* ed. Paul E. Peterson (Stanford, Calif.: Hoover Institution Press, 2002); Alan B. Krueger and David Card, "Labor Market Effects of School Quality: Theory and Evidence," in *Does Money Matter? The Link between Schools, Student Achievement and Adult Success*, ed. Gary Burtless (Washington, D.C.: Brookings Institution, 1996); Robert H. Topel, "Factor Proportions and Relative Wages: The Supply-Side Determinants of Wage Inequality," *Journal of Economic Perspectives* 11, no. 2 (1997); Kathy J. Hayes and Lori L. Taylor, "Neighborhood School Characteristics: What Signals Quality to Homebuyers?" in *Economic Review* (Dallas: Federal Reserve Bank of Dallas, 1996); Richard G. Sims, "School, Funding Taxes and Economic Growth: An Analysis of 50 States" (Washington, D.C.: National Education Association, 2004).

52. Peterson, *City Limits*.

53. Jean Anyon, *Ghetto Schooling: A Political Economy of Urban Educational Reform* (New York: Teachers College Press, 1997); Jeffrey Mirel, *The Rise and Fall of an Urban School System: Detroit, 1907–1981* (Ann Arbor: University of Michigan Press, 1993); Louis F. Miron, Patricia F. First, and Robert W. Wimpelberg, "Equity, Adequacy and Educational Need: The Courts and Urban School Finance," in *The Politics of Urban Education in the United States: Politics of Education Association Yearbook*, ed. James G. Cibulka, Rodney J. Reed, and Kenneth K. Wong (Bristol, Pa.: Taylor and Francis, 1992); William A. Fischel, "School Finance Litigation and Property Tax Revolts: How Undermining Local Control Turns Voters Away from Public Education" (paper presented at Developments in School Finance 1999–2000, Washington, D.C., July 1999 and July 2000); Carolyn M. Hoxby, "How to Do (and Not to Do) School Finance Equalization: The Legacy and Lesson of Serrano," *Quarterly Journal of Economics* 116 (2001).

54. Larry Cuban, *How Teachers Taught: Constancy and Change in American Classrooms, 1880–1990,* 2nd ed. (New York: Teachers College Press, 1993).

55. Comer et al., *Rallying the Whole Village;* Cuban, *How Teachers Taught;* Joyce Epstein et al., *School, Family and Community Partnerships: Your Handbook for Action* (Thousand Oaks, Calif.: Corwin Press, 1997).

56. Putnam, *Bowling Alone,* 22.

57. Kim Quaile Hill and Tetsuya Matsubayashi, "Civic Engagement and Mass-Elite Policy Agenda Agreement in American Communities," *American Political Science Review* 99, no. 2 (2005).

58. Joseph Reed, interview with author, October 1, 1991.

59. Terry M. Moe, "Power and Political Institutions," *Perspectives on Politics* 3, no. 2 (2005); see also Cuban, *The Blackboard and the Bottom Line.*

60. William J. Grimshaw, *Union Rule in the Schools: Big City Politics in Transformation* (Toronto: Lexington Books, 1979); Kerchner and Koppich, *A Union of Professionals;* Lieberman, *The Teachers Unions;* Loveless, *Conflicting Missions;* Murphy, *Blackboard Unions.*

61. Howlett and Ramlesh, *Studying Public Policy.*

62. Susan Moore Johnson and Susan Kardos, "Reform Bargaining and Its Promise for School Improvement," in Lovelace, *Conflicting Missions?* Kerchner and Koppich, *A Union of Professionals.*

63. Charles T. Kerchner and Douglas E. Mitchell, *The Changing Idea of a Teachers Union* (New York: Teachers College Press, 1988).

64. Julia E. Koppich, "A Tale of Two Approaches—the AFT, the NEA, and NCLB," *Peabody Journal of Education* 80, no. 2 (2005): 153; see also McDonnell and Pascal, *Teacher Unions and Educational Reform.*

65. Bruce S. Cooper, *Collective Bargaining, Strikes and Financial Costs in Public Education: A Comparative Review* (Eugene, Ore.: ERIC Clearinghouse on Educational Management, 1982), 43.

66. Nicholas R. Cannella, *171 Years of Teaching in Chicago: 1816–1987* (Chicago Teachers Union, 1987).

67. Cooper, *Collective Bargaining,* xvii; William L. Boyd, David N. Plank, and Gary Sykes, "Teachers Unions in Hard Times," in Lovelace, *Conflicting Missions?*

68. Gary Chaison and Barbara Bigelow, *Unions and Legitimacy* (Ithaca, N.Y.: ILR Press/Cornell University Press, 2002), 1; Ruth Milkman and Kim Voss, eds., *Rebuilding Labor: Organizing and Organizers in the New Union Movement* (Ithaca, N.Y.: Cornell University Press, 2004), 1.

69. Shanker quoted in Koppich, "A Tale of Two Approaches," 141.

70. Johnson and Kardos, "Reform Bargaining."

71. Boyd, Plank, and Sykes, "Teachers Unions in Hard Times," 196.

72. Nina Bascia, *Triage or Tapestry? Teachers Unions Work toward Improving Teacher Quality in an Era of Systemic Reform* (Seattle: University of Washington, Center for the Study of Teaching Policy, 2003).

73. Charles T. Kerchner and Julia E. Koppich, "Organizing around Quality: The Frontiers of Teacher Unionism," in Lovelace, *Conflicting Missions?*

74. Cooper, *Collective Bargaining,* 1.

75. Mahtesian quoted in Boyd, Plank, and Sykes, "Teachers Unions in Hard Times," 182.

76. Murphy, in *Blackboard Unions,* argues that Chicago was not as bad on racial relations as New York City's local was. See pp. 246–249.

77. Chaison and Bigelow, *Unions and Legitimacy,* 14–36.

78. Ibid., 24, 31. Nina Bascia, *Unions in Teachers' Professional Lives; Social, Intellectual and Practical Concerns* (New York: Teachers College Press, 1994).

79. Chaison and Bigelow, *Unions and Legitimacy.*

80. Johnson and Kardos, "Reform Bargaining."

81. Boyd, Plank, and Sykes, "Teachers Unions in Hard Times."

82. Kate Bronfenbrenner and Robert Hickey, "Changing to Organize: A National Assessment of Union Strategies," in *Rebuilding Labor: Organizing and Organizers in the New Labor Movement,* ed. Ruth Milkman and Kim Voss (Ithaca, N.Y.: Cornell University Press, 2004).

83. Michael Gans et al., "Against the Tide: Projects and Pathways of the New Generation of Union Leaders 1984–2001," in Milkman and Voss, *Rebuilding Labor,* 191–192.

84. Bascia, *Triage or Tapestry?*

85. Kate Rousmaniere, *Citizen Teacher: The Life and Leadership of Margaret Haley* (Albany: State University of New York Press, 2005).

86. Bronfenbrenner and Hickey, "Changing to Organize," 26–29.

APPENDIX

1. Charles E. Lindblom and Edward J. Woodhouse, *The Policy Making Process,* 3rd ed. (Englewood Cliffs, N.J.: Prentice Hall, 1993).

2. Like the Commercial Club, the Illinois Business Roundtable, formed in 1990, is an invitation-only association. See Kathryn Borman, Louis Costnell, and Karen Gallagher, "Business Involvement in School Reform: The Rise of the Business Roundtable," in *The New Politics of Race and Gender: The Politics of Education Association Yearbook,* ed. Catherine Marshall (Washington, D.C.: Falmer Press, 1993).

3. Cathie Jo Martin, *Stuck in Neutral: Business and the Politics of Human Capital Investment* (Princeton, N.J.: Princeton University Press, 2000).

4. George Counts, *School and Society in Chicago* (New York: Harcourt, Brace, 1928); David J. Hogan, *Class and Reform: School and Society in Chicago: 1880–1930* (Philadelphia: University of Pennsylvania, 1985); Paul E. Peterson, *The Politics of School Reform 1870–1940* (Chicago: University of Chicago Press, 1985); Julia Wrigley, *Class Politics and Public Schools: Chicago 1900–1950* (New Brunswick, N.J.: Rutgers University Press, 1982).

5. Robert Dahl, *Who Governs?* (New Haven, Conn.: Yale University Press, 1961); David Vogel, *Fluctuating Fortunes: The Political Power of Business in America* (New York: Basic Books, 1998).

6. The Industrial Club of Chicago was formed in 1905 as an outgrowth of a German social organization and merged with the Commercial Club twenty-seven years later. *History of the Industrial Club of Chicago* (Chicago: Lakeside Press, 1934); Vilas Johnson, *A History of the Commercial Club of Chicago: Including the First History of the Club by John J. Glessner* (Chicago: Commercial Club of Chicago, 1977); Stephen D. London, "Business and Chicago Public Schools: 1890–1966" (Ph.D. diss., University of Chicago, 1968).

7. Vogel, *Fluctuating Fortunes,* 41.

8. J. Clyde Mitchell, *Social Networks in Urban Situations* (Manchester, U.K.: Manchester University Press, 1969).

9. Alan Cawson, *Corporatism and Political Theory* (Oxford: Basil Blackwell, 1986); Wolfgang Streeck and Philippe Schmitter, eds., *Private Interest Government: Beyond Market and State* (Beverly Hills, Calif.: Sage Press, 1985).

10. Lawrence Howe, interview with author, November 9, 1991; Commercial Club of Chicago, "List of Civic Committee Members" (1991).

11. Commercial Club of Chicago, *Year Books of the Commercial Club of Chicago* (1911–1982).

12. Veronica Anderson, "CEOs Have Case of Civic Overload: A Call to Merge Do-Good Groups," *Crain's Chicago Business,* January 9, 1995; Commercial Club staff member, interview with author, December 5, 1991.

13. Carol A. Ray and Roslyn A. Mickelson, "Corporate Leaders, Resistant Youth and School Reform in Sunbelt City: The Political Economy of Education," *Social Problems* 37, no. 2 (1990); Edward C. Banfield and John Q. Wilson, *City Politics* (New York: Random House, 1963).

14. Commercial Club staff member interview; Barbara Ferman, *Challenging the Growth Machine: Neighborhood Politics in Chicago and Pittsburgh* (Lawrence: University Press of Kansas, 1996).

15. There is no record that Harper's immediate successor, Harry Pratt Judson, was a member. Commercial Club of Chicago, *Year Books.*

16. Ibid. The most recent figure is from "Business Clubs and Organizations," *Crain's Chicago Business,* March 6, 2005. Calculations of 2000 dollars using the consumer price index method are based on Samuel H. Williamson, "What Is the Relative Value?" (Economic History Services, April 2004), http://www.eh.net/hmit/compare/ (accessed June 27, 2005).

17. Clayton Marks, "Report of the Education Committee," in Commercial Club of Chicago, *Yearbook, 1911–1912,* 351.

18. Commercial Club staff member interview; Howe interview; Donald Perkins, interview with author, October 21, 1991.

19. These data were gathered from "the Group" and Chicago United budgets for 1972–1976, available in the Chicago Urban League Archives.

20. Howe interview; Joseph Reed, interview with author, October 1, 1991.

21. Commercial Club of Chicago, *Year Books;* Johnson, *A History.*

22. Letter from Mayor Martin Kennelly to Mr. Merle Trees, President of the Commercial Club of Chicago, February 11, 1948, in Commercial Club of Chicago, *Year Book, 1947–1948.*

23. Johnson, *A History,* 92.

24. Thomas Ayers, interview with author, October 18, 1991; Norman Ross, interview with author, November 15, 1991.

25. Information about Chicago United for the years 1971–1976 was gathered from deacons' meeting minutes, "the Group" meeting minutes, and Chicago United meeting minutes available in the Chicago Urban League Archives. For later years I relied on interviews and Chicago United, "Chicago United Update" (1999); Chicago United, "Chicago United: Thirty Years of Progress and Lessons" (1998).

26. Howe interview; Leon Jackson, telephone interview with author, January 3, 1992; Johnson, *A History;* Ross interview.

27. Thomas Ayers interview.

28. Chicago United, "Chicago United Update"; Chicago United, "Chicago United: Thirty Years of Progress and Lessons"; Barbara Rose, "Strained Tradition: Refashioning the Civic Leadership Network," *Crain's Chicago Business,* January 24, 1994.

29. Steven Strahler, "Commercial Club Awaits Overhaul," *Crain's Chicago Business,* April 26, 1996; John Ayers, interview with author, December 15, 1997; Commercial Club executive, interview with author, June 18, 1997.

30. Civic Committee of the Commercial Club of Chicago, "Chicago Business Leaders Applaud Renaissance 2010—Pledge Financial and Technical Support" (press release, June 24, 2004).

31. Pastora San Juan Cafferty, *The Chicago Project: A Report on Civic Life in Chicago* (Chicago: Central Areas Committee, 1986); local business lawyer, interview with author, November 5, 1991; David Paulus, interview with author, September 30, 1991.

32. Mary Lou Cowlishaw, interview with author, June 6, 1997; Carolyn Nordstrom, interview with author, June 30, 1997.

33. John Ayers interview; Charles Davis, interview with author, November 24, 1991; Nordstrom interview.

34. Chicago United, "Membership Lists" (1970–1979); Nordstrom interview.

35. Most "black companies" were assessed dues in the third and forth categories, which were labeled, respectively, "Group C—Four Largest Black Companies" and "Group D—Smaller Black Companies." Chicago United budget for 1975 (n.d.), Chicago Urban League Archives, box 6, file 17.

36. Carolyn Nordstrom, personal communication, October 19, 2000.

37. African American Chicago United leader, interview with author, December 12, 1991; Davis interview; Leon Jackson, interview with author, October 28, 1991.

38. Peter Clark, "Civic Leadership: Symbols of Legitimacy," in *Democracy in Urban America,* ed. Oliver Williams and Charles Press (Chicago: Rand-McNally, 1969).

39. Jacoby Dickins, interview with author, November 25, 1991; Lu Palmer, interview with author, November 20, 1991; Davis interview; Gary Rivlin, *Fire on the Prairie: Chicago's Harold Washington and the Politics of Race* (New York: Henry Holt, 1992).

40. Commercial Club staff member interview; Davis interview.

41. Minutes of Deacons' Policy Committee Meeting, October 10, 1974, Chicago Urban League Archives, box 46, file 3.

42. Chicago United, "Chicago United: Thirty Years of Progress and Lessons," 25.

43. Chicago United, "Chicago United Midyear Update" (2000); Chicago United, "Chicago United Update"; Nordstrom interview.

44. Leadership for Quality Education, *LQE: Leadership for Quality Education* (Chicago, 1991).

45. Jahahara Armstrong et al., "Open Letter to Ms. Diana Nelson, President of LQE," (December 13, 1993); B. Kenneth West, interview with author, November 14, 1991.

46. On the distinctions between bridging and bonding organizations, see Robert Putnam, *Bowling Alone* (New York: Simon and Schuster, 2000); Leadership for Quality Education, "Membership Lists" (1989–1998); Leadership for Quality Education, *LQE: Leadership for Quality Education.*

47. Diana Lauber, interview with author, November 3, 1991; Leadership for Quality Education, *LQE: Leadership for Quality Education;* Joseph Reed, telephone interview with author, January 3, 1992.

48. John Ayers, personal communications, December 9, 1993, and February 14, 1996.

49. Maureen Kelleher, "First Renaissance Schools Chosen as Charter Leaders Depart" (Catalyst Chicago, February 2005), http://www.catalyst-chicago.org/02-05/0205ren2010.htm (accessed June 10, 2005).

Index

AAERI (African-American Educational Reform Institute), 143
ABCs. *See* Alliance for Better Chicago Schools
Abu-Lughod, Janet, 3–4
Access to Excellence, 82
Access to Excellence II, 82
Accountability, 13, 57, 80, 91, 95, 103, 111, 118, 128, 129, 130, 144, 149, 151–152, 153, 171, 182, 184(table), 218
  adjusting, 14, 152, 157, 169
  bureaucratic, 6, 104, 123, 144, 154, 157, 160, 183, 185
  centralization and, 6, 154
  corporate, 83, 179, 199
  financial, 132
  LSCs and, 154
  management, 40
  market, 184(table), 187
  moral, 184(table), 189, 192
  performance, 112, 183
  political, 85, 129, 144, 153, 157, 171, 173, 184(table), 189
  professional, 184(table), 192
  sanctions for, 131, 157–159, 164, 168
  student, 4
  versions of, 156–159
Accountability Act (1985), 121
Accreditation process, 192
Activism, 1, 91, 103, 167, 171, 199, 212
  business, xi, 76, 213
  union, 168
  See also Civic activism; Corporate activism
Adams, Cyrus, III, 74
Addams, Jane, 18, 22, 23, 24, 182
Adopt-a-School program, 107
Advisory Commission on School Board Nominations, 57, 88, 98
Affirmative action, 109

AFL (American Federation of Labor), 62–63, 74
African American activists, 68–69, 73, 76, 107, 119, 199
  legacy of, 4
African-American Educational Reform Institute (AAERI), 143
African Americans, ix, 3–4, 30, 81, 90–91, 127, 133
  Chicago United and, 78–80, 82–83, 85, 98, 99, 107, 108, 127, 219
  class and, 91, 109, 114–115, 118, 124–125, 127, 199–200
  Commercial Club and, 76–78, 109, 216
  CSC and, 69, 87
  CTU and, 63–64, 86–87, 110, 117, 128, 161, 165, 168
  decentralization and, 107, 126
  ethnic whites and, 52–53
  housing and, 59, 71–74, 136
  Latinos and, 91, 105, 114, 115, 116, 126, 131, 133, 181
  migrations, 53, 59
  patronage and, 37, 64, 136
  political incorporation and, 89–95, 98–99, 106–109, 111, 126, 133–134
  racial complications for, 51–52, 57, 105, 111, 113, 126, 144, 161, 188, 197
  reform and, 113–116, 120–121, 122, 124, 126–127, 143, 145, 147, 151, 167, 181, 199–201
  school reform and, 116
  schools, representation in, xii, 53, 64, 75, 80, 95, 96–97, 100–107, 110, 111, 119, 126, 137, 146–147
  segregation and, 65–71, 74–75, 80–82, 84–85, 87–99, 101, 106
  unemployment rate among, 197
  violence of, 73–74, 76, 86

African Americans, *continued*
  violence toward, 54, 72
  votes of, 133
African American schools, 65
  inferiority of, 69
  LSCs and, 144
  overcrowding in, 84
  upgrades for, 82
  white schools and, 68
African American students, 90
  accountability sanctions and, 131
  performance of, 2, 103, 141, 160, 163–164,
    169, 177
  retention of, 164
AFT. *See* American Federation of Teachers
Agendas, 47, 112, 120
  action, x, 8
  African American, 108
  civic, 15
  civil rights, 103
  competing, 139–142
  corporate, 170, 172, 177, 210
  creating, 181
  empowerment, 182, 189, 190, 194, 201, 206
  entrepreneurial, 187
  financial, 137
  initiating, 185, 196
  management, xi, 112, 137, 180, 197
  market, 182, 186, 187
  multiple, 182–183
  performance, 12, 182, 192, 193–197, 201,
    208
  progressive, 209
  reform, xi, xiii, 2, 5, 6, 8, 11, 14, 45, 118,
    119, 125, 173, 175, 177, 178, 179–183,
    188, 193, 198, 199, 201, 205, 210, 218
  shifting, 14, 15
  union, 43
  vocational, 197
Alinsky, Saul, 4, 124
Alliance for Better Chicago Schools (ABCs),
    122, 126, 138, 143
  agenda of, 119, 120
  coalition of, 125, 127, 128
  corporate executives/community activists
    and, 200–201
  reform plan of, 121
Allswanger, John, 64
Altgeld, Governor, 34
American Association of School Administration,
    66

American Federation of Labor (AFL), 62–63, 74
American Federation of Teachers (AFT), 62,
    117, 174, 237n76
  CTF and, 34
  reform law and, 141–142
American School, Loeb rule and, 34
Ames, Donald C., 148
Anderson, Alan, 71, 87
Andrews, Benjamin, 30
Armour, Phillip D., 19
Arvey, Jacob, 57, 58
ASPIRA, 104, 114
Avery, Sewell, 26, 61
Ayers, John, 139, 141, 163, 221
Ayers, Thomas, 73, 76, 78, 99, 100, 103, 139, 182
  Black Coalition and, 77
  Daley and, 61–62
  housing conference and, 72
  withdrawal of, 98

Bacon, Warren, 86, 99, 103, 118, 182, 219, 220
  Chicago United and, 119, 124
  efficiency and, 100
  management reform agenda and, 112
  Washington campaign and, 109
Baldwin bill, 35, 46
Bankruptcy, 40, 112, 173
Barnes, Willie, 107
Believe in the Public Schools, 118
Bennett, William: on Chicago schools, 113
Berman, Arthur, 93, 252n156
Berry, Edwin, 70–71, 77, 78
Betancur, John, 134
Bevel, James, 71
Bigelow, Barbara: on unions, 206
Bilandic, Michael, 89, 108, 124
  Democratic machine and, 90
  financial crisis and, 98
  integration and, 81
Bilingual education, 115, 152, 164
Birth of a Nation, 53
Black belt, 3, 53, 59, 234n12
Black Caucus, 122
Black Nationalists, 106, 115
Black Panthers, 77
Black "policy" syndicates, 53
Black Power, 65, 71, 77
Blacks. *See* African-Americans
Blackstone Rangers, 77
Black Strategy Center (BSC), 77–78
Blaine, Anita McCormick, 21, 23, 182

Block grants, 105, 152
Bloom, Benjamin, 193
Bonding organizations, 198, 199, 201, 275n46
Bond ratings, 89, 92, 93, 146
Bonds, 92, 93, 94
Boosterism, ix, 11, 20, 56
Booz, Allen & Hamilton, audit by, 75
Boston Compact, 110, 111, 249n100
Boycotts, 54, 70, 74, 99
Braskamp, Larry, 151
Breakthrough schools, 264n186
Bridging organizations, 275n46
Brown v. Board of Education (1954), 69
Bryk, Anthony S., 140, 151, 194
  empowerment/performance and, 191, 193
  inspectorate and, 190
BSC (Black Strategy Center), 77–78
Buck bill, 34
Buckner, James, 79
Budgetary problems, 17, 37, 154, 170
Bureaucracy, 27, 48, 51, 84, 119, 207
  impersonal, 33–35
  reform and, 6
Bureau of Curriculum, 42
Bureau of Special Education, 42
Bureau of Vocational Guidance, 42
Burnham Plan, 37
Burroughs v. Board of Education (1962), 239n109
Business activism, xi, 76, 213. See also
    Corporate activism
Business associations, 2, 14–15, 186, 201
  class conflict and, 13
  Commercial Club and, 218
  influence of, 16
  public schools and, 14
  See also Chicago United; Commercial Club;
    Cosmopolitan Chamber of Commerce;
    Illinois Business Round Table; Illinois
    Chamber of Commerce; Illinois
    Manufacturers Association; Industrial
    Club of Chicago; Leadership for Quality
    Education; National Business Roundtable
Business-union coalitions, 205, 206
Busing, 74
Busse, Fred A., 23, 31, 32, 44
Butler, Nicholas Murray, 24
Byrd, Manfred, 81, 101, 107, 117, 118
  school reform and, 110–113
Byrne, Jane, 89, 98, 99, 107, 108, 109, 113, 124
  budget problems for, 93
  Commercial Club and, 92

integration and, 81
SFA and, 95

CAC. See Chicago Annenberg Challenge
CACI. See Chicago Association of Commerce
    and Industry
Callaway, John, 150
Carl, Jim, 114
Carson Pirie Scott, 76, 110
Caruso, Angeline, 94
Catalyst: Voices for Chicago School Reform,
    140, 141, 155, 163
  on Vallas, 154
CBUC (Chicago Black United Communities),
    98, 107
CCCO. See Coordinating Council of
    Community Organization
Center for School Improvement, 140
Centralization, 27–29, 32, 33, 43, 45, 48, 51, 57,
    61, 84, 86, 88, 102–103, 123, 124, 191,
    202, 218
  accountability and, 6
  political, xii
  resistance to, 34
Central office staff, by race/ethnic group,
    97(fig.)
CEO, 153, 154, 155, 157, 168
Cermak, Anton, 40–41, 55, 59, 85, 134, 175,
    233n170
  anti-crime campaign promise of, 53
  Commercial Club and, 41, 44
  control by, 52–53
  institutionalization and, 50
  school policy and, 42
  teachers' salaries and, 41
  Traylor and, 61
CFL. See Chicago Federation of Labor
CHA (Chicago Housing Authority), 59, 73
Chadsey, Charles: ouster of, 232n131
Chaison, Gary: on unions, 206
Chapter 1 funds, 128, 129, 130, 153
Charter Convention, 31
Charter schools, 188
Chicago and Northwest Railroad, 40, 72
Chicago Annenberg Challenge (CAC), 190, 194,
    205
  CTU and, 168
  described, 159
  funding, 160, 209
  LSCs and, 167
  progressive agenda and, 209

Chicagoans United to Reform Education
    (CURE), 104, 114, 117, 118, 119, 121
  coalition members of, 247n62
  proposal by, 115
Chicago Association of Commerce and Industry
    (CACI), 16, 24, 111, 211, 212
Chicago Association of Neighborhood
    Development Organizations, 111
Chicago Black United Communities (CBUC),
    98, 107
Chicago Board, 92
Chicago Council of Industrial Organizations
    (CIO), 55
Chicago Daily News, 82
Chicago Defender, 53, 134
  on Daley, 59–60
  Willis resignation and, 69
Chicago Federation of Labor (CFL), 45, 62, 205
  CTF and, 34
  Harper bill and, 31
  Otis bill and, 34
  school board and, 62
  vocational education and, 26
Chicago Fest, boycott of, 99
Chicago Freedom Movement, 71, 87, 108
Chicago Housing Authority (CHA), 59, 73
Chicago Manual Training School, 20, 21, 23,
    216
Chicago model, 1, 2–5
Chicago Panel for Public School Policy and
    Finance, 103, 118, 119, 123
  reform and, 159
  SBM and, 115
Chicago Partnership, 110, 219, 252n148
Chicago Political Freedom Movement, 108
Chicago Priorities Panel on School Finance,
    103, 105, 114
Chicago Public Schools Reform Working
    Group, 151
Chicago Sun-Times, 94, 103, 140, 145, 155
Chicago Teachers College, 56
Chicago Teachers Federation (CTF), 26, 36, 62,
    181, 182, 196, 208
  CFL and, 31, 34, 45
  Commercial Club and, 25
  criticism of, 32
  feminists in, 45
  Harper bill and, 30, 31
  legacy of, 231n106
  Loeb rule and, 34
  neutrality of, 188

Otis bill and, 34
  school finances and, 35–36, 39, 42
  school governance and, 29
  teachers councils and, 29, 32, 191
  tenure and, 34
  vocational eduction and, 25–27
Chicago Teachers Union (CTU), 62, 66, 74, 87,
    90, 93, 110, 116, 122, 126, 132, 136, 142,
    147, 151, 164, 189, 190, 204, 208, 209
  access for, 203
  bargaining rights and, 203
  battle within, 162
  CAC and, 168
  Chicago United and, 112
  collaboration by, 206
  collective bargaining and, 63, 205, 206
  corporate elites and, 205
  decentralization and, 117
  employment regime and, 207
  empowerment regime and, 208
  fiscal problems and, 128
  grievances and, 161
  isolation for, 204
  low-performing schools and, 164
  machine era and, 86
  1995 law and, 161
  policy making and, 64
  pressures on, 118, 207
  public trust and, 206
  reform and, 124, 201
  strikes by, 63, 92, 111–112, 125
  Vallas and, 163
Chicago Theological Seminary, 76
Chicago Title and Trust Company, 58
Chicago Tribune, 52
  on reformers, 23
  on Sargent Committee, 41
  on Willis, 69
Chicago Trinity, 19
Chicago Union League Club, 151
Chicago United, 82, 93, 95, 98, 118, 120, 122,
    127, 138, 147, 149, 152, 174, 175, 191,
    211, 213
  Bacon and, 124
  characteristics of, 219–221
  civil rights leaders and, 83
  Commercial Club and, 99–113, 198, 217
  CTU and, 112
  decentralization and, 218
  establishment of, 79, 85, 212
  the Group and, 78, 79, 80, 98, 220

integration and, 82, 83
LQE and, 137, 212, 221
membership of, 216, 219, 220–221
racial issues and, 108–109, 218
reform agenda of, 119, 125
school board/superintendent and, 95
SFA and, 98, 99
SBM and, 117
Washington and, 109
Chicago Urban League, 59, 76, 78, 98, 103,
    107, 113, 114, 119, 143, 145, 151
Black Power and, 71
CCCO/Raby and, 70
community control and, 190
housing/census data and, 65
segregation and, 67
Title I and, 106
Chico, Gery, 154, 162
Child and Welfare Services, 155
Chubb, John E., 260n99
CIO, 55
Citizen inspectors, 186
Citizen's Association of Chicago, 18
Citizen's Save Our Schools Committee, 55
Citizen's Schools Committee (CSC), 55, 58, 66,
    67, 69, 74, 86, 94, 126, 195, 209
corruption and, 175
PCC and, 114
recommendations by, 103
school board commission and, 73
vocational education and, 196
work of, 56, 68, 87
City Charter Commission, 46
City Club, 18, 34
Commercial Club and, 25
Cooley bill and, 24, 32
vocational education and, 25, 26
City services, 14, 166, 171
City-Wide Advisory Committee (CWAC), 82
Citywide Coalition for School Reform, 140,
    151, 205
City Women's Club, 24, 43, 55, 209
Civic activism, xiii, 16, 54, 120, 130, 199, 213
Commercial Club and, 91
opportunities for, 218
student outcomes and, 2
Civic actors, xiii, 43, 51, 124, 176, 212
influence of, 181
reform and, 15, 170, 180, 211
Civic betterment, education and, 18–20
Civic capacity, 7–9, 12

Civic coalitions, 8–9, 44, 45, 205, 206, 208,
    210
consolidation/action by, 87
reform and, 179–183, 185–201, 211
Civic Committee (Commercial Club), 100,
    109–110, 112, 120, 138, 139, 147, 148,
    153, 165, 211, 213, 217
corporate model and, 167
decentralization and, 219
founding of, 212
LQE and, 137, 212, 216, 218, 221
privatization and, 218
Civic Federation, 18, 28, 111
Cooley bill and, 24
Harper bill and, 31
Civic institutions, design of, 20
Civic leaders, 4, 65, 182, 191
structural prescriptions of, 169
Civic reformers, 17, 31, 51, 55
agendas of, 47
Civil disobedience, 45, 54
Civil rights, 3, 13, 73, 77, 85, 121, 141, 189,
    191, 210, 219
legislation, 81
reform and, xi
Civil Rights Act (1964), Title VI of, 70
Civil Rights Commission, 85
Civil rights leaders, 81, 86
Chicago United and, 83
integration and, 83
Civil rights movement, 52, 86, 105, 106, 108,
    113, 126, 199, 220
in Chicago, 64–75
collective bargaining and, 63
demands of, 69
Latinos and, 116
segregation and, 67
Civil service, 37, 57, 58, 109, 126, 134
Class conflict, 13, 43, 46, 51, 131, 185
Class Politics and Public Schools (Wrigley), 25
Clinton, Bill, 135, 155, 156
Coalition building, 119–122, 183, 208
Coalition partners, 47, 124–129, 205, 207
Coalition politics, 1, 2, 43–49, 183
human agency and, 10
Collective bargaining, 9, 51, 86, 88, 109,
    201–202, 203
civil rights movement and, 63
CTU and, 205, 206
Columbian Exhibition (1893–1894), 26
Comer School Development Program, 140

Commercial Club, xiii, 5, 23, 28, 45, 46, 50, 53,
    54, 62, 72, 78, 93, 94, 124, 136, 138, 147,
    149, 150, 152, 154–155, 166, 173, 175,
    177, 197, 205, 211
  activism of, 171, 212
  alliances in, 217–219
  as bonding organization, 198
  business principles and, 27
  centralization/bureaucratization and, 27
  characteristics/reform eras and,
    214–215(table)
  city charter and, 31
  committees/personal staff of, 216–217
  cost cutting/control and, 44
  decision making in, 217–219
  dues/subscriptions for, 216
  economic development and, 61
  education and, 17, 20
  elitism/cohesion of, 211
  founding of, 16, 19, 20, 212
  governance and, 47–48
  influence of, 46, 75, 101, 171, 176, 212
  initiatives by, 20, 36
  King assassination and, 76
  legislation and, 16–17
  membership of, 40–41, 211, 213, 216, 220
  organizational underpinnings of, 213
  politics and, 18
  role of, 22
Commercial Club of Boston, 19
Commercial education, 27
Commission on Educational Reorganization, 28
Commission on Human Relations, 73
Committee on Public Expenditures, 41
Committee on Slum Clearance (Commercial
    Club), 216
Commonwealth Edison, 40, 61, 98
Community activists, 201
  corporate leaders and, 167, 201
  LSCs and, 143
Community-based organizations, 2, 4, 15, 128
Community Conservation Act (1953), 58
Competition, 14, 153, 162–165
Compton, James, 137
Compulsory schooling, Latinos and, 105
Conservatism, 4, 6
Consortium on Chicago School Research, 140,
    160, 163, 194
Continental Illinois National Bank and Trust
    Company, 41, 93
Contracts, 138, 141, 148, 149, 161

Contract schools, 139
"Contract with America," 148
"Contract with Illinois," 148
Cook County Board of Commissioners, 39
Cook County Democratic Party, 60, 90
Cooley, Edwin G., 23, 28, 30–31, 66, 131
  centralization and, 32
  Commercial Club and, 24, 32–33, 175
  dual system and, 45–46
  Harper bill and, 31
  manual training and, 21–22
  reform and, 44
  survey by, 216
Cooley bill, 23
  opposition to, 24, 25, 26, 32, 48
Coordinating Council of Community
    Organization (CCCO), 69, 70, 71, 74, 76,
    87
Corporate activism, xi, 213
  economic grounds for, 132
  influence of, 170–179
  model for schools, 154–156, 260n96
  outcomes and, 179
  reform and, 166, 179–180
  resurgence of, 165–169
  revised market model and, 187
Corporate-community coalitions, 210
Corporate leaders, 1, 11, 14, 47, 107, 118, 126,
    198
  agendas of, 43, 179–180
  collaboration with, 15
  Commercial Club and, 172, 199
  community activists and, 167, 201
  CTU and, 205
  desegregation and, 88
  educational interests and, 176
  influence of, 47, 171, 174, 197
  management approach of, 200
  market experience/management training and,
    198
  performance regimes and, 197
  reform and, 201
  unions and, 206, 208
Corporate models, 48, 167, 168–169, 176, 186
Corporate sector: plan of action and, 125
  reform and, 5, 14
  unions and, xi, 208
Corporate-union coalitions, xi
Corr, Frank, 233n170
Corruption, 1, 31, 40, 45, 52, 86, 87, 104, 129,
    135, 172, 173, 175, 177, 191

city hall, 58
  Commercial Club and, 18
  consolidation and, 54–57
  containing, 35–39
  exposing, 44, 209
Cosmopolitan Chamber of Commerce, 211
Costs: cutting, 35–39, 44, 94–95
Council of Great City Schools, 82
Counts, George, 18
Cowlishaw, Mary Lou, 150, 151, 261n126
Crain's Chicago Business, on Vallas, 156
Crane, Richard T., Sr., 20, 23, 45
Crane and Company, 36
Cronyism, 104, 135
Cross-class coalitions, 2, 201, 208, 209
Cross-race coalitions, 208
CSC. *See* Citizen's Schools Committee
CTF. *See* Chicago Teachers Federation
CTU. *See* Chicago Teachers Union
Cuban, Larry, 5, 197–198
CURE. *See* Chicagoans United to Reform
    Education
Curriculum, 178, 179, 192, 208
  changes in, xiii, 48
  liberal, 48
  scripted, 194
  teachers and, 159
  tree-hugging, 194
CWAC (City-Wide Advisory Committee), 82

Daley, Richard J., 51, 78, 84, 93, 109
  African Americans and, 64, 65, 71, 77,
    z 86–87
  boycotts and, 70
  business community and, 60
  CFL and, 62
  Chicago United and, 79, 80, 83
  civil rights and, 65, 75
  Commercial Club and, 60, 61, 217
  CSC and, 73
  CTU and, 63
  death of, xii, 90
  financial crisis and, 98
  governing coalition and, 61, 63
  leadership of, 90
  machine and, 60, 85
  patronage and, 60
  race relations and, 81
  redevelopment plan and, 60
  reputation of, 61, 71
  unions and, 62–63, 92

Daley, Richard M., 101, 175, 206, 218, 219,
    220, 221
  budget negotiations and, 146, 154
  business community and, 261n115
  centralization and, xii
  civil rights coalition and, 199
  corporate activism and, 153, 154, 165, 166
  corporate/union supporters of, 134
  CTU and, 164, 203
  decentralization and, 132
  development and, 135, 155
  election of, 133, 134, 150
  ethnic whites and, 133
  governing coalition and, 166
  Latinos and, 131, 133
  1995 law and, 161, 188
  parent report cards and, 159
  privatization and, 134–135, 155
  reform and, 1, 137, 157, 182,
    261n115
  SBNC and, 145
  school closings and, 163
  school control and, 108
  SFA and, 146
  Shakman Decrees and, 135
  social promotion and, 158
  strikes and, 203
Daniels, Lee, 149, 150
Dawson, William L., 53, 59, 64–65, 70
Deanes, James, 114, 119
De Bay, Cornelia B., 22
Decentralization, ix, xii, 1, 52, 57, 75, 88, 91,
    106, 114, 116–117, 119, 127, 128, 132,
    148, 167, 177, 191, 206, 218, 219
  administrative, 112
  African Americans and, 126
  business planning and, 138
  Commercial Club and, 153
  implementing/altering, 137–147
  law, 125, 130
  political, 6, 189
  reform and, 107
  support for, 80
Decision making, 48, 123, 125, 174, 188, 191,
    201
  biracial, 220
  centralized, 102–103
  joint, 162
  managerial, 202
  participation in, 189
  patterns of, 211

Decision making, *continued*
  private, 85
  restructuring, 166
Deming, W. Edward, 178
Democratic education, 26, 29–33, 118
Democratic machine, x, xi, 5, 44, 50, 52, 54, 62,
    68, 90, 102, 133–137
  African Americans and, 81
  business/labor and, 49, 51
  centralization/bureaucracy and, 51
  Commercial Club and, 85
  disintegration of, xii, 89
  importance of, 64
  reform coalitions and, 49, 87
Democratic National Convention, 135
Dennis, Richard, 251n123
Department of Health, Education, and Welfare
    (HEW), 70, 74, 81
Department of Human Services, 155
Department of Urban Renewal, 73
Depression, 16, 38, 49, 52, 64, 89, 91, 102, 103,
    132, 201, 206
  impact of, 39–43, 45, 46, 86, 175
  public schools and, 50
  reassessments and, 40
  reform and, 14
  school services and, 4
  vocationalism and, 173
Desegregation, 1, 6, 13, 94, 101, 105
  avoiding, 79–84
  Commercial Club and, 178
  confrontations over, 3, 81–82, 89, 178
  corporate elite and, 88
  fiscal crisis and, xii
  Latinos and, 116
  plan for, 74, 81
  reform and, 89
  responding to, 112
  voluntary, 82–83
Designs for Change (DFC), 104, 118, 119, 159,
    194
  parent power of, 115
  policy entrepreneurship of, 120
  proposal by, 115
  study by, 105
  summit and, 114
Dever, William E., 38, 44
Dewey, John, 23, 26, 163
  child centeredness and, 195
  Cooley bill and, 25
  on manual training, 21
  Young and, 32

DFC. *See* Designs for Change
Discipline, 105, 169, 196, 208
Disenfranchisement, 188, 189
Doty, Earl, 76, 77
Double shifts, 65, 67, 74
Drivers' education, 152
Dropout rates, 3, 26, 79–80, 104, 105, 111, 113,
    164
Dual systems, 25, 45, 260n112
Duncan, Arne, 164, 168
Dunlap, Al, 156
Dunne, Edward, 22, 31, 44, 190
DuSable High School, 110

Early childhood education, African Americans
    and, 105
East Garfield, 59
Economic development, 7, 105, 109, 188, 197
Economic elites, influence of, 170–179
Economic functionalism, 187, 195
Economic security, 16, 37, 177
Edgar, James, 146, 148, 150, 152
Educational culture, 192
Educational problems, economic terms for,
    13–14
Education cartel, 176, 180
Education Committee (Civic Federation), 28
Education Committee (Commercial Club), 20,
    26, 33
Education parks, 87
Education Task Force (Chicago United), 99, 100
Education Task Force (Group), 79, 220
Education trust, 28
"Effective schools" research, 193
Efficiency, xi, 14, 16, 38, 114, 130, 138, 147,
    183
  business, 27–29, 46, 48, 50, 66, 69, 87,
    99–100, 129, 170–171, 174–175, 185
  budgetary, 178
  concerns about, 17, 89, 106, 175, 177–178
  managerial, 101, 172
  politics and, 28–29, 33–34, 58, 92–93,
    134–135, 172
  productivity and, 23–24, 28, 30
  scientific management and, 27
  social, 39
Electoral coalitions, 44, 65, 124, 133–137
  governing coalitions and, 10
Employment regimes, 10, 183, 185, 207
Empowerment, 122, 182, 194, 201, 206
  democratic, 190
  elite, 191

low-income, 137
parent, 189, 190
performance and, 191, 193
teacher, 175, 190–191, 208–210
Empowerment regimes, 188–192
Entrepreneurialism, 169, 186
Equity, 101, 112, 120, 129, 179
Ethnic demographics, changes in, 3
Ethnic whites, 52, 185, 186
African Americans and, 53, 65
anti-integrationist, 90
backlash of, 57
corporate/union financing of, 133
Evans, Tim, 115
Executive Committee (Commercial Club), 213, 216, 217, 220
Executive Committee (LQE), 221
Executive Committee (PEA), 33

Fairbank, N. K., 20
Federation of Men Teachers of High School, 36, 232n121
Federation of Women High School Teachers, 41
Field, Marshall, 19, 20
Finances, 39, 176
corporate leaders and, 35–43, 91–95, 149, 152, 154–155, 173, 196–197
Financial crisis, xii, 36, 43, 46, 88, 89, 91–95, 98, 103, 105, 125, 138, 146, 206
Financial Planning Committee, 110
Financial Research and Advisory Committee (FRAC), 110, 136, 138, 147, 198, 217, 221
First Chicago, 118
First National Bank, 41, 61, 76
Fiscal crisis. See Financial crisis
Fitzpatrick, John, 31
Forbes, on Vallas, 156
Fortune, on Daley/business community, 60
Foundations, 2, 188
"Four walls" approach, 68
FRAC. See Financial Research and Advisory Committee
Freedom Movement, 72
Freeman, Gaylord, Jr., 76, 77, 78
Frykund recommendations, 154

Gentrification, 135, 166
Gidwitz, Ronald, 111, 148, 149, 182
Gills, Douglas, 134
Gingrich, Newt, 148, 149
Globalization, 171

Goggin, Catherine, 29, 30, 36
Good-government groups, 2, 4, 46–47, 52, 54, 55, 84, 103
business/labor and, 47
reform and, 88, 209
urban school systems and, 13
Governance, 14, 15, 29, 91, 176
battles over, 47–48
executive/legislative branches of, 28
reform, 8, 48
Governing regimes, 10, 51, 65
types of, 184(table)
Governor's Tax Conference, 41
Grant, Sharon, 151
Grassroots groups, 139, 143, 191
Gray, Hannah, 213
Great Fire (1871), 19
Great Society, 63
"Grey Wolves," 58
Grimshaw, William, 63

Haley, Margaret, 38, 39, 46, 161, 182
criticism of, 30
CTF and, 30, 62
Harper Commission and, 29
salary increases and, 36
Hamilton Club, Cooley bill and, 24
Hampton, Fred, 77
Hannon, Joseph P., 81, 85, 93–94
appointment of, 63
Chicago United and, 83
desegregation and, 82–83
performance agenda of, 193
settlement and, 237n81
subdistrict councils and, 190
Title I allocation and, 106
Hansot, Elisabeth, 28
Harding, John C., 23
Hargraves, J. Archie, 76, 77
Harper, William Rainey, 28, 29, 274n15
Chicago Manual Training School and, 21
Commercial Club and, 213
Harper bill, 30, 32–33
Harper Commission, 28, 33, 44, 190
draft legislation and, 30
report by, 29, 173, 189
Young and, 32
Harris Bank, 41, 118, 143
Harrison, Carter H., II, 27, 33, 44, 233n170
Harris Trust and Savings, 41, 118, 143
Hauser, Phillip: report by, 67, 68–69, 70, 74

Havinghurst, Robert, 103
  report by, 67–69, 70, 74
Haymarket bombing, 25
Haymarket Group, 115
HDO (Hispanic Democratic Organization), 133
Health care, 92, 154
Healy, Robert, 110, 117
Heartland Institute, 104, 145
Heineman, Ben W., 72, 76, 77, 78
Helene Curtis, 111, 148
Henderson, Peter, 101, 108
Herrick, Mary, 41–42
HEW (Department of Health, Education, and
  Welfare), 70, 74, 81
Hirst, Charles, Jr., 79
Hispanics. See Latinos
Hispanic Democratic Organization (HDO), 133
Hogan, David, 27
House Bill 206, 151
House Elementary and Secondary Education
  Committee, 150
Housing: discrimination in, 52
  economic exploitation and, 71
  open, 73
  summit, 76
Howe, Lawrence, 110, 139, 221
Hull House, 18, 34
Hunt, Harold, 58, 66, 107
  Commercial Club and, 175, 216
Hyde Park, 108

IBEC. See Illinois Business Education Council
Illinois Blighted Areas Redevelopment Act
  (1947), 58
Illinois Business Education Council (IBEC),
  149, 150, 151, 152, 153
  Commercial Club and, 219
  school law and, 148
Illinois Business Roundtable, 147, 148, 149,
  152, 153, 197, 198
  competitive markets and, 166
Illinois Chamber of Commerce, 147, 148
Illinois Federation of Labor, 26, 34, 45
Illinois Federation of Women's Clubs, 31
Illinois Manufacturers Association (IMA), 16,
  34–35, 147, 149, 153, 167, 195, 198, 205,
  211, 212
  Baldwin bill and, 35
  competitive markets and, 166
  Cooley bill and, 24
  Public School League and, 35

Illinois Standard Achievement Test, 165
Illinois Supreme Court, 36
  Loeb rule and, 34
  reform law and, 142
IMA. See Illinois Manufacturers Association
Inclusion, xii, 13
Industrial Club of Chicago, 46, 54, 273n6
Industrial education, 21, 27
Industrial Revolution, 16
Inland Steel, 92, 99
Institutionalization, 12, 49, 50, 185, 194
Insull, Samuel, 22, 40
Integration, 71, 81, 82, 83, 247n62
  African Americans and, 106
  defending, 53
  demonstrations against, 99
  opposition to, 73
Interest groups, 62, 85
International Federation of Labor, 205
Interorganizational coordination, 218
Iowa Test of Basic Skills (ITBS), 3, 157, 158, 165
Isolation in the Schools (Young), 32
ITBS. See Iowa Test of Basic Skills

Jackson, Jesse, 71, 77, 107, 122
Jackson, Leon, 93
Jaher, Frederic, 18
Johnson, Argie, 146–147, 151
Johnson, George E., 216
Johnson, Lyndon B., 70, 73, 135
Johnson, William H., 56, 58
Joint Commission on Real Estate Valuation, 41
Joint House and Senate Investigation
  Committee, 92, 94
Judson, Harry Pratt, 274n15
Junior colleges, 42, 56
Junior high schools, 35, 38, 42, 45

Karanja, Sakoni, 117, 138
Katznelson, Ira, 9
Kelleher, Patrick, 113, 116
Kellogg School of Business (Northwestern
  University), 101
Kelly, Edward J., 53, 57, 60, 73, 84
  black students and, 54
  institutionalization and, 50
  patronage and, 62
  public construction contracts and, 61
  reputation of, 55
  Sargent Committee and, 55
  unions and, 42, 55, 56

Kennedy, John F., 66
Kennelly, Martin H., 57–58, 60, 84
  African Americans and, 59
  anti-patronage stance of, 61
  CHA and, 59
  Commercial Club and, 216
  institutionalization and, 50
  patronage and, 58
Kenwood-Oakland Community Organization
    (KOCO), 107, 113
Keppel, Francis, 70
Kimbrough, Ted, 137, 259n83
  criticism of, 146
  Latinos and, 146
  managerial tinkering and, 139
King, Martin Luther, Jr., 3, 87
  assassination of, 73, 76
  CCCO and, 71
  Chicago Freedom Movement and, 71, 108
  Daley and, 72
  demands of, 72
  desegregation and, 81
  Leadership Council and, 73
  Raby and, 69
King, Terry, 112
KOCO (Kenwood-Oakland Community
    Organization), 107, 113
Koldyke, Martin "Mike," 138, 139
Kotsakis, John, 93, 117, 142, 182

Labor, 16
  business and, 51
  See also Chicago Teachers Federation;
    Chicago Teachers Union; Unions
Labor-capital conflict, 25–35
Landry, Lawrence, 69
Latino Institute, 114, 119, 151
Latinos, xii, 109, 113, 115, 121, 136
  in Chicago United, 219–221
  in Cook County, 3
  Daley and, 131, 133–134
  desegregation and, 83, 116
  growth of, 3, 81, 133
  power of, 91, 98, 108, 131, 167
  rights of, ix
  school reform and, 103, 104, 116, 119, 120,
    127, 143, 146, 160, 167, 170, 181,
    199–200
  unemployment rate among, 197
  voting by, 165
  Washington and, 108, 116

Latino students: accountability sanctions and,
    131, 163–164
  retention of, 164
Leadership Council for Metropolitan Open
    Communities, 72–73
Leadership for Quality Education (LQE), 137,
    141, 147, 149, 163, 200, 211, 213, 217
  characteristics of, 221
  Civic Committee and, 216, 218
  Commercial Club and, 198
  credibility of, 139
  founding of, 212
  monitoring by, 138
  New Schools for Chicago and, 165
  school reform law and, 212
  survey by, 144
League of Women Voters, 55
"Learn-Earn Connection," 110
Learn-Earn Summit, 111, 118
Legislative Black Caucus, 121
Leiter, Joseph, 228n21
Leiter, Levi Z., 19, 228n21
Lenz, Linda, 140
Lesson plans, 159, 204
Localism, 6, 129, 139
Local school councils (LSCs), ix, 121, 123–126,
    128, 137–142, 146, 151, 158, 160, 181,
    189, 209
  accountability and, 154
  African American schools and, 144
  CAC and, 167
  Chapter 1 funds and, 130
  community activists and, 143
  criticism of, 144–145
  empowerment of, 122, 194
  experiments with, 75, 191
  extending, 122
  legitimacy for, 129
  principals and, 131, 153
  role of, 143, 190
  training for, 144
  voting process with, 143
  welfare reform and, 132
Loeb, Jacob, 34, 38
Loeb rule, 34, 35, 44, 62, 188
Loop, 19, 92, 76, 135, 156
Love, Ruth, 100, 101, 146
  black community and, 107
  performance agenda of, 193
LQE. See Leadership for Quality Education
LSCs. See Local school councils

Lynch, Deborah, 142, 160, 161–162, 182
    CTU and, 117, 162, 164, 168
    failing schools and, 204
    open letter by, 162
    PACT and, 162
    partnership schools and, 165, 190
    reform and, 191
    teacher empowerment and, 175

MacGregor, Robert, 98, 101
Madigan, Michael, 120, 121, 151
Magnet schools, 87
"Make No Little Plans" (Perkins), 101, 102
Management, xi–xii, 14, 35, 46, 88, 130, 162
    changes in, 30, 75, 170, 174, 175
    class conflict and, 46
    market and, 147–152, 178, 186–188
    mayors and, 52, 55, 61–62, 137, 153
    modern, 22, 47, 91, 147, 180
    path-dependency of, 174–176
    problems with, 75, 83, 86, 100, 111–
        112, 144–145, 170, 177–179, 207
    reform and, 27–28, 88, 91, 99–101, 106, 118,
        129, 139, 149–150, 166, 171, 174–175,
        177, 186, 197, 217
    restructuring of, 80, 176, 188
    scientific, 16–17, 67, 178
    site-based, 112, 115, 117, 190
    superintendents and, 32, 57, 58, 66, 69,
        111–112, 119, 153–155, 162, 175
Managerialism, 14, 165, 173, 176, 185, 204, 210
Manual training, 20–22, 42, 172, 195
March, James, 198
Mark, Clayton, 31
Market reform, 186, 187, 189, 198–201
Market regimes, 186–188
Marshall Field and Company, 58
Martinez, Peter, 116, 119
Mastery Learning, 82, 107, 193
Mayoral control, 4, 159, 178, 204
    corporate version of, 133
    promoting, 157
Mays, Jeff, 148, 153
McAndrew, William, 66, 195
    innovations by, 44–45
    pedagogical changes and, 35
    plans of, 38–39
    social efficiency and, 39
McCahey, James B., 56, 58
McCormick, Robert, 40, 61
McCormick Place, 135

McFerren, Coretta, 118, 138
McKersie, William S., 140
McPherson, Bruce, 151
Memorial Day massacre (1937), 55
Mendoza, Henry, 95
Men's and Women's High School Federations,
    205
Merchant's Club, 16, 22, 46
Mexican American hometown associations, 116
Mexican American Legal Defense Fund
    (MALDEF), 151
Migration, 43, 52, 134
    African American, 2–3, 53, 59, 64–65
    enrollment and, 59
    school initiatives and, 17
Mills, Wiley Wright, 23
Minority contract set-asides, 134
Moe, Terry M., 260n99
Monteguedo, Lourdes, 116
Montgomery Ward, fire bombing at, 76
Moody's Investors Service, 93
Moore, Donald, 104, 115, 118, 119, 182
Mortensen, Peter, 35, 38, 232n131

NAACP (National Association for the
    Advancement of Colored People), 60, 76,
    78
Naperville School Board, 150
Naperville Sun, 150
Nash, Patrick A., 42, 54, 60
National Association for the Advancement of
    Colored People (NAACP), 60, 76, 78
    CCCO/Raby and, 70
    housing/census data and, 65
    segregation and, 67
National Business Roundtable, 148
National Education Association (NEA), 56–57,
    66, 84, 175
National Guard, riots and, 72
National Research Council, ITBS and, 158
National Women's Trade Union, 31
Nation at Risk, A, 105
NCACSS (North Central Association of
    Colleges and Secondary Schools), 56, 57
NEA. See National Education Association
Near North Side, 135, 136
Nelson, Diane, 221
New Deal, 53, 55
Newhouse, Richard, 90
New Republic, Loeb rule and, 34
New Schools for Chicago, 165, 218, 221

New York Times, 55
"No Child Left Behind" law, 176–77
Norris, Frank, 228n21
North Central Association of Colleges and
    Secondary Schools (NCACSS), 56, 57
Northern Trust, 41
North Lawndale, 59
Northwestern Mutual Life Insurance Company,
    66
"No social promotion" policy, 4
Nuveen, John, 54

Office of Education, CCCO charges and, 70
Office of Intervention, 164
Office of Systemwide Reorganization, 101, 107
Operation Breadbasket, 77
Operation PUSH, 106, 107, 113, 119, 143
Organizational ties, 212–213
Otis, Joseph E., 33
Otis, Ralph, 33
Otis bill, 33–34, 46
    business alternative to, 35
    tenure and, 34
Otis law (1917), 33, 37, 45, 46, 47, 57, 84, 130,
    173, 188
Outsourcing, 135, 136, 148, 153, 154, 155, 188,
    210
Overcrowding, 84, 167
Oversight, corporate, 177, 178, 201

PACT, (ProActive Chicago Teachers), 162
Palmer, Lu, 98, 106, 107
Parent Community Council (PCC), 118, 119,
    120, 127
    CSC and, 114
    proposal by, 115
Parent report cards, 159
Parents
    empowerment of, 189, 190
    reform and, 160–161, 210
    teachers and, 132, 141, 198, 209, 210
    unions and, xi, 210
Parent-school relations, 105, 196, 251n128
Parents United for Responsible Education
    (PURE), 118
Parker, Francis, 23
Partnership schools, 152, 165
Patronage, 9, 22, 27, 28, 38, 43, 44, 50–53,
    55–59, 63, 76, 77, 84, 89, 172, 173, 177
    black politicians and, 65
    city hall, 135

controlling, 54, 60
eliminating, 58
entrepreneurship and, 102
municipal job, 64
opposition to, 61
phony, 37
pinstripe, 135, 166
unions and, 62
Paulus, David, 119, 122
PCC. *See* Parent Community Council
PEA (Public Education Association), 33, 35, 46
Pedagogies, 2, 87, 192, 193, 198
changes in, xiii, 38–39, 48, 194, 196
community-based, 167
concern about, 202
refining, 196
vocational, 47
Pensions, 149, 153
Percy, Charles, 216
Performance, 2, 157, 176
accountability for, 112, 183
agendas for, 12, 182, 192, 193–197, 201,
    208
data on, 68
empowerment and, 191, 193
evaluating, 153–154
gap in, 165
improving, 3, 12, 168, 189
poor, 164, 168, 204
reform and, 205
responsibility for, 128
student, 11–12, 132, 148, 174, 177, 192, 199,
    204, 210
teacher, 161, 192
Performance regimes, 10–11
agenda formulation and, 196
building/sustaining, 197–198
constituents of, 195, 196
corporate elites and, 197
redefining, 192–198
unions and, 195
Perkins, Donald, 93, 99, 102, 109
economic development and, 100
study by, 101
Pershing Road barracks, closing of, 156
Peterson, Paul E., 9, 63, 74
Philips, James "Pate," 149
Pickering, George, 71, 87
Pierson, Paul, 172, 174
Plan of Chicago (1909), 15, 25, 42, 55, 60, 101,
    228n25

Platoon schools, 38, 45, 208
Policy making, 8, 101, 212
    unions and, 64, 172
Political access, 79, 85–87, 95, 99–100, 114,
        116, 123, 124–126, 134, 137, 150,
        165–166, 203
    importance of, 50, 174, 175–176
    lack of, 51, 52, 108–109, 131, 151
Pond, Allan B., 33
Post, Louis F., 23
PPAC. *See* Professional Personnel Advisory
        Committee
Principals: LSCs and, 153
    by race/ethnic group, 97(fig.)
    as school managers, 118
    selecting, 121, 124, 131, 159, 209
Private actors, public actors and, 181
Privatization, xii, 6, 9, 113, 134–135, 136, 148,
        150, 153, 210, 218
    city service, 166
    Commercial Club and, 187, 200
    low-performing schools and, 167
    savings with, 155
    support for, 139, 187
ProActive Chicago Teachers (PACT), 162
Probation, 130, 158, 264n177
Professional associations, 16
    reform plans and, 15
Professional development, 158, 195, 208
Professionalism, 6, 44, 165, 204
Professional Personnel Advisory Committee
        (PPAC), 124, 141, 160, 190
Professional Personnel Leadership Committee,
        190
Progressive era, xii, xiii, 16, 45, 46, 54, 85, 86,
        126, 132, 147, 149, 154, 165, 167, 169,
        171, 181, 185, 186, 188, 189, 190, 194,
        204, 216
    control and, 48
    ethnic politics of, 133
    legacy of, 173, 174, 175
    performance agendas of, 195
    reform and, 6, 129, 208, 209, 210
    standards of, 48
Progressive schooling, 193
Property taxes, 39, 74, 91, 92, 149, 166
    freezing, 135
    reducing, 41
Protestant flight, 52
Public, The, 23
Public actors, private actors and, 181

Public Education Association (PEA), 33, 35, 46
Public libraries, reading programs by, 155
Public School League, 35
Public trust, 206–208
Pullman, George M., 19, 20
Pullman Car Company, 36
Pullman strikes, 25
PURE (Parents United for Responsible
        Education), 118
Putnam, Robert, 198, 200

Quest Center, 142, 160, 164, 165, 167, 209

Raby, Albert A., 115, 182, 190
    Daley and, 77
    King and, 69
    resignation of, 73
    on segregation, 70
Race relations, 38, 53, 76, 191, 218
    Daley and, 81
    schooling and, 212
Racial demographics, changes in, 3
Racial disparities, 129
Racial issues, xi–xii, 51–52, 64, 85, 101,
        106–110, 131
Reagan, Ronald, 105
Reassessments, 39, 40
Recentralization, 153, 189
Redmond, James F., 85
    businesses and, 79
    Chicago United and, 83
    Daley and, 75
    desegregation and, 74, 75
    LSCs and, 121
Reed, Joseph, 137, 139, 221
    on Daley/SBNC, 145
Rees, John O., 41
Reese, Thomas, 142, 161, 165
    criticism of, 162
Reform coalitions, 16, 84, 128, 181, 185,
        197
    creating, 180, 198
    cross-class, 132
    diversity of, xi, 49
    governing regimes and, 184(table)
    influence of, 126
    leaders of, 182
    middle-class, 29
    participating in, 7, 11
    performance and, 12
    resisting, 185

Reform law (1988), 122–124, 141–142, 147
    striking down of, 142
Reform Summit, 118
Regime analysis, 180–182, 197
    framework for, 207
    multiple agendas and, 182–183
Regime change, x, 9–12
    approach to, 11, 12
    mobilizing for, 202(fig.)
Renaissance 2010, 165
Responsibility, 128, 132, 193
    civic, 29, 30
Restrictive covenants, 59, 64–65, 69, 235n13
Retention, 130, 164
Retirement benefits, 92
Reyes, Victor, 133
Riots, 8, 53, 59, 72, 73, 76, 182
Robinson, Theodore W., 24, 32, 182
    advocacy by, 45
    on Commercial Club, 20, 23
    on Cooley bill, 26
Rolling, Ken, 159, 264n186
Rollow, Sharon, 140
Roosevelt, Franklin D., 42
Rosenwald, Julius, 61
Rousmaniere, Kate, 30
Royko, Mike, 72

Salaries, 41, 59
    cuts in, 50
    increase in, 36
Sargent, Fred, 40, 41, 42
Sargent Committee, 46, 86, 195
    Commercial Club and, 43
    CSC and, 56
    cuts and, 41–43, 209
    legacy of, 51, 177
    recommendations by, 41
    retrenchment of, 52
Sawyer, Eugene, 115, 121, 122, 124
SB 1839, 121, 252n156
SBM, (Site-based management), 112, 115, 117
SBNC. See School Board Nominating
    Commission
Scandals, 56, 67, 85, 86
School Board Nominating Commission
    (SBNC), 84, 123, 137, 145, 152, 153
School boards, 28, 43, 60
School councils. See Local school councils
School culture, 192, 193, 196
School Finance Authority (SFA), 100, 103, 106,

    118, 122, 123, 125, 132, 138, 139, 181,
    200
    Board of Education and, 95
    budget and, 119, 146
    Chicago United and, 98, 99
    criticism of, 113
    demise of, 154
    described, 94
    desegregation and, 178
    enabling legislation for, 95
    outcome goals by, 129
    oversight by, 127–128, 131, 149, 153
    Washington and, 110
School improvement, 2, 140
    political dynamics of, 201–210
"Schools Push for Tax Collections" (Chicago
    Sun-Times), 94
School system managers, teachers and, 202
SCLC (Southern Christian Leadership
    Conference), 71, 77
Segregation, 3, 4, 38, 53, 58, 65, 70, 74, 75, 82,
    85, 86, 182
    civil rights groups and, 67
    housing, 72
    reform and, 87–88
    report on, 67
    response to, x, 69, 71, 88
    social geography of, 9
Settlement houses, 4
SFA. See School Finance Authority
Shakman decrees (1983), 135
Shakman v. The Democratic Organization of
    Cook County et al., 64
Shanker, Al, 117, 142, 204
Shoop, John: death of, 232n131
Simon, Herbert, 198
Sinclair, Upton, 18
Singer, William S., 137
"Single tax," supporters of, 22–23
Site-based management (SBM), 112, 115, 117
Smith, Kenneth, 98
Smith-Hughes bill (1917), 26–27
Snedden, David, 24
Social activists, 135, 139
Social issues, 54, 105, 198, 208
Social reformers, 45, 46–47, 208
Soldier Field, rally at, 72
Solis, Danny, 116, 117, 119, 133, 138
    on Kimbrough, 146
    Latinos and, 134
Sonsteby, John J., 23

Southern Christian Leadership Conference
    (SCLC), 71, 77
South Park Board, 42
South Side, 53, 59, 141
South Side Academy, 21
Special education, 152, 157, 164
Special Task Force Report, 99, 100, 101, 102,
    112
Standardized tests, 158, 160, 165, 169,
    204
    scores, 3, 157, 162, 167, 170, 174
Stead, William T., 18, 19, 26
Stone, Clarence N., x
    on corporate involvement, 13
    opposition/passive resistance and, 183
    performance regime and, 11, 192
    reform and, 7, 10, 11, 180
    on teachers/agenda-setting coalitions,
        181
Strawn, Silas, 40, 61
Strawn Committee, 40, 41
Strayer, George, 41
Strikes, 25, 141, 203, 237n81
    banning, 150, 152
    firefighter, 98
    teacher, 63, 92, 111–112, 125
Structural similarities, 212–213
Students, by race/ethnic group, 96(fig.)
Suffragists, 30
Superintendents, 22, 28–29, 208
    centralization/professionalization and, 33
    as managers, 175
    school reform and, 187
Support-service employees, 89
Swift, George, 233n170
Swift and Company, 36

Tax-anticipation warrants, 36, 39, 40, 41
Tax increment financing (TIF), 135, 136,
    155
Taylor, Frederick Winslow, 23, 178
Taylor, Graham, 18
Teachers, 64, 68, 90–91, 161
    agenda-setting coalitions and, 181
    appointment of, 28
    certification of, 158
    credentialing/advancement of, 185
    curriculum and, 159
    democratic challenge by, 29–33
    empowerment of, 175, 190–191, 208–210
    influence of, 48, 181

institutional memory and, 49
parents and, xi, 132, 141, 198, 209, 210
performance regimes and, 195
quality of, 167, 172
by race/ethnic group, 96(fig.)
reform and, xi, 160–161
school system managers and, 202
unions and, 34, 172, 205, 208
Teachers councils, 29, 32, 174, 186, 208
Technical Advisory Committee on Intergroup
    Relations, 58
Tenure, 47, 195
Textbooks, selection of, 28, 29
The Woodlawn Organization (TWO), 107, 113,
    114
Thompson, James, 93, 122, 216
Thompson, William Hale, 44, 52, 53, 232n131
    corruption of, 45
    emergency funds and, 40
    Haley and, 182
    Loeb rule and, 34
    organized crime and, 37
    Otis law and, 37
    political scheme of, 38
    racial crisis and, 37
    reassessment and, 39
TIF (Tax increment financing), 135, 136,
    155
TIME. See To Improve Management of
    Education
Title I funds, 105, 106
Title VI (Civil Rights Act), 70
To Improve Management of Education (TIME),
    138, 147, 149, 154
Traditional schooling, 193
Travis, Dempsey, 234n8
Traylor, Melvin, 61
TWO (The Woodlawn Organization), 107, 113,
    114
Tyack, David, 5, 28

Unemployment, 40, 102, 197
U.S. Commission on Civil Rights, 67, 82
U.S. Council of Mayors, 155
U.S. House of Representatives, 148
U.S. Justice Department, 101, 158, 164
Unions, xi, xiii, 2, 4, 10, 14, 15, 18, 42,
    45, 48, 52, 55, 65, 112, 117, 148, 150,
    185
    antipathy to, 206
    as coalition partners, 204–206, 208–210

Commercial Club and, 36
decline of, 136, 203–204
demographics of, 208
efficacy of, 203
influence of, 50, 168
lawsuits by, 36
legitimacy of, 206–207
1995 law and, 188
patronage and, 62
reform and, 17, 88, 141–142, 201, 204, 209, 210
teachers and, 34, 172, 205, 208
United Neighborhood Organizations (UNO), 117, 119, 122
legitimacy of, 120
LSC candidates and, 144
school reform and, 159
summit and, 114
vouchers and, 116
United Progressive Caucus (UPC), 161, 162, 165
University of Chicago, Chicago Manual Training School and, 21
UNO. *See* United Neighborhood Organizations
UPC. *See* United Progressive Caucus
Urban League. *See* Chicago Urban League

Vallas, Paul, 157, 161, 193, 194
CTU and, 163
management by, 154, 155–156, 168
open letter to, 162
on outsourcing, 155
parent report cards and, 159
principals and, 158
privatization and, 156
resignation of, 163, 164
school reform promoters and, 155
social promotion and, 158
on teachers/curriculum, 159
VanderWeele, Maribeth, 145, 155, 156
Van Gorkom, Jerome W., 94
Vaughn, Jacqueline, 110, 112, 117, 128, 161
death of, 142
reform and, 113
Veblen, Thorstein, 18
Vincent, George E., 27
Vivian, C. T., 77
Vocational education, 4, 20–25, 48, 172, 173, 177, 196, 197, 209
cost of, 37
criticism of, 24–25

dual system, 26
implementation of, 21, 22, 27
survey on, 25
unions and, 26–27, 195
Vocational Education Commission, 66
Vouchers, 116, 139, 148, 165, 188

Walberg, Herbert J., 80
Wallace, George, 66
Washington, Harold, 89, 111, 123, 128, 131, 132, 136, 201, 220
business communities and, 108
Chicago United and, 109
civic participation and, xii
coalition of, 125
corporate reformers and, 177
death of, 114–115
election of, 90, 99, 108, 113
job creation/skills development and, 166
Latinos and, 108, 116, 134
legacy of, 114, 124, 133, 200
low-income empowerment and, 127, 137
reform and, 115, 182
regime formation and, 199
SFA and, 110
summit and, 113–114, 120, 181, 199
Webb v. Board of Education (1961), 239n109
Webb v. Board of Education of Chicago (1963), 239n109
Weber, Arnold, 139, 153
Weir, Margaret, 9
West, Ken, 200
on board of education, 118–119
on LSCs, 143
on unions, 138
West Side, 59
riots in, 72, 73
West Town, gentrification of, 135
White flight, 52, 70
White schools, 238n96
African American schools and, 68
Willis, Benjamin C., 63, 70, 86, 99, 107, 240n134
administration of, 68
Chicago United and, 83
Commercial Club and, 175
criticism of, 185
Daley and, 75
neighborhood schooling and, 66
racial conflict and, 74

Willis, Benjamin C., *continued*
    resignation of, 69, 71
    segregation and, 67
Willmott, Peter, 110, 118
Women's groups, 24, 34, 52, 55, 209
Women's Trade Union League, 34
Woods Fund, 159
Works Progress Administration, 55
Wrigley, Julia, 13, 25

Young, Ella Flagg, 25, 130, 190
    Cooley bill and, 32
    leadership of, 33
    Loeb rule and, 34
    professionalism and, 44
    teachers councils and, 191
    vocational education and, 24
Youth Apprentice Council, 260n112